SUPERVISION: HUMAN PERSPECTIVES

2 3 4 5 6 7 8 9 0   FGRFGR   7 8 3 2 1 0 9

This book was set in Times Roman by BookTech, Inc. (ECU).
The editors were Eric M. Munson and Barry Benjamin;
the cover was designed by Joan E. O'Connor;
the production supervisor was Dominick Petrellese.
New drawings were done by ANCO/Boston.
Fairfield Graphics was printer and binder.

Library of Congress Cataloging in Publication Data

Sergiovanni, Thomas J.
    Supervision: human perspectives.

    Published in 1971 under title: Emerging patterns of
supervision.
    Includes index.
    1. Includes supervision. 2. School management and
organization. I. Starratt, Robert J., joint author.
II. Title.
LB2805.S52 1979   371.2'013   78-18692
ISBN 0-07-056311-X

Kristina Kostopoulos

Super

Human

Second

Thomas J. Sergio
University of Illinois,

Robert J. Starr
Fordham Univers

McGraw-Hill Book Company

New York St. Louis San Francisco Auckland Bogotá Düsseldorf
Johannesburg London Madrid Mexico Montreal New Delhi
Panama Paris São Paulo Singapore Sydney Tokyo Toronto

Contents

1

HUMAN RESOURCES SUPERVISION AND ORGANIZATIONAL LEADERSHIP

2

HUMAN RESOURCES AND EDUCATIONAL LEADERSHIP

3

A HUMAN RESOURCES APPROACH TO STAFF DEVELOPMENT, CLINICAL SUPERVISION, AND TEACHER EVALUATION

Foreword

For anyone who carries a leadership responsibility in education, or who aspires to such a role, few if any topics are as important to understand or as crucial to one's professional life as supervision. Broadly defined, it encompasses all the functions and problems that are associated with the upgrading of performance; and ultimately the very quality of school programs depends on the insight, the skill, and the dedication of those persons who are charged with overseeing and helping teachers in their work with children and youth. Therefore the appearance of a first-class textbook on so crucial a subject is a welcome event, and it is a pleasure to offer some words of introduction to it. (One advantage of writing a Foreword is that you are among the first persons privileged to read the new work.)

As I reflect upon the situation in American schools and colleges today, at this point in early 1978, I perceive that many of our current problems, and embarrassments, stem from the historic neglect of supervision. Both as a theoretical concern and as a body of practical information, supervision has received much less attention than it merits; and all too few of the leaders in education, not only in the United States but worldwide, have devoted themselves to the generation of supervisory knowledge. Luckily, the rather small coterie of supervision scholars includes some extremely able people, Sergiovanni and Starratt among them, and in addition there is seminal work in other disciplines on which these scholars have been able to draw. As a result, there is a solid and growing base of both theory and methodology upon which it is possible to build more effective and productive approaches. One of the strengths of this book is that it reviews that base and brings into focus for the educator a great deal of important material whose relevance to work with teachers is only now becoming apparent.

The title chosen by these authors has rather special meaning, since the word "human" signals the overall emphasis of the book. Without diminishing their commitment as reflected in the first edition to the humanization of education, the authors have moved on to a concept of human resources supervision, the nature of which they define first in the Preface and then in the opening section. Further, there is in this second edition greater attention paid to the general notion of staff development and especially to the nature and importance of clinical (i.e., classroom-centered, hands-on) supervision as a key to all that goes on in the name of supervision.

It interested me that the authors recommend, as a way of becoming acquainted with the volume, browsing through the introductions to each of its three major parts. They also seemed to approve the idea of checking out the last chapter first, so that the reader could better sense where the volume is going. I did not do either of those things, but in retrospect I applaud the latter suggestion in particular. The nine chapters of Part 1 are in sum an excellent review of the scholarly background material to which I referred a few paragraphs back; and although some neophyte readers can probably deal with them without other preparation, it seems to me that the reasons for the inclusion of all these rich and varied materials might be clearer to such readers if they first acquire some sense of where the book is ultimately heading. Professors, graduate students, and other specialists will undoubtedly feel great appreciation, as I did, for Part 1 and the resources that it harnesses, and to them I say, "Start at the beginning."

The overall architecture of the book is intriguing to me, and as a veteran observer-participant I am already impatient to see how the *third* edition will be organized and how much more progress it will reflect. From this second edition I gain the impression that we are entering a creative period in the history of supervision and that the connections between staff development (as these authors relate supervision to it) and the other major dimensions of education (notably policy formulation, curriculum building, and instructional practice) will increasingly be recognized as vital. These authors have elected to examine first the organizational dimensions of schooling, then the curricular, and finally the supervisory-evaluative-developmental. They chose, with good reason as I see it, to spend little time on the nuts-and-bolts topics with which supervision textbooks are sometimes concerned, and instead to examine the broader questions that would-be supervisors ought to be reflecting upon. This decision has led to a provocative, profound, and ultimately dignified statement about supervision as a concept and as an enterprise. Along the way it offers excellent suggestions for supervisory practice, but it wisely avoids a cook-book-type approach. The volume will add depth and stature to the field, and one hopes it will stimulate greater interest in the research and development work on which further progress depends.

Each reader will find his own benefits and excitement in the pages that follow. I have already pointed to the welcome evidence that I found of a maturing discipline. I welcome, too, the various suggestions, mostly indirect, to the effect that collaborative supervision, like collaborative teaching, offers much promise for the future. I was pleased at the emphasis upon understanding the total context within which each supervisory act occurs, and I was inspired by the material, drawn in part from Elliot Eisner, identifying the aesthetic and artistic dimensions of supervision and challenging supervisors to become, in effect, connoisseurs of their craft as well as technical experts. I believe all practitioners will find, notably in Part 3, some extremely useful clues to the achievement of such an ideal.

Given the multidimensional nature of this volume, it seems to me that it can serve not only as a basic text in supervision courses, but also as a resource volume in other fields. Courses in school administration, particularly those concerned with personnel matters, will be enriched by reference to the Part 1 material. Courses in curriculum and instruction can profitably include material from Part 2. Seminars and advanced courses dealing with professional careers, communications, and (especially) leadership will value some of the materials in Parts 1 and 3.

Robert H. Anderson
Professor and Dean
College of Education
Texas Tech University

Preface

Humanistic aspirations characterized the first edition of this book. Such aspirations were to be fulfilled by linking more carefully educational program and instructional matters with compatible organizational and supervisory arrangements. Quoting from the preface of the first edition, "we believe that humanizing education, with its focus on self-actualization of youngsters, can be achieved only in a humanizing organization which focuses on self-actualization of teachers and other educational professionals." The second edition unfolds similarly, giving attention in Part 1 to the supervisor's role in organizational leadership, in Part 2, the supervisor's role in educational leadership, and in Part 3 (new to the second edition) the supervisor's role in instructional leadership.

To some, humanizing aspirations are viewed with suspicion, and, we believe, for good reason. Often such aspirations are articulated as little more than laissez faire or permissive sorts of arrangements which overemphasize interpersonal goals for their own sake. In our view, emphasizing interpersonal relationships with teachers in isolation from concern for their achievement, performance, and professional development is hardly humanistic. Indeed, the same principle holds true for students. Classroom designs void of personal meanings and intellectual challenge are hardly humanistic, regardless of how pleasant they might be.

In edition 2 a distinction is made between *human relations* and *human resources* supervision. Human relations, often mistaken for being humanistic, lacks the potency, involvement, maturity, and emphasis of intrinsic satisfaction found in human resources supervision. True, both are concerned with people and their needs, but unlike human relations, which seems concerned only with security and social needs, human resources supervision views people as having the desire and potential for motivation, responsibility, and success at work—all as means to intrinsic satisfaction.

Human resources supervision requires a more open and active partnership between and among students, teachers, and supervisors. Older patterns of supervision, with their stress on authority, compliance, and control, and with their identification of wisdom with hierarchical position, put teachers in the position of passively accepting the directives of the principal, supervisor, or department chairperson. In turn, teachers have tended to view their students as being in the same passive position in relation to them.

A contrast of the Table of Contents of editions 1 and 2 will reveal many changes. In addition to the refining of the concept of human resources supervision, these changes include the addition of a chapter on staff development (Chapter 15) and a chapter on clinical supervision and teacher evaluation (Chapter 16). To an unprecedented extent, we now have a young and stable teaching force whose long-term effectiveness will depend upon constant renewal. Staff development is shifting from a school district luxury to a position of critical responsibility. Supervision as staff development is an innovation which needs conceptual support and operational guidelines. Chapter 15 is a step in this direction. There is an obvious need for teacher evaluation to change from an administrative ritual of summative evaluation to a process of supervision of a formative nature. In this effort target setting, clinical supervision, group and peer supervision, and other formative practices need to be integrated, conceptualized, and put into practice. Chapter 16 is a response to this need. Included in this chapter are emerging naturalistic evaluation practices such as portfolio development and the use of aesthetic criticism techniques.

Chapter 6, entitled "A Contingency Approach to Supervisory Leadership," another new chapter, provides an update on leadership theory and on applying this theory in practice. Viewing the school as a political system and dealing with the internal politics of schooling (Chapter 7) represents still another new feature of the second edition.

Part 2 has been altered substantially. It contains three new chapters (Chapters 10 to 12): "The Controversial Context of Supervision," "The Supervisor's Educational Platform," and "Supervising Varieties of Curricula." Instead of attempting a quick overview of the complexities of curriculum development, Part 2 now assumes that basic introductions to learning theory and curriculum development are covered elsewhere. The focus of these chapters is to bring the supervisor into those areas of program supervision that are essential. The key to much of the supervisor's effectiveness with program supervision relates to the supervisor's having developed a clear "educational platform" which will guide and lend intelligibility and consistency to his or her supervisory activity.

Many features of the first edition remain. From a supervisory point of view the school is seen as encompassing three interdependent subsystems—organizational, educational, and instructional. The supervisor's unique role is portrayed as that of linking pin for all three subsystems. The book continues to rely heavily on theoretical foundations, sacrificing perhaps discussions of some job-entry competencies needed by supervisors in favor of building long-term perspectives of what supervision is and can be. Our interest, therefore, is less in the immediate intricacies of the job and more in building a career long view of supervision.

Readers are encouraged to begin in their journey through the book by first reading the introductions to each of the three parts. Part 1, "Human Resources Supervision and Organizational Leadership," sets the stage of supervision. Whatever curricular and instructional goals supervisors have, they are achieved through and with others in an organized setting. Part 2, "Human Resources and Educational Leadership," provides supervisors with the compass settings and a sense of direction so that they will be able to navigate with purpose. Refining the reader's educational platform is the intent here. Part 3, "A Human Resources Approach to Staff Development, Clinical Supervision, and Teacher Evaluation," focuses specifically on three important task areas traditionally associated with the supervisor's instructional leadership responsibilities.

For those readers who like to look at the last chapter of a book first, in order to see whether the story has a happy or a sad ending, or to check out the conclusions before groping through the labyrinth of arguments the authors marshal to reach the conclusions, we hope our concluding chapter will appeal. In that chapter we try to highlight our underlying convictions in writing the book in the first place as well as our beliefs about the future of supervision in the larger field of educational developments.

The book as a whole could not have been written without the long hours of discussion, argument, and encouragement which the authors were privileged to share with each other. Though responsibility for each chapter was shared jointly, Parts 1 and 3 were developed by T. J. Sergiovanni and Part 2 by R. J. Starratt.

The list of creditors to this book is long. Colleagues and students have contributed generously of their ideas. To all of them we are grateful.

Thomas J. Sergiovanni
Robert J. Starratt

Part One

Human Resources Supervision and Organizational Leadership

INTRODUCTION: THE NATURE OF SUPERVISION

Supervision has been a relatively dormant activity in schools, and those designated specifically as supervisors have typically been seen as minor functionaries. Supervisory staffs have become progressively smaller as the demands for economy have increased, and many supervisory activities have been assigned, at least in a titular sense, to others with more administrative responsibilities. As could be expected, overburdened administrators typically give only cursory attention to new responsibilities.

Signs exist, however, which suggest that supervision may be experiencing a mild renaissance. At the national level the Association for Supervision and Curriculum Development is placing stronger emphasis on supervision. The literature in the field is expanding and improving in quality. With respect to general supervision, for example, less emphasis is given to delineating job descriptions and task areas for supervisors and more emphasis is given to developing concepts basic to supervision and articulating supervisory processes. With respect to classroom supervision, clinical strategies and aesthetic strategies are beginning to compete successfully with the more traditional approaches to teacher evaluation.

Publications focusing on problems and issues in supervision are among the most popular offered by the Association for Supervision and Curriculum Development. Supervisory topics are appearing more frequently on the programs of this organization's national conference and series of National Curriculum Study Institutes. The founding of the Conference of Professors of Instructional Supervision in 1976 is evidence that scholars interested in problems in supervision are increasing in numbers, interested in identifying themselves, establishing better communications networks, and developing more systematic approaches to research and development.

Local school districts throughout the country are showing unprecedented interest in teacher evaluation, supervision, and staff development. Educational program design and instructional strategy development are also receiving top priority.

THE CHANGING SCENE

What are the reasons for this renewed interest in supervision? As is so often the case, "necessity is the mother of invention." One such necessity for school districts has been adjusting to declining enrollments. In Illinois, for example, enrollments increased approximately 113 percent during the 25-year period 1946–1971. Enrollments have since steadily declined and are expected to continue to decline until a leveling point is reached in the early- to mid-eighties. This situation in Illinois parallels similar national trends. School districts are faced with the necessity of rethinking present strategies for improving the quality of educational services as a result of declining enrollments and related problems such as smaller budgets, demands for accountability, closing and combining schools, teacher surpluses, and teacher entrenchment as manifested by low mobility and turnover rates. As growth-oriented organizations in an expanding economy, schools have in the past been able to obtain increases in quality of education by adding new programs, increasing staff size, and providing new services. In periods of modest growth, zero growth, or decline, however, changes in quality depend more heavily on changes in present staff and present programs. Program evaluation, teacher evaluation, staff development, curriculum development, and other activities typically associated with supervision have become critical leverage points in improving educational quality under present growth conditions. Since improvements must be made within existing human, material, and financial resources, the supervisory function increases in importance. But the situation is more complex than it first appears.

Changing present conditions provides a new set of leadership demands on the school in both an educational and organizational sense. Not only do good educational decisions need to be made but teachers need to have strong identity with, and commitment to, these decisions. The leadership burden in obtaining this commitment increasingly falls to supervisors who are closest in competence and affinity to teachers and their work.

Consider, for example, the problem of staff stability. Good teaching jobs are difficult to find, and teachers are less likely to leave once they are employed. Low teacher turnover is often viewed initially as a blessing, particularly to those who just a few years ago experienced difficulty in finding and keeping teachers. But in reality low turnover poses a serious problem for schools. Dissatisfied teachers are now less likely to leave. The reasons for staying on the job are too important. But if reasons for staying are limited to job security and other bread-and-butter concerns, we may well have large numbers of teachers who remain on the job for the wrong reasons. As a result, instructional quality is endangered. In the absence of easy turnover, the maintenance and development of job satisfaction, motivation, and commitment in teachers becomes more important. Again the burden increasingly falls on supervisors who are closest to teachers and their work.

Consider the problem of change as another example. In an expanding district one can impose structural changes on existing staff and by the process of staff attrition and careful replacement, transfers, and creative new assignments obtain internalized changes.[1] But under current conditions of stability, structural changes must be accompanied by internalized changes in the *present* teaching staff. Teachers need to accept, believe in, and be committed to new practices. This sort of change creates strong leadership challenges for the school. Again the burden falls on supervisors who are closest to teachers and their work.

As a final example consider the problem of staff development as it relates to staff stability. Many schools are faced with the prospect of a relatively young teaching staff who are likely to grow old together over the next 2 decades. Age in itself has the potential to provide natural benefits which accrue from experience and maturity. But this potential can be lost unless marked by a commitment to continuous personal and professional development. Staff development of the quality and quantity needed in the decades ahead makes strong demands on school leadership—a burden again likely to fall increasingly on supervisors.

The increased importance attributed to supervisors is attractive, if not euphoric, for those interested in this field. But whether this new emphasis will develop into promises fulfilled or promises broken will depend, we believe, on the form that supervision takes.

THREE FORMER IMAGES OF SUPERVISION

Present supervisory practices in schools are based on one, or a combination, of three general supervisory theories—traditional scientific management, human relations, and neoscientific management.[2] Traditional scientific management represents the classical autocratic philosophy of supervision in which teachers are viewed as appendages of management and as such are hired to carry out prespecified duties in accordance with the wishes of management. Control, accountability, and efficiency are emphasized in an atmosphere of clear-cut boss-subordinate relationships. Vestiges of this brand of supervision can still be found in schools, though by and large traditional scientific management is not currently in favor.

Human relations supervision has its origins in the democratic administration

---

[1] Structural changes refer to changes in design. Team teaching, open classroom, and IGE are examples of structural changes. Internalized changes refer to changes in assumption, beliefs, and behavior of teachers. Internalized changes support structural changes, and both are necessary.

[2] This section follows closely T. J. Sergiovanni, "Beyond Human Relations," in T. J. Sergiovanni (ed.), *Professional Supervision for Professional Teachers,* Washington, D.C.: Association for Supervision and Curriculum Development, 1975, pp. 1–4.

movement advocated in the thirties and is still widely preached and practiced. Human relations supervision was a successful challenge to traditional scientific management. Teachers were to be viewed as "whole people" in their own right rather than as packages of needed energy, skills, and aptitudes to be used by administrators and supervisors. Supervisors worked to create a feeling of satisfaction among teachers by showing interest in them as people. It was assumed that a satisfied staff would work harder and would be easier to work with, to lead, and to control. Participation was to be an important method, and its objective was to make teachers *feel* that they are useful and important to the school. "Personal feelings" and "comfortable relationships" were the watchwords of human relations.

Human relations supervision is still widely advocated and practiced today, though its support has diminished. Human relations promised much but delivered little. Its problems rest partly with misunderstandings as to how the approach should work and partly with faulty theoretical notions inherent in the approach itself. The movement actually resulted in widespread neglect of teachers. Participatory supervision became permissive supervision, which in practice was laissez faire supervision. Further, the focus of human relations supervision was and still is an emphasis on "winning friends" in an attempt to influence people. To many, "winning friends" was a slick tactic which made the movement seem manipulative and inauthentic, even dishonest.

In 1967 the Association for Supervision and Curriculum Development's Commission on Supervision Theory concluded its 4 years of study with a report entitled *Supervision: Perspectives and Propositions.*[3] In this report William Lucio discussed scientific-management and human relations views of supervision and spoke of a third view—that of the revisionists—which sought to combine features of both scientific management and human relations. Standard-bearers of the revisionists were Douglas McGregor, Warren Bennis, Chris Argyris, and Rensis Likert.[4]

If ever a misunderstanding existed between theorists and practitioners, the revisionist movement would be a prominent example. This was largely a paper movement which in practice rarely amounted to much more than a more sophisticated form of human relations. What the revisionist writers intended was never really understood by many or properly implemented on a wide scale. Whereas the earlier human relations movement put the emphasis on the teachers' social-interaction needs and physical comfort, the revisionist view was articulated as a superficial attempt to make teachers *feel* a part of the school primarily through relatively controlled or safe participation practices. To old human relations add one part participation and stir well. Nothing important seemed really changed. The ideas of the revisionists are still important, we think, and if properly under-

---

[3] William Lucio, ed., *Supervision: Perspectives and Propositions,* Washington, D.C.: Association for Supervision and Curriculum Development, 1967.
[4] Douglas McGregor, *The Human Side of Enterprise,* New York: McGraw-Hill, 1960; Warren Bennis, "Revisionist Theory of Leadership," *Harvard Business Review,* vol. 39, no. 2, pp. 26–38, 1961; Chris Argyris, *Personality and Organization,* New York: Harper, 1957; and Rensis Likert, *New Patterns of Management,* New York: McGraw-Hill, 1961.

stood and implemented, they can lead us away from our present inadequacies in supervisory practice.

Neoscientific management, the most recent image of supervision, is in large part a reaction against human relations supervision, particularly its neglect of the teacher in the classroom. Neoscientific management shares with traditional scientific management an interest in control, accountability, and efficiency. The code words of this movement are "teacher competencies," "performance objectives," and "cost-benefit analysis." The task dimension, concern for job, and concern for highly specified performance objectives, all so lacking in human relations supervision, are strongly emphasized in neoscientific management though often at the expense of the human dimension. Neoscientific management relies heavily on externally imposed authority and as a result often lacks acceptance from teachers.

The three images of supervision share a lack of faith and trust in the teacher's ability and willingness to display as much interest in the welfare of the school and its educational programs as that presumed by administrators, supervisors, and the public. In traditional scientific management, teachers are heavily supervised in an effort to ensure for administrators, supervisors, and the public that good teaching will take place. In human relations supervision, teachers are nurtured and involved in efforts to increase their job satisfaction so that they might be more pliable in the hands of administrators and supervisors, thus ensuring that good teaching will take place. In neoscientific management, impersonal, technical, or rational control mechanisms substitute for face-to-face close supervision. Here it is assumed that if visible standards of performance, objectives, or competencies can be identified, then the work of teachers can be controlled by holding them accountable to these standards, thus ensuring, for administrators and supervisors and the public, better teaching.

HUMAN RESOURCES SUPERVISION

In the first edition of this book we referred to emerging patterns of supervision which showed promise for moving schools away from scientific-management images of supervision. The emerging patterns were clearly a part of the revisionist movement and were described as enlightened supervision. Many scholars and practitioners have confused enlightened supervision with human relations supervision. Because of this confusion and because of our better understanding of concepts and practices associated with enlightened patterns, we have chosen to refer to them as human resources supervision. The distinction between human relations supervision and human resources supervision is critical.[5] Whereas human relations and human resources supervision are, for example, both concerned with teacher satisfaction, human relations views satisfaction as a means to a smoother and more effective school. The human relations supervisor might adopt

[5] This distinction was first made by Raymond Miles, "Human Relations or Human Resources?" *Harvard Business Review,* vol. 43, no. 4, pp. 148–163, 1965, and by Mason Haire, Edwin Ghiselli, and Lyman Porter, *Managerial Thinking: An International Study,* New York: Wiley, 1966. See Chapter 8 for further elaboration of this distinction.

shared decision making because it would increase teacher satisfaction. Satisfied teachers, it is assumed, would in turn be easier to work with, and indeed to lead, and therefore effectiveness would be increased.

The Human Relations Supervisor

The rationale behind this strategy is that teachers want to *feel* important and involved. This feeling in turn promotes in teachers a better attitude toward the school, and therefore they become easier to manage.

The human resources supervisor, by contrast, views satisfaction as a desirable end toward which teachers will work. Satisfaction, according to this view, results from the successful accomplishment of important and meaningful work, and this sort of accomplishment is the key component of school effectiveness. The human resources supervisor would adopt shared decision-making practices because of their potential to increase school effectiveness. He assumes that better decisions will be made, teacher ownership and commitment to these decisions will be increased, and the likelihood of success at work, an antecedent to school effectiveness, will increase.

The Human Resources Supervisor

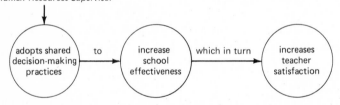

Much of the success of the now-popular neoscientific-management images of supervision—those which rely on impersonal quality-control mechanisms, such as performance contracts, accountability to predetermined objectives, and competency standards—results from the confusion which exists between human relations and human resources supervision. Indeed, many of the forces contributing to a revival of interest in supervision articulated earlier in this introduction require that we abandon human relations notions in favor of more job-centered and task-oriented approaches. But the problems we see in adapting neoscientific approaches are that, while they provide a needed emphasis on the work of the school, they assume a rationality and perspective which neglect the human dimension in organization, educational program, and instruction. Neoscientific management, for example, often assumes a list of competencies, performance criteria, and other specifications that apply to all teachers, to all teaching situations, to all students, at all times—assumptions both unrealistic and undesirable. The human resources view, as we shall argue, provides the needed integration between person and organization, and personality and accomplishment, as applied to teachers and schools, as well as to students and classrooms.

SUMMARY

In this introduction important trends influencing supervisory practice were discussed. It was noted that such factors as declining enrollments, staff stability, and limited resources have contributed to a renewed interest in supervision. Three former images of supervision (scientific management, human relations, and neo-scientific management) were discussed and judged inadequate as models to meet present conditions. A fourth image, human resources supervision, was proposed.

Chapter 1

Perspectives for Supervision

Many of the issues associated with supervision over the years remain intact at this writing. Confusion in role definition still plagues the field, and uncertainty exists in determining who are supervisors, what are the key components of their jobs, how much authority they should have and what their relationship to administrators and teachers should be. Further at issue is whether supervision should be viewed as a special role or as a process component of several roles.

VIEWPOINTS OF SELECTED AUTHORS

In this section selected statements from key authors in the field of supervision are provided as a means to suggest what each views as the essential components of supervision. The statements are provided without editorial comment. Readers may wish to compare points of view among the authors, and between them and the points of view expressed in this book. What do these views share with human resources supervision and how are they different?

1   Ben Harris defines *supervision* as:[1]

---

[1] Ben N. Harris, *Supervisory Behavior in Education,* 2d ed., Englewood Cliffs, N.J.: Prentice-Hall, 1975, pp. 10–11.

What school personnel do with *adults* and *things* to maintain or change the school operation in ways that directly influence the teaching processes employed to promote pupil learning. Supervision is highly instruction-related but not highly pupil-related. Supervision is a major function of the school operation, not a task or a specific job or a set of techniques. Supervision of instruction is directed toward both maintaining and improving the teaching-learning processes of the school.

2   Kimball Wiles views supervision as those activities which are designed to improve instruction at all levels of the school enterprise. He describes supervisors as follows:[2]

> They are the expediters. They help establish communication. They help people hear each other. They serve as liaison to get persons into contact with others who have similar problems or with resource people who can help. They stimulate staff members to look at the extent to which ideas and resources are being shared, and the degree to which persons are encouraged and supported as they try new things. They make it easier to carry out the agreements that emerge from evaluation sessions. They listen to individuals discuss their problems and recommend other resources that may help in the search for solutions. They bring to individual teachers, whose confidence they possess, appropriate suggestions and materials. They sense, as far as they are able, the feelings that teachers have about the system and its policies, and they recommend that the administration examine irritations among staff members. They provide expertness in group operation, and provide the type of meeting place and structure that facilitate communication. They are, above all, concerned with helping people to accept each other, because they know that when individuals value each other, they will grow through their interaction together and will provide a better emotional climate for pupil growth. The supervisor's role has become *supporting, assisting,* and *sharing,* rather than directing. The authority of the supervisor's position has not decreased, but it is used in another way. It is used to promote growth through assuming responsibility and creativity rather than through dependency and conformity.

3   William Burton and Leo Brueckner, two pioneers in the area of supervision whose classic 1955 book, *Supervision: A Social Process,*[3] seems remarkably contemporary, identify certain principles which govern the operation of supervision as follows:

PRINCIPLES GOVERNING THE OPERATION OF SUPERVISION

1 Administration is *ordinarily* concerned with providing material facilities and with operation in general.

2 Supervision is *ordinarily* concerned with improving the setting for learning in particular.

3 Administration and supervision considered *functionally* cannot be separated or set off from each other. The two are co-ordinate, correlative, complementary, mutually shared functions in the operation of educational systems. The provision of any and all conditions favorable to learning is the common purpose of both.

[2] Kimball Wiles, *Supervision for Better Schools,* 3d ed., Englewood Cliffs, N.J.: Prentice-Hall, 1967.

[3] William H. Burton and Leo J. Brueckner, *Supervision: A Social Process,* 3d ed., New York: Appleton-Century-Crofts, 1955, pp. 85, 88. Reprinted by permission of Appleton-Century-Crofts, Division of Meredith Corporation.

4 Good supervision is based on philosophy and science.

   a Supervision will be sensitive to ultimate aims and values, to policies, with special reference to their adequacy.

   b Supervision will be sensitive to "factness" and to law, with special reference to their accuracy.

   c Supervision will be sensitive to the emergent, evolutionary, nature of the universe and of democratic society in particular, hence should be permeated with the experimental attitude, and engage constantly in re-evaluation of aims and values, of policies, of materials and methods.

5 Good supervision is (in the United States) based upon the democratic philosophy.

   a Supervision will respect personality and individual differences between personalities, will seek to provide opportunities for the best expression of each unique personality.

   b Supervision will be based upon the assumption that educational workers are capable of growth. It will accept idiosyncrasies, reluctance to cooperate, and antagonism as human characteristics, just as it accepts reasonableness, co-operation, and energetic activity. The former are challenges; the latter, assets.

   c Supervision will endeavor to develop in all a democratic conscience, that is, recognition that democracy includes important obligations as well as rights.

   d Supervision will provide full opportunity for the cooperative formulation of policies and plans, will welcome and utilize free expression and contributions from all.

   e Supervision will stimulate initiative, self-reliance and individual responsibility on the part of all persons in the discharge of their duties.

   f Supervision will substitute leadership for authority. Authority will be recognized as the authority of the situation and of the facts within the situation. Personal authority if necessary will be derived from group planning.

   g Supervision will work toward co-operatively determined functional groupings of the staff, with flexible regrouping as necessary; will invite specialists when advisable.

6 Good supervision will employ scientific methods and attitudes in so far as those methods and attitudes are applicable to the dynamic social processes of education; will utilize and adapt to specific situations scientific findings concerning the learner, his learning processes, the nature and development of personality; will co-operate occasionally in pure research.

7 Good supervision, in situations where the precise controlled methods of science are not applicable, will employ processes of dynamic problem-solving in studying, improving, and evaluating its products and processes. Supervision either by scientific methods or through orderly thought processes will constantly derive and use data and conclusions which are more objective, more precise, more sufficient, more impartial, more expertly secured, and more systematically organized than are the data and conclusions of uncontrolled opinion.

8 Good supervision will be creative and not prescriptive.

   a Supervision will determine procedures in the light of the needs of each supervisory teaching-learning situation.

   b Supervision will provide opportunity for the exercise of originality and for the development of unique contributions, of creative self-expression; will seek latent talent.

c   Supervision will deliberately shape and manipulate the environment.

9 Good supervision proceeds by means of an orderly, co-operatively planned and executed series of activities.

10 Good supervision will be judged by the results it secures.

11 Good supervision is becoming professional. That is, it is increasingly seeking to evaluate its personnel, procedures, and results; it is moving toward standards and toward self-supervision.

PRINCIPLES GOVERNING THE PURPOSES OF SUPERVISION[4]

1 The ultimate purpose of supervision is the promotion of pupil growth and hence eventually the improvement of society.

2 A second general purpose of supervision is to supply leadership in securing continuity and constant readaptation in the educational program over a period of years; from level to level within the system; and from one area of learning experience and content to another.

3 The immediate purpose of supervision is co-operatively to develop favorable settings for teaching and learning.

a   Supervision, through all means available, will seek improved methods of teaching and learning.

b   Supervision willl create a physical, social, and psychological climate or environment favorable to learning.

c   Supervision will co-ordinate and integrate all educational efforts and materials, will supply continuity.

d   Supervision will enlist the co-operation of all staff members in serving their own needs and those of the situation; will provide ample, natural opportunities for growth by all concerned in the correction and prevention of teaching difficulties, and for growth in the assumption of new responsibilities.

e   Supervision will aid, inspire, lead, and develop that security which liberates the creative spirit.

4   More recently John Lovell in revising Kimball Wiles's book views supervision as an instructional behavior system.[5]

> *Instructional supervisory behavior is assumed to be an additional behavior system formally provided by the organization for the purpose of interacting with the teaching behavior system in such a way as to maintain, change, and improve the provision and actualization of learning opportunities for students.* The instructional supervisor, operating from his own unique conceptual base, works to achieve certain tasks through various operations and activities. From this frame of reference, instructional supervisory behavior can be a dimension of many roles in the eduational organization. A superintendent of schools, with special competence in the teaching of reading, working with a group of primary teachers to evaluate a proposed "reading program," would be participating in instructional supervisory behavior. A teacher appointed by the administration to chair a curriculum planning committee would be participating in instructional

---

[4] Ibid.

[5] Kimball Wiles and John T. Lovell, *Supervision for Better Schools,* 4th ed., Englewood Cliffs, N.J.: Prentice-Hall, 1975, pp. 6, 8.

supervisory behavior to achieve the task. The critical factor is not the title of the role but the nature of the behavior.

5 Following Lovell, Robert Alfonso, Gerald Firth, and Richard Neville also view supervision as an instructional behavior system which interacts with the school's counseling, teaching, administrative, and student behavior system. In their view:[6]

> Instructional supervision is herein defined as: *Behavior officially designated by the organization that directly affects teacher behavior in such a way as to facilitate pupil learning and achieve the goals of the organization.*
>
>   There are three key elements in this definition. First, the behavior exhibited is "officially designated." It is not random, casually determined activity, but it bears the stamp of organizational request and formal authority. Secondly, it "directly influences teacher behavior." This rules out the multitude of tasks performed by supervisors that, while they may be important to the organization, are *not* supervision. It provides a test as to whether one is really engaging in supervisory behavior—does it clearly affect the teachers?—the teacher behavior subsystem. Thirdly, it specifies an ultimate outcome tied directly to the reason for the existence of the school: the facilitation of student learning. This element also provides focus for influencing teacher behavior—not willy-nilly, but purposeful change in teacher behavior in order to improve learning.

The authors agree that supervision is a set of activities and role specifications specifically designed to influence instruction. Harris's statement best summarizes this view. Wiles, and Burton and Brueckner provide a human relations portrait of supervision immersed in the principles of democracy and equality as a means to influence instruction. More recent works, as represented by Lovell, and Alfonso, Firth, and Neville, view supervision as a special kind of behavior which is distinguished from other behavior by its deliberate focus on the school's teaching behavior system. These authors rely heavily on a broad social science base characterized by scientific rationality or objectivity in prescribing principles of supervisory behavior.

Human resources supervision shares many of the features of the points of view discussed. It, too, focuses on the improvement of instruction, though it views the links between organization, leadership, educational program, and instruction as being far more deliberate and interdependent. An assumption basic to human resources supervision, for example, is that humane classrooms and humane curriculum designs can only be accomplished in humanistic organizations.

Human resources supervision builds upon many of the ideas of Wiles, and Burton and Brueckner, though in human resources, more emphasis is given to integrating individual needs with school objectives and tasks. One way that this is done is by emphasizing the importance of meaningful work to teachers and by viewing teacher satisfaction, *derived from accomplishment,* as a critical key to building motivation and commitment and therefore improving instruction.

---

[6] Robert J. Alfonso, Gerald R. Firth, and Richard F. Neville, *Instructional Supervision: A Behavioral System,* Boston: Allyn and Bacon, 1975, pp. 35–36.

Human resources supervision shares an interest in the social sciences with the views of Lovell and of Alfonso, Firth, and Neville though in a much more *subjective* fashion. In the view of human resources supervision values, too, play an important part and social science concepts need to be evaluated for appropriateness to educational settings before they can be put into practice. In this sense, educational administration and supervision are applied sciences drawing upon both science (research and theory) and art (experience and intuition) for concepts and ideas which are evaluated for consistency with *educational values* before they are adapted to practice.[7]

Confusion often exists in our field between supervisory roles and supervisory processes. In the sections which follow, various images of supervision with implications for practice are discussed and an attempt is made to differentiate supervisory processes from those considered administrative.

THE ROLE-PROCESS DILEMMA

Supervision on the one hand is often viewed as a process component of a variety of roles and on the other hand as a useful label to categorize a group of school roles whose primary function is the improvement of instruction. Essentially, incumbents of roles whose primary function is the improvement of instruction also engage in supervisory processes. Chairpersons, curriculum directors, subject-matter supervisors, and many elementary school principals are examples of people whose roles are considered supervisory. They engage in such supervisory processes as staff development, motivation, and shared decision making but typically within the context of instructional improvement. Superintendents, however, engage in similar processes as they "supervise" central office staff. In short, many of the characteristics of supervision are shared by a number of roles, though typically those labeled supervisors engage in these activities more deliberately within the context of instructional improvement.

It seems useful to us to distinguish between modes of behavior which can be described as supervisory and others which cannot. Deciding on what constitutes supervisory behavior helps us to realize the scope and breadth of supervision. Below are several statements which help to clarify our view of the concept of supervision. In each case the distinctions we make are conceptual and are designed to increase our understanding. In operation the distinctions are less clear.

1 Viewing supervision as a process is in some respects more meaningful than viewing supervision as a role or the supervisor as a particular role incumbent.

When supervision is viewed as a process, then all personnel who practice supervision in schools (superintendents, principals, librarians, staff personnel, department or division chairpersons, classroom teachers, and others, including nonprofessional personnel) are supervisors at one time or another.

[7] See, for example, T. J. Sergiovanni and F. D. Carver, *The New School Executive: A Theory of Administration,* New York: Harper & Row, 1973, esp. Chap. 1, "Applied Science and the Role of Value Judgements," and Chap. 2, "A Belief Pattern for Decision-Making."

2 Supervision is a process used by those in schools who have responsibility for one or another aspect of the school's goals and who *depend directly upon others* to help them achieve these goals.

A crucial aspect which differentiates supervisory behavior from other forms of organizational behavior is *action to achieve goals through other people.* A principal who works to improve the effectiveness of the educational program for students by helping teachers become more effective in the classroom is behaving in a supervisory way. A critical aspect of this relationship is that the principal is dependent upon the teacher in attempting to increase program effectiveness.

3 Since behavior is a significant part of the supervisory process, it is often useful as an analytical method for understanding the process as a whole to focus on this aspect of supervision.

The supervisory process requires attention to the social, cultural, attitudinal, and behavioral ethos of the total supervisory environment, but it is often analytically easier to discuss the process in terms of behavior. Thus supervisory behavior is an important construct in this book and, as such, forms the basis for analyzing other aspects of the supervisory process and their relationship to supervisory effectiveness.

4 Behavior of administrators and others in school organizations which is characterized by action toward achievement of school goals but is *not* dependent upon others for success is described as administrative rather than supervisory.

When administrators and supervisors work with things and ideas rather than people in pursuing school goals, they tend to be operating in an administrative way rather than in a supervisory way. Work on the budget, the master schedule, or the program for a summer workshop and preparation of a memo for the superintendent may all be related to achieving or facilitating school purposes, but the principal is often justified in carrying out these activities and responsibilities in a way which does not require dependence upon others for success.

5 Depending upon the circumstances, one may choose to behave in an administrative way—directly—or in a supervisory way—through people—to achieve school goals.

Certain aspects of school goals are more effectively (and in some cases exclusively) accomplished through administrative behavior, while other aspects are more effectively accomplished through behavior described as supervisory. The choice between one pattern of behavior and the other is critical for decision making in school organizations. To be sure, as schools mature and develop as professional organizations, the supervisory way of behaving becomes the dominant pattern of operation for all school personnel. Figure 1-1 illustrates this relationship.

We need at this point to differentiate between working with and through people to achieve school goals and using people to achieve these goals. Using people is consistent with classical-traditional management styles (and, to a lesser

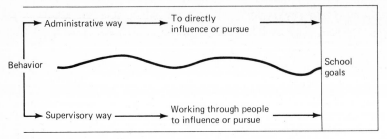

Figure 1-1 Behaving in an administrative way or supervisory way.

extent, contemporary management patterns), which considered people as appendages of administrators as they, the administrators, pursued school goals. Modes of operation consistent with this pattern are not effective in marshaling the human organization to work on behalf of the school's purposes. While such modes of operation may show signs of high performance efficiency, these results are usually short-term, with long-term results that are disastrous for the leader, the led, the organization, and, in our case, the young clients who pass through the nation's schools.

6 When administrators and supervisors choose to operate in an administrative way to achieve school purposes, their actions may or may not involve change; but when they choose to operate in a supervisory way, their actions usually involve some aspects of change in behavior (see Figure 1-2).

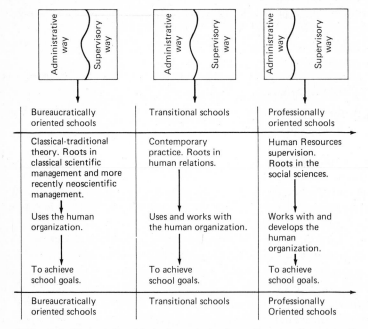

Figure 1-2 The relationship between behavior patterns and organizational maturity.

A major effort of any supervisory act is the changing of some aspect of a person's concept of self, way of behaving, attitude set, or relationship to the school and within the school as an organization. Whether a supervisor is working to improve the performance of teacher A, the effectiveness of classroom B, the attitude of group C, or the direction of school D, each purpose requires fundamental attention to the nature of change, strategies for change, and resistance to change. When administrators and supervisors decide to behave in a supervisory way, they adopt the perspective of change agent. Processes of change and their relationships to supervisory attitudes and behavior are explored in detail in later chapters.

We have discussed and described perspectives for understanding the concept of supervision. An effort has been made to differentiate between alternative ways of behaving in order to accomplish school goals. Actions on the part of school administrators, teachers, and supervisors which involve and depend upon the acceptance, identity, and commitment of people in order to achieve these goals are described as *supervisory*. Actions on the part of administrators, teachers, and supervisors which do not involve, or are not dependent upon, these aspects of the human organization to achieve school goals are described as *administrative*.

In addition, it was noted that though administrators and teachers engage in supervisory processes, the label "supervisor" is generally affixed to those who engage in supervisory processes primarily within the context of instructional improvement.

As schools progress toward professional maturity, the dominant pattern of behavior for all school personnel will be supervisory rather than administrative. Notice that supervisory ways of behaving are not the province of a particular person or a particular position (principal, science supervisor, teacher) but are natural modes of behavior for all who work with, and are a part of, the human organization of any school.

CHARACTERISTICS OF SUPERVISORY ROLES

Supervisors work primarily in the area of instructional improvement. Organizational demands require most personnel in schools to be involved in some aspects of administrative behavior, but for those who work in the area of instructional improvement, supervisory behavior will tend to predominate. Supervisory roles can be further differentiated from the more administrative roles by such characteristics as (1) heavy reliance on expertness as an educational program leader and instructional leader, (2) the necessity of living in two worlds and of speaking two languages, and (3) limits imposed on their authority.

Supervisors in education, as in other fields ranging from medicine to industry, are expected to be experts in the production system of their organizations. A high school principal can get along quite well with only a conversational acquaintance with classroom organizational patterns, problems, and prospects, but a department chairperson needs a more detailed perspective to be successful. Supervisors are expected to be experts in educational and instructional matters. As educational and instructional leaders, their work exhibits a high concern for:

Curriculum and teaching objectives
Educational program content, coordination, and scope
Alternatives and options
Curriculum and teaching innovations
Structured knowledge
Grouping and scheduling patterns
Lesson and unit planning
Evaluating and selecting learning materials
Patterns of teacher and student classroom influence
Developing and evaluating educational encounters
Teaching styles, methods, and procedures
Classroom learning climates
Teacher, student, and program evaluation[8]

A second characteristic differentiating supervisory from other roles is the necessity of living in two worlds and of speaking two languages—the language of teachers and the language of administrators. Teachers and administrators operate from different perspectives each of which often makes one unintelligible to the other. True, most administrators have been teachers previously, but having been cast into a different arena and subjected to different pressures, they often have difficulty in understanding the problems teachers face. Teachers, on the other hand, view the school from a limited, often unrealistic, perspective. Their perspective is frequently accompanied by an unsympathetic view of the administrator and his or her role. Supervisors are forced to live in both worlds and to mediate difficulties in communication and perspective between the two worlds without alienating either—no small order!

A third characteristic, cited earlier, involves limitations placed on the supervisor's authority: Supervisors are often considered "staff" rather than "line" officers, though admittedly the difference between the two is more muddled than neat. As such, they rely heavily on functional authority conferred by their knowledge as educational and instructional leaders and on personal leadership characteristics as sources of authority to influence both teachers and administrators. Effective administrators rely similarly on functional authority, but this is enhanced or backed up by formal authority derived from their more clearly superordinate position in the hierarchy. We will discuss supervisory authority more fully in Chapter 7.

THE SUPERVISOR IN THE HIERARCHY

Just what is the supervisor's place in the hierarchy of the school? Keith Davis identifies five different views of the supervisor's role which range from affording

---

[8] See, for example, Thomas J. Sergiovanni, *Handbook for Effective Department Leadership,* Boston: Allyn and Bacon, 1977, p. 4. Parts Two and Three of this book give attention to building a conceptual base for understanding and enriching the supervisor's potential for educational and instructional leadership.

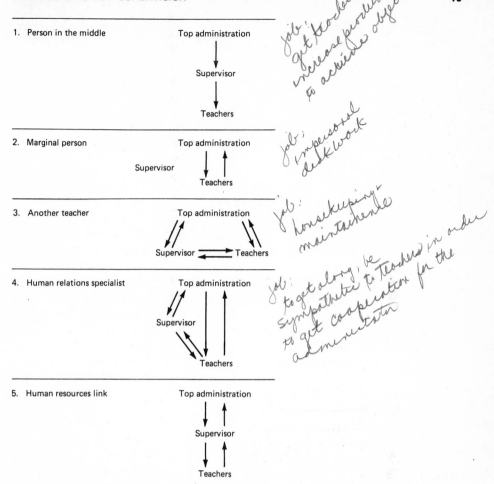

Job: teachers to get increase production to achieve objectives

Job: impersonal deskwork

Job: housekeeping + maintenance

Job: to get along, be sympathetic to teachers in order to get cooperation for the administration

Figure 1-3 Viewpoints on the supervisor's role. _(From Keith Davis, Human Behavior at Work: Human Relations and Organizational Behavior, 4th ed., N.Y.: McGraw-Hill, 1972.)_

the supervisor a critical place in the hierarchy to affording the supervisor a marginal place.[9] The viewpoints are illustrated in Figure 1-3.

The _person-in-the-middle_ view of the supervisor is characterized by a process of mediating between the two opposing worlds of teachers and administrators. Here administrators are seen as emphasizing task-oriented leadership and a variety of quality-control mechanisms in efforts to push teacher and school closer to achieving objectives and increasing production. Teachers as human beings, however, are seeking a more relaxed, trusting, and congenial atmosphere within which to work—one that is secure from tension and is responsive to their needs.

[9] Keith Davis, _Human Behavior at Work: Human Relations and Organizational Behavior,_ 4th ed., New York: McGraw-Hill, 1972, pp. 120–123.

Supervisors are caught in the middle, struggling valiantly to reconcile what may well be impossible differences. In this sense, supervisors are seen as buffers, or persons in the middle.

As a *marginal person,* the supervisor is also in the middle but is excluded from or on the margin of important decisions affecting the school. Here the supervisor is not accepted by either group and is ignored for the most part by both groups. As a result the marginal-person supervisor often spends more time as a curriculum administrator, as a materials procurer, or being engaged in some other impersonal activity associated with desk work.

The *another-teacher* view of supervision is characterized by affording supervisors low authority and status and by permitting them only minimum discretion. Supervisors, in this view, are often considered liaison persons upon whom administrators rely to get the word down to teachers. Housekeeping chores and maintenance activities, rather than leadership responsibilities, occupy the attention of this type of supervisor. Many secondary school chairpersons, for example, can be characterized as supervisors of this sort.

As a *human relations specialist* the supervisor is considered a staff specialist charged with the caring for, and maintaining of, the human side of the school enterprise. The need for such a specialist is based on the assumption that in any organization job demands and human demands are in conflict. Teachers have needs and feelings and are subject to frustration, disappointment, and other maladies which can endanger morale. According to this view, poor morale is not good for the school and should be avoided. The supervisor's job as human relations specialist is to get along with teachers, be sympathetic to their problems, and otherwise tend to their idiosyncrasies in an attempt to gain their cooperation and compliance to administrative directives.

As a *human resources link,* the supervisor is not viewed as an administrative tool or organizational buffer but as a key member of the school's leadership team. Here the supervisor is a critical link between the school's organizational and management subsystem and its educational-instructional subsystem. This is indeed an in-the-middle view, but here the supervisor serves an integrating rather than buffering role. It is assumed that though educational programs and instruction exist within an organized setting, organization and mangement exist to serve educational programs and instruction. That being the case, the integrating role of the supervisor is considered critical in the administrative hierarchy, and he or she assumes a key role in school district decision making. The reasons why the school exists constitute the supervisor's primary area of responsibility.

The supervisor should be viewed as a human resources link in the administrative hierarchy and as such should assume a critical role in district decision making. This is a normative view of supervisors which prevails in the literature, is believed by many including top administration, and fits a growing number, but still a minority, of schools.[10] A descriptive view represents a more realistic ap-

---

[10] As noted in the Introduction to Part One, more emphasis is presently being given to supervision as a key role in building school effectiveness not only by professional organization and journals but by changes in practice in school districts throughout the country.

praisal which reveals that most supervisors are viewed either as marginal members of the school hierarchy or as persons in the middle. A large number are viewed as human relations specialists, and this may well be a first step toward upgrading supervisory roles in a fashion which approximates the human resources viewpoint. The other-teacher image of supervision is fading as collective bargaining becomes widespread.

SUMMARY

This chapter presented perspectives on supervision. Viewpoints of selected authors were provided and contrasted. Supervision can be viewed, on the one hand, as a process component of a variety of administrative and supervisory roles and, on the other hand, as a label to categorize roles the primary responsibility of which is the improvement of instruction. The dependency relationship which exists between leader and individual or group distinguishes administrative behavior from supervisory behavior. Supervisory behavior was prescribed, for instance, when the leader needed to obtain individual or group commitment to goals and tasks in order to be effective.

The extent to which supervisory, as opposed to administrative, behavior dominates provides a basis for classifying schools as bureaucratic, transitional, or professional. It was noted that the more professional schools were dominated by supervisory behavior.

Supervisory roles were characterized by three distinguishing features: (1) heavy reliance on expertness as an educational program and instructional leader, (2) the necessity to live in two worlds and to speak two languages, and (3) limits imposed on their authority. Five viewpoints of supervisory roles within the administrative hierarchy were then described. They included the person in the middle, marginal person, another teacher, human relations specialist, and human resources link. The human resources link perspective was then proposed as the most effective model for supervision.

STUDY GUIDE

Recall the concepts, ideas, and meanings associated with each of the following phrases and terms included in this chapter. Can you discuss each of them with a colleague and apply them to the supervisory context of your school? If you cannot, review them in the text and record the page number for future reference.

1 Buffering role _____
2 Dependency relationship _____
3 Descriptive view of supervision _____
4 Distinguishing characteristics of supervisory roles _____
5 Educational-leadership concerns _____
6 Human relations specialist _____
7 Human resources link _____
8 Instructional supervisory behavior _____
9 Integrating role _____

10 Marginal person _____
11 Normative view of supervision _____
12 Person in the middle _____
13 Purposes of supervision _____
14 Role-process dilemma _____
15 Supervision as instruction-related _____
16 Supervisors as expediters _____
17 Supervisory authority _____
18 Supervisory patterns in bureaucratic schools _____
19 Supervisory patterns in professional schools _____
20 Supervisory patterns in transitional schools _____
21 Teacher behavior subsystem _____
22 Worlds and languages of supervisors _____

EXERCISES

1 Who are the persons in your school or district that are considered primarily as supervisors? How is their work distinguished from those considered primarily as administrators?

2 Review persons in your school or district in both supervisory and administrative roles. Develop a chart listing the role, the type of supervisory activities demonstrated in the role, and the percentage of time spent on each supervisory activity in a typical week. Base your estimates of percentage on the total time spent in all activities (administrative and supervisory) for each role.

3 Using Figure 1-3 as a guide, classify each person in your school or district whom you have identified primarily as a supervisor.

4 Describe the "ideal" supervisor as seen by the average teacher in your school or district. How does this description measure up to your analysis of supervisory roles in 2 and 3 above? How does this description measure up to your view of the "ideal" supervisor?

Chapter 2

A Theory of Supervision

A number of frameworks for conceptualizing supervision and supervisory behavior are presented in this book. Among them are Jacob Getzels and Egon Guba's social system formulation; Amitai Etzioni's compliance theory; Rensis Likert's System 4; Robert Blake and Jane Mouton's managerial grid; the contingency leadership theories of Fred Fiedler and W. J. Reddin; the concept of organizational health, as proposed by Matthew Miles; conflict models proposed by Chris Argyris and Ronald Corwin; Gerald Hage's axiomatic theory of organizations; McGregor's Theories X and Y; the motivational theories of Abraham Maslow, Frederick Herzberg, and Victor Vroom; and other conceptual frameworks not readily associated with specific names.[1] Each of these modes of thought varies considerably in depth and focus, but each provides readers with "power concepts" which facilitate the explanation of organizational, administrative, and supervisory phenomena. An understanding of these phenomena can form the basis for improved supervisory performance. These frameworks are an integral part of the theory which follows and are discussed and applied in subsequent chapters. None of the formulations currently available to educators is extensive enough, however, to provide us with a general theory of supervision. Each should be viewed as a middle-range theory. The theory of supervision we propose in this

[1] A bibliography for these authors appears at the end of Chapter 2.

chapter is composed of several middle-range theories integrated into a broader design.

THE IMPORTANCE OF THEORY

Hands-on experiences and practical suggestions characterized by immediacy of application to the situation being confronted are what busy and hard-pressed supervisory practitioners seek. This orientation is valuable indeed but inadequate and shortsighted *as an exclusive view.* The effective supervisor needs to practice his or her profession from a foundation of concepts and ideas strong enough to stand the test of time and powerful enough to account for a variety of situations, many of which will be new and unfamiliar.

Consider, for example, the differences between training and education. Training is a process of accumulating a series of programmed behaviors which can be applied with reliability to a series of highly predictable situations.[2] The preparation of masons, refrigerator repairmen, and computer console operators is characterized by training. Jobs suitable for training can be precisely defined and analyzed, and a best way can be determined for implementing each job's activities.

Education, by contrast, is a process of accumulating understandings and interpretations of knowledge. Definitive answers are not provided in education, but rather the emphasis is on acquiring knowledge paradigms, value perspectives, structures, concepts, and ways of thinking which help the educated person to generate pertinent strategies for new and often unfamiliar situations.

Some aspects of supervision, charting classroom interactions using the Flanders method, for example, are quite programmed and suitable to training. But supervision is largely a varied, situational, and unpredictable discipline. It is difficult to generate universal laws and principles of procedure for supervision, and for this reason the supervisory setting is more suitable to education than training. Conceptual considerations and theoretical frameworks are not only powerful and economical ways to understand supervisory problems and practices but are necessary components of the supervisor's education.

Theories are modes of thinking that lead to the generation of propositions amenable to testing either in the laboratory or in practice. In developing a theocal basis for human resources supervision, our intent is to construct a systematic conceptual framework to assist readers in increasing understanding of present practice and in generating additional practices.

Many view theory as a set of abstractions that occur in some mysterious way, from which principles are derived which seem only remotely related to practice. In fact, however, theory is usually derived from practice. Practices become established sometimes as a result of hunches and often as a result of trial and error. Those who observe practice fairly systematically form additional hunches about the relationship between and among practices. Hunches can lead directly to propositions and principles relating to practice, but as hunches are

---

[2] Many rigidly structured and articulated competency-based "training" programs can be so categorized.

formalized and linked together, they become the basis for theory. Propositions and principles are derived from theory, and their testing in the laboratory or real world leads to the establishment and extension of practice. The cycle continues with practices leading to new hunches, more theory, additional propositions, testing, and further modification and extension of practice.

SKILL LEVELS FOR SUPERVISORS

Scholars have attempted to identify the traits of successful supervision and more recently have turned their attention to identifying competencies for successful supervision. The complex, varied, and unpredictable nature of supervision, however, has made such attempts difficult. Adequate maps of successful supervision remain elusive.

An alternate strategy is to focus less on traits and competencies and more on skills and their related domains of knowledge. Katz has identified three basic skills upon which he believes successful supervision rests—technical, human, and conceptual.[3] The skills are actually quite interdependent but can be treated separately for analytical purposes. Each of the skill domains applies to educational and organizational leadership roles of supervisors as well.

Technical skills assume ability to use knowledge, methods, and techniques to perform specific tasks. The mechanics associated with writing a lesson plan, developing a study unit, equipping a learning-resource center, purchasing laboratory equipment, preparing a meeting agenda, scheduling a cycle of clinical supervision, and filling out an annual report might be examples of technical skills.

Human skills refer to one's ability and judgment in working with and through people. This skill requires self-understanding and acceptance as well as consideration for others. Its knowledge base includes an understanding of, and facility for, leadership effectiveness, adult motivation, attitudinal development, group dynamics, and the development of human resources.

Conceptual skills refer to the supervisor's ability to view the school, the district, and the educational program as a whole. This skill includes the effective mapping of the interdependence between the components of the school as an organizational system, the educational program as an instructional system, and the human organization as a functioning human system. Understanding the interdependencies which exist between establishing a humane organization, articulating a humane administrative-supervisory system, and developing a humane educational program is an example of conceptual skill.

Katz argues that, though each of the skill levels is universally present in administrative and supervisory positions, conceptual skills are emphasized more by administrators and technical skills more by supervisory personnel, who are for the most part concerned with the day-by-day work of the school. This relationship is illustrated in Figure 2-1.

Notice that regardless of level a common and strong emphasis is required on human skills. Part One of this book, "Human Resources Supervision and Organi-

---

[3] Robert L. Katz, "Skills of an Effective Administrator," *Harvard Business Review,* vol. 33, no. 1, pp. 33–42, 1955.

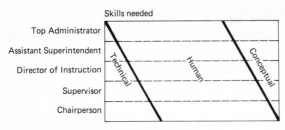

Figure 2-1   Skills Needed at Various Levels.

zational Leadership," gives strong attention to the knowledge domains associated with this skill level. The conceptual skill level, particularly important to Part Two, "Human Resources and Educational Leadership," is strongly emphasized throughout the book. The theme that human organization, human supervision, and human educational programs are interdependent and inseparable is an example. Some attention is given to technical skills, particularly in Part Three, "Human Resources Approach to Staff Development, Clinical Supervision, and Teacher Evaluation," but this attention is limited by the need to relate technical skills to specific supervisory situations—a task better accomplished through class discussion and simulation, and in-service education programs.

A SYNTHESIZING THEORY OF SUPERVISION

What follows in the form of a theory of supervision represents a blueprint for the development of subsequent chapters as well as a basis for supervisory strategies which, it is hoped, will *be developed by the reader.* The theory proposed is one which depends heavily upon a number of existing formulations, concepts, and ideas which have been synthesized and related to provide an integrated and systematic effort toward improving supervisory effectiveness.

The theory identifies and describes three sets of variables. One set is the *initiating* variables. Initiating variables are what supervisors start out with. They include the assumptions, values, and beliefs which determine the leadership style and pattern and the priorities of supervisors, and the kinds of decisions they are likely to make. With regard to organizational structure, for example, how supervisors view and use rules and regulations, the decision-making traditions and procedures they establish, and the patterns of authority they develop and enforce are considered initiating variables.

Reactions of persons influenced by the initiating variables make up the second set of variables referred to as *mediating*. The third set, the *effectiveness* variables, represents the "output" which results from school efforts and activities. These are the key components of the school's human organization.

The following list of variables is not conclusive or exhaustive but represents examples which fall into each of the three categories. In each case the emphasis is on teachers and other adults, but the categories and the theory itself apply to students as well.

EXAMPLES OF INITIATING VARIABLES

1 Assumptions which supervisors hold in reference to their peers, subordinates, and themselves.

2 Administrative and supervisory behavior patterns which are consistently displayed by supervisors.

3 The nature of the authority system which prevails in the school and the resulting strategies for compliance used by supervisors.

4 The nature of goals and directions for the school and patterns for the emergence of these goals.

5 Character of motivational topics and motivational strategies used by supervisors.

6 The supervisor's view of change and the articulation of his or her change-agent role.

7 The structure and functioning of decision making.

8 The supervisor's perspectives on the organizational character of the school or unit. Consider, for example, the emphasis the supervisor gives to each of the following:

a Formalization (the extent to which the supervisor emphasizes rules and regulations).

b Stratification (the importance the supervisor places on status systems and the rights of those in superordinate positions).

c Centralization (the extent to which the supervisor emphasizes shared decision-making, as opposed to superordinate decision-making, prerogatives).

d Productivity (the emphasis the supervisor gives to the number, but not necessarily the quality, of units processed. The number of learning objectives, the number of children served, the amount of time spent, and the number of months gained could be considered as examples).

e Efficiency (the extent to which the supervisor emphasizes quantity of output at least cost. Large classes and lecture methods are more efficient means to cover the text material than small classes).

f Adaptability (the emphasis the supervisor gives to school responsiveness to changing needs and requirements of students, advances in educational technology and pedagogy, and changes in community. Individualized instruction, team teaching, and active participation of parents and students are often common indicators of adaptability).

g Complexity (the extent to which the supervisor relies on the personal and professional expertness of subordinates and respects their stature as educational specialists).

h Job Satisfaction (the emphasis the supervisor gives to providing teachers and other organizational members with opportunities for achieving *intrinsic* satisfaction at work).

EXAMPLES OF MEDIATING VARIABLES

1 Attitudes which teachers and other employees have toward their jobs and toward their superiors, peers, and subordinates

2 The extent to which the staff is committed to school goals and purposes

3 Levels of performance goals held by teachers and other educational workers

4 Levels of group loyalty and group commitment which exist in the school

5 The extent to which teachers have confidence and trust in themselves, their peers, and their superiors

6 The extent to which teachers feel that they have control over their immediate work environment and can meaningfully influence the larger school environment
7 The extent to which a system for communications exists at all levels of the school enterprise and in all directions

EXAMPLES OF EFFECTIVENESS VARIABLES

1 Performance levels of teachers and other employees
2 Performance levels of students
3 Personal growth levels of teachers and students
4 Absence and dropout rates of the students
5 Quality of school-community relations
6 Quality of teacher-management relations
7 Levels of intrinsic job satisfaction for teachers

TRADITIONAL SUPERVISORY PATTERNS

Confusion often results when one attempts to map the relationships which exist between variables of one set and those of other sets. Indeed, the relationships between and among these sets of variables are just beginning to be understood. A common practice, which is now considered to be suspect, is for supervisors to work from initiating variables directly to effectiveness variables. This practice is associated with the classical scientific-management (and the now-popular neo-scientific-management) approach to supervision and is illustrated as follows:

Initiating variables ⟶ Effectiveness variables

Social science theorists seem now to suggest that the attainment of effectiveness variables is dependent upon the health of the school's human resources as reflected in teachers' skills, loyalty, trust, support, commitment to objectives, and motivation to work. This requires that supervision be concerned with conscious and direct efforts to influence the mediating variables.

HUMAN RESOURCES SUPERVISORY PATTERNS

Patterns of supervision associated with human resources are based on the premise that consistent and long-term achievement of school success is dependent upon the positive presence of the mediating variables.

The human organization of schools, which includes the quality of communications, group loyalty, levels of job satisfaction, and commitment to task, for example, exerts a direct influence over the determining of the nature and quality of school success. In turn, these mediating variables are influenced and determined by the nature and quality of attitudes, practices, and conditions which the initiating variables comprise. For conceptual purposes the variables are arranged unilaterally, but in practice they are interactive. We usually speak of the initiating variables affecting the mediating, but overlook the influence of the mediating on the initiating variables. This interacting relationship can be viewed as follows:

The direct approach may be illustrated by a principal who, in attempting to improve learning experiences for youngsters, wishes to adopt innovation A for his or her school. This principal may, by behaving in an administrative way, choose to use hierarchical position and legal prerogative to require this change (he or she might proceed with the adoption of the change over the summer recess and present the new teaching pattern, innovation A, to the teachers upon their return in the fall), or might, by behaving in a supervisory way, approach the human organization concerning the problem of improving learning experiences for children with an expectation of the professional response of others to this problem.

The first approach—the strategy which moves directly from the intervening variable set to the school-success variables—risks creating apathy or alienation in the human organization. Teachers will tend not to identify with changes imposed on them from above. The effectiveness of the school, therefore, may actually be reduced rather than improved as originally intended by our fictitious principal. A well-meaning administrator who ignores the human organization often finds that his or her efforts are unappreciated as well as ineffectual in terms of school performance.

The key to understanding the theory is to differentiate between long- and short-term effectiveness. Often, working directly from initiating to effectiveness variables is more effective in the short run than working to effect changes in the mediating variables. But over time, this strategy can result in serious erosion of the school's human organization. Consider, for example, the now-classic Morse and Reimer study[4] which analyzed the effectiveness (the productivity and well-being of the human organization) of employees subjected to two different styles of supervision. Group 1, subjected to a style of supervision described as hierarchical by the investigators, outdistanced Group 2, subjected to a participatory style, in productivity, but showed a commensurate decline in the quality of its human organization. Over time, this corrosion of the human organization in the hierarchically controlled environment took its toll in performance. In commenting on this phenomenon, Likert notes that "the attitudes, loyalties, and motivation which improved the most in the participative program and deteriorated the most in the hierarchical controlled program are those which these studies have consistently shown to be most clearly related *in the long run* to employee motivation and productivity."[5]

Human resources supervision, that which fully coordinates, develops, and utilizes the resources of the human organization, requires an investment in time

---

[4] Nancy Morse and E. Reimer, "The Experimental Change of a Major Organizational Variable," *Journal of Abnormal and Social Psychology,* vol. 52, no. 1, pp. 120–129, 1956.
[5] Rensis Likert, *New Patterns of Management,* New York: McGraw-Hill, 1961, p. 68.

by school ófficials before appreciable results can be realized. As the mellowing process sets in, the school's investment in its human organization will likely show improvement in each of the effectiveness variables.

THE THEORY ILLUSTRATED

The accompanying flowchart (Table 2-1) suggests samples of alternative attitudes and ways of behaving for those who supervise in schools, as well as several organizational styles which schools may adopt. The potential effects of each of these initiating variables on a host of mediating variables are described. And finally, changes which can be expected to result in the school-effectiveness variables are indicated. The theory, as illustrated in Table 2-1, forms the basis for Part One of this book. Each of the concepts which compose the theory is cross-referenced to later chapters. There the concepts will be illustrated, explained, and applied to supervision for better schools. As you read the flowchart highlighting key characteristics of the theory, note that across the top are listed the three variables of concern: the initiating variables, how the mediating variables are affected by the initiating variables, and the resulting quality of school effectiveness. The initiating variables are further subdivided into schools of thought, or supervisory theories, with which they are most associated. Supervisory assumption, for example, might be associated with classical, contemporary, or human resource theories. Mediating variables, listed to the right of initiating variables in Table 2-1, are affected by initiating variables in three ways represented as Types 1, 2, and 3. The mediating variables in turn influence the quality of school effectiveness. That is, over time, the school may exhibit high, medium, or low effectiveness depending upon the reaction of the mediating variables to those listed as initiating. Quality of school effectiveness is listed to the extreme right of Table 2-1.

Further discussion of the mediating variables and the types of reactions they provide to what the supervisor initiates are described below.

Mediating Variables—Type 1 Reaction[6]

Type 1 reactions—those prompted by classical-traditional supervisory patterns— are typically characterized by considerable teacher job dissatisfaction with working conditions, supervision, school policies, and administration. Further, dissatisfaction with job security, with interpersonal relations with peers and subordinates, and with superiors, status, and salary can be expected. Some of these factors are symptomatic of a supervisory climate which encourages alienation of the teaching staff. Supervisors do not work deliberately to cause Type 1 reactions. Such reactions are usually unanticipated consequences of ignoring the human organization of the school. The Type 1 reaction results, over time, in lower levels of performance; resistance to change; higher turnover; antiorganizational, informal group activity; and formal labor problems for the school.

---

[6] The evidence does not substantiate a link between morale—that is, satisfaction—and performance—that is, productivity—unless satisfaction is dependent upon performance. See, for example, Bernard M. Bass, *Organizational Psychology,* New York: Allyn and Bacon, 1965, p. 38.

see p. 27 chart:

Table 2-1 A Synthesizing Theory of Supervisory Effectiveness

Initiating variables	Supervision			How the mediating variables are affected	Results: Types 1-3	Quality of effectiveness variables	Overtime
	Classical	Contemporary	Human resources				Low / Medium / High
1. Administrative and supervisory assumptions (McGregor)	Theory X (p. 101)	Consistent choice	Theory Y	Type 1 (p. 30) → Type 3 (p. 31) →		Low High	
Management assumptions (Argyris)	Infancy assumptions (p. 103)		Growth assumptions	Type 1 → Type 3 →		Low High	
2. Administrative and supervisory orientation: Style propensity (Gibb)	Defensive		Participatory	Type 1 → Type 3 →		Low High	
Value system	School Community Society Individual			Type 1 →		Low	
			Individual Society Community School	Type 3 →		High	
Skill level (Katz)	Technical only (p. 25)			Type 1 →		Low	

Handwritten annotations:

1) performator
2) postperator
3) performance level

→ How those Supervised are affected

What supervisors start out with — "mentaling"

results

Summary of whole text

31

Table 2-1 (continued)

Initiating variables	Supervision			How the mediating variables are affected	Results: Types 1-3	Quality of effectiveness variables	Low Medium High
	Classical	Contemporary	Human resources				
3. Administrative and supervisory behavior:		Human only		Type 2		Medium	
			Technical Human and conceptual	Type 3		High	
(p. 25)							
Social system (Getzels)	Nomothetic			Type 1		Low	
		Ideographic		Type 2 (p. 36)		Medium	
(p. 63)			Transactional	Type 3		High	
Managerial grid style (Blake and Mouton)	9, 1.			Type 1		Low	
		1,9.		Type 2		Medium	
(p. 112)			9,9.	Type 3		High	
Contingency leadership theory (Fiedler, Reddin)	Separated and/or Task (p. 119)	Related		Type 1		Low	
			Contingency with related and integrated prominent	Type 2		Medium	
Patterns of supervision (Likert)			Type 3		High		
Man-to-man style of supervision (p. 175)				Type 1		Low	
		Group supervision		Type 3		High	

Table 2-1 (continued)

Initiating variables	Supervision			How the mediating variables are affected	Results: Types 1-3	Quality of effectiveness variables
	Classical	Contemporary	Human resources			
4. Authority systems (Thompson)	Legally defined authority based on position-hierarchy	Organizationally defined authority based on ability	Functional authority	Type 1	→	Low
	(p. 61)			Type 3	→	High
Peabody formulation	Formal authority Legitimacy Position	Competence Person		Type 1	→	Low
	(p. 134)			Type 3	→	High
Power base (French and Raven)	Legitimate Coercive Reward	Expert Referent		Type 1	→	Low
	(p. 138)			Type 3	→	High
Compliance system (Etzioni)	Coercive	Utilitarian Normative		Type 1	→	Low
	(p. 142)			Type 2	→	Medium
				Type 3	→	High
5. Motivational perspective Maslow theory of human motivation	Security (p. 153)			Type 1	→	Low

{ Low Medium High

Table 2-1 (continued)

Initiating variables	Supervision			How the mediating variables are affected	Results: Types 1-3	Quality of effectiveness variables
	Classical	Contemporary	Human resources		{	{ Low / Medium / High
		Social and Esteem		Type 2 →		Medium
		Esteem	Autonomy	Type 3 →		High
			Self-Actualization			
Motivation-hygiene theory (Herzberg)	Coercive (p. 163)			Type 1 →		Low
		Hygiene		Type 2 →		Medium
			Motivation and Hygiene	Type 3 →		High
Expectancy theory (Vroom)	Satisfaction = production (p. 170)			Type 2 →		Medium
		Production = satisfaction		Type 3 →		High
6. Change strategy	Coercive (p. 148)			Type 1 →		
		Avoidance		Type 2 →		
			Participative	Type 3 →		High
Change perspective	Extrapersonal political view			Type 1 →		Low
		Interpersonal human relation view		Type 2 →		Medium
			Intrapersonal paradigm shift view	Type 3 →		High

Table 2-1 (continued)

Initiating variables	Supervision		Human resources	How the mediating variables are affected	Results: Types 1-3	Quality of effectiveness variables { Low Medium High }
	Classical	Contemporary				
7. Manifestation of organizational style, managerial emphasis on mechanistic or organic, bureaucratic or professional (Hage)	Mechanistic Formalization Stratification Centralization Production Efficiency ($)		Organic	Type 1 →		Low
	(p. 51)		Adaptability Complexity Job satisfaction	Type 3 →		High
8. Management system (Likert)	System 1 System 2	System 3 System 4		Type 1 → Type 2 → Type 3 →		Low Medium High
9. Organizational climate (Halpin and Croft)	Closed	Open		Type 1 → Type 3 →		Low High

Mediating Variables—Type 2 Reaction

Contemporary supervisory patterns which rely heavily on human relations perspectives evoke Type 2 responses from teachers. The Type 2 reaction involves a feeling of apathy toward the welfare of the school and toward the vigorous pursuit of school goals. Supervisors who emphasize a socially oriented group life characterized by high morale, good feelings, and low tension often elicit this response. Teachers are relieved from job dissatisfaction, performance expectations are low, work pressure is eliminated, and security is guaranteed. Yet teachers feel no compulsion to exert commitment, energy, and effort beyond that which is minimally required to carry on day by day. Little opportunity exists for teachers to grow personally and professionally and to enjoy deep satisfaction from their work.[7] Supervisors who evoke a Type 2 reaction from teachers often fail to distinguish between using people and working with people to achieve school goals. This is a confused pattern, characterized by ambivalence and uncertainty.

Mediating Variables—Type 3 Reaction

Human resources supervisory patterns—those which work to achieve school-effectiveness variables through encouraging the growth and development of the human organization—evoke responses from subordinates which are labeled Type 3. This type of response is characterized by high commitment to the work of the school, high loyalty to the school and to the membership subunit, high performance goals, and a desire, combined with an opportunity, for personal and professional growth. Job satisfaction centers around growth opportunities, achievement, recognition, responsibility, and advancement. The reward system which encourages Type 3 responses depends heavily upon achievement.[8] Supervisory behavior which evokes a Type 3 response from the human organization is most associated with school effectiveness.

CAUTIONS IN IMPLEMENTING HUMAN RESOURCES SUPERVISION

Enthusiasm is both virtuous and dangerous. One purpose of this book is to promote enthusiasm for the concept of human resources supervision. We will argue that human resources supervision is not only humane and fitting for educational organizations with their "people intensive" characteristics and distinctively human undertakings but that this view is supported by a formidable body of theory and research and enjoys claims of success from practitioners in many fields. But why the caution?

It would be a mistake, we believe, to view the assumptions, concepts, and practices associated with human resources supervision as universally applicable. Human beings are much too complex for that sort of blanket prescription.

---

[7] Type 2 response is characterized by the relative absence of dissatisfaction, combined with little opportunity for achieving satisfaction. The phenomenon is discussed in detail in Chapter 8. See, for example, Frederick Herzberg, Bernard Mausner, and Barbara Synderman, *The Motivation to Work,* New York: Wiley, 1959.

[8] See footnote 6.

Consider, for example, the problem of motivation and human resources supervision. A distinct and powerful point of view of motivation will be presented, complete with documentation on three counts—value system, theory, and empirical evidence. Though the point of view will be applicable to most teachers, still, many will not respond. One's set of values and work norms, for example, affects one's orientation toward his or her job. Some teachers will never be properly motivated to work and others will usually be motivated to work regardless of what supervisors do. Indeed, a good rule of thumb is, if you want motivated teachers, hire motivated people, if you can. The majority of teachers, however, desire and seek satisfying work and will respond to human resources supervision. But many will not, and alternative supervisory methods and procedures that suit these teachers will need to be provided. In such cases, patterns of supervision associated with classical-management or human relations theory may well be appropriate.

Human resources supervision is not an elixir to be administered indiscriminately to all. But it is a powerful conception of supervision which, by using the concepts of motivation and job enrichment, can markedly improve the identity, commitment, and performance of most teachers and the effectiveness of schools.

A further note—though supervisors may find many teachers to whom the theory will not apply, they need to be careful if this number increases. The problem may well be with the teachers the supervisors encounter, but, on the other hand, it could be with the supervisors and their perceptions of teachers. More about this when we discuss supervisory assumptions in Chapter 5.

SUMMARY

Many scholars have proposed theories and models which have the potential to be used in a powerful way by those who supervise in the nation's schools, but no one schema has been offered as a general theory of supervision. Chapter 2 builds upon the work of scholars from a variety of social science fields by integrating and relating their ideas into a synthesizing theory of supervisory effectiveness. The theory identifies and relates three sets of variables: initiating (supervisory and organizational), mediating (human organization), and school effectiveness, which permit the conceptual mapping of effective supervision.

The concepts, models, and schemata which comprise the initiating variables in the synthesizing theory are the focus of Chapters 3 to 7. Chapters 8 and 9 deal with the mediating variables and the school-success variables.

STUDY GUIDE

Recall the concepts, ideas, and meanings associated with each of the following phrases and terms included in this chapter. Can you discuss each of them with a colleague and apply them to the supervisory context of your school? If you cannot, review them in the text and record the page numbers for future reference.

1 Conceptual skills _____
2 Educating supervisors _____

3 Effectiveness variables _____
4 Human organization _____
5 Human skills _____
6 Initiating variables _____
7 Mediating variables _____
8 Middle-range theories _____
9 Synthesizing theory of supervision _____
10 Technical skills _____
11 Theory _____
12 Training supervisors _____
13 Type 1 reaction _____
14 Type 2 reaction _____
15 Type 3 reaction _____

SELECTED REFERENCES

Argyris, Chris: *Personality and Organization,* New York: Harper, 1957.

Blake, Robert, and Jane Mouton: *The Managerial Grid,* Houston: Gulf, 1966.

Corwin, Ronald: "Professional Persons in Public Organizations," *Educational Administration Quarterly,* 1965, vol. 1, pp. 1–22.

Etzioni, Amitai: *A Comparative Analysis of Complex Organizations,* New York: Free Press, 1961.

Fiedler, Fred: *A Theory of Leadership Effectiveness,* New York: McGraw-Hill, 1967.

Getzels, Jacob W., and Egon G. Guba: "Social Behavior and Administrative Process," *School Review,* Winter 1957, vol. 65, pp. 423–441.

Hage, Gerald: "An Axiomatic Theory of Organization," *Administrative Science Quarterly,* 1967, vol. 10, pp. 289–320.

Halpin, Andrew W.: *Theory and Research in Administration,* New York: Macmillan, 1967.

Herzberg, Frederick, Bernard Mausner, and Barbara Snyderman: *The Motivation to Work,* New York: Wiley, 1959.

Likert, Rensis: *The Human Organization: Its Management and Value,* New York: McGraw-Hill, 1968.

McGregor, Douglas: *The Human Side of Enterprise,* New York: McGraw-Hill, 1960.

Maslow, Abraham: *Motivation and Personality,* New York: Harper & Row, 1954.

Miles, Matthew B: "Organizational Health: Figure and Ground," in *Change Processes in the Public Schools,* Eugene: University of Oregon, Center for the Advanced Study of Educational Administration, 1965.

Reddin, William J.: *Managerial Effectiveness,* New York: McGraw-Hill, 1970.

Vroom, Victor: *Work and Motivation,* New York: Wiley, 1964.

EXERCISES

1 Paul Mort is often quoted as saying, "Action without theory is like a rat scurrying through a maze." Another favorite quote of theorists is, "There is nothing as practical as good theory." In your own words, develop a working definition of theory. Give examples of how theory is dependent upon practice.

2 Develop a list of competencies for two or three supervisory roles (perhaps department chairperson, elementary school principal, and central office director of instruction). Sort the competencies for each role into each of the three skill levels—technical, human, and conceptual. Compare your analyses of supervisory skills with the discussions in this chapter.

3 Develop a paragraph or two describing three real or imagined teachers, one whose reaction to organizational life is Type 1, another whose reaction is Type 2, and a third, Type 3. To what extent are these reactions related to administrative, organizational, and supervisory characteristics as described in the synthesizing theory, and to what extent are reactions related to other factors? Other factors might include the teacher's interest in teaching, the teacher's personality, or perhaps competing demands from forces outside the school.

Chapter 3

The Organizational
Environment for Supervision

Supervisory behavior takes place within a complex system which involves the interaction between and among initiating, human, and school-effectiveness variables. The supervisor, for example, behaves (1) in an organizational environment, (2) from an authority base, (3) in specific ways, (4) in an attempt to modify the mediating variables in a fashion which increases staff identity and commitment, and (5) with the goal of increasing some dimension of school effectiveness. Our concern in this chapter is with those variables initiated by the supervisor which are concerned with the more organizational aspects of the school. Ultimately the purpose of supervision is to enhance educational programs and instructional effectiveness in the school. These educational concerns are very much influenced by broader characteristics which make up the school's organizational subsystem. Humanism in educational programs design and implementation, for example, depends upon humanism in organizational design and school structure. This chapter deals selectively with the application of analytical concepts from organizational theory. The language of organizational theory will be foreign to many but worth deciphering, for the ideas are important to understanding the context of modern supervision.

THE SCHOOL AS A COMPLEX ORGANIZATION

We live in an organized world and the world is full of organizations. To quote from a recent book on organization: "Children are born into the physical confines of large medical organizations—hospitals—spend much of their growing years in even larger organizations—schools—and graduate, most of them, into the employ of even larger businesses or government organizations. Many of our large high schools are as populous as small towns, universities are veritable cities, and multinational corporations are virtual nation states."[1]

Romantic vestiges of the little red schoolhouse still exist in America, but most schools, like most organizations, have experienced phenomenal growth in size, areas serviced, and professional complexity. The emergence and spread of the large high school, for example, has accelerated to the point where this unit dominates American secondary education. The operation of the large high school is usually characterized by an emphasis on conserving resources through sophisticated management techniques, scientific staff utilization, computerized scheduling, diverse program offerings, and a variety of student services. Elementary schools share many of these features, though on a smaller scale.

Modern organizations are characterized by a high degree of specialization as well as by size. Schools are not unlike other organizations in this regard in that they have their share of experts who claim monopolies over certain aspects of the management system (directors, vice-principals, division heads for instructional units, student personnel administrators, finance experts, and so on) as well as over certain aspects of the technical system (subject-matter specialists, hardware experts, early childhood–disadvantaged–compensatory education specialists, and sociopsychological practitioners, for example).[2] The number of new positions and functional roles which have appeared in the last 2 decades in American education have made schools, as organizations, more complex.

In larger communities, the diversity of the schools' goals, combined with the large number of employees, often makes them comparable in complexity with other organizations. Size in itself, however, is not a sufficient criterion for identifying complexity. Schools are complex primarily because of the sophistication of their technology, the diversification of their goals, the varied nature of their tasks, and their patterns of structure.

BUREAUCRATIC ELEMENTS AND TENDENCIES IN SCHOOLS

What does the word "bureaucracy" mean to you? Chances are, this word conjures up negative feelings and reactions from most Americans. The antibureaucracy bias, unfortunately, limits and inhibits rational discussion of the positive

---

[1] H. Randolf Bobbitt, Jr., Robert Breinholt, Robert Doktor, and James McNaul, *Organizational Behavior: Understanding and Predicting,* Englewood Cliffs, N.J.: Prentice-Hall, 1974, p. 1.

[2] The terms "management systems" and "technical systems" are used, after Parsons, to differentiate between the administrative sphere and the educotechnical sphere. See Talcott Parsons, "Some Ingredients of a General Theory of Organization," in Andrew W. Halpin (ed.), *Administrative Theory in Education,* Chicago: University of Chicago, Midwest Administration Center, 1958.

and negative bureaucratic characteristics of schools. We perhaps contribute to this bias by designating schools as either bureaucratically oriented or profession-ally oriented. For purposes of this discussion, the bureaucratic designation for schools is used in a negative sense, in that human resources supervision will tend not to thrive there. The professional designation for schools is used in a positive sense to indicate an ideal environment for supervision. Yet underlying these per-spectives, the authors recognize that schools are actually on a continuum extend-ing from more bureaucratic to less bureaucratic. We also concede that except for large high schools and for large school districts, schools, when compared with many other community institutions, seem considerably less bureaucratic.

The person responsible for introducing the concept of bureaucracy, with its accompanying characteristics, to the political and social science literature was Max Weber. He believed that "the decisive reason for the advance of bureau-cratic organization has always been its purely technical superiority over other forms of organization."[3] Weber's ideal bureaucracy is characterized as follows: (1) the division of labor and the specific allocation of responsibility; (2) reliance on fairly exact hierarchical levels of graded authority; (3) administrative thought and action based on written policies, rules, and regulations; (4) an impersonal, universalistic bureaucratic environment for all inhabitants; and (5) the devel-opment and longevity of administrative careers.[4]

The extent to which schools follow the bureaucratic model varies, of course, from school to school. Yet all schools exhibit some bureaucratic tendencies.[5] A comparison of general bureaucratic characteristics and bureaucratic tendencies of schools follows:

Characteristics of Bureaucracy	*Applied to Schools*
1 Organization tasks are distrib-uted among the various posi-tions as official duties. Implied is a clear-cut division of labor among positions, which makes possible a high degree of special-ization. Specialization, in turn, promotes expertness among the staff, both directly and by en-abling the organization to hire employees on the basis of their technical qualifications.	1 The school organization has clearly been influenced by the need for specialization and the division of tasks. The division of the school into elementary and secondary units; the estab-lishment of science, mathemat-ics, music, and other depart-ments within a school; the intro-duction of guidance programs and psychological services; and, indeed, the separation of the ad-

---

[3] Max Weber, "Bureaucracy," in Hans Gerth and C. Wright Mills (eds.), *From Max Weber,* New York: Oxford, 1946, p. 214.

[4] Max Weber, *Theory of Social and Economic Organization,* trans. by A. M. Henderson and T. Parsons, New York: Oxford, 1947, pp. 333–336.

[5] Any list of items which characterize or describe bureaucracy in reference to "ideal type" is limited in that no one organization fits the description exactly.

2 The positions or offices are organized into a hierarchical authority structure. In the usual case this hierarchy takes on the shape of a pyramid, wherein each official is responsible for his subordinates' decisions and actions as well as his own to the superior above him in the pyramid, and wherein each official has authority over the officials under him. The scope of authority of superiors over subordinates is clearly circumscribed.

3 A formally established system of rules and regulations governs official decisions and actions. In principle the operations in such administrative organizations involve the application -of these general regulations to particular cases. The regulations ensure the uniformity of operations and, together with the authority structure, make possible the coordination of various activities. They also provide for continuity in operations regardless of changes of personnel, thus promoting a stability lacking . . . in charismatic movements.

4 Officials are expected to assume an impersonal orientation in their contacts with clients and with other officials. Clients are to be treated as cases, the officials being expected to disregard all personal considerations and to maintain complete emotional detachment, and subordinates are to be treated in a similar impersonal fashion. The social distance between hierarchical levels and that between officials and their clients is intended to foster ministrative function from the teaching function all represent responses to this need.

2 The school organization has developed a clearly defined and rigid hierarchy of authority. Although the term "hierarchy" is seldom used in the lexicon of the educational administrator, the practices to which it refers are prevalent. The typical organization chart is intended specifically to clarify lines of authority and channels of communication. Even in the absence of such a chart, school employees have a clear conception of the nature of the hierarchy in their school systems. In fact, rigid adherence to hierarchical principles has been stressed to the point that failure to adhere to recognized lines of authority is viewed as the epitome of immoral organizational behavior.

3 The school organization has leaned heavily upon the use of general rules to control the behavior of members of the organization and to develop standards which would assure reasonable uniformity in the performance of tasks. Whether they have taken the form of policy manuals, rules and regulations, staff handbooks, or some other type of document, general rules have been used extensively to provide for the orderly induction of new employees into the organization and to eliminate capricious behavior on the part of all school personnel, including administrators and members of boards of education.

such formality. Impersonal detachment is designed to prevent the personal feelings of officials from distorting their rational judgment in carrying out their duties.

5 Employment within the organization constitutes a career for officials. Typically an official is a full-time employee and looks forward to a lifelong career in the agency. Employment is based on the technical qualifications of the candidate rather than on political, family, or other connections. Usually such qualifications are tested by examination or are verified by certificates that demonstrate the candidate's educational attainment—college degrees, for example. Such educational qualifications create a certain amount of class homogeneity among officials, since relatively few persons of working-class origin have college degrees, although their number is increasing. Officials are appointed to positions, not elected, and thus are dependent on superiors in the organization rather than on a body of constituents. After a trial period officials gain tenure of position and are protected against arbitrary dismissal. Remuneration is in the form of a salary, and pensions are provided after retirement. Career advancements are "according to seniority or to achievement or both."[6]

4 Despite frequent proclamations regarding togetherness and democracy, the school organization has made extensive application of Weber's principle of impersonality in organizational relationships. Authority has been established on the basis of rational considerations rather than on the basis of charismatic qualities or traditional imperatives; interpersonal interactions have tended to be functionally specific rather than functionally diffuse; and official relationships have been governed largely by universalistic, as contrasted with particularistic, considerations. Thus, by operating in a spirit of "formalistic impersonality," the typical school system has succeeded, in part, in separating organizational rights and obligations from the private lives of individual employees.

5 Employment in the educational organization has been based upon technical competence and has constituted for most members a professional career. Promotions have been determined by seniority and by achievement; tenure has been provided; and fixed compensation and retirement benefits have been assured.[7]

---

[6] Peter M. Blau and W. Richard Scott, *Formal Organizations: A Comparative Approach,* San Francisco: Chandler, 1962, pp. 32–33. Copyright © 1962 by Chandler Publishing Company.

[7] Max G. Abbott, "Hierarchical Impediments to Innovation in Educational Organizations," in M. G. Abbott and John Lovell (eds.), *Change Perspectives in Educational Administration,* Auburn, Ala.: Auburn University School of Education, 1965, pp. 44–45.

BUREAUCRATIC DYSFUNCTION

The modern organization is seen by some people as a marvel of accomplishment and efficiency, and by others as a beast which dehumanizes the spirit, cripples creativity, and warps the personality. Supervisors should not be advocates or enemies of organizations but rather should accept the reality that most schools are fairly complex organizations and as such have benefits and costs. Certain goals, objectives, and educational activities can be successfully pursued only in an organized setting, but others suffer somewhat because of this organized setting. Are the benefits worth the cost? Can the costs be lived with? Are the benefits of long-term value? Are some costs so high that benefits need to be forsaken? These are important questions for supervisors.

Bureaucracy provides us with costs and benefits. Its benefits are in the orderliness and efficiency that it brings to the schools. Its costs are in its deterministic and programming characteristics, which often result in rigid and impersonal organizational structures. The basic dimensions of bureaucracy seem less offensive than the excessive application of its underlying assumptions of rationality by many administrators and supervisors. Cyert and March,[8] March and Simon,[9] and Thompson,[10] for example, suggest that a basic fallacy behind early attempts to study organizations has been our tendency to view them as rational structures. In this context, we have assumed that problem-solving activity in schools included carefully delineating *all* the alternative solutions to a given problem, anticipating the effects of these solutions to a given problem, and weighing each of the alternatives systematically. The alternative with the highest score is then chosen as the best solution. This process represents a most formidable task, quite beyond the capabilities of all but superhumans and superorganizations. Indeed, one needs to exercise caution when viewing schools as maximizing organizations. People tend to seek not the best needle in a haystack, but rather one that satisfies the reason for their search. Schools tend to seek not maximizing solutions to their problems, but rather solutions which they can accept as satisfying current needs. *Organizations are notoriously "satisficing" as they follow their own impulses,* and in this sense the bureaucratic image of rational organization seems not to approximate reality.

It should be pointed out however that though schools may be better characterized as "satisficing" rather than maximizing organizations, this does not preclude their ability to value and strive for that which is good, just, and excellent. Indeed, basic to the human resources view is the acceptance of the human capacity to set goals, to believe, and to strive, even though it seems afflicted somewhat by this "satisficing" tendency.[11] Weber's concept of bureaucracy provides a framework for prescribing action, but much of what is intended by administra-

[8] Richard M. Cyert and James G. March, *A Behavioral Theory of the Firm,* Englewood Cliffs, N.J.: Prentice-Hall, 1963.

[9] James G. March and Herbert A. Simon, *Organizations,* New York: Wiley, 1958.

[10] James Thompson, *Organizations in Action,* New York: McGraw-Hill, 1968.

[11] See, for example, Thomas J. Sergiovanni, "The Odyssey of Organizational Theory in Education: Implications for Humanizing Education," in Richard H. Weller (ed.), *Humanistic Education: Visions and Realities,* Berkeley, Calif.: McCutchan, 1977, pp. 197–232.

tors and supervisors may result in unanticipated reactions from the human organization and dysfunctional consequences for the school. It is difficult to conceive of any supervisor consciously intending school dysfunction. The actions of supervisors are undoubtedly well intended when such dysfunction does occur, but working under the norms of rationality typically associated with the bureaucratic view, they may be unaware of the possibility of unanticipated results.

We discuss in detail in the last section of this chapter the nature of dysfunction which contributes to teacher militancy, student militancy, and other symptoms of general disengagement between and among teachers, administrators, and students. Here, our discussion will be limited to only one aspect of the problem—what we intend to accomplish and do not intend to accomplish as we work to increase control over the achievement of school goals through an emphasis on *reliability, delegation of authority,* and the use of *universal impersonal rules.*[12] Each of these variables is a crucial component of the ideal bureaucracy.

EMPHASIS ON RELIABILITY

As administrators and supervisors attempt to increase control over achievement of the school's goals, they frequently work to increase reliability in decision-making processes and in behavior of teachers and students. This is often accomplished by instituting and implementing policies, standard operating procedures, rules, and regulations to guide behavior within the human organization. Uniformity of behavior is seen as a powerful means to move large numbers of people toward goals, with a minimum amount of confusion and conflict.

Organizational and client reactions to an emphasis on reliability of behavior through the development of rules is illustrated in Figure 3-1.[13] The intended result of reliability through rules is uniform and programmed decision making. This in turn decreases the search for alternatives to problems and results in more programmed behavior on the part of supervisors. The entire system also provides supervisors with a mechanism which permits them to escape personal accountability for their actions. If teachers do not like rules enforced by supervisors, they blame the rules structure or the system. With reference to classroom rules, it is presumed that students will vent hostility on the rules, the system, or the establishment, rather than on the teacher when he or she enforces dress codes, gum-chewing regulations, marking policies, and other policies characteristic of a "tyranny of rules." Supervisors optimistically work under the same assumption in applying the rules to teachers.[14]

---

[12] This discussion relies heavily on James G. March and Herbert A. Simon's discussion of the Merton, Selznick, and Gouldner formulations which appears in *Organizations,* New York: Wiley, 1958, pp. 36–47.

[13] This model and the three which follow are adapted from March and Simon, op. cit., pp. 36–47.

[14] We do not suggest that unanticipated consequences always occur. Such consequences may or may not occur, depending upon a number of contingency variables. In this case, where egalitarian values are strong, clients will resent increases in visible power by superordinates. Where egalitarian values are not strong, the unanticipated consequences are less likely to occur. The same caution applies as well to the Selznick and Gouldner formulations which follow.

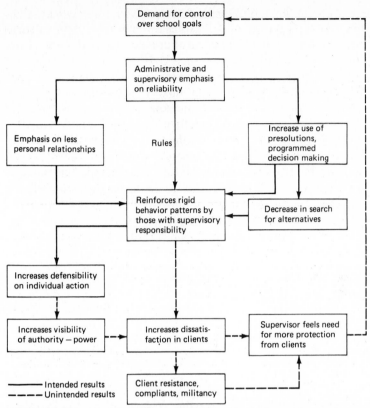

Figure 3-1 Merton: Emphasis on reliability. *(From James G. March and Herbert A. Simon, Organizations, New York: Wiley, 1958.)*

The unanticipated consequences of an emphasis on reliability are described by Merton as (1) increases in the visibility of power and authority which supervisors have by virtue of position; (2) increases in levels of dissatisfaction and frustration of clients; (3) resistance, complaints, militancy, and conspiracy among clients as a result of this dissatisfaction and frustration; (4) a need felt by supervisors for more protection from client hostility; which (5) results in an increase in control; and so the cycle continues. This is an example of a school getting better and getting worse at the same time.

EMPHASIS ON DELEGATION OF AUTHORITY

Schools have been formally characterized by a division of labor since the introduction of the graded system. As professional and technical skill expands, the division of tasks becomes eclipsed by personal and professional specialization. Both represent a form of delegation of authority in that division carries with it some autonomy and responsibility for action. The rationale for delegation is that the competency of the specialist will be utilized in order to increase his or her performance and thus close the gap between performance and school goals. In the large high school the typical form of delegation is found in departmentalization. Selznick describes organizational and client reaction to delegation of authority and division of labor in Figure 3-2.

The danger of departmentalization, delegation, and division is the emergence of subgoals for the newly formed subgroups. As these subgoals become internalized, they tend to assume priority over the total school mission. Some of this is natural, of course, particularly at budget time; but over the long run such goal conflict actually lowers the performance of the total school goals. A number of variables tend to increase or decrease the possibility of unanticipated consequences of delegation as described by Selznick. If total school goals, for example, are remote or are beyond realizing, teachers tend to focus on their own department or grade-level goals as they seek guides to their professional performance.

High school departments, grade levels in elementary schools, bureaus in the central office, special teacher groups, the new academic and vocational division units (divisions of humanities, social science, physical science, vocational education, and so on) appearing as substitutes for departments in many high schools, schools within the school, teaching teams, and the like, all run the risk of negative consequences as described by Selznick.

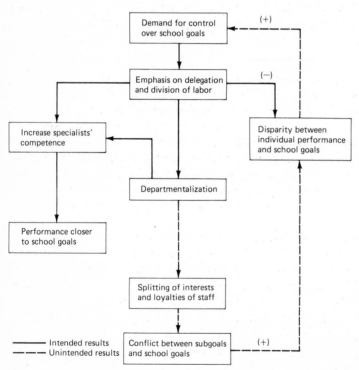

Figure 3-2   Selznick: Emphasis on delegation. *(From James G. March and Herbert A. Simon, Organizations, New York: Wiley, 1958.)*

EMPHASIS ON GENERAL AND IMPERSONAL RULES

The literature is nearly unanimous in suggesting to administrators and others that the legitimacy of their supervisory role as perceived by subordinates is largely a function of low visibility of power (nonauthoritarianism) and low levels of interpersonal tension. As a result of this, those in authority tend to rely on the use of general and impersonal rules in order to regulate or modify the behavior of subordinates. This phenomenon and its interesting potential consequences are described by Gouldner in Figure 3-3.

Gouldner's model portrays the inherent dangers in relying on general-impersonal rules. It suggests that when supervisors attempt to decrease power visibility and interpersonal tension in order to obtain satisfaction and compliance in teachers through the use of general rules, they obtain results opposite to those intended. When one wishes to regulate the behavior of a few through the use of rules which apply to all, one announces and legitimizes *minimum* organizational expectations for everyone. This in turn may lead to teachers focusing on or meeting minimum requirements exclusively, which often results in reduced performance. Any reduction in performance is likely to receive an organizational response in the form of close supervision. Close supervision tends to increase power visibility and interpersonal tension. This tends to decrease the legitimacy of supervision, particularly in egalitarian cultures such as ours, and decreases teacher satisfac-

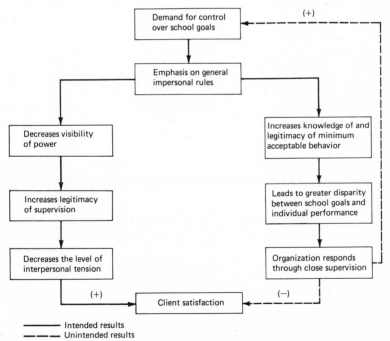

Figure 3-3 Gouldner: Emphasis on general and impersonal rules. *(From James G. March and Herbert A. Simon, Organizations, New York: Wiley, 1958.)*

tion. The model works remarkably well when applied to classroom management, with students as clients.

The likelihood of the Gouldner reaction is considerably reduced if members have high commitment and loyalty to the school and have largely internalized the goals of the school. One of the dangers of discussing examples of unanticipated consequences is that the simple examples we use might be viewed as fixed relationships. There are numerous variables—many still undiscovered—which have an effect as to whether one or another of the models presented will come out as we have described. Perhaps in summary it is sufficient to caution that seemingly simple administrative-supervisory acts, however well intended, have complex and often negative ramifications in the human organization of the school and in the school itself. Such ramifications can be reduced by viewing the school more realistically as an organization which possesses some bureaucratic characteristics but which in reality is far less rational in organization, structure, and functioning than is typically assumed.

PROFESSIONAL ELEMENTS AND TENDENCIES IN SCHOOLS

Though the school contains many bureaucratic characteristics, it possesses some distinguishing characteristics common to professional organizations as well.

Professional organizations, or more appropriately those which are professionally oriented, tend to differ from other organizations primarily in the nature of their authority and power systems. This type of organization is characterized by the development and application of a pluralistic power structure which is (1) dispersed throughout the organization on the basis of ability and competence, (2) dynamic, in the sense that it shifts from person to person and from time to time on the basis of task, (3) interdependent, in that usually coalitions of individuals are needed to marshal sufficient competence to command authority at a given time, and (4) functional, in that it tends not to keep well in storage but needs to be constantly examined for "goodness of fit" in terms of competence and task. The professionally oriented organization tends to rely on task-oriented rather than people-oriented power bases.[15]

Professionally oriented people can be characterized as having (1) considerable advanced formal preparation, (2) skills not readily available in others, including other professionals, (3) a commitment to their profession, discipline, or area which often assumes priority over a commitment to their place of employment, and (4) an interest in a reward system which emphasizes growth and development, achievement, and responsibility but does not ignore bread-and-butter items such as security and salary.

---

[15] Like any "rule" or "truism," this one has exceptions. As competency becomes established in people—that is, as their professional reputation increases—their authority base may shift to themselves as people (who they are rather than what they can contribute) or may include themselves as people (who they are and what they can contribute). At the group level, if one pessimistically applies "Michel's iron law of oligarchy" to this process, one is led to conclude that what starts as ability authority soon turns into status authority.

Not all teachers can be described as professionals but many can. In some schools teachers have outdistanced schools in moving toward professionalization. Where this is the case, we are confronted with a large number of professionally oriented employees who are expected to operate and grow in schools which are by and large bureaucratically oriented.

AN AXIOMATIC THEORY OF ORGANIZATIONS

At this point we have established that most schools and school districts can be described as fairly complex organizations which contain both bureaucratic and professional characteristics. But schools vary in the extent to which one or another of these characteristics is emphasized. In this section an *axiomatic theory of organization* is presented as a useful framework for describing the professionally oriented school, contrasting it with the bureaucratically oriented school, and describing an organizational system of interaction which helps to map the sociological environment of schools for supervision.

THE STRUCTURAL-FUNCTIONAL SYSTEM

Organizations have structures and functions. Emphasizing some structures contributes more to certain functions than others. Further, when some structures are emphasized others are de-emphasized. Knowing the relationships between and among organizational structures and functions can provide supervisors with powerful understandings and tools for action.

Gerald Hage has proposed a theory of organizations which maps out these relationships very effectively.[16] His theory identifies, describes, and charts patterns of interaction between eight key components found in schools and other organizations. Four of these components are *structural* and constitute the means by which schools organize to achieve ends. Structurally, schools, departments, and units are concerned with degrees of centralization, formalization, stratification, and complexity as means to achieve ends. Four other components are *functional* and constitute categories within which school ends might be sorted. Functionally, schools, departments, and units are concerned with the emphasis given to production, efficiency, adoption, and satisfaction goals. The structural and functional characteristics of organization are described as follows:

THE SCHOOL'S STRUCTURAL-FUNCTIONAL SYSTEM

Structure-Organizational Means

Complexity   This refers to how specialized the school is organizationally and administratively as well as to the degree of professional and technical specialization which exists in the teaching staff. Complexity is concerned with *specialization in people,* not in jobs or tasks. The heart surgeon is a person specialist, the assembly line worker is a task specialist. Normally, the teacher who is an expert on constitutional

[16] This discussion is based primarily on Gerald Hage, "An Axiomatic Theory of Organizations," *Administrative Science Quarterly,* vol. 10, no. 3, pp. 289–320, December 1965.

government is a person specialist, but normally the teacher who teaches nothing but sophomore American history is a task specialist. The more professional the staff, the more complex the organization. The more complex the organization, the more influence professionals have in decisions relating to their work.

Centralization   The extent to which levels of decision making correspond to predetermined hierarchical arrangements or organizational charts determines the school's centralization tendencies. When responsibility and authority for important decision making is dispersed throughout the school we have low centralization. When important decision making is primarily the prerogative of the central office or principal, we have high centralization. Schools can be characterized by low centralization with regard to adults (teachers heavily involved) but high centralization with regard to students (students not involved).

Formalization   This refers to the extent a school relies on standardized rules and regulations or standard operating procedures in order to increase uniformity in decision making and similarity in behavior. High formalization is related to high centralization because it programs the decision making of teachers, students, and often administrators, and funnels upward any situations which are varied and cannot be accounted for by the rules or by standard operating procedures.

Stratification   This refers to the amount of status differences which exist between and among hierarchical levels in the school. As status differences increase, that is, as rights and privileges of people at one level increase over those at other levels, stratification increases.

Function-Organizational Ends

Production   This refers to school output which can be counted and easily measured. The number of students graduated, the number of courses offered, the number of Carnegie units accumulated, the number of pages read or problems completed are examples of production. *Production does not refer to quality.* When schools are more concerned with the quality of services they render to students, and work to improve this quality as opposed to increasing the *number* of services rendered or the *number* of clients served, they are de-emphasizing production.

Efficiency   This refers to costs per unit of output. Costs include not only money, but utilization of staff, time, materials, and space as well. A teacher-student ratio of 35 to 1 is more efficient than one of 25 to 1.

Adaptiveness   This refers to the school's ability to respond and its emphasis on responding to changing professional and societal environments. An adaptive school is one which utilizes the most advanced professional and technical knowledge and know-how and whose educational program adjusts to changing student needs.

Satisfaction   This refers to the extent the school focuses on the worth of its human organization as a manifest school goal. Need fulfillment and professional and personal growth and development of teaching staff are considered legitimate and important goals which are ranked with student learning, growth, and development.

The eight structural-functional characteristics of schools are related in fairly predictable ways. For example, as a school department or unit increases its emphasis on *centralized* control and decision making, it is likely to become more *formalized* and its *stratification* system is likely to become more pronounced. At the same time, its emphasis on *complexity*, or person autonomy and specialization, will decrease. Higher centralization, formalization, and stratification and lower complexity are very likely to increase the school's *production* and *efficiency* levels, but the school will become less responsive and *adaptive* and people will become less *satisfied*.

The basic propositions of the theory as proposed by Hage are as follows:

The higher the centralization, the higher the production.
The higher the formalization, the higher the efficiency.
The higher the centralization, the higher the formalization.
The higher the stratification, the lower the job satisfaction.
The higher the stratification, the higher the production.
The higher the stratification, the lower the adaptiveness.
The higher the complexity, the lower the centralization.[17]

Perhaps the easiest way to understand the relationship between and among the eight organizational dimensions is to view them as being in two groups—one more characteristic of bureaucratically oriented schools and the other, of professionally oriented schools. The group associated with bureaucratically oriented schools is composed of centralization, formalization, stratification, production, and efficiency. The professional group is composed of complexity, adaptibility, and satisfaction. When one dimension in the bureaucratic group increases, each of the others with the same sign also increases. Those with the opposite sign decrease. The same relationships hold for dimensions in the professional group— changes in one produce similar changes in each of the others. *Further, any change in the bureaucratic group produces opposite changes in the professional group and vice versa.* All of the groups are shown below ("L" = lower; "H" = higher):

Bureaucratically Oriented Schools

L　complexity	L　adaptiveness
H　centralization	H　production
H　formalization	H　efficiency
H　stratification	L　job satisfaction

Professionally Oriented Schools

H　complexity	H　adaptiveness
L　centralization	L　production
L　formalization	L　efficiency
L　stratification	H　job satisfaction

THE IDEAL SCHOOL TYPES SUMMARIZED

Bureaucratically oriented schools tend to be precise in defining roles, obligations, and rights and relations (high formalization and high stratification); are detailed detailed in prescribing rules and regulations in seeking to program decision making for teachers and students (high formalization); seek to funnel decision making which is varied and unpredictable to the top while standardizing decision

[17] Ibid., pp. 297–299.

making at lower levels (high centralization); and are concerned with processing the largest number of students at the least cost in terms of personnel, money, equipment, space, and the like (high production and high efficiency). Since all the structural features of schools are interdependent, a change in one variable results in changes in other variables. Thus, bureaucratically oriented schools, while increasing in formalization, centralization, and the like, display a low tolerance for innovativeness and change (low adaptiveness); an unwillingness to permit power to be diffused to lower organizational levels and thus an unwillingness to encourage authority based on ability rather than simply position (low complexity); and thereby encourage a reluctance to provide teachers with meaningful reward systems which will permit them to function as respected, autonomous, and responsible professionals (low job satisfaction).

The ideal professional type of school stresses adaptiveness rather than production and is characterized by its complexity and the level of job satisfaction available to its members. The emergence and spread of professionally oriented organizations in education are a reflection of four closely related trends in teaching as an occupation: (1) the increased specialization of semiprofessional and professional workers; (2) the quality and sophistication of their academic and professional training; (3) the knowledge explosion which has occurred in virtually all curriculum areas, teaching fields, and educational technologies; and (4) the belief (real or imagined) that schools as they are currently functioning do not meet their commitment to provide all students with an intellectual, social, and emotional experience appropriate for growth in society as we know it today or in the years ahead. These trends are compounded by a prevalent desire for autonomy which seems to permeate every aspect of our society.

The professionally oriented large school, for example, is one which seeks to accommodate the need for expression which professional workers require. It is complex (in terms of its administrative diversification as well as the degree of personal specialization which exists in the staff) and highly innovative, and provides teachers, students, and other members with opportunities for their personal as well as professional fulfillment. This type of school tends also to be wasteful and expensive;[18] it ignores or circumscribes hierarchically defined status and authority systems; and it tolerates no more than a minimum use of rules and other forms of programmed decision making. Advocates of the professional model argue that the production emphasis of the bureaucratic model is incompatible with providing high-quality education for youth and is in fact damaging and demoralizing to teachers and students. Schools seem to be shifting from orientations we describe as bureaucratic to orientations we describe as professional. That professionalization is being realized at different rates for different schools, school systems, and communities should not be allowed to mask the long-term trend.

---

[18] When the same standards are applied to professionally oriented and bureaucratically oriented schools, the former are found lacking in the efficiency category. In terms of quality of output, however, the professionally oriented school seems immeasurably more able.

A CONTINGENCY APPROACH TO ORGANIZATIONAL STRUCTURE

A popular organizational principle to which we subscribe is that *form should follow function.* Form follows function when the school is organized and operated in a way which facilitates the goals, objectives, and activities of people. Function follows form when the work of people is modified to fit the structure and operating style of the organization. In reality, however, the relationship between form and function is less direct. Indeed, the two interact constantly with each making demands on the other. At any given moment function may be determined by the demands of form, but over the long haul supervisors need to work at keeping the balance in favor of form following function. Organizational structure is the central nervous system of the school, and when it is functioning properly, it permits the organization to perform a variety of related motions and activities—often simultaneously. But like any nervous system, it has limits. Some motions and activities are modified or prohibited because they make excessive demands on the school's nervous system—its organizational structure. Take the principles of individualized instruction and teacher autonomy, for example. The school can be and should be much more responsive to, and flexible in, providing teachers with discretion and autonomy. But we cannot individualize to the point at which a separate school would be created for each student or each teacher. To do so would, in essence, destroy the school as an organized institution.

The overall purposes and functions of the school seem better served by organizational and structural forms described as professionally oriented. These structures seem best able to accommodate the unique characteristics of the technology of educational organizations. "Technology" refers to methods and characteristics associated with the school's professional and instructional subsystem. Adjusting the structure of an organization to fit unique aspects or demands of that organization's technology is a concept associated with sociotechnical theories of organization.[19]

James Thompson, in the tradition of sociotechnical thinking, identifies three major categories of technology: long-linked, mediating, and intensive.

An organization with a long-linked technology is characterized by fixed demands in product, certainty in goals, and programmed activities or, in Thompson's words, "serial interdependence in the sense that act Z can be performed only after successful completion of act Y, which in turn rests on X, and so on"[20] Scientific management in one or another of its forms seems compatible with organizations of this type.

An organization with a mediating technology has as its primary function the linking of clients or customers who are interdependent. Banks, post offices, insur-

[19] See, for example, Paul Lawrence and Jay Lorsch, "Differentiation and Integration in Complex Organizations," *Administrative Science Quarterly,* vol. 12, no. 1, 1967; Joan Woodward, *Industrial Organization: Theory and Practice,* London: Oxford, 1965; and F. E. Emery and E. L. Trist, "The Causal Texture of Organizational Environments," *Human Relations,* vol. 18, no. 3. 1963. This discussion of sociotechnical theory follows that which appears in T. J. Sergiovanni, op. cit.

[20] James D. Thompson, *Organizations in Action,* New York: McGraw-Hill, 1967, p. 16.

ance companies, and telephone utilities are examples of organizations with mediating technologies. In each case the organization is faced with the challenge of handling diverse inputs in standard ways. Borrowers' needs may vary, but standard rules govern the loan. Organizations of this type find needed comfort within the bureaucratic model.

Organizations with intensive technologies bring to bear a variety of resources in order to bring about a change in a particular object. The selection, combination, and order of application of these resources, however, are determined on the basis of interaction with this object. When the object in question is human, according to Thompson, the intensive technology is regarded as therapeutic, as is the case in a general hospital. In Thompson's words, "the intensive technology is a custom technology. Its successful employment rests in part on the availability of all the capacities potentially needed, but equally on the appropriate custom combination of selected capacities as required by the individual case or project."[21] The professionally oriented view of organizations, particularly as articulated by human resources theorists, seems most suited to intensive technologies.

SOCIOTECHNICAL THEORY AND THE SCHOOL

The sociotechnical and other contingency theorists differ from the classical-management and behavioral theorists in that they deny that there is a universal image of effective supervision and organization. Indeed, in their view, the effectiveness question is dependent upon institutional-level demands for adaptiveness and performance on the one hand and unique properties of the organization's professional subsystem (technology) on the other. The sociotechnical view elevates the importance of a school's technology, or professional subsystem, and accords it the positions of key determiner of organizational structure and equal partner in the mediation between the organization and its institutional level. Indeed, this view emphasizes the principle that form follows function.

What are the patterns of institutional-level demands for the school, and what technical properties do they possess? Schools are complex organizations in that they pursue a variety of goals and are subjected to multiple expectations. Variability exists between schools with regard to which expectations are emphasized, but all schools feel some pressure to perform and adapt. Performance-oriented expectations are, for example, concerned with the achievement of predetermined objectives[22] and with the learning of culturally defined meanings.[23] Schools and communities vary in the extent to which they define and standardize the core of knowledge which they believe is worth knowing, but some core exists neverthe-

---

[21] Ibid., p. 18.

[22] Abraham Maslow, "Some Basic Propositions of a Growth and Self Actualizing Psychology," in Arthur Combs (ed.), *Perceiving, Behaving, Becoming,* Washington, D.C.: Association for Supervision and Curriculum Development, 1962.

[23] James MacDonald, "An Image of Man: The Learner Himself," in Ronald Doll (ed.), *Individualized Instruction,* Washington, D.C.: Association for Supervision and Curriculum Development, 1964.

less. Adaptive-oriented expectations are more concerned, for example, with in-trinsic objectives, or learning for its own value, and with the students' personal meanings. Again variability exists in the extent to which adaptive expectations are emphasized, but recognition is nonetheless always given to the notion that students vary greatly in ability, motivation, values, and interests.

An imbalance currently exists in most schools in favor of emphasis on per-formance expectations. Here the professional subsystem of the school is likely to approximate the long-linked technology, and scientific-management principles are likely to be appropriate. Or in some quarters the adaptive qualities of young-sters are seen as a problem to be dealt with and somehow weakened. Here the school works to take this varied input in student dispositions and mediate it in standardized ways. The professional subsystem of the school is likely to take on mediating technology characteristics, and bureaucratic principles are seen as ap-propriate.

But schools that take on long-linked, or mediating, qualities in the organiza-tion of their professional subsystems still need to deal with the human factor. Waller describes this dilemma as the plight of the teacher who must work in an impersonal, bureaucratic structure but who needs the cooperation of students in order to be effective.[24] Work concerns are therefore separated from human con-cerns and are dealt with sequentially rather than simultaneously, to avoid con-flict. Counseling is institutionalized as a special function. Homeroom is the time scheduled for personal conerns. Personal interests are pursued through extracur-ricular activities or during free time. Recess is the time for fun, and school is the time for work, and so on. These are human relations devices intended to appease social needs so that people will be more accepting of controls with regard to the work of the organization.

Not so common but seen as desirable by many humanists is a school charac-terized by a clear imbalance in favor of adaptive goals and expectations. Given this imbalance, the school would take on the characteristics of a *simple*-intensive technology, which would be characterized by client feedback and custom tailor-ing of client services. Clearly this would be a client-centered organization whose survival would depend upon client assurance that his or her specifications, prefer-ences, and needs would be met. Further, since client preferences and needs can be expected to vary, the school would engage in craftlike or tailor-made activities to ensure particularistic products. Some combination of human relations and human resources supervision, perhaps with human relations dominating, might be appropriate for this simple-intensive technology.

But none of these is desirable as the exclusive image of a school. We prefer to view the school as a *complex*-intensive organization characterized by a moder-ately open system, one with a fairly steady-state flow of input in the form of community expectations, clients, and financial resources, but one that is able to effectively interact with and influence this input. The degree of the school's im-pact will depend upon the strength of its professional subsystem and upon its

---

[24] Willard Waller, *The Sociology of Teaching*, New York, Wiley, 1932.

having administrators and supervisors who are capable of arguing convincingly on behalf of certain educational-program values and intents.

Since the demands for neither performance nor adaptability seem unreasonable if balanced, then an important function of this professional subsystem is to define the balance. If both performance and adaptability are to be honored, then an organizational structure capable of integrating the two must be sought. Such a structure should possess the capacity to shift its form and focus in accordance with a variety of technical-level demands. A school or classroom, for example, would have the capacity to function either simultaneously or sequentially in a long-linked fashion for certain kinds of activities and in a custom-tailored fashion for others.

Consider, for example, one important property of the school's professional subsystem—the nature of goals and objectives. To the extent that it is appropriate for objectives to be predetermined and stated precisely, then the instructional system, together with its organizational features, should take on long-linked characteristics in accordance with scientific-management principles. In instances where it is desirable to leave the discovery of objectives entirely to students, a more laissez faire instruction system more in tune with human relations principles might be suitable. And where it is desirable for teachers and students to interact together to establish or discover objectives, human resources concepts would likely be suitable.

Much value exists in viewing the school under the rubrics of sociotechnical thinking as an intensive-complex organization which adjusts its organizational form and educational-program structure according to technical demands. Such an organization would be considered professional in character because of its adaptive capacities. Further, such adjustments require a distribution of authority and talent throughout the organization, which precludes relying as a matter of policy on standardization, formalization, stratification, centralization, and other traditional bureaucratic characteristics.

An additional professional subsystem property particularly important to human organizations such as schools is the question of values. Schools are normative organizations. People involved in normative organizations are concerned with questions of appropriateness as well as efficiency and efficacy. Indeed, it is not uncommon for the former concern to take precedence over the latter two.

In this sense, then, organization and supervision in education is a normative science concerned with the consequences of choice in terms of preferred values.[25] Each of the views of supervision and organization discussed in this chapter has much to contribute to good practice in education, though only human resources theory possesses, in our opinion, the value richness to serve as the overall framework for supervision in the school. Therefore, the extent to which sociotechnical thinking can be applied humanistically in education will depend upon the extent to which its principles are articulated within a broad commitment to the values of human resources theory.

[25] See, for example, T. J. Sergiovanni and Fred D. Carver, *The New School Executive: A Theory of Administration,* New York: Harper & Row, 1973.

THE SUPERVISOR'S ORGANIZATIONAL RESPONSIBILITIES

The focus of this chapter has been in an area not typically of concern to those with supervisory responsibilities. Yet supervisors are invariably charged with some aspect of change and are required to work for it in constant interaction with the structural-functional system of the school. To be sure, the focuses of supervision are people and program. Supervisors work with other professionals through an educational program to effect positive change in students. Success largely depends upon the realization that this work does not take place in a vacuum. Realism requires that the supervisor does not ignore the organizational context of schools. Human resources supervision is dependent upon a realistic appraisal and understanding of the school as an organization.

The sociotechnical view of organizations with its accompanying principle that form follows function requires that the supervisor assume a more active role in organizational matters. The supervisor is in a position to best understand critical aspects of the school's technology and professional subsystem and therefore is in a position to help administrators develop supporting and accommodating organizational structures and to evaluate existing structures to determine how well they fit with the school's educational-program intents and activities.

SUPERVISORY CONFLICT

Supervisors will often find themselves face to face with the stresses and strains which accompany life in formal organizations. Particularly common are strains associated with three organizational dilemmas related to professional and bureaucratic roles, ability and authority, and autonomy and coordination.

1 *Professional and bureaucratic role dilemma.* Some evidence seems to exist that contemporary organizations in American society are undergoing a process of simultaneous professionalization and bureaucratization.[26] Corwin[27] suggests that this is indeed the case for schools. He observes that administrators hold primarily bureaucratic expectations for behavior in schools, while teachers hold primarily professional expectations. This comparison is presented in Table 3-1.

In an analysis of school conflict identified through research based on this comparison, Corwin makes the following observation:

Approximately forty-five percent of all the incidents involved teachers in opposition to members of the administration; about one-fifth of these disputes were "open" discussions involving direct confrontations of parties in an argument or "heated" discussions (as judged by content analysis), or "major incidents" including a third party in addition to those teachers and administrators initially involved; this is a

[26] Litwak, for example, proposes several models of bureaucracy, one of which is the professional model which combines Weberian concepts with those of the human relations movement. He maintains that this model is most effective where jobs deal with both uniform and nonuniform events or with social skills as well as the traditional knowledge area. Eugene W. Litwak, "Models of Bureaucracy which Permit Conflict," *The American Journal of Sociology,* vol. 67, no. 3, pp. 177–184, September 1961.

[27] Ronald Corwin, "Professional Persons in Public Organizations," *Educational Administration Quarterly,* vol. 1, no. 3, pp. 1–23, Autumn 1965.

Table 3-1. Contrasts in the Bureaucratic- and Professional-Employee Principles of Organization

Organizational characteristics	Bureaucratic-employee expectations	Professional-employee expectations
Standardization		
Routine of work	Stress on uniformity of clients' problems	Stress on uniqueness of clients' problems
Continuity of procedure	Stress on records and files	Stress on research and change
Specificity of rules	Rules stated as universals; and specific	Rules stated as alternatives; and diffuse
Specialization		
Basis of division of labor	Stress on efficiency of techniques; task orientation	Stress on achievement of goals; client orientation
Basis of skill	Skill based primarily on practice	Skill based primarily on monopoly of knowledge
Authority		
Responsibility for decision making	Decisions concerning application of rules to routine problems	Decisions concerning policy in professional matters and unique problems
Basis of authority	Rules sanctioned by the public	Rules sanctioned by legally sanctioned professions
	Loyalty to the organization and to superiors	Loyalty to professional associations and clients
	Authority from office (position)	Authority from personal competence

From Ronald Corwin, "Professional Persons in Public Organizations," *Educational Administration Quarterly*, vol. 1, no. 3, p. 7, Autumn 1965.

larger number of open conflicts than reported among teachers themselves. About one-half of all incidents involved *groups* of teachers (teachers' organizations in seven percent of the cases).

Twenty-four percent of all conflict incidents fell in the categories of classroom control, curriculum management, and authority in the school; these incidents embraced such issues as the use of proper teaching techniques and procedures, changing the curriculum and selection of textbooks. About half of these involved administrators. Of the 159 incidents that were in the open, about one-fourth were with the administration over these issues of authority.[28]

The higher the professional orientation of teachers, according to Corwin's findings, the higher the rates of conflict. He concludes, "The weight of evidence from this very limited sample suggests that there is a consistent pattern of conflict between teachers and administrators over the control of work, and that professionalization is a militant process."[29] The dilemma for the supervisor is, of course, reconciling for himself or herself and for the human curriculum and its beneficiaries the increasing bureaucratization and professionalism which Corwin and others see as two simultaneous but conflicting thrusts for schools.

2 *The ability-authority dilemma.* This dilemma is a result of a distinction being emphasized in schools between the right to decide and the power and expertise to do. Teachers have, on the basis of authority derived from ability, successfully co-opted many functions previously reserved for administrators. Administrative reaction to increased teacher authority is generally mixed with pessimism and often with fear. Most of what administrators have yielded deals with curriculum and teaching matters, although no administrative responsibility is immune from co-optation on the basis of ability authority.

The dilemma, of course, is how those who administer and supervise as part of their legal responsibility are to maintain control over school developments. Human resources supervision offers clues to solving the dilemma in that it advocates the development and extension of ability monopolies for administrators. These ability monopolies will lie not so much in instructional and curriculum areas but rather in the management, growth, and development of the human organization of the school. The distinction which Parsons makes between the management system and the technical system in organizations seems useful here.[30] Administrators and to some extent supervisors, on the basis of ability authority, contribute to school goals through the management system. Teachers and to some extent supervisors, on the basis of ability authority, contribute to school goals through the technical system. Human resources supervision recognizes and respects the legitimacy of a number of sources of authority, but it focuses primarily on ability authority.

---

[28] Ibid., p. 12.
[29] Ibid., p. 15.
[30] The terms "management systems" and "technical systems" are used here, after Parsons, to differentiate between the administrative sphere and the educotechnical sphere in schools. See Talcott Parsons, "Some Ingredients of a General Theory of Organization," in Andrew W. Halpin (ed.), *Administrative Theory in Education,* Chicago: University of Chicago, Midwest Administration Center, 1958.

3 *The autonomy-coordination dilemma.* As teachers become more sophisticated and specialized in terms of professional and academic training, interests, and performance, and as their personal specialization and ability bases expand, teachers increase their demands for autonomy from administrators. Yet as the personal specialization phenomenon increases, teachers become more interdependent in order to achieve school goals. The typical organizational reaction to interdependence among specialists is one of coordination.[31] However, coordination of professional specialists imposes limits on the autonomy of each and is a threat to their ability monopolies. The supervisory dilemma can be reduced to this: how is it possible to cope with a situation in which teachers are becoming more autonomous in their specialization as they become less autonomous in the larger sphere of accomplishing schoolwide goals?

Pusic portrays the drama of professional specialization versus coordination as follows:

> Professional specialization leaves the specialist in possession of the necessary knowledge and skill to perform complex and meaningful activities. He is much less in danger of being separated from the meaning of his work and, therefore, much more independent. He knows his work and does not need to wait for others to assign tasks to him. Still the work of the individual specialist has to be co-ordinated and integrated into larger contexts. An individual physician in a hospital, a social worker in an agency, a scientist in a laboratory, a teacher in a school, an administrator in an office can make their full contribution only as their work is brought into rational relationships with the work of others. The very independence of their individual activities, however, makes co-ordination both more necessary and more difficult. The classical school of administrative science early became aware that the span of control—the number of people to be co-ordinated by one superior—was in inverse proportion to the professional level of the work co-ordinated.[32]

Recognizing the importance of coordination to administrators and to the organization, Pusic nevertheless sees dangers in overemphasis. Addressing himself to welfare agencies, he makes the following comments:

> The methods of co-ordination practiced within the traditional structure of organization seem to be ill adapted to the task of tying together the work of professional specialists. The work of individuals is co-ordinated within an organization by a hierarchy of superiors who are responsible for the allocation of work tasks to those below them as well as for the control and necessary correction of their work performances. With the increasing complexity of organizations and of the work done by their individual members the hierarchical method of co-ordination and of reports up the line becomes more abundant. More time is spent in meetings and other forms of face-to-face contact. More writing and reading for purposes of co-ordination have to be done at all levels. Administrative procedures become more involved, formalities more numerous as the organizational system tries to counteract the centrifugal tendencies of specialization. This increase of co-ordinating activities, however, has to find its

---

[31] The phenomenal growth of directors, staff assistants, and other coordinators in schools seems to substantiate this trend.

[32] Eugen Pusic, "The Political Community and Future of Welfare," in John Morgan (ed.), *Welfare and Wisdom,* Toronto: University of Toronto Press, 1967, p. 67.

place within the fixed time-budget at the disposal of the organization. Co-ordination can ultimately expand only at the expense of the main activity, which is the initial social reason for the existence of the system. More co-ordination means less health work, less social welfare services, less education, less research by the respective organizations. The point of diminishing returns can be clearly seen: it is the moment when the balance between co-ordination and basic activity becomes so unfavorable that organization will no longer be the socially most economical method of human co-operation.[33]

Additional supervisory dilemmas in the organizational context of schools can be identified and discussed. Of particular interest to supervision are the relationships which exist between the demands and needs of organization and those of their human inhabitants. The interface is discussed in the next section, where the school is considered as a social system.

THE SCHOOL AS A SOCIAL SYSTEM

The most widely recognized and perhaps the most useful framework for studying and understanding administrative and supervisory behavior is the social systems analysis developed for educators by Jacob Getzels and Egon Guba.[34] This formulation is reviewed and modified for supervision below.

The social systems theorists[35] view administration and supervision as a social process which occurs within a social system. Process and context can be examined, according to this view, from structural, functional, and operational perspectives. Structurally, administration and supervision are considered to be a series of superordinate-subordinate relationships within a social system. Functionally, this hierarchy of relationships (principal to teacher, teacher to student, and so on) is the basis for allocating and integrating roles, personnel, and facilities to accomplish school goals. Operationally, the process occurs in person-to-person interaction.

The term *social system* is used by Getzels and Guba in a conceptual rather than a descriptive way. They conceive of this system as containing two interdependent but interacting dimensions. The first dimension consists of the *institution,* which is defined in terms of its *roles,* which are in turn defined in terms of *role expectations,* all of which are carefully designed to fulfill the goals of the institution.

[33] Ibid., p. 68.
[34] The following discussion is based on a number of sources. Documentation is loose in view of the general familiarity and acceptance of the Getzels and Guba social systems model. See, for example, J. W. Getzels, "A Psycho-sociological Framework for the Study of Educational Administration," *Harvard Educational Review,* vol. 22, pp. 235–246, Fall 1952; J. W. Getzels and E. G. Guba, "Social Behavior and the Administrative Process," *The School Review,* vol. 65, pp. 423–441, 1957; J. W. Getzels, "Administration as a Social Processs," in Andrew W. Halpin (ed.), *Administrative Theory in Education,* Chicago: University of Chicago, Midwest Administration Center, 1958; and more recently J. W. Getzels et al., *Educational Administration as a Social Process: Theory, Research, Practice,* New York: Harper & Row, 1968. Especially basic to this discussion is the Getzels and Guba 1957 article.
[35] Cf. Talcott Parsons, *The Social System,* New York: Free Press, 1951.

Institution $\longrightarrow$ Roles $\longrightarrow$ Role expectations $\longrightarrow$ Institutional goal achievement

All institutions have certain characteristics and imperative functions in common:

1 *Institutions have purposes.* They are established to perform certain functions and are legitimized by client groups and societal groups on the basis of these functions. Purposes for schools are generally of two kinds: those which are manifest—the educational and custodial functions which win community and societal support—and those which are latent—the power gratification and growth rewards which members (teachers and administrators) seek.

2 *Institutions are structural.* Institutional goals are achieved through task diversification. Therefore roles are established with appropriate role descriptions. Each role is assigned certain responsibilities and resources, including authority for implementing given tasks. The ideas are conceived and responsibilities allocated in terms of actors, as defined below, rather than of personalities.[36]

3 *Institutions are normative.* Roles serve as norms for the behavior of those who occupy the roles. Each actor or role incumbent is expected to behave in certain predetermined ways in order to retain a legitimate position in the school. Teachers, for example, who adopt modes of behavior typical of the student culture have difficulty in maintaining their legitimate position in the eyes of other teachers, administrators, and perhaps even of students.

4 *Institutions are sanction-bearing.* Institutions have at their disposal appropriate positive and negative sanctions for ensuring compliance with established norms. Teachers who are rate-busters in the eyes of other teachers, for example, may be subject to a silent treatment or to a whisper campaign. Those who appear to be deviants to the principal wait longer for school supplies, are given undesirable class assignments, and are swamped with classroom visitations.

The operation of institutions is defined and analyzed in terms of the subunit role. Roles represent the various positions, offices, and status prerogatives which exist within the institution and are themselves defined in terms of role expectations. Roles are generally institutional givens and, therefore, are not formulated to fit one or another personality. Behaviors associated with a given role are arranged on a conceptual continuum extending from those required to those prohibited. Certain behaviors are considered absolutely mandatory (that the teacher at least show up for school), and others are absolutely forbidden (that the teacher not become romantically involved with students). Between these extremes are other behavior patterns—some recommended, others disapproved, but all to varying degrees permissible. Roles are best understood when examined in relation to other roles. The student role helps us to understand the teacher role, and so on.

In the absence of individuals with complex and unique personalities, the organizational dimension described above provides for maximum organizational predictability. This aspect of the social system is called the nomothetic dimen-

---

[36] A survey of a typical first-grade class on the first day of school will reveal reliable, even though sterotyped, descriptions of the role of principal as compared with the role of teacher.

sion. The second aspect, the ideographic dimension, adds the human element to the social system formulation.[37] As the institutional dimension was analyzed in terms of role and expectation, so the individual dimension is similarly analyzed and defined operationally in terms of personality and need disposition.

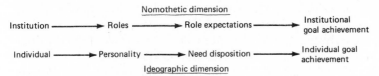

The ideographic dimension is similar in format (but not in substance) to the nomothetic dimension in that individuals, like institutions, have goals which they express through their personalities and pursue according to their unique need dispositions.

The two dimensions of the social system are assumed to be in constant interaction. In its nomothetic dimension the organization strives to socialize the individual to its own image and ends, while in its ideographic dimension the individual strives to socialize the organization to his or her own image and ends.[38] Behavior, then, in any social system is a function of the interaction between unique personalities and preestablished roles. Conformity to the institution, its roles, and its expectations leads to organizational effectiveness, while conformity to individuals, their personalities, and their need dispositions leads to individual efficiency.

Getzels and Guba identify a number of conflict situations which could potentially result from the organization's interaction with its human inhabitants. Among them are role-personality conflicts which result from a discrepancy between the pattern of expectations attached to a given role and the pattern of need dispositions of the role incumbent. An assistant principal with a high dependence orientation would find a role characterized by autonomous and independent action quite uncomfortable; teachers with a professional and technical need to interact with school policy makers who are defensive, authoritarian, and non-communicative experience similar role-personality conflict. Multiple but conflicting expectations for the same role are another source of role conflict. Supervisors who are expected by some teachers to visit classes and by others to stay away experience conflict of this type. The young mother-teacher faces role conflict of this type as she struggles to justly fulfill two demanding roles. The school as an organization is frequently subject to role conflict of this type as it attempts to appease multiple and conflicting expectations from its many publics.

[37] Guba describes the process by which the terms *nomothetic* and *ideographic* were chosen for the theory as follows: "The terms 'ideographic' and 'nomothetic' were picked from *Roget's Thesaurus* by me one wintry afternoon when I had nothing better to do than to try to find some new and interesting terms to use in our theory. We justified this at the time by claiming that we had to find terms 'untainted' by value connotations."—E. G. Guba, "Development, Diffusion, and Evaluation," in T. L. Eidell and J. M. Kitchell (eds.), *Knowledge Production and Utilization in Educational Administration,* Eugene, Oregon: Center for the Advanced Study of Educational Administration, 1968, p. 38.

[38] E. W. Bakke, "Concept of the Social Organization," in Mason Haire (ed.), *Modern Organization Theory,* New York: Wiley, 1961, p. 60.

SUMMARY

We have, for illustrative purposes, discussed the school's life as something quite independent from that which results from those who live and work in the school. As the school "becomes alive," it takes on many of the characteristics of a human organism. As such, the school develops a unique organizational personality which is expressed by and, indeed, is imposed upon those who come to live and work within its boundaries. Further, in the absence of more than token human direction and control, the school pursues a series of satellite goals which revolve around the simple but omnipresent need for growth and survival.[39] Within this context the school's goals are generally pursued in a mechanical way, with changes occurring largely because the nature of growth and survival needs change. When changes do occur, they are seemingly unaffected by, and reflect little interest in, the wishes and requirements of the school's human inhabitants, except as such concerns contribute to the school's growth and survival. If left to its own whims, the school evolves into a monolithic structure which captures and uses its human participants to accomplish its, rather than their, ends. This phenomenon is illustrated by the *natural* tendency of schools to adopt conservative perspectives, to exert a major emphasis on maintenance activities, to avoid change, and thereby to avoid controversy and conflict. School conservatism is illustrated by the now-classic Mort studies, which showed a 50-year gap between an educational invention and widespread adoption of that educational practice.[40]

A fundamental concern of supervision is the question of whether schools use people to accomplish organizational ends or whether people use schools to accomplish human ends. This concern is placed in perspective by the following phrase from the *Cardinal Principles of Secondary Education,* 1918: "The objectives must determine the organization or else the organization will determine the objectives."

Human resources supervisors work to develop the human dimension in schools. They are concerned with the appropriateness of school goals, the welfare and growth of school workers, and, indeed, the intellectual, social, and emotional self-actualization of school clients. Such human concerns require the school as an organization to serve its students, unlike traditional supervisory patterns, which required individuals to serve the school.

The purpose of this chapter was to introduce those who supervise to the broader environment within which supervision takes place. The school was described as a complex organization which shares many characteristics of bureaucracy and professionalism. One hazard in viewing the school as a bureaucracy is to attribute to it degrees of rationality which do not match with reality. It was

---

[39] While *school growth* refers to extension of curricular offerings, school boundaries, size of staff, and the like, it also refers to increases in influence, status, and prestige. *Survival,* for schools, refers to continued community financial and moral support and the avoidance of conflict, controversy, and uncertainty, as well as guaranteed tenure for the present school establishment. Both can be maintained by giving only token attention to a quality educational program.

[40] The Mort studies are summarized in Paul R. Mort, "Studies in Educational Innovation from the Institute of Administrative Research: An Overview," in Matthew B. Miles (ed.), *Innovation in Education,* New York: Teachers College Press, 1964, pp. 317–328.

pointed out that schools are more accurately characterized as "satisficing" rather than maximizing organizations, but this "satisficing" tendency does not prevent people from valuing and striving for excellence. Indeed basic to the human resources view is the belief in the human capacity for setting goals, for striving for greater achievement even though people are subjected to "satisficing" limitations.

Professional elements and tendencies in schools were described and contrasted with bureaucratic elements by viewing the school as a structural-functional system. Though it is considered most appropriate for schools to be professionally oriented, a contingency approach to organization, relying on sociotechnical theory, was proposed. The school was then viewed as a social system, and key areas of conflict for supervisors were presented. Discussed were conflicts between professional and bureaucratic values, between the socializing tendency of organizations and individual personality, between ability and authority, and between autonomy and coordination.

STUDY GUIDE

Recall the concepts, ideas, and meanings associated with each of the following phrases and terms included in this chapter. Can you discuss each of them with a colleague and apply them to the supervisory context of your school? If you cannot, review them in the text and record the page number for future reference.

1 Ability-authority conflict _____
2 Axiomatic theory of organization _____
3 Bureaucratic dysfunction _____
4 Educational subsystem _____
5 Intensive technology _____
6 Maximizing _____
7 Nomothetic _____
8 Professional-bureaucratic conflict _____
9 Social system formulation _____
10 Structural-functional system _____
11 Unanticipated consequences _____
12 Autonomy-coordination conflict _____
13 Bureaucratically oriented school _____
14 Contingency approach _____
15 Ideographic _____
16 Long-linked technology _____
17 Mediating technology _____
18 Organizational subsystem _____
19 Satisficing _____
20 Sociotechnical theory _____
21 Technology of schools _____

EXERCISES

1 This chapter emphasizes the negative aspects of bureaucracy in schools. But bureaucracy provides us with benefits too. Consider, for example, an inexperienced teacher in

conference with parents who are influential in the community (perhaps the local banker and spouse, a former teacher). How can the school as an organization with bureaucratic characteristics help provide this teacher with authority?

2 "People tend to seek not the best needle in a haystack, but rather one that satisfies the reason for their search." This metaphor was used to suggest the "satisficing" rather than maximizing nature of decision making in schools. Carefully observe one or two administrators or supervisors for a week. Describe the extent to which decisions they make are "satisficing."

3 Prepare a two-page case study involving supervisors and teachers in a situation which illustrates the ability-authority dilemma.

Chapter 4

Building a Climate
for Supervision

The structure of the school and its functioning as a formal organization influence the character of the school, dispositions of teacher and students, and the flow, design, and articulation of the school's educational program. Organizational structure and function, however, are relatively objective characteristics whose effects on the school are more likely to be felt in the form of perceptions and feelings of teacher and students. This chapter is concerned with these more subjective impressions of the school's *climate*. The following questions are considered: What is climate? Why is it important? How is it effected? What roles does supervision play in building climate? How might climate be conceptualized? How might climate be charted and monitored?

WHAT IS ORGANIZATIONAL CLIMATE?

Since the climate of a school is a matter of impression, it is often difficult to define with precision. Climate might be viewed on the one hand as the enduring characteristics which describe a particular school, distinguish it from other schools, and influence the behavior of teachers and students, and on the other hand as the "feel" which teachers and students have for that school. Litwin and Stringer, for example, define climate as: "The perceived subjective effects of the formal system, the informal 'style' of managers, and other important environmental factors on the attitudes, beliefs, values, and motivation of people who work in a particular organization."[1]

According to this view, climate represents a composite of mediating variables which intervene between the structure of an organization and the style and other characteristics of leaders, and teacher performance and satisfaction.[2]

THE IMPORTANCE OF CLIMATE

Many supervisors do not like to be cast into a leadership role which requires that they give attention to organizational climate. They prefer instead to devote full attention to what they feel really matters—educational program and students. This concern is commendable, and indeed educational and instructional roles of supervision are most important. But supervisors will have a difficult time exercising this leadership without a sufficient supportive climate within which to work. Further, excluding or neglecting organizational climate in favor of educational tasks can actually limit the total amount of leadership talent available in the school.

The need for an organizational-climate emphasis is clear. A healthy climate frees supervisor and teacher to work more fully on educational matters. Further, a direct focus by supervisors on educational-leadership responsibilities is often viewed by teachers as authoritarian, and therefore the leadership initiatives of supervisors are limited. An organizational-climate emphasis, on the other hand, not only permits the supervisor to take a direct lead in educational matters when appropriate, but draws out the leadership talents of others as well. Here leadership becomes a process rather than a set of prerogatives associated with the supervisor's role.

Direct instructional leadership is still at the core of the supervisor's role, but the focus is less on who assumes the role and more on whether it is indeed assumed. The supervisor may display instructional leadership directly or by working to see that leadership does emerge from within the teaching staff. Fundamental to this position is the belief that a major aspect of the supervisor's job is to provide the circumstances and climate for leadership.

THE SUPERVISOR AND SCHOOL CLIMATE

Climate is a necessary link between organizational structure and teacher attitude and behavior. George and Bishop, for example, found that formal structural characteristics of the schools they studied had an important influence on the way in which teachers perceived the school's climate. The 296 teachers in their study were more likely to view the climates of bureaucratically oriented school districts as closed and constricting. Professionally oriented school districts, on the other

[1] George H. Litwin and Robert A. Stringer, Jr., *Motivation and Organizational Climate,* Boston: Harvard University, Division of Research, Graduate School of Business Administration, 1968, p. 5.

[2] In this sense, organizational climate comprises the mediating variables, which intervene between the initiating variables and school-effectiveness variables, according to the synthesizing theory of supervision presented in Chapter 2.

hand, were viewed as being more trusting and open and as producing less anxiety in teachers.[3]

But climate would be of more interest to top administrators than to supervisors if it were primarily affected by organizational structure. Supervisors are interested because of the link which exists between leadership assumptions, characteristics, and behavior, and school climate, and indeed the link is strong. Halpin, for example, finds that it is the behavior of elementary school principals (the extent to which they are seen as aloof, emphasizing production and close supervision, setting an example through their own hard work, and showing consideration) which in a large measure sets a climate tone for a school.[4]

In a more direct investigation of leader behavior and organizational climate Litwin and Stringer found that by varying the leadership style in each of three simulated organizations, they were able to create three different climates, each with distinct implications for member performance and satisfaction.[5] In organization A the leader strongly emphasized structure, status, assigned roles, position authority, vertical communications, and a punitive system of rules and regulations. Organization A resembled the classical-management, or bureaucratic, view of management and organization. In organization B the leader strongly emphasized an informal, loose structure and promoted shared decision making, team work, and friendliness. This organization was fashioned pretty much in accordance with human relation beliefs. Organization C was also characterized by interpersonal support and cooperation, but here the leader provided an added emphasis on quality performance and encouraged creativity. Organization C approximated the human resources model. In each case the organizations varied in the mode of leadership provided by the designated leader.

Members in organization A viewed the climate as punitive and nonsupportive and as offering little chance for individual initiative. The leader was viewed as aloof, and interpersonal conflict was common despite efforts of the leader to suppress it. Members of organization B viewed the climate as warm, cooperative, participatory, tension-free, and friendly. Members of organization C viewed the climate as being somewhat cooperative and loosely structured but bounded by norms of responsibility, personal initiative, and risk taking. Though members found the organization rewarding, it was characterized by moderate conflict.

Each of the climates was, in turn, associated with quite different outcomes for the three organizations. Job satisfaction and performance were low in organization A. Performance was also low in organization B, but in this case innovation was moderately high and satisfaction very high. Organization C was characterized by very high performance and innovation and high satisfaction. These relationships are summarized in Table 4-1.

Supervisors frequently are not able to influence broader questions of organizational structure and function in schools to the extent they wish. But they can

---

[3] J. George and L. Bishop, "Relationship of Organizational Structure and Teacher Personality Characteristics to Organizational Climate," *Administrative Science Quarterly,* vol. 16, pp. 467–476, 1971.

[4] Andrew W. Halpin and Donald B. Croft, *Organizational Climate of Schools,* Chicago: University of Chicago, Midwest Administration Center, 1963.

[5] Litwin and Stringer, op. cit.

Table 4-1.   Leadership, Climate and Effectiveness: Litwin and Stringer

Leadership	Climate	Effectiveness
Organization A Bureaucratic leadership	Closed	Performance low Satisfaction low
Organization B Human relations leadership	Warm Supportive Friendly	Performance low Satisfaction very high Innovation high
Organization C Human resources Leadership	Supportive Goal-oriented	Performance very high Satisfaction high Innovation very high

still exert a strong influence on school climate through the nature and quality of leadership they exercise.

ORGANIZATIONAL CLIMATE AND SCHOOLS

Two well-known constructs for conceptualizing organizational climate for schools can be found in the work of Matthew Miles[6] and of Andrew Halpin and Don Croft.[7]

Halpin, for example, views schools as being on a conceptual climate continuum that extends from open to closed.[8] This framework is not unlike that which considers individual personalities as being on a continuum from open-mindedness to closed-mindedness. At a very simple level, organization climate refers to the feeling which exists in a given school and the variability in this feeling as one moves from school to school. Halpin, in describing climate, notes that "as one moves to other schools, one finds that each has a 'personality' of its own. It is this 'personality' that we describe here as the 'organizational climate' of the school. Analogously, personality is to the individual what organizational climate is to the organization."[9]

The Organizational Climate Description Questionnaire was developed by Halpin and Croft as a means to measure and chart the difference in "feel" which characterizes individual schools. The instrument examines eight dimensions of organizational climate, four of which focus on teacher behavior and four on the behavior of the principal. These are presented in Table 4-2.

Each of the eight dimensions of climate is represented in the instrument as a subtest.[10] Various combinations of emphasis on each of the subtests, as perceived

[6] Matthew Miles, "Planned Change and Organizational Health: Figure and Ground," *Change Processes in the Public Schools,* Eugene: The University of Oregon, Center for the Advanced Study of Educational Administration, 1965, pp. 11–34.

[7] Halpin and Croft, op. cit. For a condensed version see Halpin's *Theory and Research in Administration,* New York: Macmillan, 1967, pp. 131–249.

[8] The Halpin climate "continuum," as measured by the Organizational Climate Description Questionnaire, moves from open, through autonomous, controlled, familiar, and paternal, to closed.

[9] Halpin, *Theory and Research in Administration,* p. 131.

[10] Ibid., p. 150. The dimension which seems to have the strongest relationship to open climate is esprit.

by the teachers responding to the instrument, reveal for the school a climate-similarity score which determines the relative position of the school on the open-to-closed continuum. The school with an open climate, for example, is characterized by low disengagement, low hindrance, very high esprit, high intimacy, low aloofness, low production emphasis, very high thrust, and high consideration, The closed school exhibits very high disengagement, high hindrance, very low esprit, high intimacy, high aloofness, high production emphasis, low thrust, and low consideration. Open- and closed-school climates are described by Halpin as follows:

> The Open Climate depicts a situation in which the members enjoy extremely high *Esprit*. The teachers work well together without bickering and griping (low disengagement). They are not burdened by mountains of busywork or by routine reports; the principal's policies facilitate the teachers' accomplishment of their tasks (low hindrance). On the whole, the group members enjoy friendly relations of intimacy. The teachers obtain considerable job satisfaction, and are sufficiently motivated to overcome difficulties and frustration. They possess the incentive to work things out and to keep the organization "moving." Furthermore, the teachers are proud to be associated with their school.[11]
>
> The Closed Climate marks a situation in which the group members obtain little satisfaction in respect to either task-achievement or social-needs. In short, the principal is ineffective in directing the activities of the teachers; at the same time, he is not

[11] Ibid., pp. 174–175.

Table 4-2.   The Eight Dimensions of Organizational Climate

	Intensity scale	
	Open	Closed
Teachers' Behavior		
1. *Disengagement* refers to the teachers' tendency to be "not with it." This dimension describes a group which is "going through the motions," a group that is "not in gear" with respect to the task at hand. It corresponds to the more general concept of *anomie* as first described by Durkheim.* In short, this subtest focuses upon the teachers' behavior in a task-oriented situation.	–	++
2. *Hindrance* refers to the teachers' feeling that the principal burdens them with routine duties, committee demands, and other requirements which the teachers construe as unnecessary "busywork." The teachers preceive that the principal is hindering rather than facilitating their work.	–	+
3. *Esprit* refers to morale. The teachers feel that their social needs are being satisfied, and that they are, at the same time, enjoying a sense of accomplishment in their job.	++	--
4. *Intimacy* refers to the teachers' enjoyment of friendly social relations with each other. This dimension describes a social-needs satisfaction which is not necessarily associated with task-accomplishment.	+	+

Table 4-2. (*continued*)

	Intensity scale	
	Open	Closed

Principal's Behavior

5. *Aloofness* refers to behavior by the principal which is characterized as formal and impersonal. He "goes by the book" and prefers to be guided by rules and policies rather than to deal with the teachers in an informal, face-to-face situation. His behavior, in brief, is universalistic rather than particularistic; nomothetic rather than idiosyncratic. To maintain this style, he keeps himself—at least "emotionally"—at a distance from his staff.   [Open: −] [Closed: +]

6. *Production emphasis* refers to behavior by the principal which is characterized by close supervision of the staff. He is highly directive and plays the role of a "straw boss." His communication tends to go in only one direction, and he is not sensitive to feedback from the staff.   [Open: −] [Closed: +]

7. *Thrust* refers to behavior by the principal which is characterized by his evident effort in trying to "move the organization." Thrust behavior is marked not by close supervision, but by the principal's attempt to motivate the teachers through the example which he personally sets. Apparently, because he does not ask the teachers to give of themselves any more than he willingly gives of himself, his behavior, though starkly task-oriented, is nonetheless viewed favorably by the teachers.   [Open: ++] [Closed: −]

8. *Consideration* refers to behavior by the principal which is characterized by an inclination to treat the teachers "humanly," to try to do a little something extra for them in human terms.   [Open: +] [Closed: −]

*Emile Durkheim, *Le Suicide,* Paris, Libraire Felix Alcan, 1930, p. 277. *Anomie* describes a planlessness in living, a method of living which defeats itself because achievement has no longer any criterion of value; happiness always lies beyond any present achievement. Defeat takes the form of ultimate disillusion—a disgust with the futility of endless pursuit.

++ Very high emphasis
+ High
− Low
−− Very low

Source: Andrew Halpin, *Theory and Research in Administration*, New York: Macmillan, 1967, pp. 150–151. The intensity scale is an addition to the original Halpin table.

inclined to look out for their personal welfare. This climate is the most closed and the least genuine climate that we have identified.[12]

The values associated with human resources supervision suggest that the work of the school needs to be accomplished within the framework of open

[12] Ibid., p. 180. We should caution at this time that the OCDQ was developed for use with elementary schools. Some controversy seems to exist over whether the instrument can be used in other school settings, but the instrument tends not to be valid for large secondary schools and perhaps (in our opinion) even for large elementary schools. As schools increase in size and/or complexity, the referent-point principal should perhaps be changed to someone closer to the teachers. See J. Foster Watkins, "The OCDQ—an Application for Some Implications," *Educational Administration Quarterly,* vol. 4, pp. 46–60, Spring 1968. Also, Fred D. Carver and T. Sergiovanni, "Some Notes on the OCDQ," *Journal of Educational Administration,* vol. 7, no. 1, May 1969.

climates. Attention to climate is particularly crucial in that the classroom door does not provide a sufficient buffer to protect the classroom from the prevailing school climate. Closed climates in organizations tend to breed closed learning climates. Open climates in organizations tend to breed open learning climates. A significant direction for leadership-supervisory behavior is moving toward the development and maintenance of the climate most conducive to dynamic instructional leadership.

ORGANIZATIONAL HEALTH: A SUPERVISORY GOAL

A similar but broader approach to understanding the prevailing flavor, attitude, sentiment, and orientation of a given school is that which Miles proposes as the concept of organizational health. Miles describes the healthy school as one which exhibits reasonably clear and reasonably accepted goals (goal focus); communication that is relatively distortion-free vertically, horizontally, and across boundary lines (communication adequacy); equitable distribution of influence to all levels of the organization (optimal power equalization); and effective and efficient use of inputs, both human and material (resource utilization). The healthy school likewise reflects reciprocally satisfying vectors of influence between the inhabitants and the school (cohesiveness), a feeling of well-being among the staff (morale), self-renewing properties (innovativeness), and an active response to its environment (autonomy and adaptation). Finally, the healthy school maintains and strengthens its problem-solving capabilities (problem-solving adequacies).

Each of the 10 dimensions of health is described in detail below. They form a major share of the content which composes the process of supervision. From Miles, they are:[13]

1 *Goal focus.* In a healthy organization, the goal (or more usually goals) of the system would be reasonably clear to the system members, and reasonably well accepted by them. This clarity and acceptance, however, should be seen as a necessary but insufficient condition for organization health. The goals must also be *achievable* with existing or available resources, and be *appropriate*—more or less congruent with the demands of the environment.

2 *Communication adequacy.* Since organizations are not simultaneous face-to-face systems like small groups, the movement of information within them becomes crucial. This dimension of organization health implies that there is relatively distortion-free communication "vertically," "horizontally," and across the boundary of the system to and from the surrounding environment. That is, information travels reasonably well—just as the healthy person "knows himself" with a minimum level of repression, distortion, etc. In the healthy organization, there is good and prompt sensing of internal strains; there are enough data about problems of the system to insure that a good diagnosis of system difficulties can be made. People have the information they need, and have gotten it without exerting undue efforts, such as those involved in moseying up to the superintendent's secretary, reading the local newspaper, or calling excessive numbers of special meetings.

3 *Optimal power equalization.* In a healthy organization the distribution of influence is relatively equitable. Subordinates (if there is a formal authority chart)

[13] Miles, op. cit., pp. 18–21.

can influence upward, and even more important—as Likert has demonstrated—they perceive that their boss can do likewise with his *boss*. In such an organization, intergroup struggles for power would not be bitter, though intergroup conflict, (as in every human system known to man) would undoubtedly be present. The basic stance of persons in such an organization, as they look up, sideways and down, is that of collaboration rather than explicit or implicit coercion.

    4 *Resource utilization.* We say of a healthy person, such as a second-grader, that he is "working up to his potential." To put this another way, the classroom system is evoking a contribution from him at an appropriate and goal-directed level of tension. At the organization level, "health" would imply that the system's inputs, particularly the personnel, are used effectively. The overall coordination is such that people are neither overloaded nor idling. There is a minimal sense of strain, generally speaking (in the sense that trying to do something with a weak or inappropriate structure puts strain on that structure). In the healthy organization, people may be working very hard indeed, but they feel that they are not working against themselves, or against the organization. The fit between people's own dispositions and the role demands of the system is good. Beyond this, people feel reasonably "self-actualized"; they not only "feel good" in their jobs, but they have a genuine sense of learning, growing, and developing as persons in the process of making their organizational contribution.

    5 *Cohesiveness.* We think of a healthy person as one who has a clear sense of identity; he knows who he is, underneath all the specific goals he sets for himself. Beyond this, he *likes himself;* his stance toward life does not require self-derogation, even when there are aspects of his behavior which are unlovely or ineffective. By analogy at the organization level, system health would imply that the organization knows "who it is." Its members feel attracted to membership in the organization. They want to stay with it, be influenced by it, and exert their own influence in the collaborative style suggested above.

    6 *Morale.* The implied notion is one of well-being or satisfaction. Satisfaction is not enough for health, of course; a person may report feelings of well-being and satisfaction in his life, while successfully denying deep-lying hostilities, anxieties, and conflicts. Yet it still seems useful to evoke, at the organization level, the idea of morale: a summated set of individual sentiments, centering around feelings of well-being, satisfaction, and pleasure, as opposed to feelings of discomfort, unwished-for strain, and dissatisfaction.

    7 *Innovativeness.* A healthy system would tend to invent new procedures, move toward new goals, produce new kinds of products, diversify itself, and become more rather than less differentiated over time. In a sense, such a system could be said to grow, develop, and change, rather than remaining routinized and standard.

    8 *Autonomy.* The healthy person acts "from his own center outward." Seen in a training or therapy group, for example, such a person appears nearly free of the need to submit dependently to authority figures, *and* from the need to rebel and destroy symbolic fathers of any kind. A healthy organization, similarly, would not respond passively to demands from the outside, feeling itself the tool of the environment, and it would not respond destructively or rebelliously to perceived demands either. It would tend to have a kind of independence from the environment, in the same sense that the healthy person, while he has transactions with others, does not treat their responses as *determinative* of his own behavior.

    9 *Adaptation.* The notions of autonomy and innovativeness are both connected with the idea that a healthy person, group, or organization is in realistic, effective contact with the surroundings. When environmental demands and organization resources do not match, a problem-solving, restructuring approach evolves in which *both* the environment and the organization become different in some respect. More adequate, continued coping of the organization, as a result of changes in the local system, the relevant portions of the environment, or more usually both, occurs. And such a system has sufficient stability and stress tolerance to manage the difficulties which occur during the adaption process.

    10 *Problem-solving adequacy.* Finally, any healthy organism—even one as theoretically impervious to fallibility as a computer—*always* has problems, strains, difficulties, and instances of ineffective coping. The issue is not the presence or absence of problems, therefore, but the *manner* in which the person, group, or organization copes with problems. Argyris has suggested that in an effective system, problems are solved with minimal energy; they stay solved; and the problem-solving mechanisms used are not weakened, but maintained or strengthened. An adequate organization, then, has well-developed structures and procedures for sensing the existence of problems, for inventing possible solutions, for deciding on the solutions, for implementing them, and for evaluating their effectiveness.

Each of the dimensions of organizational health for any school operates in a system of dynamic interaction characterized by a high degree of interdependence. Clear goal focus, for example, depends upon the extent to which the school communicates its goals and permits inhabitants to modify and rearrange them. At another level, a high degree of organizational health encourages school adaptiveness, while school adaptiveness contributes to, and is essential to, organizational health.

THE SYSTEM 4 CLIMATE: AN INTEGRATED APPROACH TO SCHOOL SUPERVISION

In 1961 *New Patterns of Management*[14] by Rensis Likert appeared as part of the general literature in supervision. The book made a significant and widespread impact on noneducational settings and a small but nevertheless significant inroad in the literature and in the practice of educational supervision. The signifiance of this book to educational supervision is that it offered for the first time an intergrated, research-based system of supervision applicable to schools. This system is based on the development of highly effective work groups who are committed to the goals of the school and who work toward these goals as a means to professional growth and development and personal self-fulfillment. These groups are linked together in an overlapping pattern which permits them to function, on the one hand, as relatively small and cohesive primary groups and, on the other hand, as dynamic contributors to, and influencers of, the total school enterprise.

    A highly effective school work group is described as one which: (1) members

---

[14] Rensis Likert, *New Patterns of Management,* New York: McGraw-Hill, 1961. In the early chapters of *New Patterns of Management,* Professor Likert summarizes, synthesizes, and articulates hundreds of studies performed through the institute which have relevance to supervision. In the remaining chapters, Likert uses this mass of findings to develop and support a theory of supervision based on three fundamental principles: (1) the principle of supportive relationships, (2) the principle of group decision making and group supervision, and (3) the principle of high performance goals for individuals, groups, and the organization.

perceive as supportive and which builds and maintains their sense of personal worth, (2) has high performance goals which are consistent with those of the school and/or the profession, (3) uses group decision making, and (4) is linked to other school groups through multiple and overlapping group structures.

From these ideas Likert was able to develop a theory of supervision which relies heavily on the concept of organizational climate as an intervening variable between what supervisors and administrators do and organizational effectiveness. The theory was described in Likert's 1967 book entitled *The Human Organization: Its Management and Value.*[15] Here Likert proposed four different climates known as Management Systems 1, 2, 3, and 4. The characteristics of each of these systems, or climates, together with corresponding initiating variables, can be found in the profile of organizational characteristics, which appears as Table 4-3. In each case it is assumed that scores close to System 4 (those to the right of the scale in Table 4-3) will promote greater organizational effectiveness.[16]

It would be helpful if the reader would take a moment to respond to the profile in accordance with Likert's directions. "Please think of the *most* productive (effective) department, division, or organization you have known well. Then place the letter *h* on the line under each organizational variable in the following table to show where this organization would fall. Treat each item as a continuous variable from the left extreme of System 1 to the right extreme of System 4."[17]

The reader may also wish to respond to the form a second time, placing an *l* at the point which describes the least effective educational unit or school organization for each of the organizational variables.[18]

---

[15] Rensis Likert, *The Human Organization: Its Management and Value,* New York: McGraw-Hill, 1967.

[16] As Likert develops the theory, he identifies and classifies organizational variables into three types: "causal," "intervening," and "end-result," as follows: The "causal variables are independent variables which determine the course of developments within an organization and the results achieved by the organization. These causal variables include only those independent variables which can be altered or changed by the organization.

The "intervening" variables reflect the internal state and health of the organization, e.g., the loyalties, attitudes, motivations, performance goals, and perceptions of all members, and their collective capacity for effective interaction, communication, and decision making.

The "end-result" variables are the dependent variables which reflect the achievements of the organization, such as its productivity, costs, scrap loss, and earning. Likert, *The Human Organization,* p. 29.

This classification of variables resembles the framework for the synthesizing theory presented in Chapter 2. We referred to the three classes as initiating variables, mediating variables, and school-effectiveness variables.

All the variables which the Likert theory comprises are presented in the profile of organizational characteristics, which appears as Table 4-3. Next to each variable is an intensity index which indicates the nature of the variable and the amount of the variable present in a given organization.

[17] Ibid., p. 3. Numerous other uses of the form are apparent. Ideal management systems can be compared with real management systems. Superordinates' perceptions of ideal or real can be compared with subordinates' perceptions of ideal or real, and so on.

[18] Table 4-3 is a reproduction of Appendix II of Rensis Likert's *The Human Organization: Its Management and Value,* pp. 197–211. It appears here with only minor modifications in format. Appendix II is a combination of Tables 3-1 and 7-1 of the same book. We are grateful to Professor Likert and to McGraw-Hill Book Company for permitting us to reproduce material which is so fundamental to their book. Table 4-3 of course, may not be reproduced in any way without permission from the publisher. The Profile of a School, an inventory in several versions, has since been developed specifically for school use and is available from Rensis Likert Associates Inc., Ann Arbor, Michigan.

Respondents generally perceive high-performing departments, units, and organizations as lying toward the right end of the table on each of the organizational variables and low-performing units lying toward the left. Likert reports research which supports these perceptions and notes that as organizations move toward System 4, they are more productive, are characterized by high-performing work groups, have lower costs, have more favorable attitudes, and display improved labor-management relationships, with System 4 organizations achieving excellent records in each of these dimensions. The converse seems to be true for organizations displaying management systems that lie well toward System 1.[19] We would, of course, expect similar responses from educators and similar findings in educational organizations.

SHIFTING MANAGEMENT SYSTEMS

The management systems described in Table 4-3 are composed of individual characteristics and tendencies, each dependent upon the existence of others of a similar intensity. As a result of this interdependence among the organizational variable types, it is not likely, except for incidental responses, that a given school can be described as possessing some characteristics of System 1, others of System 2, and still others of System 4. Typically, a pattern of response to Table 4-3 would emerge for a given school which would clearly type the school into one or another system category. In explaining this phenomenon Likert observes: "The communications processes of System 1 are compatible with all other aspects of System 1 but are not compatible with any aspect of System 3 or System 4. The same is true of the decision-making processes and the compensation plans. *The Management system of an organization must have compatible component parts if it is to function effectively.*"[20]

It is not likely that enduring changes can be made, for example, in the levels of teachers' commitment to school goals without substantial changes in supervisory assumptions. People should expect to see the alteration of their supervisory assumptions reflected in each of the mediating variables, including in the commitment levels of teachers. As a further illustration, it is not likely that supervisory efforts to improve the problem-solving capabilities of staff will be effective if each of the other variables which comprise this system is ignored. The hard facts of the matter suggest that a System 2 supervisor who wishes to adopt one dimension of System 4 will not have success unless he or she adopts each of the other dimensions. By the same token, a supervisor who tries to adopt all the System 4 dimensions with the exception of one or two (who continues, for example, to lack confidence and trust in subordinates—a System 1 characteristic) will not succeed.[21]

Systems 1 and 2

System 1 is referred to as exploitive-authoritarian and System 2 as benevolent-authoritarian. Differences between the two exist, but they are close enough to be

[19] Ibid., see, for example, pp. 13–46.
[20] Ibid., p. 123.
[21] This ineffectiveness will tend to reinforce belief of such supervisors that you cannot trust people anyway, and that System 1 is better after all. They will have evidence to support this contention in that they did give System 4 a try, but it just does not work.

TABLE 4-3. PROFILE OF ORGANIZATIONAL CHARACTERISTICS

Organizational variable	System 1	System 2	System 3	System 4	Item no.
1. Leadership processes used					
a. Extent to which superiors have confidence and trust in *subordinates*	Have no confidence and trust in subordinates	Have condescending confidence and trust, such as master has in servant	Substantial but not complete confidence and trust; still wishes to keep control of decisions	Complete confidence and trust in all matters	1
b. Extent to which subordinates, in turn, have confidence and trust in *superiors*	Have no confidence and trust in superiors	Have subservient confidence and trust, such as servant has in master	Substantial but not complete confidence and trust	Complete confidence and trust	2
c. Extent to which superiors display supportive behavior toward others	Display no supportive behavior or virtually none	Display supportive behavior in condescending manner and situations only	Display supportive behavior quite generally	Display supportive behavior fully and in all situations	3
d. Extent to which superiors behave so that subordinates feel free to discuss important things about their jobs with their immediate superior	Subordinates do not feel at all free to discuss things about the job with their superior	Subordinates do not feel very free to discuss things about the job with their superior	Subordinates feel rather free to discuss things about the job with their superior	Subordinates feel completely free to discuss things about the job with their superior	4

e. Extent to which immediate superior in solving job problems generally tries to get subordinates' ideas and opinions and make constructive use of them

| Seldom gets ideas and opinions of subordinates in solving job problems | Sometimes gets ideas and opinions of subordinates in solving job problems | Usually gets ideas and opinions and usually tries to make constructive use of them | Always gets ideas and opinions and always tries to make constructive use of them |

2. Character of motivational forces

a. Underlying motives tapped

| Physical security, economic needs, and some use of the desire for status | Economic needs and moderate use of ego motives, e.g., desire for status, affiliation, and achievement | Economic needs and considerable use of ego and other major motives, e.g., desire for new experiences | Full use of economic, ego, and other major motives, as, for example, motivational forces arising from group goals |

b. Manner in which motives are used

| Fear, threats, punishment, and occasional rewards | Rewards and some actual or potential punishment | Rewards, occasional punishment, and some involvement | Economic rewards based on compensation system developed through participation; group participation and involvement in setting goals, improving methods, appraising progress toward goals, etc. |

TABLE 4-3. (continued)

Organizational variable	System 1	System 2	System 3	System 4	Item no.
c. Kinds of attitudes developed toward organization and its goals	Attitudes usually are hostile and counter to organization's goals	Attitudes are sometimes hostile and counter to organization's goals and are sometimes favorable to the organization's goals and support the behavior necessary to achieve them	Attitudes usually are favorable and support behavior implementing organization's goals	Attitudes are strongly favorable and provide powerful stimulation to behavior implementing organization's goals	8
d. Extent to which motivational forces conflict with or reinforce one another	Marked conflict of forces substantially reducing those motivational forces leading to behavior in support of the organization's goals	Conflict often exists; occasionally forces will reinforce each other, at least partially	Some conflict, but often motivational forces will reinforce each other	Motivational forces generally reinforce each other in a substantial and cumulative manner	9
e. Amount of responsibility felt by each member of organization for achieving organization's goals	High levels of management feel responsibility; lower levels feel less; rank and file feel little and often welcome opportunity to behave in ways to defeat organization's goals	Managerial personnel usually feel responsibility; rank and file usually feel relatively little responsibility for achieving organization's goals	Substantial proportion of personnel, especially at higher levels, feel responsibility and generally behave in ways to achieve the organization's goals	Personnel at all levels feel real responsibility for organization's goals and behave in ways to implement them	10

82

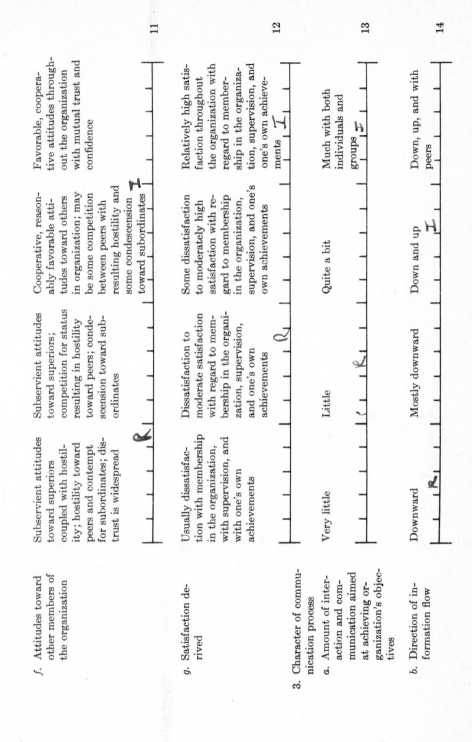

f. Attitudes toward other members of the organization — 11

Subservient attitudes toward superiors coupled with hostility; hostility toward peers and contempt for subordinates; distrust is widespread	Subservient attitudes toward superiors; competition for status resulting in hostility toward peers; condescension toward subordinates	Cooperative, reasonably favorable attitudes toward others in organization; may be some competition between peers with resulting hostility and some condescension toward subordinates	Favorable, cooperative attitudes throughout the organization with mutual trust and confidence

g. Satisfaction derived — 12

Usually dissatisfaction with membership in the organization, with supervision, and with one's own achievements	Dissatisfaction to moderate satisfaction with regard to membership in the organization, supervision, and one's own achievements	Some dissatisfaction to moderately high satisfaction with regard to membership in the organization, supervision, and one's own achievements	Relatively high satisfaction throughout the organization with regard to membership in the organization, supervision, and one's own achievements

3. Character of communication process

a. Amount of interaction and communication aimed at achieving organization's objectives — 13

Very little	Little	Quite a bit	Much with both individuals and groups

b. Direction of information flow — 14

Downward	Mostly downward	Down and up	Down, up, and with peers

83

TABLE 4-3. (continued)

Organizational variable	System 1	System 2	System 3	System 4	Item no.
c. Downward communication					
(1) Where initiated	At top of organization or to implement top directive	Primarily at top or patterned on communication from top	Patterned on communication from top but with some initiative at lower levels	Initiated at all levels	15
(2) Extent to which superiors willingly share information with subordinates	Provide minimum of information	Give subordinates only information superior feels they need	Give information needed and answer most questions	Seek to give subordinates all relevant information and all information they want	16
(3) Extent to which communications are accepted by subordinates	Viewed with great suspicion	Some accepted and some viewed with suspicion	Often accepted but, if not, may or may not be openly questioned	Generally accepted, but if not, openly and candidly questioned	17
d. Upward communication					
(1) Adequacy of upward communication via line organization	Very little	Limited	Some	A great deal	18

(2) Subordinates' feeling of responsibility for initiating accurate upward communication	None at all	Relatively little, usually communicates "filtered" information and only when requested; may "yes" the boss	Some to moderate degree of responsibility to initiate accurate upward communication	Considerable responsibility felt and much initiative; group communicates all relevant information	19
(3) Forces leading to accurate or distorted upward information	Powerful forces to distort information and deceive superiors	Many forces to distort; also forces for honest communication	Occasional forces to distort along with many forces to communicate accurately	Virtually no forces to distort and powerful forces to communicate accurately	20
(4) Accuracy of upward communication via line	Tends to be inaccurate	Information that boss wants to hear flows; other information is restricted and filtered	Information that boss wants to hear flows; other information may be limited or cautiously given	Accurate	21
(5) Need for supplementary upward communication system	Great need to supplement upward communication by spy system, suggestion system, and similar devices	Upward communication often supplemented by suggestion system and similar devices	Slight need for supplementary system; suggestion systems may be used	No need for any supplementary system	22
e. Sideward communication, its adequacy and accuracy	Usually poor because of competition between peers, corresponding hostility	Fairly poor because of competition between peers	Fair to good	Good to excellent	23

TABLE 4-3. (continued)

Organizational variable	System 1	System 2	System 3	System 4	Item no.
f. Psychological closeness of superiors to subordinates (i.e., friendliness between superiors and subordinates)	Far apart	Can be moderately close if proper roles are kept	Fairly close	Usually very close	24
(1) How well does superior know and understand problems faced by subordinates	Has no knowledge or understanding of problems of subordinates	Has some knowledge and understanding of problems of subordinates	Knows and understands problems of subordinates quite well	Knows and understands problems of subordinates very well	25
(2) How accurate are the perceptions by superiors and subordinates of each other?	Often in error	Often in error on some points	Moderately accurate	Usually quite accurate	26
4. Character of interaction-influence process					
a. Amount and character of interaction	Little interaction and always with fear and distrust	Little interaction and usually with some condescension by superiors; fear and caution by subordinates	Moderate interaction, often with fair amount of confidence and trust	Extensive, friendly interaction with high degree of confidence and trust	27

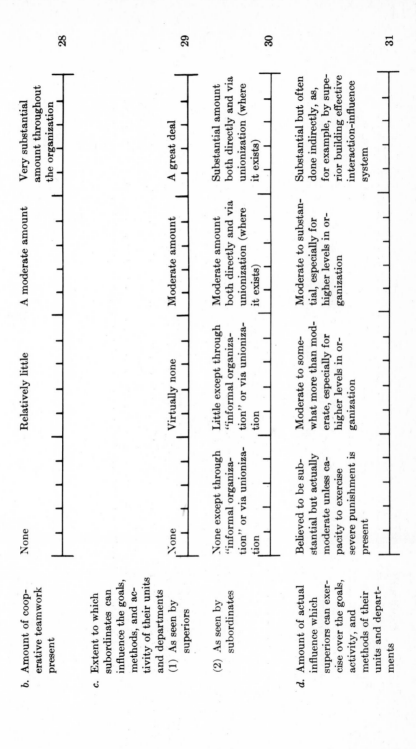

b. Amount of cooperative teamwork present

28

| None | Relatively little | A moderate amount | Very substantial amount throughout the organization |

c. Extent to which subordinates can influence the goals, methods, and activity of their units and departments

(1) As seen by superiors

29

| None | Virtually none | Moderate amount | A great deal |

(2) As seen by subordinates

30

| None except through "informal organization" or via unionization | Little except through "informal organization" or via unionization | Moderate amount both directly and via unionization (where it exists) | Substantial amount both directly and via unionization (where it exists) |

d. Amount of actual influence which superiors can exercise over the goals, activity, and methods of their units and departments

31

| Believed to be substantial but actually moderate unless capacity to exercise severe punishment is present | Moderate to somewhat more than moderate, especially for higher levels in organization | Moderate to substantial, especially for higher levels in organization | Substantial but often done indirectly, as, for example, by superior building effective interaction-influence system |

TABLE 4-3. **(continued)**

Organizational variable	System 1	System 2	System 3	System 4	Item no.
e. Extent to which an effective structure exists enabling one part of organization to exert influence upon other parts	Effective structure virtually not present	Limited capacity exists; influence exerted largely via vertical lines and primarily downward	Moderately effective structure exists; influence exerted largely through vertical lines	Highly effective structure exists enabling exercise of influence in all directions	32
5. Character of decision-making process					
a. At what level in organization are decisions formally made?	Bulk of decisions at top of organization	Policy at top, many decisions within prescribed framework made at lower levels but usually checked with top before action	Broad policy decisions at top, more specific decisions at lower levels	Decision making widely done throughout organization, although well integrated through linking process provided by overlapping groups	33
b. How adequate and accurate is the information available for decision making at *the place where the decisions are made?*	Information is generally inadequate and inaccurate	Information is often somewhat inadequate and inaccurate	Reasonably adequate and accurate information available	Relatively complete and accurate information available based both on measurements and efficient flow of information in organization	34

	Often are unaware or only partially aware	Aware of some, unaware of others	Moderately aware of problems	Generally quite well aware of problems	
c. To what extent are decision makers aware of problems, particularly those at lower levels in the organization?					35
d. Extent to which technical and professional knowledge is used in decision making	Used only if possessed at higher levels	Much of what is available in higher and middle levels is used	Much of what is available in higher, middle, and lower levels is used	Most of what is available anywhere within the organization is used	36
e. Are decisions made at the best level in the organization as far as (1) Availability of the most adequate and accurate information bearing on the decision	Decisions usually made at levels appreciably higher than levels where most adequate and accurate information exists	Decisions often made at levels appreciably higher than levels where most adequate and accurate information exists	Some tendency for decisions to be made at higher levels than where most adequate and accurate information exists	Overlapping groups and group decision processes tend to push decisions to point where information is most adequate or to pass the relevant information to the decision-making point	37

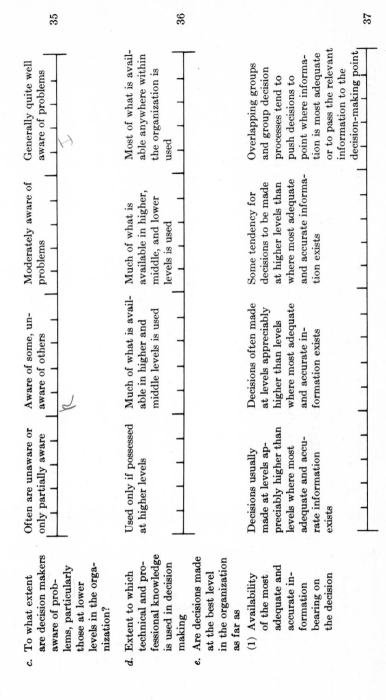

89

TABLE 4-3. (continued)

Organizational variable	System 1	System 2	System 3	System 4	Item no.
(2) The motivational consequences (i.e., does the decision-making process help to create the necessary motivations in those persons who have to carry out the decision?)	Decision making contributes little or nothing to the motivation to implement the decision, usually yields adverse motivation	Decision making contributes relatively little motivation	Some contribution by decision making to motivation to implement	Substantial contribution by decision-making processes to motivation to implement	38
f. To what extent are subordinates involved in decisions related to their work?	Not at all	Never involved in decisions; occasionally consulted	Usually are consulted but ordinarily not involved in the decision making	Are involved fully in all decisions related to their work	39
g. Is decision making based on man-to-man or group pattern of operation? Does it encourage or discourage teamwork?	Man-to-man only, discourages teamwork	Man-to-man almost entirely, discourages teamwork	Both man-to-man and group, partially encourages teamwork	Largely based on group pattern, encourages teamwork	40

Organizational variable					
6. Character of goal setting or ordering					
a. Manner in which usually done	Orders issued	Orders issued, opportunity to comment may or may not exist	Goals are set or orders issued after discussion with subordinates of problems and planned action	Except in emergencies, goals are usually established by means of group participation	41
b. To what extent do the different hierarchical levels tend to strive for high performance goals?	High goals pressed by top, generally resisted by subordinates	High goals sought by top and often resisted moderately by subordinates	High goals sought by higher levels but with occasional resistance by lower levels	High goals sought by all levels, with lower levels sometimes pressing for higher goals than top levels	42
c. Are there forces to accept, resist, or reject goals?	Goals are overtly accepted but are covertly resisted strongly	Goals are overtly accepted but often covertly resisted to at least a moderate degree	Goals are overtly accepted but at times with some covert resistance	Goals are fully accepted both overtly and covertly	43
7. Character of control processes					
a. At what hierarchical levels in organization does major or primary concern exist with regard to the performance of the control function?	At the very top only	Primarily or largely at the top	Primarily at the top but some shared feeling of responsibility felt at middle and to a lesser extent at lower levels	Concern for performance of control functions likely to be felt throughout organization	44

TABLE 4-3. **(continued)**

Organizational variable	System 1	System 2	System 3	System 4	Item no.
b. How accurate are the measurements and information used to guide and perform the control function, and to what extent do forces exist in the organization to distort and falsify this information?	Very strong forces exist to distort and falsify; as a consequence, measurements and information are usually incomplete and often inaccurate	Fairly strong forces exist to distort and falsify; hence measurements and information are often incomplete and inaccurate	Some pressure to protect self and colleagues and hence some pressures to distort; information is only moderately complete and contains some inaccuracies	Strong pressures to obtain complete and accurate information to guide own behavior and behavior of own and related work groups; hence information and measurements tend to be complete and accurate	45
c. Extent to which the review and control functions are concentrated	Highly concentrated in top management	Relatively highly concentrated, with some delegated control to middle and lower levels	Moderate downward delegation of review and control processes; lower as well as higher levels perform these tasks	Review and control down at all levels with lower units at times imposing more vigorous reviews and tighter controls than top management	46
d. Extent to which there is an informal organization present and supporting or opposing goals of formal organization	Informal organization present and opposing goals of formal organization	Informal organization usually present and partially resisting goals	Informal organization may be present and may either support or partially resist goals of formal organization	Informal and formal organization are one and the same; hence all social forces support efforts to achieve organization's goals	47

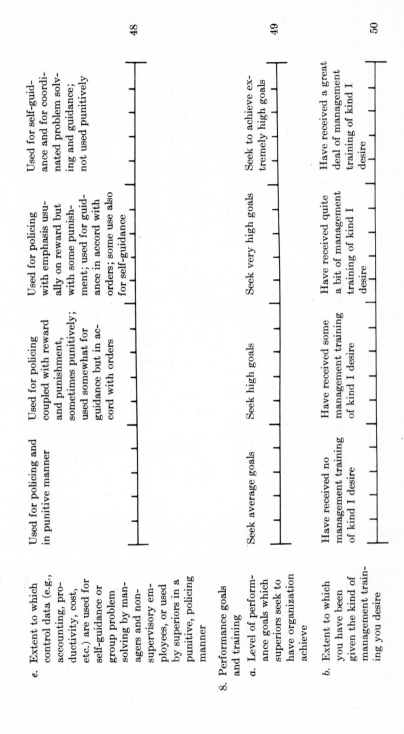

e. Extent to which control data (e.g., accounting, cost, productivity, etc.) are used for self-guidance or group problem solving by managers and non-supervisory employees, or used by superiors in a punitive, policing manner

Used for policing and in punitive manner	Used for policing coupled with reward and punishment, sometimes punitively; used somewhat for guidance but in accord with orders	Used for policing with emphasis usually on reward but with some punishment; used for guidance in accord with orders; some use also for self-guidance	Used for self-guidance and for coordinated problem solving and guidance; not used punitively

48

8. Performance goals and training

a. Level of performance goals which superiors seek to have organization achieve

Seek average goals	Seek high goals	Seek very high goals	Seek to achieve extremely high goals

49

b. Extent to which you have been given the kind of management training you desire

Have received no management training of kind I desire	Have received some management training of kind I desire	Have received quite a bit of management training of kind I desire	Have received a great deal of management training of kind I desire

50

93

TABLE 4-3. **(continued)**

Organizational variable	System 1	System 2	System 3	System 4	Item no.
c. Adequacy of training resources provided to assist you in training your subordinates	Training resources provided are only fairly good	Training resources provided are good	Training resources provided are very good	Training resources provided are excellent	51

The table above can be used for other purposes by appropriate modifications in the instructions:

Form S Instructions:

On the line below each organizational variable (item), please indicate the kind of organization you are trying to create by the management you are providing. Treat each item as a continuous variable from the extreme at one end to that at the other. Place a check mark on each line to show the kind of management you are using and the kind of organization you are creating.

Form D Instructions:

On the line below each organizational variable (item), please indicate by a check mark where you would *like* to have your organization fall with regard to that item. Treat each item as a continuous variable from the extreme at one end to that at the other.

NOTE: When the Profile of Organizational Characteristics is used as a survey instrument, responses to certain items selected at random are reversed.

From Rensis Likert, *The Human Organization: Its Management and Value.* Copyright © 1967 by McGraw-Hill, Inc. Used with permission of McGraw-Hill Book Company. No further reproduction or distribution authorized without permission of McGraw-Hill.

described together. Supervisors (principals, teachers, and others) who adopt System 1 or System 2 perspectives[22] rely on high-control methods; hierarchical pressures and authority; Theory X assumptions in regard to subordinates, domination, regulation, and distortion of communication channels; and programmed, delimited, and centralized decision making as they work to achieve school goals.

Systems 1 and 2 supervisors can expect from subordinates (administrators, teachers, students, and others) less group loyalty, lower performance goals, less cooperation, more conflict, less teamwork and mutual assistance among peers, more feeling of unreasonable pressure, less favorable attitudes toward supervisors and the school, and lower motivational potential for performance.[23] This response from the human organization of the school takes its toll in poor performance on each of the school-success variables.

Systems 3 and 4

System 3 is described as consultive, while System 4 is labeled participative. System 3 is somewhat descriptive of supervisory practice which characterizes schools well on their way toward developing professional organization. It is a transitional management system which is often characterized as being "better than before" but still clings to many of the features of the earlier type of management. System 3 fails in attempting to maximize the achievement of school goals, student actualization, and teacher self-fulfillment, but it at least performs satisfactorily in each of these pursuits while maintaining dimensions and features which are organizationally and administratively familiar.

System 4 is indeed close to our concept of human resources supervision. Administrators, teachers, and others who adopt this perspective rely on the principle of supportive relationships, on group methods of supervision, on Theory Y assumptions, on self-control methods, on ability authority, and on other principles of System 4. The human organization of the school reacts to this perspective by displaying greater group loyalty, high performance goals, greater cooperation, more teamwork and sharing, less feeling of unreasonable pressure, more favorable attitudes toward the supervisor and the school, and higher levels of motivation for performance.[24] The result, of course, is increases in the dimensions of school success. System 4 is, of course, an ideal difficult to achieve in practice. Therefore it may be more useful in actual situations to speak of *tendencies toward System 4* rather than speaking of actually meeting this goal.

CHARTING ORGANIZATIONAL CLIMATE

Careful study of the profile of organizational characteristics in Table 4-3 provides operationally defined descriptions of four supervisory-management systems.

[22] We do not portray educators of this configuration as "bad guys" because often they are well-meaning and have high performance expectations for themselves, the school, and its inhabitants. Some do, indeed, adopt Systems 1 and 2 as a result of their own inadequacies. These systems permit supervisors to behave defensively and ensure that they will remain immune to a relatively hostile interpersonal world. See Jack Gibb, "Dynamics of Leadership," in *In Search of Leaders,* Washington, D.C.: National Education Association, American Association for Higher Education, 1967.

[23] Likert, *The Human Organization,* p. 76.

[24] Ibid., p. 76.

Their usefulness in prescribing supervisory behavior in detail and in an integrated way is enormous. System 4, for example, paints an extensive portrait of a major segment of human resources supervision. Each of the four systems is able to describe the supervisory environment of teachers not only in relation to administrators, supervisors, and others, but also as supervisors in relation to their young clients.

Table 4-3 can also serve as a guideline for measuring organizational position on the management continuum and movement along the continuum. The table can also serve as a target-setting device by measuring (1) where a school or educational subunit is on the continuum, (2) where it would like to be, and (3) progress at intervals toward this goal. Basic to this discussion is the concept that change toward System 4 tends not to occur on a random, broken-front basis, but as a total assault on all the variables which compose the system.

The Likert approach, as illustrated in Table 4-3, offers an operational definition of the supervisor's job, provides a practical means for generating and ordering supervisory goals, and serves as a useful tool for measuring supervisory effectiveness. Further, the human curriculum, with its emphasis on student self-actualization, depends upon a System 4–oriented supervisory environment for success.

SUMMARY

In this chapter the importance of organizational climate to school effectiveness was discussed. Climate was viewed as a combination of the enduring characteristics which describe a particular school and distinguish it from other schools, and the feeling which teacher and student have for that school. Accordingly, climate represents a composite of mediating variables which intervene between initiating and school effectiveness variables. It was pointed out that although supervisors have difficulty in affecting climate by initiating changes in organizational structure and function, they can exert direct influence on school climate through the leadership they provide. Bureaucratic leadership, for example, tends to be associated with relatively closed climate and low performance and satisfaction. Human relations leadership tends to be associated with a warm, supportive, and friendly climate and with low performance but high satisfaction and some innovation. Human resources leadership tends to be associated with a supportive, goal-oriented climate and high performance, satisfaction, and some innovation. Views of organizational climate, as conceptualized by Halpin and Croft, and Miles, were then presented as examples of ways of thinking and descriptive statements of climate components. Likert's profile of organizational characteristics was then presented as a method for charting and monitoring school climate. This instrument was accompanied by a discussion of four organizational climates, Systems 1, 2, 3, and 4, each associated with a particular pattern of leadership. System 4 was then discussed as the ideal toward which human resources supervisors work.

STUDY GUIDE

Recall the concepts, ideas, and meanings associated with each of the following phrases and terms included in Chapter 4. Can you discuss each of them with a colleague and apply them to the supervisory content of your school? If you cannot, review them in the text and record the page numbers for future reference.

1   Bureaucratic leadership _____
2   Climate defined _____
3   Closed climate _____
4   Effectiveness variables and climate _____
5   Healthy climate _____
6   Human relations leadership _____
7   Human resources leadership _____
8   Initiating variables and climate _____
9   Management systems _____
10 Mediating variables and climate _____
11 Open climate _____
12 Organizational Climate Description Questionnaire _____
13 Organizational health _____
14 Profile of organizational characteristics _____
15 Systems 1, 2, 3, and 4 _____

EXERCISES

1   Describe the climate of your school using the eight dimensions of organizational climate included in Table 4-2. Provide specific examples or describe specific critical incidents which illustrate each climate dimension.
2   Have a group of teachers from the same school fill out the profile of organizational characteristics provided in Table 4-3, indicating for each item the way their school actually is (real) and the way they would prefer it to be (ideal). Average responses, and develop a real and ideal profile for that school. How might such a profile be used as a planning device for the supervisor?
3   Compare organizational climate as conceptualized and operationalized by Halpin, Miles, and Likert. How are these views similar and how are they different? Using these views, develop a 10-item questionnaire which you believe summarizes the most important dimensions of organizational climate.

Chapter 5

Leadership Behavior and Supervisory Effectiveness

At this point we have discussed a number of initiating variables of importance to supervision under the rubrics of organizational structure and function (Chapter 3) and organizational climate (Chapter 4). It was suggested that though both have important implications for supervisory effectiveness, climate is more accessible to influence by supervisors than is structure and function. In this chapter a third category of initiating variables, supervisory assumptions and leadership behavior, will be discussed. Leadership is of particular importance to supervisors not only because it is accessible to them but, in addition, because of its far-reaching effects throughout the school. Leadership directly touches the school's human organization, has a pronounced effect on each of the mediating variables, and is closely associated with school climate. In this sense, leadership is a potent force for increasing supervisory effectiveness.

The following questions are considered in this chapter: What assumptions do supervisors and other make about human nature and, particularly, the behavior of people in their world of work? How do these assumptions affect the supervisor's behavior? What are the effects of this behavior on the human organization of the school? What are the predominant behavioral orientations that supervisors and others bring to school problems? How do these orientations affect supervisory behavior? And, again, how does this behavior affect the human organization of the school? Human resources supervision is concerned with the worth, growth, and development of the human organization, for it is upon this growth that the success of the school enterprise depends.

PROBLEMS IN DEFINITION

In the 1964 yearbook of the National Society for the Study of Education, Lipham[1] carefully differentiates between behavior he considers administrative and that which he describes as leadership. After Hemphill,[2] Lipham defines leadership as "the initiation of a new structure or procedure for accomplishing an organization's goals and objectives or for changing an organization's goals or objectives."[3] On the other hand, the administrator "may be identified as the individual who utilizes existing structures or procedures to achieve an organizational goal or objective."[4] The emphasis for leadership, according to Lipham, is on newness or change, while administration is primarily concerned with maintaining and using existing structures. Both behavioral modes are directed toward the achievement of school goals, and the appropriateness of each depends upon the circumstances.[5] Moreover, both leadership and administrative behavioral patterns use the same organizational and individual variables in working toward school goals.

This differentiation between leadership and administrative behavior is not entirely consistent with our definition[6] of supervisory ways of behaving as opposed to administrative ways of behaving, but the two are not contradictory. Leadership behavior that accords with the Hemphill-Lipham definition is more likely to occur as a result of behaving in a supervisory way (by our definition, supervisory ways of behaving involve change in one or another aspect of the human organization), although it may also occur in schools as a result of administrative ways of behaving. For example, a high school department chairperson divides a class into two sections according to ability and thus alters teacher A's assignment and the work flow of the department. If he makes this decision independently of his colleagues, he has initiated change in an administrative way. If as a teacher, independently of his students, he alters class goals or procedures, he

---

[1] James Lipham, "Leadership and Administration," in *Behavioral Science and Educational Administration,* Chicago: National Society for the Study of Education, 1964 Yearbook, 1965, pp. 119–141.

[2] James K. Hemphill, "Administration as Problem Solving," in Andrew Halpin (ed.), *Administrative Theory in Education,* Chicago: University of Chicago, Midwest Administration Center, 1958, p. 98.

[3] Lipham, op. cit., p. 122.

[4] Ibid.

[5] To be sure, however, both administrative and leadership styles are essential to the school, and although the question of correct mix is complex, schools need to maintain themselves internally and to balance this maintenance with appropriate external adaption.

[6] One should be realistically aware of the limitations inherent in the concept of leadership as we presently know it. As Warren Bennis observes, "Of all the hazy and confounding areas in social psychology, leadership theory undoubtedly contends for top nomination. And ironically, probably more has been written and less is known about leadership than about any other topic in the behavioral sciences." See his "Leadership Theory and Administrative Behavior," *Administrative Science Quarterly,* vol. 4, pp. 259–260, December 1959.

displays leadership according to the Lipham description, but nevertheless he has chosen not to operate in a supervisory way.

Separating leadership from administration in the manner proposed by Lipham has a number of advantages. The two are so interrelated in practice, however, that for the purposes of discussion in this chapter both are considered as variations of leadership style.[7]

MANAGEMENT PHILOSOPHY AND SUPERVISORY ASSUMPTIONS

Whatever a person does makes sense to that person. This explains why two educators with similar supervisory responsibilities in similar schools with similar goals and similar personnel when confronted with an identical problem, may operate in dissimilar ways. Both believe that their own method of operation is the one suitable to the task and circumstances. How do supervisors, principals, teachers, and others come to establish styles of supervision?[8] These are partly the result of management philosophies and of supervisory assumptions which individuals have accumulated or learned over the years.

Teachers, for example, whose classrooms are characterized as "open" have learned to consider students differently from their counterparts with "controlled" classrooms. These teachers have different management philosophies and different conceptions of their roles and the roles of their students. This is true, too, for principals who operate open, as opposed to closed schools.[9] Interestingly, in each case teachers often respond to the supervisor's expectations in such a way that they prove him or her correct. This simply reinforces that supervisor's use of a given supervisory style. Understanding this self-fulfilling prophecy is crucial to understanding the relationship between management philosophy and supervisory behavior.[10] Rensis Likert's study of supervisors of highly effective work groups in industry, for example, strongly suggests that subordinates generally respond positively to the supervisor's high evaluation and confidence in them and work harder to justify the supervisor's expectations.[11] In the next section we present and discuss Douglas McGregor's comparison of two ideal-type management philosophies, along with supervisory assumptions which emerge from these philoso-

---

[7] "Management style" is a term which encompasses both leadership and administration as defined by Lipham. Educators, however, find the word "management" alien, and therefore we substitute "leadership style," to refer to both leadership and administration.

[8] By *supervisory* or *leadership style* we refer simply to predominant patterns of behavior associated with a given person, role, or school. Any given style permits and absorbs occasional departures in behavior, provided that it does not alter the prevailing or basic behavior pattern.

[9] "Open" and "closed" are used here within the framework of the Organizational Climate Description Questionnaire. See Andrew Halpin and John Croft, *The Organizational Climate of Schools,* Chicago: University of Chicago, Midwest Administration Center, 1963.

[10] An interesting application of the self-fulfilling prophecy is in the operation of controlled-environment examinations. When heavy cheating is expected, elaborate controls are implemented and the cheating rate will tend to rise. The rate declines as expectations for cheating decline and controls are minimized. For an extensive treatment of the self-fulfilling prophecy as it applies to teacher expectations of student performance, see Robert Rosenthal and Lenore Jacobson, *Pygmalion in the Classroom,* New York: Holt, 1968.

[11] Rensis Likert, *New Patterns of Management,* New York: McGraw-Hill, 1961. See, for example, Chap. 1.

phies.[12] He describes them as Theories X and Y in order to minimize semantic and value confusion.

THEORY X AND SCHOOLS

McGregor's language may seem more descriptive of nonschool environments, but his ideas have wide application to schools.[13] Examine his assumptions and propositions below, first in reference to school administrators and supervisors and teachers, and then in reference to teachers and students.

Management Propositions—Theory X

    1 Management is responsible for organizing the elements of productive enter-prise—money, materials, equipment, people—in the interest of economic [education-al] ends.

    2 With respect to people, this is a process of directing their efforts, motivating them, controlling their actions, modifying their behavior to fit the needs of the orga-nization.

    3 Without this active intervention by management, people would be passive—rewarded, punished, controlled—their activities must be directed. This is management's task in managing subordinate managers or workers. We often sum it up by saying that management consists of getting things done through other people.

Supervisory Assumptions—Theory X

Behind this conventional theory are several additional beliefs—less explicit but widespread:

    4 The average man is by nature indolent—he works as little as possible.

    5 He lacks ambition, dislikes responsibility, prefers to be led.

    6 He is inherently self-centered, indifferent to organizational needs.

    7 He is by nature resistant to change.

    8 He is gullible, not very bright, the ready dupe of the charlatan and the demagogue.[14]

    One cannot avoid noticing that schools tend toward the pessimistic assumptions of Theory X. In answering the question of whether this pessimistic image of humanity is correct, McGregor suggests that human behavior in organizations is approximately what management perceives it to be. Social scientists who have

    [12] An ideal type represents a conceptualization of a number of interrelated ideas in a polarized fashion. While the risk of stereotyping is present in the use of ideal types, they are nevertheless most useful in describing and grouping phenomena. Therefore, no one individual or case may provide a mirror image for any ideal type, and it is recognized that ideal descriptions tend to overstate their arguments. But such individuals or cases may be usefully described as approximating one or another type.

    [13] This discussion is based largely on Douglas McGregor, *The Human Side of Enterprise,* New York: McGraw-Hill, 1960. Also, Warren G. Bennis and Edgar H. Schein (eds.), *Leadership and Motivation: Essays of Douglas McGregor,* Cambridge, Mass.: M.I.T., 1966.

    [14] These assumptions are quoted from McGregor's essay, "The Human Side of Enterprise," which appears in Bennis and Schein, op. cit., p. 5. The essay first appeared in *Adventure in Thought and Action,* Proceedings of the Fifth Anniversary Convocation of the School of Industrial Manage-ment, M.I.T., Apr. 9, 1957. We added the word "education" to item 1 in McGregor's list. The article has been reprinted in *The Management Review,* vol. 46, no. 11, pp. 22–28, 1951.

confirmed management's Theory X suspicions are sure that this behavior is not a consequence of inherent human nature. In schools, such behavior on the part of students or teachers is in part a consequence of our administrative, supervisory, and educational philosophy, policy, and practice. Thus supervisory styles stemming from Theory X are based on mistaken notions of what is cause and what is effect. Fundamental to Theory X is a philosophy of direction and control. This philosophy is administered in a variety of forms and rests upon a theory of motivation which is inadequate for most adults, particularly professional adults, and indeed is quickly outgrown by students.[15]

The behavior typically manifested in Theory X assumptions is labeled by Argyris as Pattern A.[16] Pattern A takes two forms: hard and soft. In the school, the hard version is a no-nonsense approach characterized by strong leadership, tight controls, and close supervision by the teacher in a classroom setting and by the supervisor in a total school setting. The soft approach relies heavily on buying, persuading, or winning people through good (albeit superficial) human relations and benevolent paternalism to obtain compliance and acceptance of direction from superiors. The emphasis in both soft and hard versions of Pattern A is on manipulating, controlling, and managing people. The assumptions supervisors hold remain the same regardless of whether the hard or soft approach is used.

There are many problems with Theory X and Pattern A as management systems in organizations in general, though the problems seem more acute in the school. As basic philosophies, Theory X and Pattern A seem inconsistent with the hopes of teachers, administrators, and supervisors who are interested in raising the quality of life for young people in schools, and therefore they are not compatible with human resources supervision.

THEORY Y AND SCHOOLS

An alternate management philosophy based on more adequate assumptions of human nature is needed in order for schools to meet their professional growth commitment to teachers and to improve the intellectual, social, and emotional welfare of their young clients. This optimistic philosophy is called Theory Y after McGregor. Its main components are outlined below:

Philosophy and Assumptions—Theory Y

1 Management is responsible for organizing the elements of productive enterprise—money, materials, equipment, people—in the interest of economic [educational] ends.

2 People are *not* by nature passive or resistant to organizational needs. They have become so as a result of experience in organizations.

3 The motivation, the potential for development, the capacity for assuming responsibility, the readiness to direct behavior toward organizational goals are all present in people. Management does not put them there. It is a responsibility of

---

[15] We discuss the motivational assumptions which are the bases for Theories X and Y in a later chapter. See A. H. Maslow, *Motivation and Personality,* New York: Harper, 1954.

[16] Chris Argyris, *Management and Organizational Development,* New York: McGraw-Hill, 1971, pp. 1–26.

management to make it possible for people to recognize and develop these human characteristics for themselves.

4 The essential task of management is to arrange organizational conditions and methods of operation so that people can achieve their own goals *best* by directing *their* own efforts toward organizational objectives.[17]

Indeed, there are formidable obstacles which stand in the way of full implementation of this theory in every cubic inch of our schools. We have made progress in this direction, even if it has been slow, but additional modifications will need to be made in the attitudes of the school establishment, its publics, administrators, teachers, and students alike.

Pattern B is the label which Argyris gives to behavior associated with Theory Y assumptions. Basic to Pattern B is the dependence upon building identification and commitment to worthwhile objectives in the work context and upon building mutual trust and respect in the interpersonal context. Success in the work and interpersonal contexts is assumed to be dependent on whether meaningful satisfaction for individuals is achieved within the context of accomplishing important work as well as upon authentic relationships and the exchange of valid information. "More trust, concern for feelings, and internal commitment; more openness to, and experimenting with, new ideas and feelings *in such a way that others could do the same,* were recommended if valid information was to be produced and internal commitment to decisions generated."[18]

The differences between Theory X assumptions and behavior of the hard, or tough, variety and Theory Y assumptions and behavior are readily observable and understood. Theory X *soft* and Theory Y, however, are often deceptively similar. Theory X soft is consistent with human relations practices and Theory Y with human resources practices. These approaches are contrasted in Table 5-1.

INFANCY MANAGEMENT ASSUMPTIONS

A perhaps harsher analysis of assumptions inherent in management is offered by Argyris.[19] He notes that the ordinary worker (in the school's case teachers and students) is often considered to have little substantial ability for self-direction and self-discipline. Further, individuals largely prefer to be told what to do rather than to think for themselves, and when they do have ideas, they are generally naive or unrealistic. Gellerman, in interpreting the Argyris position, makes the following comments:

[17] McGregor in Bennis and Schein, op. cit., p. 15. Again we add the word "educational" to item number 1.
[18] Argyris, op. cit., p. 18. Argyris does not recommend that people be completely open and trusting, but that they be open to an extent that permits others to be open. He argues that trust and openness exist only in interpersonal relationships and, therefore, the question is, "How open is the relationship between person A and person B?" In Argyris's words, "To say what you believe is to be honest; to say what you believe in such a way that the other can do the same is to be authentic."
[19] This discussion is based largely on Chris Argyris, *Personality and Organization,* New York: Harper, 1957. See also, "Individual Actualization in Complex Organizations," *Mental Hygiene,* vol. 44, no. 2, pp. 226–237, April 1960; and *Integrating the Individual and Education,* New York: Wiley, 1964.

Table 5-1 Supervisory Assumptions

Theory X Soft Human relations model	*Theory Y* Human resources model
Attitudes toward people	
1. People in our culture, teachers and students among them, share a common set of needs—to belong, to be liked, to be respected.	1. In addition to sharing common needs for belonging and respect, most people in our culture, teachers and students among them, desire to contribute effectively and creatively to the accomplishment of worthwhile objectives.
2. While teachers and students desire individual recognition, they more importantly want to *feel* useful to the school and to their own work group.	2. The majority of teachers and students are capable of exercising far more initiative, responsibility, and creativity than their present jobs or work circumstances require or allow.
3. They tend to cooperate willingly and comply with school goals if these important needs are fulfilled.	3. These capabilities represent untapped resources which are presently being wasted.
Kind and amount of participation	
1. The supervisor's basic task (or in reference to students, the teacher's basic task) is to make each worker believe that he or she is a useful and important part of the team.	1. The supervisor's basic task (or in reference to students, the teacher's basic task) is to create an environment in which subordinates can contribute their full range of talents to the accomplishment of school goals. He or she works to uncover the creative resources of subordinates.
2. The supervisor is willing to explain his or her decisions and to discuss subordinates' objections to the plans. On routine matters, he or she encourages subordinates in planning and in decision making. In reference to students, the teacher behaves similarly.	2. The supervisor allows and encourages teachers to participate in important as well as routine decisions. In fact, the more important a decision is to the school, the greater the supervisor's efforts to tap faculty resources. In reference to students, the teacher behaves similarly.
3. Within narrow limits, the faculty or individual teachers who make up the faculty should be allowed to exercise self-direction and self-control in carrying out plans. A similar relationship exists for teachers and students.	3. Supervisors work continually to expand the areas over which teachers exercise self-direction and self-control as they develop and demonstrate greater insight and ability. A similar relationship exists for teachers and students.
Expectations	
1. Sharing information with teachers and involving them in school decision making will help satisfy their basic needs for belonging and for individual recognition.	1. The overall quality of decision making and performance will improve as supervisors and teachers make use of the full range of experience, insight, and creative ability which exists in their schools.

Table 5-1 Supervisory Assumptions

Theory X Soft Human relations model	*Theory Y* Human resources model
Expectations	
2. Satisfying these needs will improve faculty and student morale and will reduce resistance to formal authority.	**2.** Teachers will exercise responsible self-direction and self-control in the accomplishment of worthwhile objectives that they understand and have helped establish.
3. High faculty and student moral and reduced resistance to formal authority may lead to improved school performance. It will at least reduce friction and make the supervisor's job easier.	**3.** Faculty satisfaction and student satisfaction will increase as a by-product of improved performance and the opportunity to contribute creatively to this improvement.

Source: Adapted from Raymond E. Miles, "Human Relations or Human Resources?" *Harvard Business Review,* vol. 43, no. 4, pp. 148–163, 1965, esp. exhibits I and II.

Most organizations, especially at the lower levels, are geared for men who make a very childlike adjustment to life: They leave very little leeway for choosing, for using discretion, or for adapting rules to fit circumstances. Most employees are expected to do just as they are told and leave the thinking to the foreman, whose capacity for doing so is a perennially moot point among the people he supervises. In any case millions of grown men are required to spend forty hours a week suppressing their brainpower in order to maintain a system that is not nearly as efficient as it looks.[20]

The Argyris position is essentially that the human personality is not given sufficient opportunity to mature in most formal organizations. Schools in general do offer relatively more opportunities for personal growth than most other organizations. Yet proportionally—that is, when one considers that schools are essentially human organizations—*our record on this matter is less than impressive.*

In noting the distinction between the mature and immature personality, Argyris lists seven processes that normally occur as the infant grows into the young adult, as the young adult grows into full adulthood, and as the adult increases his or her capabilities and effectiveness over the course of his or her lifetime. The seven dimensions and directions of human growth follow:[21]

First, healthy human beings tend to develop from a state of passivity as infants to a state of activity as adults. They move from being stimulated, motivated, or disciplined to relying on self-initiative and self-determination. As they mature, they rely less on supervision (teacher's, principal's, or parent's) to control them. Given clear expectations and the opportunity to develop commitment, mature adults act on their own.

[20] Saul Gellerman, *Motivation and Productivity,* New York: American Management Association, 1963, p. 73.
[21] Our discussion of the seven directions and dimensions of the mature personality follows closely that which appears in Chris Argyris, "Individual Actualization in Complex Organizations," pp. 226–227.

Second, they move from a state of dependence upon others in infancy to an adult state of relative independence, and finally to interdependence. They are able to stand on their own feet and yet to acknowledge healthy dependencies. As part of this development, they internalize a set of values which become the bases of their behavior.

Third, they tend to develop from being capable of behaving in only a few ways as infants to being capable of behaving in many different ways as adults. They actually prefer to vary their style and do not care for fixed or rigid job assignments. They prefer to develop their own means to achieve ends rather than to be limited by the *best* way as defined by the organization.

Fourth, they tend to develop from having unpredictable, shallow, casual interests of short duration as infants to having deeper interests as adults. The mature personality is characterized by responding to an endless series of challenges, and reward comes from doing something for its own sake. Adults need a work environment which is challenging to skill and creativity.

Fifth, healthy human beings tend to develop from having a short-term perspective as infants—one in which the present largely determines their behavior—to a much larger time perspective as adults—one in which behavior is affected by past events and future hopes.

Sixth, they tend to develop from being in a subordinate position in the family and society as infants to aspiring to occupy an equal and/or superordinate position in reference to their peers. They are willing to accept leadership from others if they perceive it as legitimate, but they find being "bossed" offensive.

Seventh, they tend to develop from a lack of awareness of self as infants to an awareness of, and control over, self as adults. They are sensitive about their concepts of self and aware of their individuality. They therefore experience with displeasure attempts to lessen their self-worth. They cannot be expected to simply do the work that is put before them. They need to experience ego-involvement in their work.

School assumptions which require teachers and students to behave in ways which tend toward the infancy end of the Argyris continuum usually have negative consequences for the human organization and ultimately retard school effectiveness. Such assumptions are reflected administratively in the formal organizational structures of the school in directive leadership and in managerial control through budget, incentive systems, inspection, and review procedures. Argyris describes the effects of "infancy" managerial assumptions as follows:

> Healthy human beings (in our culture) tend to find dependence, subordination and submissiveness frustrating. They would prefer to be relatively independent, to be active, to use many of their deeper abilities; and they aspire to positions equal with or higher than their peers. Frustration leads to regression, aggression, and tension. These in turn lead to conflict (the individual prefers to leave but fears doing so). Moreover, it can be shown that under these conditions, the individual will tend to experience psychological failure and short-time perspective.[22]

[22] Ibid.

Our focus in this discussion has been on adults in school organizations, but the analogy is perhaps more important in its application to students. Argyris has captured the function of American schools—to move youngsters from infancy to maturity, intellectually, socially, and emotionally. Let us examine some of the alternatives that teachers on the one hand and students on the other have in adapting to school environments which frustrate mature development.[23]

For teachers	For students
1. Leave the school. Absence and turnover.	1. Same.
2. Climb the organizational ladder into administration and supervision.	2. Submit and "play ball" with the system.
3. Become defensive, daydream, become aggressive, nurture grievances, regress, project, feel low self-worth.	3. Same.
4. Become apathetic, disinterested, non-ego-involved in the school and its goals.	4. Same.
5. Create informal groups for mutual protection from the organization.	5. Same.
6. Formalize into militant associations and unions.	6. Go underground or dissent in newspapers, organized demonstrations, student unions.
7. De-emphasize in their own minds the importance of self-growth and creativity and emphasize the importance of money and other material rewards.	7. De-emphasize intrinsic learning goals and other values and emphasize grades, credits, and the like, to beat the system.
8. Accept the above-described ways of behaving as being proper for their lives outside the organization.	8. The depressing aspect of this cycle of events is that youngsters may accept socialization into the value system of infancy management and thus reinforce and perpetuate the system for another generation.

Some writers maintain that what Argyris criticizes so vehemently is exactly what workers in organizations want. Dubin, for example, argues:

> The fact of the matter is this. Work for probably a majority of workers, and even extending into the ranks of management, may represent an institutional setting that is not a central life interest for its participants. The consequence of this is that while participating in work, a general attitude of apathy and indifference prevails. The response to the demands of the institution is to satisfy the minimum expectations of required behavior without reacting affectively to these demands.[24]

Of course not everyone is capable of mature behavior or is able to respond to Theory Y assumptions, but what Dubin fails to add is that this reaction is

[23] The list which follows is an adaptation of one which appears in Argyris, "Individual Actualization in Complex Organizations," p. 227.

[24] Robert Dubin, "Person and Organization," in William Greenwood (ed.), *Management and Organizational Behavior Theories,* Cincinnati: South-Western Publishing Co., 1965, p. 487. See also George Strauss, "Some Notes on Power-Equalization," in Harold J. Leavitt (ed.), *The Social Science of Organizations,* Englewood Cliffs, N.J.: Prentice-Hall, 1963, pp. 45–59.

learned as a result of one's experience with organizations. People are not *inherently* removed from organizational life.

MISTAKES IN IMPLEMENTING THEORY Y

It is important to point out that Theory Y is not a universal theory of how to administer and supervise. A common misunderstanding is that Pattern B behavior, the behavior most closely associated with Theory Y, should be used at all times in all cases and that it elicits a uniformly positive reaction from subordinates. What is not understood is that Theory Y refers to the *inherent potential* and *capacity* of people rather than their present condition or their disposition at a given point in time.

Consider the example of motivation:

> Motivation in teachers depends upon a complex set of factors and conditions, many of which are well beyond the control of the school and the supervisor. One's set of values and work norms, for example, affects one's orientation toward his or her job. Some teachers will never be properly motivated to work and others will usually be motivated to work regardless of what supervisors do. Indeed a good rule of thumb is, if you want motivated teachers, hire motivated people if you can. Wisdom aside, we still face the problem of increasing the identity, commitment, and performance of large numbers of teachers already tenured on the job. The majority of teachers desire and seek satisfying work and will respond to human resources supervision. But many will not and alternate supervisory methods and procedures that suit these teachers will need to be provided. Human resources supervision is not an elixir to be administered indiscriminately to all. But it is a powerful conception of supervision which by using the concepts of motivation and job enrichment can markedly improve the identity, commitment, and performance of most teachers and the effectiveness of schools.[25]

Pattern A behavior, the behavior most associated with Theory X, is not in itself inconsistent with Theory Y. Supervisors need to behave in a variety of ways, sometimes in a rather direct fashion, other times in a supportive or considerate fashion, and at still other times in a manner described as participative or team building. No one best approach applicable to all situations exists, but rather the effectiveness of an approach is dependent upon its suitability to the situation at hand. But the approach or style suited to the particular situation at hand is different from one's overriding assumptions and the beliefs upon which one's behavior is based. In human organizations such as schools it is clear that leadership styles and other behavioral patterns, though they may vary depending upon the situation, are generated from within the broad perspectives of Theory Y.

[25] Thomas J. Sergiovanni, "Human Resources Supervision," in T. J. Sergiovanni (ed.), *Professional Supervision for Professional Teachers,* Washington, D.C.: Association for Supervision and Curriculum Development, 1975, p. 30. Human resources supervision follows closely the premises of Theory Y. See also Edgar Schein, "The Hawthorne Studies Revisited: A Defense of Theory Y," in Eugene Cass and Frederick Zimmer (eds.), *Man and Work in Society,* New York: Van Nostrand, 1975, pp. 78–94.

DETERMINANTS OF SUPERVISORY PATTERNS

This chapter is concerned with the values, assumptions, and management philosophies which are a part of the supervisor's concept of self. As these dimensions are internalized, they largely determine dominant supervisory behavior patterns. Other forces, however, such as those which exist within the client and those which exist in the environment, contribute to selecting appropriate supervisory style. These forces are delineated and described in the following sections.[26]

Forces in the Supervisor

When supervisors face a problem, their approach, behavior, or style is largely affected by each of the following internalized forces:

1 *Value system.* How strongly does a supervisor feel that individuals should have a share in making the decisions which affect them? Or, how convinced is that supervisor that the official who is paid to assume responsibility should personally carry the burden of decision making? The behavior of the supervisor will also be influenced by the relative importance that he or she attaches to organizational efficiency, personal growth of subordinates, and company profits.

2 *Confidence in his subordinates.* Managers differ greatly in the amount of trust they have in other people generally, and this carries over to the particular employees they supervise at a given time. In viewing their particular group of subordinates, managers are likely to consider their knowledge and competence with respect to the problem. A central question managers might ask themselves is, "Who is best qualified to deal with this problem?" Often managers may, justifiably or not, have more confidence in their own capabilities than in those of their subordinates.

3 *Leadership inclinations.* There are some managers who seem to function more comfortably and naturally as highly directive leaders. Resolving problems and issuing orders come easily to them. Other managers seem to operate more comfortably in a team role where they are continually sharing many of their functions with their subordinates.

4 *Feelings of security in an uncertain situation.* The manager who releases control over the decision-making process thereby reduces the predictability of the outcome. Some managers have a greater need than others for predictability and stability in their environment. This "tolerance for ambiguity" is being viewed increasingly by psychologists as a key variable in a person's manner of dealing with problems.[27]

Such an impressive list of internalized forces may provoke feelings of helplessness in supervisors, but each of these dimensions can be altered and modified.

---

[26] This discussion follows Robert Tannenbaum and Warren Schmidt, "How to Choose a Leadership Pattern," *Harvard Business Review,* vol. 36, no. 2, pp. 95–101, 1958. Tannenbaum identifies three forces which managers should consider in deciding how to manage: (1) forces in the manager, (2) forces in the subordinates, and (3) forces in the situation. See also Tannenbaum and Fred Massarick, "Participation by Subordinates in the Managerial Decision-making Process," *Canadian Journal of Economics and Political Science,* vol. 16, pp. 408–418, August 1950.

[27] Tannenbaum and Schmidt, op. cit. The label "manager" tends to have negative connotations to many school people but the descriptions are equally appropriate if one substitutes the term "school supervisor" for "manager."

A first step toward this end is awareness and understanding. As supervisors come to understand the nature of the values, prejudices, and management styles which have become a part of their conscious or unconscious selves, they are in a better position to evaluate and change their present approach to supervision.

Forces in the Supervisory Environment

The organizational forces which we have described in Chapter 3 are a major influence on supervisory style. The organizational style of the school, the school's normative culture, its role expectations, its belief pattern, and its authority and power systems serve as boundaries which often delimit choice of supervisory action. Further, the nature of the problem, the consequences of the task, and the character of the goal are additional determinants of appropriate supervisory behavior. A teacher, for example, may be required by default to consult with students when class activities are varied and complex, but such consultation is little more than perfunctory when activities are routine and simple.

Forces in Others

The extent to which school supervisors may permit their respective clients to exercise more freedom and control over their own destiny and that of the school depends largely on the following conditions:

1 Whether the subordinates have relatively high needs for independence. (As we all know, people differ greatly in the amount of direction that they desire.)

2 Whether the subordinates have a readiness to assume responsibility for decision making. (Some see additional responsibility as a tribute to their ability; others see it as "passing the buck.")

3 Whether they have a relatively high tolerance for ambiguity. (Some employees prefer to have clear-cut directives given to them; others prefer a wider area of freedom.)

4 Whether they are interested in the problem and feel that it is important.

5 Whether they understand and identify with the goals of the organization.

6 Whether they have the necessary knowledge and experience to deal with the problem.

7 Whether they have learned to expect to share in decision making. (Persons who have come to expect strong leadership and are then suddenly confronted with the request to share more fully in decision making are often upset by this new experience. On the other hand, persons who have enjoyed a considerable amount of freedom resent the boss who begins to make all the decisions alone.)[28]

Indeed the choice of one supervisory pattern over another is partly a function of forces in the client to be supervised, but this rationale should not provide a convenient "out" for those whose dominant supervisory patterns fall outside the range of human resources supervision.

Human resources supervision recognizes that forces in the client may require the supervisor to behave in a variety of ways. Highly dependent teachers may well need paternalistic supervisory environments, and uncommitted students will require close-controlled supervisory environments. Human resources supervisors,

[28] Ibid.

however, are not resigned to these patterns in that they do not accept dependency in teachers as being natural or inherent; they do not accept uncommittedness in students as being natural or inherent. Dependency of teachers and lack of commitment of students are perceived as symptoms of client immaturity and/or perhaps supervisory immaturity and organizational immaturity. With this perception, the human resources supervisor works to diminish client dependency and to increase client commitment, for in the synthesizing theory these are important means to affect the school-effectiveness variables positively.

We shall now discuss and explore different supervisory leadership behavior patterns and examine their effects on the human organization which constitutes the school.

LEADERSHIP AND SUPERVISORY BEHAVIOR OBSERVED

Jack Gibb, in writing for the American Association for Higher Education 1967 Yearbook, *In Search of Leaders,* identifies and describes two ideal types of leadership style used by school administrators. The emergence of one or another of these styles in a given individual largely depends upon how that individual feels about his or her own adequacy and how much he or she trusts others.

Gibb classifies the first view, sometimes described as authoritarian, or paternalistic, as *defensive.* "Dynamically the view defends the administrator against his own fears and distrusts and against perceived or anticipated attack from the outside."[29] In this view, defensive leadership patterns are based on fear and distrust, thrive on the distortion of information, and use strategies of persuasion and high control.

The alternative to defensive supervisory practices is described by Gibb as being *participatory.* The key to this leadership style is high trust and confidence in people. "The self-adequate person tends to assume that others are also adequate and, other things being equal, that they will be responsible, loyal, appropriately work-oriented when work is to be performed, and adequate to carry out jobs that are commensurate with their levels of experience and growth."[30]

Gibb's description of the two ideal types of supervisory behavior is not without substantial support in the literature of leadership-supervisory styles. The Gibb analysis however emphasizes the forces within supervisors which determine their behavior. We move now to examining this behavior and its effects on the school.

THE DIMENSIONS OF LEADERSHIP

The research tradition dealing with leadership style in educational and noneducational settings has identified two key dimensions of leadership. These dimensions have been given a variety of labels. Subtle differences may exist in the labels, but by and large experts agree that leadership style is defined by the extent

[29] Jack R. Gibb, "Dynamics of Leadership," in *In Search of Leaders,* Washington, D.C.: National Education Association, American Association for Higher Education, 1967, p. 56.
[30] Ibid., p. 62

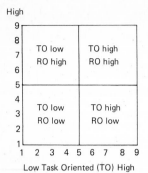

Figure 5-1 The leadership grid. *(From T. J. Sergiovanni and David Elliot, Educational and Organizational Leadership in Elementary Schools. Englewood Cliffs, N.J.: Prentice-Hall, 1975.)*

to which the leader seems to show concern for, focuses on, or seems oriented toward getting work done or accomplishing tasks and the extent to which the leader seems to show concern for, focuses on, or seems oriented toward the needs or feelings of people and his or her relationships with them.

In this discussion we will use the phrases "task-oriented" (TO) to refer to tendencies the leader shows for work and "relations-oriented" (RO) for the leader's tendency to show concern for people in displaying leadership behavior. Each of these dimensions of leadership style is illustrated conceptually in Figure 5-1.

The horizontal marginal axis line (abscissa) which forms the base of the grid represents the extent to which the leader's behavior shows a concern for task accomplishment (TO), with a high concern to the right and low concern to the left. You might estimate the extent to which your leadership style shows concern for task by checking one of the numbers (1 to 9) on this line. The vertical marginal axis line (ordinate) which forms the left side of the grid represents the extent to which the leader's behavior shows a concern for people and relationships (RO), with the top representing high concern and the bottom, low concern. Again, estimate the extent to which you show concern for people and relationships in expressing leadership by checking one of the numbers on this line. To find your location in the grid based on the estimates you have made, simply find the point where lines drawn from each of the numbers you checked would intersect. For example, if you checked a 7 on the TO line and 6 on the RO line, your position on the grid would be indicated by the *x* which appears on the grid.

THE MANAGERIAL GRID

A more descriptive attempt to conceptualize the task dimension and the people dimension of supervisory behavior has resulted in a formulation referred to as the *managerial grid*.[31] The grid focuses on five ideal-type theories of supervisory behavior, each based on the two dimensions which we have identified and dis-

---

[31] Robert Blake and Jane Mouton, *The Managerial Grid,* Houston: Gulf, 1964.

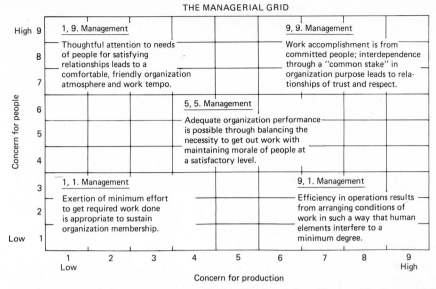

THE MANAGERIAL GRID

Figure 5-2 The managerial grid. *(From Robert Blake and Jane Mouton, The Managerial Grid, Houston, Gulf, 1964.)*

cussed as crucial variables found in organizations: (1) task and (2) people. Blake and Mouton, the proposers of the grid formulation, show the relationship between the two variables and present the five ideal-type combinations of style in Figure 5-2.

Notice that the horizontal axis, concern for production, is similar to the task-oriented construct, and that the vertical axis, concern for people, to the relationship-oriented construct. By locating degree of intensity for each of these two dimensions (from 1 to 9), we can see that the grid has potential for generating 81 different styles.

When asked to describe ideal leadership behavior in principals, teachers tend to express a preference for the integrated style which combines both TO and RO.[32] This preference seems to hold even though teachers may vary in terms of personality or need orientations. This observation lends support to the optimistic assumptions which make up the McGregor-Argyris management philosophy. That is, teachers seem able to describe ideal leadership behavior as emphasizing task—the organizational and structural aspects of the school—as well as provid-

[32] This generalization of *ideal* style results from the Leadership Behavior Description Questionnaire research tradition of Ralph Stogdill and of Andrew Halpin. The Leadership Behavior Description Questionnaire was developed by the Personnel Research Board at Ohio State University and is published by the Bureau of Business Research at that university. See John K. Hemphill and Alvin E. Coons, *Leader Behavior Description,* Columbus: Ohio State University, Personnel Research Board, 1950. See also Andrew Halpin, *Theory and Research in Administration,* New York: Macmillan, 1967, p. 86. Halpin's efforts with the LBDQ and education are pioneering. See his *The Leadership Behavior of School Superintendents,* Chicago: University of Chicago, Midwest Administration Center, 1959. Also "The Leader Behavior and Leadership Ideology of Educational Administrators and Aircraft Commanders," *Harvard Educational Review,* vol. 25, pp. 18–32, Winter 1955.

ing for individual needs, regardless of their own personality shortcomings or strengths. Human resources supervision maintains that providing for needs of mature teachers is dependent upon efforts toward achieving school goals: the two dimensions then are viewed as interdependent, since goal achievement over time is dependent upon provision for teacher need, and teacher need over time is dependent upon the achievement of school goals.

REDDIN'S 3-D THEORY OF LEADERSHIP

The managerial grid is considered to be a normative theory of leadership in the sense that it prescribes the 9.9 image of leadership as the one best style. In this section we describe a more descriptive theory (Reddin's 3-D Theory) which shares many of the features of the managerial grid but which assumes that no one best style exists.[33] Reddin views leadership style as consisting of a task and relationship emphasis similar to that illustrated previously in the quadrants of Figure 5-1.[34]

The lower-right-hand quadrant (TO high and RO low) represents a style of supervision which is characterized by a good deal of drive and emphasis on work and little overt concern for the relationship dimension. This is called the *dedicated* leadership style and is characterized by an emphasis on organizing, initiating, directing, completing, and evaluating the work of others.

The upper-left-hand quadrant (TO low and RO high) represents a style of supervision which emphasizes concern for people and little overt concern for the task dimension. This is called the *related* leadership style and is characterized by an emphasis on listening, accepting, trusting, advising, and encouraging.

The upper-right-hand quadrant (TO high and RO high) represents a combination approach to supervision, whereby people concerns are expressed through emphasizing meaningful work, and work concerns are emphasized by bringing together and stimulating committed groups of individuals. This is called the *integrated* leadership style and is characterized by an emphasis on interaction, motivation, integration, participation, and innovation.

The lower-left-hand quadrant (TO low and RO low) represents a style of supervision which expresses very little concern for either dimension. In a sense the leader removes himself or herself from both task and people. This is called the *separated* leadership style and is characterized by an emphasis on examining, measuring, administering, controlling, and maintaining.

The behavior indicators that Reddin suggests are associated with each of the four basic leadership styles shown in grid four in Figure 5-3.

Reddin proposes that the effectiveness of a given leadership style can be understood only within the context of the leadership situation. He assumes that related, integrated, separated, and dedicated are four basic styles only, each with

---

[33] W. J. Reddin, *Managerial Effectiveness,* New York: McGraw-Hill, 1970.

[34] This discussion follows that which appears in T. J. Sergiovanni, *Handbook for Effective Department Leadership: Concepts and Practices in Today's Secondary Schools,* Boston: Allyn and Bacon, 1977, p. 141. See also, Sergiovanni, "Leader Behavior and Organizational Effectiveness," *Notre Dame Journal of Education,* vol. 4, no. 1, 1973; and Sergiovanni and Elliott, *Educational and Organizational Leadership in Elementary Schools,* Englewood Cliffs, N.J.: Prentice-Hall, 1975, pp. 98–116.

	Related	Integrated
High	To listen	To interact
	To accept	To motivate
	To trust	To integrate
	To advise	To participate
	To encourage	To innovate
RO	To examine	To organize
	To measure	To initiate
	To administer	To direct
	To control	To complete
	To maintain	To evaluate
	Separated	Dedicated

Low ——————— TO ———→ High

Figure 5-3 Basic style behavior indicators. *(From W. J. Reddin, Managerial Effectiveness, New York: McGraw-Hill, 1970.)*

an effective and an ineffective equivalent depending upon the situation in which it is used. These effective and ineffective equivalents result in eight operational leadership styles, as shown in Figure 5-4.

In Reddin's terms the basic *integrated* styles when displayed in an inappropriate setting might lead to *compromise* but when displayed in an appropriate setting lead to *executive* effectiveness. As *executives*, supervisors are seen as good motivators who set high standards, who treat teachers as individuals, and who prefer team approaches in operating their units. As *compromisers*, supervisors are seen as poor decision makers who allow pressures in the situation to influence them too much.

The basic *related* style expressed inappropriately may be perceived as *missionary* behavior, but when the situation is ripe for this style, *development* of

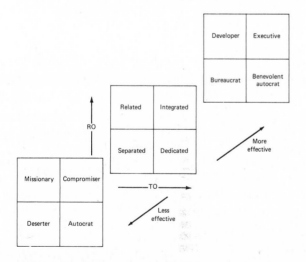

Figure 5-4 Reddin's 3-D theory of leadership. *(From W. J. Reddin, Managerial Effectiveness, New York: McGraw-Hill, 1970.)*

people takes place. As *developers,* supervisors are seen as being primarily concerned with developing teachers as individuals and professionals. As *missionaries,* supervisors are seen as being primarily interested in harmony.

If supervisors behave in a *separated* way given appropriate conditions, they are displaying an appropriate *bureaucratic* response, but if their involvement in task or people or both is needed but not forthcoming, they are seen as *deserters.* As *bureaucrats,* supervisors are seen as being primarily interested in rules and procedures for their own sake and as wanting to maintain and control the situation by their use, and they are viewed as being conscientious. As *deserters,* supervisors are seen as being uninvolved and passive.

Dedicated supervisors who are inspirational and driving forces given appropriate circumstances are seen as *benevolent autocrats,* but when this style is displayed in inappropriate situations, they are viewed as interfering, dominant, and *repressive autocrats.* In the first instance supervisors are seen as people who know what they want and know how to get it without causing resentment. In the second instance they are seen as people who have no confidence in others, as unpleasant, and as being interested only in the immediate job.

At first glance the theory seems complex and the labels chosen by Reddin confusing and on occasion inappropriate. But the language system is worth deciphering, for the concepts and ideas basic to the theory are powerful and important. A key to this theory is the notion that the *same* style expressed in different situations may be effective or ineffective. For example, a supervisor who uses the integrated style with a teacher who is in need of personal support may be seen as *compromising* the personal dimension by not giving exclusive attention to the needs of the individual. This same supervisor who relies exclusively on support and understanding when a teacher is searching for a task solution to a problem may be seen as a *missionary* lacking in forceful leadership. This related style, however, would have been perceived as being most effective in the first instance.

UNDERSTANDING SITUATIONAL LEADERSHIP VARIABLES

The situational determinants of leadership style effectiveness are difficult to identify and formally catalogue. Nevertheless, some useful generalizations can be made about situational variables and their relationship to leadership style. With a little practice one's ability to match appropriate style to situation can be improved considerably.

Generally speaking, we can assume that educational settings and particularly leadership situations in schools will only occasionally call for separated and dedicated styles, for in each of these cases the human dimension is neglected. This generalization is consistent with the human resources model for supervision. Occasions will exist when styles that show low concern for people are appropriate, but the focus of leadership *in general* will be in the related and integrated quadrants.

A number of exceptions to this generalization come to mind. In each case the job demands are such that the dedicated style, which emphasizes task but not people, will probably be most effective. One exception deals with routine situations where goals and objectives are simple, clear, and uncontroversial, and where the paths to reach the goal are few in number and clearly marked. Another exception relates to situations where very favorable leader-member relationships exist. Here, members trust the leader and are willing to follow him or her. A third exception relates to situations characterized by excessive interpersonal tension, confusion, and stress. Short-term success in these situations can be accomplished through use of the dedicated style. The leader's formal position in the school hierarchy is another important condition. When too much positional or hierarchical distance exists between leader and members, it is often less stressful for everyone if the leader uses a more directive or task-oriented style. Other important considerations which influence choice of style include time constraints and competency and motivational levels of teachers. These and other variables which one must consider in matching style to situation are discussed in the next chapter, entitled "A Contingency Approach to Supervisory Leadership."

SUMMARY

Leadership is of particular importance to effective supervision. When compared with other conditions which influence the mediating variables, organizational structure and function, for example, leadership is more directly accessible to supervision. An important conceptual distinction was made between leadership and administrative behavior, but for operational purposes both were considered as variations in leadership style.

The importance of supervisory assumptions in influencing leadership style was emphasized by discussing McGregor's Theories X and Y and Argyris's infancy management assumptions. In addition, the assumptions basic to Theory X soft (human relations) were compared with those of Theory Y (human resources). It was pointed out that though Theory Y seems more clearly appropriate to human organizations such as schools, this does not preclude the use of a number of leadership approaches.

Forces in the supervisor, in the environment, and in subordinates were discussed as additional factors impinging upon choice of style. The leadership theories of Blake and Mouton (The Managerial Grid) and W. J. Reddin (3-D Theory) were then discussed. Both theories are concerned with the task and relationship emphasis of the supervisor. Each describes basic styles of leadership as comprising a mix of emphases. In 3-D Theory it was suggested that though four basic styles (dedicated, related, integrated, and separated) could be identified, no one best style appropriate for all cases existed. The dependence of leadership effectiveness upon the correct matching of style to the characteristics of the situation at hand was discussed. A number of situational leadership variables were suggested, and it was promised that they would be further delineated in Chapter 6.

STUDY GUIDE

Recall the concepts, ideas, and meanings associated with each of the following phrases and terms included in this chapter. Can you discuss each of them with a colleague and apply them to the supervisory context of your school? If you cannot, review them in the text and record the page number for future reference.

1 Dedicated style _____
2 Forces in the environment _____
3 Forces in others _____
4 Forces in the supervisor _____
5 Grid numbers _____
6 Infancy management assumption _____
7 Integrated style _____
8 Leadership definitions _____
9 Leadership quadrants _____
10 Managerial grid _____
11 Misunderstandings of Theory Y _____
12 Pattern A _____
13 Pattern B _____
14 Relations-oriented _____
15 Related style _____
16 Self-fulfilling prophecy _____
17 Separated style _____
18 Situational leadership variables _____
19 Theory X soft _____
20 Theory Y _____
21 3-D Theory _____

EXERCISES

1 Contrast Theory X, Theory X soft, and Theory Y supervisory assumptions. Develop three teacher-evaluation policy statements with implementation guidelines—each based on one of the assumption sets.
2 Though the authors are committed to the values of Theory Y, they suggest that on occasions, *behavior* based on Theories X and X soft is justified. Provide examples suggesting when X or X soft behavior is appropriate.
3 Explain the differences between normative and situational theories of leadership.
4 List each of the behavioral indicators contained in Figure 5-2 on a separate sheet of paper, mixing the items so that they are not categorized. Role-play, or actually ask teachers to select 5 of the 20 indicators which they expect supervisors to emphasize. Repeat this procedure with administrators and supervisors. Re-sort the selected indicators into the four grid categories. You should now have three sets of expectations for the supervisor's role. In what ways are these expectations similar and in what ways are they different? Where differences occur (role conflict), how might they be resolved?

Chapter 6

A Contingency Approach
to Supervisory Leadership

In Chapter 5 it was pointed out that no one best style of leadership could be identified but rather that effectiveness of style was determined by its appropriateness to the situation at hand. Indeed, any one style might be appropriate for situation A but not B and another for situation B but not A. Using Reddin's 3-D Theory of Leadership, we identified four basic styles, each with an effective and ineffective expression.[1] The styles, with their effective and ineffective counterparts, are summarized in Table 6-1.

In this chapter we are concerned with the identification of situational variables and with helping supervisors match styles to situational demands. This is a contingency approach to supervisory leadership.

CONTINGENCY LEADERSHIP THEORY (FIEDLER)

A new theory of leadership effectiveness has emerged from some 15 years of research conducted at the University of Illinois through its Group Effectiveness Laboratory and from work done at the University of Washington since 1970. This theory, developed by Fred Fiedler and his associates,[2] stems from a research

[1] W. J. Reddin, *Managerial Effectiveness,* New York: McGraw-Hill, 1970.
[2] See Fred E. Fiedler, *A Theory of Leadership Effectiveness,* New York: McGraw-Hill, 1967, for a comprehensive treatment of this theory. More popular versions of the theory are found in Fiedler's

Table 6-1 Effective and Ineffective Expression of Leadership Style

When used inappropriately ↓	Basic styles	When used appropriately ↓
Compromiser ←	INTEGRATED →	Executive
Deserter ←	SEPARATED →	Bureaucrat
Autocrat ←	DEDICATED →	Benevolent autocrat
Missionary ←	RELATED →	Developer
Less effective		More effective

From W. J. Reddin, *Management Effectiveness*, New York: McGraw-Hill, 1970, p. 40.

tradition primarily associated with that of small-group psychology. The theory suggests that both task-oriented and relationship-oriented leaders are able to perform effectively in a group given conditions appropriate to and supportive of their leadership style. Further, the theory accepts the style of the leader as a given, and therefore recommends that the arrangement of tasks and situations accommodate leader styles rather than that styles change to fit situations.[3] Fiedler would suggest, for example, that the supervisor who is effective on a one-to-one basis with teachers because of the increased status this arrangement provides but is ineffective working with teachers as a group (group situations often decrease status differences between designated leaders and followers) should arrange for a pattern of supervision which favors the first situation and avoids the second.

The task-oriented leader in Fiedler's research corresponds to the dedicated-leadership designation of Reddin's theory, and the relationship-oriented leader to the related designation. Fiedler does not examine the separated and integrated styles.

Fiedler's extensive research strongly indicates that task-oriented leaders perform best in group situations that are either very favorable or very unfavorable to the leader. Relationship-oriented leaders, on the other hand, perform best in group situations that are intermediate in favorableness. Favorableness is defined by the degree to which the situation enables the leader to exert influence over the group.

"Engineering the Job to Fit the Manager," *Harvard Business Review,* vol. 43, no. 5, pp. 115–122, September 1965; "Style or Circumstance: The Leadership Enigma," *Psychology Today,* vol. 2, no. 10, pp. 38–43, March 1969; and Fiedler and Martin Chemers, *Leadership and Effective Management,* Glenview, Ill.: Scott, Foresman, 1974. These references form the basis of our discussion which follows.

[3] Leadership styles are measured by an instrument which yields a Least Preferred Co-Worker (LPC) score for respondents. Using an Osgood Semantic Differential format, respondents are asked to describe their least preferred co-worker on each of 16 dimensions. Those who describe this worker in a relatively positive sense are typed as relationship-oriented, while those who describe him in a negative sense are typed as task-oriented. Fiedler presents impressive evidence supporting this method in Chap. 3 of his book, *A Theory of Leadership Effectiveness.*

Three major situational variables seem to determine whether a given situation is favorable or unfavorable to the leader. In order of importance they are listed as follows: (1) leader-member relations, which in our case refers to the extent teachers accept, admire, like, and are willing to follow individual supervisors because of the kind of people they are and the relationship they have developed with the teachers; (2) task structure, which in our case refers to the extent the work of the unit or person being supervised is structured, how clearly the objectives are defined, and how limited the processes available for achieving these objectives are; (3) position power, which in our case refers to the amount of formal authority and status the supervisor has.

Fiedler's Contingency Model

A simplified version of Fiedler's contingency model is presented in Figure 6-1.[4] This figure shows the effectiveness of relationship-oriented leadership versus task-oriented leadership for group situations characterized by different combinations of leader-member personal relationships, task structure, and leader position power.

Eight group situations are identified and categorized according to whether they are high or low on each of the three critical dimensions which determine favorableness of a given style. The group situations are arranged in declining order of the leader's influence, with Cell 1 providing the leader with the most influence and Cell 8 the least influence. The leader, for example, who is well liked by group members, who is working in structured tasks, and who has a great deal of authority can exert strong influence on the group, while the opposite, the leader who is not liked, who has an unstructured assignment, and who comes with little authority has difficulty in exerting influence.

[4] The contingency model is constructed by plotting correlations of leadership style against the taxonomy of group situations. The approximate median correlations between leader LPC score and group performance plotted for each group situation (Cells 1 to 8 in Fig. 6-1) are $-.55$, $-.60$, $-.30$, .43, .40; none available for Cell 6, 0.3, and -5.0. (Fiedler, *A Theory of Leadership Effectiveness*, p. 146.)

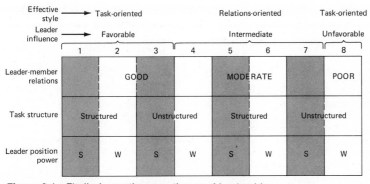

Figure 6-1   Fiedler's contingency theory of leadership.

The contingency model suggests that task-oriented leaders perform best in situations which provide them with substantial influence *and* in situations which provide them with very little influence. Relationship-oriented leaders, on the other hand, are most effective in mixed situations which afford them moderate influence over the group. Leadership contexts 1 to 3, for example, provide the leader with the most favorable opportunities for the leader to influence the group, and Fiedler finds that task-oriented leadership is the most effective style. Leadership context 8 provides the leader with the least amount of influence on group members, and again the task-oriented or directive style is found to be effective. The remaining four contexts, according to the contingency leadership theory, seem best suited to the relationship-oriented style.

When supervisors have the respect and good wishes of teachers and a great deal of formal authority to back them up, exerting influence is easy. Personal relationships with teachers are such that teachers are more willing to follow. In addition position power is such that teachers more readily yield to the supervisor the right to lead. Combine these with a structured task, as in context 1, which tends not to call for much participation anyway, and we have the perfect setting for more task-oriented or dedicated leadership. Contexts 2 and 3 are not quite as favorable as 1 but possess enough of the same ingredient to permit easy influence.

Contexts 4 to 7, on the other hand, each require the supervisor to earn the right to lead, to win the loyalty and commitment of teachers, or, as in contexts 4 and 7, where tasks are unstructured, to depend upon the knowledge and abilities of others in order to be effective. In each case related and integrated styles are found to be more effective. Context 8 is so unfavorable that, at least for a short period of time, the more directive task style is recommended. As the supervisor works to improve the situation so that it approximates context 4, his or her style needs to change accordingly.

THE ZONE OF INDIFFERENCE

All teachers do not have a uniform desire to participate in the decision-making processes of the school nor for that matter do all teachers wish to be involved in the same things. When the context of decision making is of little or no concern to a teacher (that is, when it is in his or her zone of indifference), a more task-oriented approach from the leader would be appropriate.[5] Teachers, for example, are not likely to be terribly interested in many of the purely administrative or technical aspects of operating a particular unit and would probably be pleased by a supervisor who can regulate them in a dedicated but unobtrusive way. Teachers often resent being involved in events and activities they consider to be unimportant. As one's zone of indifference with reference to a particular issue decreases, however, one's desire to be involved increases, and this necessitates use of the more related and integrated styles. These relationships are shown in Figure 6-2.

A broad range of styles exists between the two extremes of task orientation and relationship orientation. It is difficult to conceptualize leadership on the task

[5] This discussion follows Sergiovanni and D. Elliott, *Organizational and Educational Leadership in Elementary Schools,* Englewood Cliffs, N.J.: Prentice-Hall, pp. 108–109, 1975.

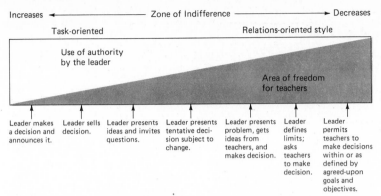

Figure 6-2 The zone of indifference. *(Adapted from Robert Tannenbaum and Warren Schmidt, "How to Choose a Leadership Pattern," Harvard Business Review. vol. 36, no. 2, 1957.)*

and relationship continuum only. For example, as one moves to the extreme right on Figure 6-2 to where the supervisor defines limits and asks teachers to make decisions and to where the supervisor permits teachers to function within limits defined by agreed-upon goals and objectives, concern for task and concern for people are both present. These are the essential characteristics of the integrated style. Nevertheless, it seems appropriate to generalize that as the substance of decision making moves closer to the classroom activities of teachers and as proposed changes in operation and procedure require attitudinal and behavioral changes from teachers, the zone of indifference is likely to decrease. Teachers will be more concerned with the issues at hand and will want to be involved. In such cases, leadership styles which include a generous component of relationship orientation (the related and integrated styles) are most likely to be effective. Moreover, the relationship between styles of supervision and the level of teachers' interest holds for the relationship between styles of supervision and the competency, maturity, and commitment levels of teachers. The more competent teachers are, given a particular set of problems or tasks, the more appropriate are related and integrated styles. The less competent teachers are, given a set of problems and tasks, the more appropriate is the dedicated style.

CONTINGENCY LEADERSHIP THEORY (VROOM)

One important characteristic of leadership style is the emphasis, or lack of emphasis, given to the participation of subordinates in decision making. Dedicated and separated styles tend not to emphasize participation. Related and integrated styles, on the other hand, tend to emphasize participation.

Victor Vroom's theory of leadership focuses on this one important dimension of leader behavior, the degree to which the supervisor should encourage participation of teachers in decision making.[6] In a typology similar to that proposed by Tannenbaum and Schmidt[7] as adapted in Figure 6-2, Vroom identifies five decision styles, or processes, which might be available for use by supervisors. This is a contingency approach in the sense that no one decision-making process is best under all circumstances and that effectiveness of one's choice is dependent upon properties of the situation at hand. The decision styles are described as follows:

1 The supervisor solves the problem or makes the decision using information available at the time. This is an approach consistent with the dedicated style.

2 The supervisor obtains necessary information from teacher(s), then decides on the solution to the problem. The supervisor may or may not tell teachers much about the problem when obtaining information from them. The role of teachers in this case is in providing information—rather than generating or evaluating solutions. This approach combines aspects of the dedicated and separated leadership styles.

3 The supervisor shares the problems with relevant teachers individually, obtaining their ideas and suggestions without bringing them together as a group. Then the supervisor, at times being influenced by their advice and at other times, not, makes the decision. This approach combines aspects of the dedicated and related leadership styles.

4 The supervisor shares the problem with teachers as a group, obtaining ideas and suggestions and then makes the decision which may or may not reflect the influence of teachers. The approach combines aspects of the integrated and dedicated leadership styles.

5 The supervisor shares the problem with teachers as a group. Together they generate and evaluate alternatives and attempt to reach agreement on a solution. The supervisor does not try to pressure the group to adopt his or her solution and is willing to accept and implement any solution that has the support of the group. This approach combines aspects of the related and integrated leadership styles.[8]

The supervisor determines which decision style is best for a particular situation on the basis of answers to seven critical questions, each of which defines and helps diagnose aspects of the problem at hand. Depending upon how the critical questions are answered, the supervisor is able to determine the best decision styles for this situation. This process, along with the critical questions, is illustrated in the form of a decision tree in Figure 6-3.

Letters A through H representing the eight critical questions are arranged along the top of Figure 6-3 in a fashion which elicits "yes" or "no" responses. To

[6] See, for example, Victor Vroom, "A New Look at Managerial Decision-Making," *Organizational Dynamics,* vol. 1, 1973; Vroom and P. W. Yetton, "A Normative Model for Leadership Styles," in H. J. Leavitt and L. Pondy (eds.), *Readings in Managerial Psychology,* 2d ed., Chicago: University of Chicago Press, 1973; and Vroom, "Leadership Revisited," in Eugene Carr and Frederick Zimmer (eds.), *Man and Work in Society,* New York: Van Nostrand, 1975, pp. 220–234.

[7] Robert Tannenbaum and Warren Schmidt, "How to Choose a Leadership Pattern," *Harvard Business Review,* vol. 36, no. 2, pp. 95–101, 1957.

[8] Adapted from Vroom, "Leadership Revisited," in Carr and Zimmer (eds.), op. cit., p. 225.

Critical questions: A. Is there a quality requirement such that one solution is likely to be more rational than another?
B. Do I have sufficient info to make a high quality decision?
C. Is the problem structured?
D. Is acceptance of decision by subordinates critical to effective implementation?
E. If I were to make the decision by myself, is it reasonably certain that it would be accepted by my subordinates?
F. Do subordinates share the organizational goals to be attained in solving this problem?
G. Is conflict among subordinates likely in preferred soltuions? (This question is irrelevant to individual problems.)
H. Do subordinates have sufficient info to make a high quality decision?

Decision tree

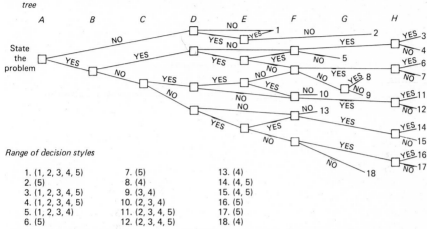

Range of decision styles

1. (1, 2, 3, 4, 5)	7. (5)	13. (4)
2. (5)	8. (4)	14. (4, 5)
3. (1, 2, 3, 4, 5)	9. (3, 4)	15. (4, 5)
4. (1, 2, 3, 4, 5)	10. (2, 3, 4)	16. (5)
5. (1, 2, 3, 4)	11. (2, 3, 4, 5)	17. (5)
6. (5)	12. (2, 3, 4, 5)	18. (4)

Figure 6-3   Vroom: Decision process flow chart. *(From Victor Vroom and Arthur Jago, "Decision-Making as a Social Process: Normative and Descriptive Models of Leadership Behavior." Technical Report #5, Organizational Effectiveness Research Programs, Office of Naval Research. N0014-67-A-0097-0027, May, 1974.)*

use the model, start with the box on the left-hand side of the diagram and ask question A. The answer, either "yes" or "no," determines the path to take on the decision tree. Continue to the right until you encounter a second box. Answer the question associated with that box and continue the process until a terminal node is reached. At that node you will find a number designating a range of feasible decision styles. This number and the range of decision styles are listed below the decision tree and correspond to the five decision styles discussed previously.

As an example, assume that in starting with square 1 to the left of the model, the answer to question A is "no." The supervisor would then follow the "no" branch of the decision tree to square 2 and respond to question D. A "yes" response to this question leads to square 3 and question E. A "no" response to this question leads to a terminal node to the far right of the diagram. Here the supervisor finds the number 2, which prescribes the appropriate decision style range. Consulting the lower portion of Figure 6-3, we find that the number 2 suggests *only* decision style 5, which requires the supervisor to share the problem with the group and seek a consensus solution. Beginning again at square 1 to the far left of the model, we find that a "yes" answer to question A leads to square 2 under question B and so on, until the process has continued through the decision tree to another terminal node.

Notice that in a number of cases several decision styles are listed. Vroom suggests that though the listed styles represent the feasible range of options available, the supervisor must still select one decision style for implementation. Each of the styles is arranged in *ascending* order of time required for implementation and *descending* order in terms of potential for *development* of teachers. Decision style 1 is most efficient in time but promises the least in developing teachers. By contrast, decision style 5 is most costly in time but has the most potential for developing teachers. Vroom suggests that one should select the decision style furthest to the left (closest to 1) from among those identified as feasible on the decision tree when time is scarce and furthest to the right (closest to 5) when time is plentiful.

In the case of schools where the development of human resources is particularly critical, the prudent supervisor will make every effort to choose decision styles closest to 5—that is, those with the greatest potential for developing teachers.

JOB DEMANDS AND LEADERSHIP EFFECTIVENESS

An additional set of concerns for supervisors interested in selecting leadership strategies in a manner consistent with contingency theory are the unique characteristics which define the job or task at hand. Job demands vary as objectives and tasks change or as attention shifts from one set of problems or objectives to another. In one situation, for example, the supervisor might be more expert than teachers, and in another case, they may be more expert than the supervisor.

Reddin suggests that as a general guide, if the problem and objectives currently in focus result in the following job demands and conditions, then the related style will probably be the most effective:[9]

- Teachers have high expertness or unusual technical skills.
- Teacher identification and commitment are necessary for success.
- The job is arranged in a way that teachers can largely decide how tasks will be accomplished.
- It is difficult to evaluate performance outcomes precisely.
- Teachers need to be creative and inventive in their work.

If the situation is such that the following job demands and conditions are present, then the separated style will probably be the most effective:

- The teacher's job is programmed in a routine fashion and requires the following of established procedures, curriculum formats, teaching strategies.
- The teacher's job is easy to perform and easy to regulate.
- Automatic feedback is provided so that the teacher can readily note her or his progress.

[9] Charting job demands and relating them to leadership styles is an integral part of Reddin, *Managerial Effectiveness,* New York: McGraw-Hill, 1970, pp. 69–88. This section follows T. J. Sergiovanni, *Handbook for Effective Department Leadership in the Secondary Schools: Concepts and Practices,* Boston: Allyn & Bacon, 1977, pp. 151–152.

- Intellectual privacy and thinking are much more important than the teacher being actively involved in something.

If the situation is such that the following job demands and conditions are present, then the integrated style will probably be most effective:

- Teachers need to interact with each other in order to complete their tasks.
- Teachers are interdependent; the success of one depends upon the help of others, and vice versa.
- Successful completion of tasks requires that the supervisor must interact with teachers as a group.
- Several solutions are possible, and the number of solutions proposed and evaluated is improved by interaction among group members.
- Teachers can set their own pace as the group pursues its task.

If the situation is such that the following job demands and conditions are present, then the dedicated style will probably be most effective:

- The supervisor knows more about the task or problems at hand than the teachers do.
- Numerous unplanned and unanticipated events are likely to occur which require attention from the supervisor.
- Teachers need to be given direction frequently in order for them to complete their task.
- The teacher's performance is readily measurable, and corrective actions by the supervisor are visible and can be easily evaluated.

NOTES ON CONTINGENCY THEORY

Contingency theories of leadership appear at the same time complex and accessible. On the one hand they portray leadership effectiveness in a fashion which causes one to grasp for the security of styles and modes that are familiar, and on the other hand their sophistication carries promises of success far beyond that which one might realistically expect. Nevertheless, contingency theories are an improvement over "one best style" theories. They are indeed complex but can be learned and used by most supervisors. They do promise much and therefore may well disappoint many users. On balance we believe that mastery and use of contingency theories can help improve effectiveness, particularly if supervisors keep in mind that the phenomena of leadership still remain somewhat of a mystery and that to date all theories are at best partial explanations, unable to account for all the forces impinging upon leader effectiveness.

One consequence of focusing on the behavioral aspects of leadership and on developing leadership strategies is that the substance of leadership decisions may get slighted. Leadership skills are important, but they cannot guarantee genuine leadership if the leader does not have a clear sense of purpose and direction.

A decisive factor which distinguishes a leader is his or her vision of, or belief in, what is possible. Besides having technical competence in management or supervisory skills, a leader possesses a deep sense of the significance of what the group is doing. In communicating that sense of significance, the leader enlists the commitment of the group to achieving those significant results. Among the military, that significance may center on the defense of democratic freedom or the defense of one's homeland. Among medical scientists, it may be the discovery of a new cure for cancer. Among government workers, the significance might center on the improvement of the quality of life for citizens in the community or even a simpler way to pay taxes. Usually what will gain the commitment of a group to its task is the general belief that its work makes a difference in the lives of other people.

What solidifies the group commitment to its work is the living out of the belief in its significance by the leader. If leaders do not practice what they preach, then the group loyalty to them and to the achievement of the significant results they talk about will evaporate. On the other hand, the moral persuasion of their consistent example will lead to greater identification with their vision of, or belief in, the significance of what the group is doing. Gradually the group will appropriate and internalize the motivation of the leader, especially when it coincides with sources of motivation in themselves which, perhaps, have lain dormant.

Usually the leader can communicate a sense of drama inherent in his or her vision of what is possible. Routine and repetition are what tend to deaden work and decrease enthusiasm. What once was challenging is reduced to habit, to an automatic response, to ordinariness. Frequently, it is the leader who will help the group recapture a sense of pride in its work or a sense of purpose, if not enthusiasm.

Perhaps an example can clarify. Consider what happens to the consciousness of an audience which is attending an exceptional dramatic performance. During and after the play they experience the value and significance inherent in many situations which they have come to accept as "ordinary." In the play, words, gestures, and decisions make a difference, sometimes a profound difference, in the lives of the characters. One word might save a life; if one gesture had been otherwise, it might have made all the difference; a door left open instead of closed might have changed the whole course of a character's life. What the characters in the play do or say has dramatic significance; the drama of human life gathers to a new fullness. Greatness, heroism, or evil is made vividly possible on the stage. The audience experiences the beautiful or tragic possibilities inherent in human life. They leave the performance with a more intense awareness of what might have happened or might be happening to their own lives.

Leaders tend to live with this more intense consciousness of the drama inherent in the human condition, of the significance of human choices, of the exciting possibilities challenging human imagination. This kind of dramatic consciousness illumines and suffuses the technical performance of their management or administrative tasks. They dwell on the significance of the task, appreciate the inherent drama in the accomplishment of the task, and communicate an appreciation and sense of excitement about the task to the group.

Supervisor leadership behavior in education, then, involves not only the supervisor's appreciation of the considerable human resources of subordinates but also the supervisor's own beliefs about, and vision of, the dramatic possibilities inherent in all educational activity. This vision, or set of beliefs, provides the substance of supervisory leadership. The forms of supervisory leadership will vary frequently, depending on the situation, but the substance or content of that leadership behavior will steadily flow out of the vision.

While the authors do not offer fully developed educational philosophy in this book, they do affirm the critical importance of it for supervisory personnel who wish to exert leadership. Without some basic vision of their own, it would seem impossible for supervisors to develop with subordinates a shared sense of purpose that flows out of the significance of what they are doing for and in the lives of students.

SUMMARY

This chapter examined contingency approaches to leadership effectiveness. Contingency theory assumes that no one best style of leadership suitable to all situations can be identified but rather that effectiveness of style is determined by its appropriateness to the situation at hand. The four basic styles proposed by Reddin and their effective and ineffective counterparts were then reviewed. Using Fiedler's contingency theory of leadership, the related (RO) and dedicated (TO) styles were selected for further examination. Leadership situations were defined by three critical variables—the quality of leader-member relationships, the extent to which the group task is structured or unstructured, and the position power of the leader. Using the three variables, we identified eight situations for leadership in descending order of ease of influence by the leader. It was determined that the dedicated style (TO) is more effective in situations which are favorable and unfavorable to influence by the leader. Situations characterized as only moderately favorable were associated with the related (RO) leadership style.

The zone of indifference of teachers was also discussed as a further consideration in choosing an appropriate style. The dedicated style was found more suitable for situations characterized by teacher indifference, but as decision making moved closer to areas considered more important to teachers, related styles were judged more appropriate. Competency, maturity, and commitment levels of teachers were cited as examples of additional contingency variables to be considered.

Vroom's contingency theory of leadership was then discussed as one approach which focuses on an aspect of leader behavior of particular importance to supervisors, the degree to which the leader should encourage participation of subordinates in decision making. Five decision styles were described, each effective in some situations but not in others. Vroom provides a methodology which uses a decision tree along which a subject is guided by answers to seven critical questions, for determining which decision style is most appropriate to the situation at hand.

Still an additional set of concerns to be considered in using contingency theory are the unique characteristics or job demands which define the job or task at hand. Lists of job conditions typically associated with the related, integrated, separated, and dedicated leadership styles were provided. Some cautions in implementing contingency theory were then discussed.

Finally, visions or beliefs of leaders were highlighted as constant sources for leadership behavior. Their consciousness of the dramatic possibilities for human growth in any educational setting—or their philosophies of education—energize their leadership behavior in whatever styles the contingencies of the situation encourage them to adopt.

STUDY GUIDE

Recall the concepts, ideas, and meanings associated with each of the following phrases and terms included in this chapter. Can you discuss each of them with a colleague and apply them to the supervisory context of your school? If you cannot, review them in the text and record the page number for future reference.

1 Contingency theory _____
2 Decision styles _____
3 Decision-free _____
4 Dedicated style _____
5 Fiedler's theory _____
6 Integrated style _____
7 Job demands _____
8 Leader-member relation _____
9 Position power _____
10 Related style _____
11 RO _____
12 Separated style _____
13 Situational favorableness _____
14 Situational variable _____
15 Task structure _____
16 Terminal node _____
17 TO _____
18 Vroom's theory _____
19 Zone of indifference _____

EXERCISES

1 Develop thumbnail sketches of four supervisors, each with leadership styles categorized as basically integrated, separated, dedicated, or related. Include in each sketch one or two examples showing situations where that supervisor's basic leadership style might be effective and situations where that style might be ineffective.
2 Identify two or three decision-making problems, and analyze each using Vroom's decision tree. How would your analysis differ if you were using Fiedler's contingency theory? Which of the two approaches do you find more useful?

3 Review the job demands listed under the chapter heading "Job Demands and Leadership Effectiveness." Which of the demands best characterizes your school? What implications would these demands have for your leadership style?

4 The leader's sense of purpose and mission is what elevates the mechanics of leadership (style, contingency theory, and so on) from mere social engineering to a human activity, and indeed this is the note upon which Chapter 6 ends. Where do you stand on the purpose and mission question? What hopes and aspirations do you have as a supervisor?

Chapter 7

Power, Authority, and Conflict in Supervision

Though many seek power, few speak of it. Our democratic culture and egalitarian norms are such that the word "power," like "politics," has become tainted. Yet power is the energy upon which organizational decision making and functioning operate. Schools, like other organizations, require a reasonable amount of order and conformity. They represent organized ways in which to accomplish certain ends. Thus directions are given, actions coordinated, suggestions made, activities assigned, meetings held, standards set, programs adapted, performance appraised, resources distributed, and plans developed within an organized structure in a systematic attempt to effect the schools' purposes. Each of these tasks and functions requires exchanges in influence in order to obtain the compliance of one person to the wishes of another and to influence the decision-making process. In the first instance we speak of a deliberate attempt by one person to influence another or a group, and in the second instance, a more general attempt to make an impact upon the functioning of the school through its decision-making processes.

In this chapter the phenomena of authority and the bases of social power available to supervisors and others are discussed. Though authority typically rests in the hands of a few, the bases of social power are more widely distributed and are accessible to many. Competing sources of authority and accessibility to bases of power often lead to competing claims of influence and to conflict between individuals. Therefore attention is also given to the development of conflict-management techniques. In addition a section on organizational politics and the management of political behavior in the school is included.

DEFINING POWER AND AUTHORITY

Power and authority are concepts often difficult to separate in practice, but useful differences exist between the two which can help in understanding their respective origins, expressions, and effects. Authority is the right to act or to require others to act on behalf of school purposes. Weber defines authority as the willing compliance of people based on the belief that it is legitimate for the designated leader to impose his or her will on subordinates.[1] The most common view of authority is that it is related to one's position and the inherent rights associated with that position.[2]

Power, on the other hand, refers to one's ability to influence the decision-making process. Sometimes this ability comes from authority associated with one's formal position in the hierarchy of the school but at other times from other sources. Indeed, often those with little authority exert considerable influence (power) on the decision-making processes of the school. Many supervisory roles are defined in such a manner that authority is weak. Chairpersons, curriculum coordinators, resource persons, and instructional supervisors might be examples. Contrast the authority which incumbents of staff-type roles have with that of superintendent for instruction, principal, general superintendent, and other line positions.[3] Lacking sufficient organizationally derived authority, supervisors are often required to look elsewhere in order to generate enough influence to affect educational decisions.

Since influence is a natural and important aspect of life in schools, supervisors need to understand the nature of authority—its many origins, form, operational feasibility, and acceptance. As schools have matured into complex professional organizations, newer forms of authority have emerged to challenge traditional authority sources. Entrepreneurial administrative behavior, the one-person show, hierarchical authority which rests largely in the position one occupies, and bureaucratic rules are seriously challenged by professional authority, ability authority, and authority owing to other sources.[4]

[1] Max Weber, *The Theory of Social and Economic Organization,* Talcott Parsons (ed.), trans. by A. M. Henderson and T. Parsons, Glencoe, Ill.: Free Press, 1947.

[2] Chester Barnard provides a contrasting view of authority. In his "acceptance theory" he assumes that authority comes from below rather than above. Authority in itself does not exist but is based on the willingness of subordinates to accept. Without acceptance, in his view, no authority exists. See, for example, Chester Barnard, *The Function of the Executive,* Cambridge, Mass.: Harvard, 1938.

[3] Traditionally a distinction has been made between *line* and *staff* positions. Line authority is straightforward and consists of a direct superordinate-subordinate relationship between individuals. Staff authority is more complex and is designed to support line authority by advising administrators and teachers, providing special services, at the request of either administrators or teachers. Operationally the distinction is more muddled, as our discussion of social power and authority will reveal.

[4] See, for example, John Kenneth Galbraith, *The New Industrial State,* Boston: Houghton Mifflin, 1967, particularly pp. 68–75. Also, Victor Thompson, *Modern Organization,* New York: Knopf, 1961, Chaps. 3 and 4.

WEBER'S AUTHORITY TYPES

Max Weber distinguishes among three types of authority on the basis of their acceptance as a common value orientation for a particular group.[5] They are described as follows:

Traditional. This authority base is legitimized by the belief in the sanctity of tradition. A given person or caste of people, usually on the basis of heredity, is preordained to rule over the others. The divine right of kings is a classical example of traditional authority. In contemporary organizations, the management caste treasures and passes on traditional prerogatives which other employees are perceived not to have. This is particularly visible in patriarchal family businesses and in paternalistic schools.

Charismatic. This authority base rests on a profession of faith which considers the pronouncements of a given leader to be inspired by supernatural powers. Disciples willingly follow the charismatic leader as they become converted to and champions of his cause. In contemporary organizations, the innovator, the champion of new educational and social movements, may be able to tap the charismatic power base. Charismatic movements eventually evolve into traditional or bureaucratic management systems.

Legal. This authority base is legitimized by a formalistic belief in the supremacy of norms and laws. In legal systems, compliance occurs as a result of a body of impersonal and universal principles and rules rather than of loyalty to the traditional or charismatic leader. Legal authority forms the basis for the ideal bureaucratic organization.

The Weber formulation provides a background for most scholarly discussions of organizational authority and power. In recent years a fourth source of organizational authority has emerged—one based on professional norms and skill. Professional authority is similar to legal authority in that both are legitimized by codes, rules, and norms. This similarity is a major cause of conflict between the two. In schools organizational norms and rules often conflict with professional norms. Consider, for example, the guidance counselor who feels it unethical or harmful to disclose test scores to parents but who is required to do so by the school code or by administrative decree. We begin our discussion by examining two general types of authority in schools—formal and functional.

FORMAL AUTHORITY VERSUS FUNCTIONAL AUTHORITY

Peabody,[6] in summarizing the work of Weber, Urwick, Simon, Bennis, and Presthus, identifies four broad categories of authority: "(1) authority of legitimacy; (2) authority of position, including the sanctions inherent in position; (3) authority of competence, including both technical skills and experience; and (4) authority of person, including leadership and human relations skills."[7] The Peabody summary appears in Table 7-1.

[5] Max Weber, op. cit.
[6] Robert L. Peabody, "Perceptions of Organizational Authority: A Comparative Analysis," *Administrative Science Quarterly,* vol. 6, no. 4, March 1962.
[7] Ibid., p. 466.

Table 7-1   The Bases of Authority

	Formal authority		Functional authority	
	Legitimacy	Position	Competence	Person
Weber*	Legal		Rational authority	Traditional authority
	Legal order	Hierarchical office	Technical knowledge, experience	Charismatic authority
Urwick†		Formal, conferred by the organization	Technical, implicit in special knowledge or skill	Personal, conferred by seniority or popularity
Simon‡	Authority of legitimacy, social approval	Authority of sanctions	Authority of confidence (technical competence)	Techniques, persuasion (as distinct from authority)
Bennis§		Role incumbency	Knowledge of performance criteria	Knowledge of the human aspect of administration
Presthus¶	Generalized deference toward authority	Formal role or position	Technical expertise	Rapport with subordinates, ability to mediate individual needs

*Max Weber, *The Theory of Social and Economic Organization*, A. M. Henderson and Talcott Parsons, trans., Talcott Parsons (ed.), Glencoe, Ill: Free Press, 1947, pp. 328, 339.

†L. Urwick, *The Elements of Administration*, London, 1944, p. 42.

‡Herbert A. Simon, "Authority," in Conrad M. Arensberg et al. (eds.), *Research in Industrial Human Relations*, New York, 1957, pp. 104–106; H. A. Simon et al., *Public Administration*, New York: Knopf, 1950, pp. 189–201.

§Warren G. Bennis, "Leadership Theory and Administrative Behavior: The Problem of Authority," *Administrative Science Quarterly*, vol. 4, pp. 288–289, 1959.

¶Robert V. Presthus, "Authority in Organizations," *Public Administration Review*, vol. 20, pp. 88–91, 1960.

Source: Robert L. Peabody, "Perceptions of Organizational Authority: A Comparative Analysis," *Administrative Science Quarterly*, vol. 6, no. 4, p. 467, March 1962.

According to Peabody, bases of formal authority (hierarchical authority, legitimacy, position, and office) are distinguished from sources of functional authority. Examples of the latter are professional competence, experience, and human relations skills. Peabody examined and compared perceptions of the bases for authority in three public service organizations: a police department, a welfare office, and an elementary school. A summary of his findings appears in Table 7-2. An overview of this table indicates that teachers seem to value authority of competence over authority of person, position, or legitimacy. Peabody offers the following explanation:

Perhaps the most striking contrast between these three public service agencies was the relative importance attached to authority of professional competence in the elementary school. Almost half of the twenty-member school staff singled out this basis

Table 7-2 Perceptions of the Bases of Authority in Three Public Service Organizations

Bases of authority	Police department, % (N = 33)	Welfare office, % (N = 23)	Elementary school, %* (N = 20)
Authority of legitimacy			
Generalized legitimacy	12	9	10
Law, state legislation, city ordinances, the state, county, city	15	17	15
Administrative codes, rules, regulations, manuals	0	17	0
Governing boards, policies of board	0	0	10
Authority of position			
Top external executive or executives, organization as a whole†	0	17	15
Top internal executive, ranking officers, administration as a whole‡	27	13	30
Immediate supervisor	9	39	0§
Inherent in position or job characteristics	30	26	15
Authority of competence			
Professional or technical competence, experience	15	22	45
Authority of person			
Personal characteristics or way in which authority is exercised	42	13	15
Other sources	6	4	0
No source supplied	18	22	15

*Percentages total more than 100 percent because some respondents indicated more than one base of authority.

†The category of "top *external* executive" included the chief executives of the parent organizations, for example, the county manager, director of public welfare, city manager, and school superintendent.

‡The category of "top *internal* executive" included the police chief, the district director, and the principal.

§Coded as "top *internal* executive" in the case of the elementary school.

Source: Robert L. Peabody, "Perceptions of Organizational Authority: A Comparative Analysis," *Administrative Science Quarterly,* vol. 6, no. 4, p. 477, March 1962.

as compared with 22 per cent of the welfare workers and only 15 per cent of the police officers. In part this was related to the fact that 75 per cent of the school staff had had graduate training, including nine teachers with the equivalent of master's degrees or beyond. Furthermore, all school staff members except the secretary and the custodian belonged to two or more professional organizations, as compared with about half the members of the police department and about one-quarter of the welfare workers who belonged to one or more professional organizations. While the principal of this school played a more passive "democratic" leadership role than either the police chief or the district director, his position or the school administration as a whole was the next most frequently mentioned source of authority in the school. The diffusion of authority which seemed to characterize this school may be the dominant pattern of authority relations in such highly professionalized organizations as research institutions, psychiatric and medical clinics, and universities.[8]

Of similar significance is the strong support among elementary school teachers for position authority as opposed to authority of person. Current supervisory trends do not substantiate this finding, and one can interpret the wide teacher recognition of position authority as a vestige of classical and contemporary supervision. Human resources supervision relies heavily on competence and person as sources of authority. Though the bases of authority remain somewhat stable in human resources supervision, the authority actors change as function changes. Hartmann describes the fluid nature of functional authority as follows:

> One of the most important characteristics of functional authority is its relativity. Authority of this kind is always dependent on the successful accomplishment of given ends. Performance is the immediate judge and executioner of such authority.
>
> Actually, the concept of functional authority makes it hard to understand why there should be hierarchies at all. The functional interplay of the productive process has an intrinsic order inasmuch as the specific contributions of all productive agents are geared to the exigencies of the over-all task. But there is nothing intrinsic to these functions (qua functions) to suggest that they should be ranked in such a way that some of these contributions should be subordinate to others.[9]

The elimination of an educational hierarchy appeals to many, particularly to professionally oriented teachers. Hierarchy however does offer stability to schools and provides continuity over time. Human resources supervision recognizes and supports legitimate and position authority, but it stresses and attempts to develop competence and person authority. Mary Parker Follett captures the spirit of authority systems in human resources supervision as follows:

> Another corollary from this conception of authority and responsibility as a moment in interweaving experience is that you have no authority as a mere left-over. You cannot take the authority which you won yesterday and apply it today. . . . In the ideal organization authority is always fresh, always being distilled anew.[10]

THE EROSION OF AUTHORITY BASES FOR ADMINISTRATORS AND SUPERVISORS

Authority bases for those who administer and for those who supervise in our schools are changing, shifting, and, in many cases, diminishing. Particularly susceptible to change and erosion is the principal's position. The principal at one time proudly possessed rather strong credentials as the legal and legitimate head

---

[8] Ibid., pp. 480–481.

[9] Heinz Hartmann, *Authority and Organization in German Management*, Princeton, N.J.: Princeton, 1959, p. 284.

[10] Henry C. Metcalf and L. Urwick, *Dynamic Administration: The Collected Papers of Mary Parker Follett,* New York: Harper, 1942.

of the school, in having broad powers by virtue of his or her *position* to impose sanctions and rewards, in displaying superior *competence* as a remarkable teacher, and in being a rather persuasive, if not paternal, personality.

As the technical structure (the teaching and educational program structure) increases in complexity and diversification, teachers by virtue of competence and person authority have assumed more responsibility for these areas. This increase in educational sophistication has required administrative arrangements beyond the traditional definition of the principal's role. Thus new positions and new policies are formed or added (on legitimate and position-authority bases) above the principal's position and located in the central office. The former trend is suggested by growth of the teacher autonomy movement and the latter by increases in central office staffs.

THE BASES OF SUPERVISORY POWER

It seems useful to consider authority as a broad basis for action not directed at any one or another individual. Power, on the other hand, at least in an administrative sense, is directed at winning individual or group compliance to superiors in the organization.[11]

French and Raven identify and describe five bases for the social power which person O can exert over person P:

> (a) reward power, based on P's perception that O has the ability to mediate rewards for him; (b) coercive power, based on P's perception that O has the ability to mediate punishments for him; (c) legitimate power, based on the perception by P that O has a legitimate right to prescribe behavior for him; (d) referent power, based on P's identification with O; (e) expert power based on the perception that O has some special knowledge or expertness.[12]

Reward power is a particular characteristic of benevolent but paternalistic administrative and supervisory environments in schools. Rewards, of course, need to be acceptable to teachers or to be desired by them. Pay increase, recognition, special favors, better schools, favorable work assignments and schedules, better equipment, and so on, are among the reward incentives available to administrators. Reward power may also provide relief from disagreeable circumstances. *Coercive power* is simply the ability to impose sanctions on teachers. Coercive power systems are the reverse of reward power systems. They often go hand in hand. The department budgets of chairpersons who comply with the wishes of the principal are increased. If they defy the wishes of the principal, their department budgets are cut, and so on.

---

[11] This definition is not limited to compliance between and among superordinates and subordinates. Teacher A may have a powerful influence on teacher B and thus be assured of teacher B's reliable compliance, yet both are officially at the same hierarchical level.

[12] J. R. P. French, Jr., and B. Raven, "The Bases of Social Power," in D. Cartwright and A. F. Zander (eds.), *Group Dynamics: Research and Theory,* 2d ed., Evanston, Ill.: Row, Peterson, 1960, p. 612. In more recent work Raven speaks of a sixth source of social power he calls *informational power.* See, for example, Raven, "Social Influence and Power," in I. D. Steiner and M. Fishbein (eds.), *Current Studies in Social Psychology,* New York: Holt, 1965, pp. 371–382.

Expert power, a concept very similar to the competence authority base, is the ability to command compliance on the basis of professional knowledge, information, and skills. Administrators and supervisors who are able to command the admiration and respect of others operate from a *referent power base.* This power source is often a result of expert power—that is, we respect and admire an individual's competence. Referent power is nevertheless conceptually independent of expert power. Many supervisors gain the support of others simply because they are admired as people.

Legitimate power refers to an administrative prerogative of command and influence as a right of the office. When the new teacher meets the superintendent at the September orientation tea, be assured that the new teacher understands fully (and understandably exaggerates) the concept of legitimate power.

BASES OF SUPERVISORY POWER, SATISFACTION, AND PERFORMANCE

In an attempt to answer the question "Why do people comply with the requests of supervisors, and how are these reasons related to organizational effectiveness and individual satisfaction?" Bachman, Bowers, and Marcus[13] examined the bases of supervisory power in five organizational settings. The investigators asked subordinates why they complied with their supervisor's wishes. Additional measurements were obtained for worker satisfaction and, in three of the organizations, for worker performance. Table 7-3 shows the mean ratings of bases of power for each of the five organizations on each of the five power variables. Note that power variables are adopted from French and Raven.

The investigators observe that the most important reason for complying with the wishes of superiors was response to legitimate power and expert power. Re-

[13] Jerald D. Bachman et al., "Bases of Supervisory Power: A Comparative Study in Five Organizational Settings," in Arnold S. Tannenbaum (ed.), *Control in Organizations,* New York: McGraw-Hill, 1968, p. 229.

Table 7-3   Mean Ratings of Bases of Power*

Bases of power	Organizational settings				
	1 Branch offices	2 Colleges	3 Insurance agencies	4 Production work units	5 Utility company work groups
Legitimate	4.1	3.6	3.3	3.4	4.7
Expert	3.5	4.1	3.8	3.4	3.0
Referent	2.9	3.5	2.5	2.7	2.1
Reward	2.7	2.3	2.8	2.8	2.7
Coercive	1.9	1.6	1.8	2.3	2.5

*All ratings have been adjusted so that a value of 5.0 represents the highest possible rating and 1.0 represents the lowest possible rating. Respondents in organizational settings 1, 2, and 5 used a ranking procedure; those in settings 3 and 4 used a procedure that permitted independent ratings of the five bases of power.

Source: Jerald D. Bachman et al., "Bases of Supervisory Power: A Comparative Study in Five Organizational Settings," in A. S. Tannenbaum (ed.), *Control in Organizations,* New York: McGraw-Hill, 1968, p. 234.

ferent and reward power were cited less often, with coercive power the least likely reason for compliance. This trend seems more pronounced for organizations described as professional—the branch office, the college, and the insurance agency. Public schools would be expected to respond similarly.

Correlations between the five bases of supervisory power and measures of satisfaction with the supervisor or with the job appear in Table 7-4.

This table shows that expert power and referent power seem to provide the strongest and most consistent positive correlation with worker satisfaction. Coercive power, particularly for the educational organizations studied, draws the most negative correlation with satisfaction. The investigators summarize their findings as follows:

> This summary of data obtained in five organizational studies has provided a number of fairly consistent findings. (1) Legitimate power was rated one of the two most important bases of power; however, it did not seem a consistent factor in organizational effectiveness, nor was it related significantly to total amount of control. (2) Expert power was the other very prominent basis of power, and it was strongly and consistently correlated with satisfaction and performance. Of the five bases, expert power was most positively related to total amount of control. (3) Referent power was of intermediate importance as a reason for complying with a supervisor's wishes, but in most cases it was positively correlated with criteria of organizational effectiveness. In two sites it was significantly and positively related to total amount of control. (4) Reward power was also of intermediate importance; in this case the correlations with organizational effectiveness and with total control were not consistent. (5) Coercive power was clearly the least prominent reason for compliance; moreover, this basis of power was often negatively related to criteria of effectiveness and in two cases negatively related to total amount of control.[14]

In another study using the French and Raven formulation, Bachman, Smith, and Slesinger[15] examined the relationship among bases for social power and

[14] Ibid., p. 236.
[15] Jerald D. Bachman et al., "Control, Performance, and Satisfaction: An Analysis of Structural and Individual Effects," in Arnold S. Tannenbaum, op. cit., p. 213.

Table 7-4 Correlations with Satisfaction Measures

Bases of power	Organizational settings				
	1 Branch offices (N = 36)	2 Colleges (N = 12)	3 Insurance agencies (N = 40)	4 Production work units (N = 40)	5 Utility company work groups (N = 20)
Legitimate	−.57*	−.52	.04	.40†	−.35
Expert	.69*	.75*	.88*	.67*	.30
Referent	.75*	.67†	.43†	.57*	.11
Reward	−.57*	−.80*	.48*	.27	−.12
Coercive	−.31	−.70†	−.52*	.01	−.23

*$p < .01$, two-tailed.
†$p < .05$, two-tailed.
Source: Jerald D. Bachman et al., "Bases of Supervisory Power: A Comparative Study in Five Organizational Settings," in A. S. Tannenbaum (ed.), Control in Organizations, New York: McGraw-Hill, 1968, p. 235.

Table 7-5   Power, Performance, and Satisfaction

Bases of manager's power	Mean standardized performance	Mean satisfaction with manager
Referent	.40*	.75*
Expert	.36*	.69*
Reward	-.55†	-.51†
Coercive	-.31	-.71†
Legitimate	-.17	-.57†

Note: Sell entries are product-moment correlation.
*$p < .05$, two-tailed.
†$p < .01$, two-tailed.
   Source: Bachman et al., "Control, Performance, and Satisfaction: An Analysis of Structural and Individual Effects," in A. S. Tannenbaum (ed.), *Control in Organizations*, New York: McGraw-Hill, 1968, p. 213.

satisfaction and performance in a professional sales office.[16] Correlations among worker perception of office-manager power, office mean-performance scores, and office mean-satisfaction scores are provided in Table 7-5. This table again suggests that referent power and expert power yield higher positive and significant correlations with performance and satisfaction, while reward, coercive, and legitimate power bases yield some significant but all negative correlations with performance and satisfaction. The investigators conclude the following:

> Total control, performance, and satisfaction with the office manager were all relatively high for the office manager whose leadership was perceived as resting largely upon his skill and expertise (expert power) and upon his personal attractiveness (referent power). Conversely, the less effective office manager was one who appeared to rely more heavily upon the use of rewards and sanctions (reward power and coercive power) and upon the formal authority of his position (legitimate power) as a formal description of his role might indicate. At the level of interoffice comparison, this overall relationship was substantial and highly consistent.[17]

In examining the relationship between influence and satisfaction in secondary schools, Hornstein and his associates conclude:

> These data, which are in full accord with the findings of previous studies, suggest that the effects of superior-subordinate relations in school systems are very much like those of various industrial, sales, and voluntary organizations. Teachers report greatest satisfaction with their principal and school system when they perceive that they and their principals are mutually influential, especially when their principal's power to influence emanates from their perceiving him as an expert. Moreover, this same principal-teacher relationship is associated with a perception of higher student satisfaction.[18]

They also note that teachers' perceptions of the principal's use of coercive power were highly related to their dissatisfaction with the principal and the school and with their perceptions of students' dissatisfaction with teachers.

   [16] The salesmen in this study earned from $10,000 to $25,000 per year prior to 1961. Thirty-six branch offices of a national firm were used.
   [17] Bachman et al., op. cit., p. 225.
   [18] Harvey A. Hornstein et al., "Influence and Satisfaction in Organizations: A Replication," *Sociology of Education*, vol. 41, no. 4, p. 389, Fall 1968.

In a Canadian study which investigated sources of power used by elementary school principals and their relationship to teachers' perceptions of satisfaction and performance, Balderson notes:

> Schools with principals whose power was perceived to rest on relevant expertise received *high* scores for teacher morale, teacher satisfaction with principal's performance, and the degree to which the principal favored (1) teacher doing an effective job helping students learn, (2) teacher experimenting with new ideas and techniques, and (3) teacher suggesting ideas to improve the school. In addition these schools also received *high* scores for the degree to which teachers feel their principals are open to their ideas and the degree to which they feel their principals have delegated enough authority to teachers to enable them to do their work. Without exception, those schools with principals who were perceived to exercise coercion in attempting to influence teachers revealed the lowest scores on these measures.[19]

Studies of this sort make it difficult to determine cause and effect, but the relationship between expert authority and other factors associated with school effectiveness seems clear. Balderson concludes that "if we also note that supervisors are involved in the task of achieving better instruction by working through others, that is teachers, it seems evident from these data that the effectiveness of supervisory practice will be enhanced by the adoption of practices based on expertise,"[20] a view entirely consistent with human resources supervision.

It seems apparent that supervisory behavior which relies on functional authority and on expert and referent power bases will have positive effects on the human organization of the school. Such efforts should lead to positive effects on the school-effectiveness variables, which are outlined in the synthesizing theory of Chapter 2.

COMPLIANCE THEORY (ETZIONI)

We have given emphasis to one or another base for supervisory action, but a number of strategies, power bases, and authority systems may be appropriate, depending upon the nature of goals to be achieved and the tasks which constitute action toward the goals. The "goodness of fit" of a given compliance or *power* strategy depends upon three major variables: *goals, involvement, and task.* The four components are arranged in a formulation of compliance theory by Etzioni.[21] The components and characteristics derived from his compliance theory are summarized in Table 7-6.

The appropriateness of a given compliance strategy will depend largely on organizational costs in relation to goal achievement. If, for example, the goal is order and the task a routine one, the most efficient compliance strategy is coercive. Yet before one chooses this strategy, one must be prepared to pay the price of alienating subordinates. If it is worth the price to accomplish the goal, then the

[19] James H. Balderson, "Principal Power Bases: Some Observations," *The Canadian Administrator,* vol. 14, no. 7, pp. 3–4, 1975.

[20] Ibid., p. 5.

[21] Amitai Etzioni, *A Comparative Analysis of Complex Organizations,* New York: Free Press, 1961.

Table 7-6   The Components and Characteristics of Etzioni's Compliance Theory*

Component	Type A	Type B	Type C
Goal	Order	Economic	Cultural
Power	Coercive	Utilitarian	Normative
Involvement	Alienative	Calculative	Moral
Task	Routine	Instrumental	Expressive

*Order goals are oriented toward control of actors in the organization. Economic goals refer to increasing or maintaining output at favorable cost to the organization. Cultural goals refer to the socializing, institutionalizing, preserving, extending, and applying of value systems and life systems.

Source: Amitai Etzioni, A Comparative Analysis of Compex Organizations, New York: Free Press, 1961.

coercive strategy (at least within the limits of this formulation) is legitimate. The key, of course, rests with the time variable. Any system can absorb short periods of alienation in subordinates, but over time, alienation results in a collapse of the system. Schools, for example, can hardly operate as dynamic learning institutions with alienated students, parents, or teachers.

The goals of schools are generally considered to be predominantly cultural in nature. The tasks of teachers and students are largely expressive in that they define, legitimize, and strengthen commitment to the cultural goals of the school. Expressive tasks and cultural goals require, according to this formulation, normative compliance strategies and obtain moral commitment from school inhabitants. One can argue that each of the three goals is legitimate for schools. Human resources supervision, however, although recognizing the occasional legitimacy of each, does not view them as equally balanced, but leans heavily on the cultural, normative, expressive, and moral compliance strategies.

THE SCHOOL AS A POLITICAL SYSTEM

Earlier in this chapter we spoke of the accessibility of power in schools to those willing and able to tap appropriate sources. It is true that persons with authority derived from their positions have a distinct advantage in acquiring and using some sources of power, but nevertheless power monopolies tend not to exist. Increased reliance on functional authority, participatory decision making, and other power-equalization strategies associated with human resources supervision has enabled teachers to become more powerful. Further, as schools move farther away from bureaucratically oriented images of structure and teaching, power equalization increases.

As power equalization increases in the school, the *potential* for expressing political behavior increases. Political scientists tend to define politics as self-serving behavior, protecting one's own domain, building support through a constituency, influencing and maneuvering, and/or building coalitions.[22] The acquisition and maintenance of power seems central in their view. In contrast to this view we define *organizational politics,* after Robbins, as *internal* to the organiza-

---

[22] Political behavior associated with organizational politics differs from political behavior associated with government and political science in its broadest sense. The former is concerned with the activities of individuals inside the organization, the latter with external constituencies.

tion and as any behavior of an organizational member that is *self-serving*. In his words, "when individuals act to enhance their own position, regardless of costs to the organization or to others, they are acting politically."[23] In this context political behavior is often dysfunctional to the organization, though at times one's self-interest may coincide with organizational purposes.

One can debate the benefits and evils of political behavior in schools. To simplify matters, schools benefit when the correspondence between self and organizational interests is great and suffer when this correspondence is slight. Though political behavior may be functional at a given point in time, it is too risky to be considered as a widespread strategy. Political behavior is based on self-interest rather than organizational norms, goals, and beliefs, and though benefits accrue when the two are matched, organizational goals are likely to be sacrificed if self-interest so mandates.

But political behavior exists nevertheless, and indeed its *potential* for expression in the school *increases* as power equalization increases and as roles become more ambiguous. Faced with the prospect of increases in political behavior in the school, administrators and supervisors can slow down or suppress such behavior by reversing the trend toward power equalization and by clarification of roles. But this suggests a return to more classically and bureaucratically oriented schools—a trend not palatable to those who advocate human resources supervision. A second alternate is to "manage" political behavior so that it becomes less popular and to the extent that it exists, matches more closely school purposes.

In developing a concept of organizational politics, Rogers describes five systems found with various degrees of emphasis in all organizations: ideological, social, technical (educational), judicial (legal), and political.[24] These are illustrated in Figure 7-1. The systems are not operationally discrete but can nevertheless be readily differentiated. We suggest as a basic proposition that the more manifest the ideological, legal, educational, and social systems are, and the greater the degree of commitment to them, the less chance of dysfunctional behavior in the political system. Since many aspects of the legal system are fixed, or given, the relationship suggested above is likely to be stronger for the ideological, social, and educational systems.

To the extent that the propositions we propose are true, dysfunctional political behavior can be controlled by making more explicit and increasing commitment to the ideological, social, and educational systems. In the school, the ideological system comprises the assumptions, values, and beliefs which represent a platform from which organizational decisions are made. Theory Y assumptions, for example, as part of a school's management platform would belong in the ideological system. The social system (greatly affected by the ideological system and corresponding closely to the mediating variables described in the synthesizing theory of supervision discussed in Chapter 2) includes the attachments, rela-

---

[23] Stephen P. Robbins, *The Administrative Process Integrating Theory and Practice*, Englewood Cliffs, N.J.: Prentice-Hall, 1976, p. 64. This discussion follows closely Robbins's ideas as expressed on p. 64–66.

[24] Rolf E. Rogers, *The Political Process in Modern Organizations*, New York: Exposition Press, 1971. This reference is the source for the discussion which follows.

Figure 7-1 The school's five organization systems.

tionships, loyalties, and norms which characterize the school's human organization. The greater the group loyalty, the greater the support and trust which exists within the group and between the group and administrators and supervisors, the less likely will dysfunctional political behavior be expressed. The educational system includes the intents, assumptions, values, and beliefs which compose the school's educational platform. The more agreement which exists over educational intents, the less likely will dysfunctional political behavior be expressed.

Though one might speak idealistically of eliminating political behavior in schools, realistically the emphasis should be more on creating a better match between such behavior and the norms which constitute the school's ideological, social, and educational systems. The more explicit the norms and the greater the agreement between them, the more likely that self-interest will conform to school purposes than purposes to self-interest.

CONFLICT-HANDLING STYLES

As power becomes more widely dispersed in schools and political behavior becomes more manifest, the potential for interpersonal conflict increases accordingly. Like political behavior, conflict is now assumed to be a natural part of modern organization and indeed is at times credited with positive effects upon the organization. Positive effects aside, the school can hardly operate effectively in a state of siege, and therefore the resolution or management of interpersonal conflict and the cultivation of conflict-handling styles becomes a major concern of human resources supervision.

Following Blake and Mouton,[25] David Jamieson and Kenneth Thomas view conflict-handling styles as consisting of two critical dimensions. One dimension is concerned with the extent to which an individual attempts to satisfy the interest of the other party or partner in the conflict.[26] This is the *cooperative* dimension. A person's concern here can be described on a conceptual continuum ranging from uncooperative to cooperative. The second dimension focuses on the extent to which an individual emphasizes the satisfaction of his or her own concerns. This is the *assertiveness* dimension. A person's concern here can be described on a conceptual continuum ranging from unassertive to assertive. As illustrated in Figure 7-2, five specific conflict-handling styles, competing, accommodating,

[25] Robert Blake and Jane Mouton, *The Managerial Grid,* Houston: Gulf, 1964. See also Blake and Mouton, "The Fifth Achievement," *Journal of Applied Behavioral Science,* vol. 6, no. 4, pp. 413–426, 1970; and Blake, Mouton, and Herbert Shepard, *Managing Intergroup Conflict in Industry,* Houston: Gulf, 1964.

[26] David W. Jamieson and Kenneth W. Thomas, "Power and Conflict in the Student-Teacher Relationship," *Journal of Applied Behavioral Science,* vol. 10, no. 3, pp. 321–336, 1974.

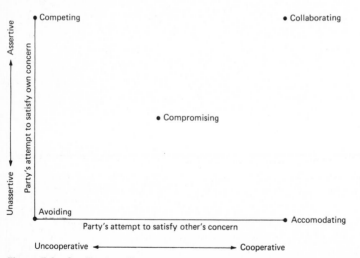

Figure 7-2 Conflict handling modes, plotted according to party's attempt to satisfy own and other's concern. *(Reproduced by special permission from David W. Jamieson and Kenneth W. Thomas, "Power and Conflict in the Student-Teacher Relationships," Journal of Applied Behavioral Science, vol. 10, no. 3, p. 326, 1974.)*

avoiding, collaborating, and compromising, can be identified from combinations of the two dimensions.

Each of the styles is based on certain assumptions and is characterized by distinctive actions.[27] Styles characterized as competing are based on assumptions that differences between people are natural and can be expected, that some people have knowledge and others do not, and that some issues are right and others wrong. Therefore the supervisor owes it to herself or himself to prevail in conflicts with others whose opinions and knowledge and goals are in doubt. Further, persuasion and force are acceptable tools in resolving conflict. Competing supervisors engage in a win-lose strategy and are quite willing to endanger some relationships and to sacrifice others in order to have their personal goals realized.

Accommodating supervisors, by contrast, feel that differences drive people apart and that good relationships cannot be ignored. The slogan of accommodating supervisors is "To differ is to reject." Conflict requires that such supervisors sacrifice their personal convictions and goals in order to accommodate those of others, and, if necessary, ignore differences in order to preserve harmony. Accommodating supervisors strive to maintain relationships at any cost.

Compromising supervisors feel that at times some parties (themselves included) are obliged to set aside their own view in the interest of the majority, and that people should be allowed to express their views but they should not be allowed to block progress. Compromising supervisors will change course and alter plans if necessary but maintain enough consensus to keep moving, in the belief that motion is more important than destination and therefore decisions should be made and purpose and direction compromised in order to maintain the consensus needed to keep moving.

Collaborating supervisors believe that differences are natural and healthy and view them as neither good nor bad. Conflict requires honest confrontation and objective problem solving. Such supervisors do not see an inherent difference in their personal goals and aspirations for the school and the view of others and are hopeful that both views can be integrated into some common good.

Avoiding supervisors see no virtue in conflict and do not personally face up to it. If avoiding supervisors cannot handle conflict in some impersonal manner (relying on rules and precedents for example), they are likely to simply withdraw from the situation.

It is difficult to decide which of the conflict-handling styles is best. Often different situations require different styles. *Constant* use of the accommodating, avoiding, or competing styles, however, is not likely to be very effective. Still, when the issues are important enough for one's view to prevail, or the situation is such that the other party is not sufficiently knowledgeable, the competitive style may be necessary. Sometimes the task or issues at stake are not important and

---

[27] This discussion is based on Blake and Mouton, "The Fifth Achievement," *Journal of Applied Behavioral Science;* Jay Hall, *Conflict Management Survey,* Houston: Teleometrics, 1968; and David Kolb, Irwin Rubin, and James McIntyre, *Organizational Psychology: An Experiential Approach,* Englewood Cliffs, N.J.: Prentice-Hall, 1971.

much can be gained by emphasizing relationships, and here the accommodating style might be best. In sum, any of the conflict-handling styles might be appropriate in different circumstances.

SUMMARY

Power was described in this chapter as the energy upon which organizational decision making and functioning operate. Though many negative effects can be attributed to power abuses, care was taken to portray power, authority, and political behavior as in themselves neither good nor bad.

Authority was defined as the right to act or require others to act on behalf of school purposes. Authority is normally derived from one's position in an organization or status in a guild (profession) or social system. Power on the other hand refers to one's ability to influence the decision-making process. Though power is often derived from authority, other sources (expert and referent) were also cited.

Formal authority was differentiated from functional authority and various conceptualizations of authority were outlined. Among these were Weber's charismatic, traditional, and legal distinctions and Peabody's listing, which includes legal and position as examples of formal authority, and competence and person as examples of functional authority. The five bases of supervisory power were then discussed. These include legitimate, expert, referent, reward, and coercive. It was pointed out that expressions of power by supervisors based on expert and referent bases are positively associated with increased satisfaction and higher performance levels in subordinates. The association between use of power and level of identity of organizational members was then discussed in terms of Etzioni's compliance theory.

Power-equalization strategies such as shared decision making and reliance on functional rather than formal authority were associated with potential increases in political behavior of teachers. For organizational purposes, political behavior was described as any behavior of a teacher or other person which is self-serving. Such behavior was judged functional when matched to organizational purposes and dysfunctional when not. It was suggested in accordance with the ideas of Rolf Rogers that dysfunctional political behavior could be reduced by bringing greater commitment to the school's organizational philosophy and value system and to the intents, beliefs, and values which make up its educational platform. The chapter concluded with a discussion of five conflict-handling styles available to supervisors. These include competition, accommodation, compromise, collaboration, and avoidance.

STUDY GUIDE

Recall the concepts, ideas, and meanings associated with each of the following phrases and terms included in Chapter 7. Can you discuss each of them with a colleague and apply them to the supervisory context of your school? If you cannot, review them in the text and record the page number for future reference.

1 Acceptance theory _____
2 Assertiveness dimension _____
3 Authority _____
4 Coercive power _____
5 Compliance theory _____
6 Conflict-handling styles _____
7 Cooperative dimension _____
8 Educational system _____
9 Expert power _____
10 Formal authority _____
11 Functional authority _____
12 Ideological system _____
13 Legitimate power _____
14 Line authority _____
15 Organizational politics _____
16 Peabody's authority types _____
17 Political behavior _____
18 Political system _____
19 Power _____
20 Power and performance _____
21 Power and satisfaction _____
22 Power equalization _____
23 Referent power _____
24 Reward power _____
25 Staff authority _____
26 Weber's authority types _____

EXERCISES

1 In a typical elementary school setting the cast of characters might include teachers, students, custodians, principal-supervisor, parents, secretaries, and superintendent. What authority does each of these groups have over classroom decisions? How does this authority differ from the actual influence patterns (power) you observe?
2 Describe the political atmosphere in your school. Who are the main characters? What agendas do they have? How do they influence decision making? How does this political activity affect the supervisor's ability to use each of the five bases of supervisory power suggested by French and Raven?
3 Which of the descriptions of conflict-handling modes best fits the way you operate (or are likely to operate)?

Chapter 8

The Human Organization of Schools

The human organization of the school is the connecting link—in the synthesizing theory, the set of mediating variables—between how supervisors think, believe, and behave and the school's progress toward achievement of its goals. Further, the dynamics of the school as an organization and the organizational milieu which determines behavior in schools are also connected, for better or for worse, to the achievement of school goals by the human organization.

As an illustration, whether Johnny learns X or not depends largely upon how Johnny feels about learning X. Teachers as supervisors play a major role in affecting Johnny's learning by affecting Johnny's feelings. Our explanation of Johnny's learning suffers from lack of detail in outlining the complexities and contingencies of the matter, but our point should be clear nevertheless. Johnny's learning of X is largely affected by his concept of self, his levels of aspiration, his unique motivational orientation, the perceived relevancy of what is being offered for learning to his need structure, his level of commitment, his stage of cognitive and moral development, his previous experience with similar learning situations, his level of maturation, his value-belief system, and his interpersonal entanglements and commitments to others.

Teachers also believe in certain things, behave in certain ways, and perform at certain levels for largely the same reasons. The material presented in this chapter applies to all who compose the human organization of the school, but our emphasis will be on the teacher. We are interested in how teachers react to the initiating variable set and the effect that this reaction has on school effectiveness.

TEACHERS AND THEIR WORLD OF WORK

Teaching can be boring work for many teachers. Routine, dull, monotonous, or flat may be more appropriate descriptions. It is, of course, unfair to assume that all teachers react in the same way, for so many are hardworking, committed, and dedicated. Nevertheless, teaching is often boring to large numbers of teachers and to their students. The zip and excitement are gone.

This chapter is concerned with the problems and challenges of motivating teachers to invest their best talent in increasingly better and more effective teaching. It is based on the following assumptions: (1) poor motivation in youngsters is largely a symptom of school, teacher, and educational program problems rather than any inherent condition in those youngsters. It is probably true that *some* youngsters cannot be motivated within the limitations of what we know at this time about youngsters and schooling. Large numbers of poorly motivated youngsters, however, are indications that the school is not performing adequately. Teacher motivation, or lack of it, may be the prime trouble spot. (2) Significant changes in school effectiveness will not come about quite so much as a result of increasing salaries (according to merit or otherwise) of teachers, decreasing class size, introducing new teaching materials, demanding more academic training or certification credentials of teachers, reducing the work load, introducing clerical assistants, or using performance contracts. These are all important and can contribute a certain amount to effectiveness, but their potency cannot compare with powerful social-psychological variables such as internal commitment and motivation to work. (3) Developing highly motivated teachers should be a high priority of supervisors and administration. Simply stated, quality education and effective schools depend largely upon the presence of competent administrators, supervisors, and teachers who are committed and motivated to work.

In the introduction to Part One we spoke of the declining-enrollment problem which afflicts most schools at this time and its ancillary problem, staff stability.

In the sixties teachers were in short supply, and teacher turnover was relatively high. Teachers were not quite as hesitant as they are now about moving to another school district in order to improve their financial condition, opportunity for promotion, job assignment, or the location of their job. If a teacher had an undesirable position, the solution was to change jobs. Schools worked hard to compete for qualified teachers, and once they were hired, schools attempted to improve working conditions as a means to retain them.

We are now in a period of retrenchment and of teacher surplus. In many parts of the country, good teaching jobs are already difficult to find, and teachers are increasingly less willing to move once they obtain employment. Low turnover poses a serious problem for schools. Dissatisfied teachers are less likely to leave.

The reasons for staying on the job are too important. But if reasons for staying are limited to job security and other bread-and-butter items, large numbers of teachers may remain on the job for the wrong reasons. As a result, instructional quality is endangered. Motivation and commitment have always been important concerns of supervisors, but now, without the safety valve of turnover, they are necessities.

The world of work has enormous potential for providing individuals with enrichment, challenge, and self-development. This observation is particularly true for professionally oriented occupations such as teaching. If one accepts the premise that most teachers (at least initially) seek meaningful satisfaction from work and wish to view themselves as competent, significant, and worthwhile contributors to society, then it is easy to understand why, when confronted with work environments characterized by distrust, arbitrariness, passivity, conformity, and paternalism, they often look to recreation, hobbies, and fraternal or social groups for this satisfaction. Many seek broader alternatives as they attempt to increase their control over the reward-granting structures of schools. Still another group chooses to play the "organizational game" in hopes that they may be promoted to positions which afford more potential for meaningful satisfaction.[1]

This chapter is concerned with building motivation and commitment in teachers. Many of the decisions made in the initiating variable set of the synthesizing theory proposed in Chapter 2 will need to be evaluated with reference to their impact on teacher motivation and commitment. The chapter begins with a general analysis of human motivation and then proceeds to propose more specific theories upon which the supervisor might build strategies for developing and maintaining a high level of motivation and commitment. It is particularly important at the onset to distinguish between concepts of morale and job satisfaction as commonly associated with human relations supervision and the human resources concepts of motivation and commitment. The former concepts have to do with satisfaction derived from the *job context* and the latter, from the *work itself.* This distinction, a basic key to human resources supervision, will receive further elaboration in each of the sections which follow.

HUMAN MOTIVATION AND TEACHERS

A commonsense approach to identifying human needs would undoubtedly reveal a list of factors such as air, water, shelter, food, protection, love, acceptance, importance, success, recognition, and control. This approach provides a random and undifferentiated list, and a significant effort is required to condense it into guidelines for supervisory behavior. Abraham Maslow, the distinguished psychologist, proposed a theory of human motivation which integrates the commonsense approach with human needs. His theory can help form an operational basis for supervisory behavior.

---

[1] Fred D. Carver and Thomas J. Sergiovanni (eds.), *Organizations and Human Behavior: Focus on Schools,* New York: McGraw-Hill, 1969, p. 185.

THE MASLOW THEORY

Maslow's theory differs from other motivational formulations in that it does not consider an individual's motivation on a one-to-one basis or as a series of independent drives. Each of the human needs which the theory comprises is examined in relation to others, and they are classified and arranged into a hierarchy of prepotency. Thus before need B can be satisfied, one must first satisfy need A, and so on.

> Human needs arrange themselves in hierarchies of prepotency. That is to say, the appearance of one need usually rests on the prior satisfaction of another, more prepotent need. Man is a perpetually wanting animal. Also no need or drive can be treated as if it were isolated or discrete; every drive is related to the state of satisfaction or dissatisfaction of other drives.[2]

Maslow proposed a hierarchy of needs consisting of five levels. Specific need dimensions which compose each of the five levels are bound together by similarities in description, but, more importantly, by similarities in potency potential. Essentially, the most prepotent need occupies, and to a certain extent monopolizes, an individual's attention, while less prepotent needs are minimized. When a need is fairly well satisfied, the next prepotent need emerges and tends to dominate the individual's conscious life. Gratified needs, according to this theory, are not active motivators of behavior. Douglas McGregor describes each of the five Maslow levels and the prepotency feature of the theory simply and concisely as follows:[3]

Physiological Needs

> Man is a wanting animal—as soon as one of his needs is satisfied, another appears in its place. This process is unending. It continues from birth to death.

> Man's needs are organized in a series of levels—a hierarchy of importance. At the lowest level, but pre-eminent in importance when they are thwarted, are his *physiological needs.* Man lives for bread alone, when there is no bread. Unless the circumstances are unusual, his needs for love, for status, for recognition are inoperative when his stomach has been empty for a while. But when he eats regularly and adequately, hunger ceases to be an important motivation. The same is true of the other physiological needs of man—for rest, exercise, shelter, protection from the elements.

> *A satisfied need is not a motivator of behavior!* This is a fact of profound significance that is regularly ignored on the conventional approach to the management of people. Consider your own need for air: Except as you are deprived of it, it has no appreciable motivating effect upon your behavior.

Safety Needs

> When the physiological needs are reasonably satisfied, needs at the next higher level begin to dominate man's behavior—to motivate him. These are called *safety needs.*

---

[2] Abraham H. Maslow, "A Preface to Motivation Theory," *Psychosomatic Medicine,* vol. 5, p. 85, 1953. See especially his *Motivation and Personality,* New York: Haper & Row, 1954.

[3] Douglas McGregor, *The Human Side of Enterprise,* New York: McGraw-Hill, 1960, pp. 36–39.

They are needs for protection against danger, threat, deprivation. Some people mistakenly refer to these as needs for security. However, unless man is in a dependent relationship where he fears arbitrary deprivation, he does not demand security. The need is for the "fairest possible break." When he is confident of this, he is more than willing to take risks. But when he feels threatened or dependent, his greatest need is for guarantees, for protection, for security.

The fact needs little emphasis that, since every industrial employee is in a dependent relationship, safety needs may assume considerable importance. Arbitrary management actions, behavior which arouses uncertainty with respect to continued employment or which reflects favoritism or discrimination, unpredictable administration of policy—these can be powerful motivators of the safety needs in the employment relationship at *every level,* from worker to vice president.

Social Needs

When man's physiological needs are satisfied and he is no longer fearful about his physical welfare, his *social needs* become important motivators of his behavior—needs for belonging, for association, for acceptance by his fellows, for giving and receiving friendship and love.

Management knows today of the existence of these needs, but it often assumes quite wrongly that they represent a threat to the organization. Many studies have demonstrated that the tightly knit, cohesive work group may, under proper conditions, be far more effective than an equal number of separate individuals in achieving organizational goals.

Yet management, fearing group hostility to its own objectives, often goes to considerable length to control and direct human efforts in ways that are inimical to the natural "groupiness" of human beings. When man's social needs—and perhaps his safety needs, too—are thus thwarted, he behaves in ways which tend to defeat organizational objectives. He becomes resistant, antagonistic, uncooperative. But this behavior is a consequence, not a cause.

Ego Needs

Above the social needs—in the sense that they do not become motivators until lower levels are reasonably satisfied—are the needs of greatest significance to management and to man himself. They are the *egoistic needs,* and they are of two kinds:

    1 Those needs that relate to one's self-esteem—needs for self-confidence, for independence, for achievement, for competence, for knowledge.
    2 Those needs that relate to one's reputation—needs for status, for recognition, for appreciation, for the deserved respect of one's fellows.

    Unlike the lower needs, these are rarely satisfied; man seeks indefinitely for more satisfaction of these needs once they have become important to him. But they do not appear in any significant way until physiological, safety, and social are all reasonably satisfied.

The typical industrial organization offers few opportunities for the satisfaction of these egoistic needs to people at lower levels in the hierarchy. The conventional methods of organizing work, particularly in mass-production industries, give little heed to these aspects of human motivation. If the practices of scientific management were deliberately calculated to thwart these needs, they could hardly accomplish this purpose better than they do.

Self-fulfillment Needs

Finally—a capstone, as it were, on the hierarchy of man's needs—there are what we may call the needs for *self-fulfillment.* These are the needs for realizing one's own potentialities, for continued self-development, for being creative in the broadest sense of that term.

It is clear that the conditions of modern life give only limited opportunity for these relatively weak needs to obtain expression. The deprivation most people experience with respect to other lower-level needs diverts their energies into the struggle to satisfy those needs, and the needs for self-fulfillment remain dormant.

Although McGregor's analysis forces the needs into specific steps, Maslow considered all of them as being somewhat interdependent and, in fact, overlapping. It is nevertheless useful, at least conceptually, to consider human needs as being arranged into fairly delimited prepotency levels.

THE IMPORTANCE OF AUTONOMY

Some controversy exists as to whether needs which are at the lower levels of the hierarchy are ever activated enough to be considered work motivators. Porter,[4] for example, in adopting the Maslow hierarchy of needs for his research, has eliminated physiological needs from the list. Presumably, Porter feels that in our society this category lacks the prepotency to motivate behavior for most people. He substitutes instead a category of needs labeled "autonomy." The Porter modification seems to have particular relevance to education, for while physiological needs have tended to depreciate in importance,[5] teachers and students have expressed a demand for control over their work environment and, indeed, over their destiny. The need for autonomy which many educational participants express is based on the principle of self-government, self-control, and self-determination. Teachers, in particular, display formidable credentials in terms of professional expertness as justification for expression of this need.

In Figure 8-1 we use Porter's revision of the Maslow categories to illustrate the hierarchical relationships which constitute the theory of human needs.

THE PARTICIPATION AND PERFORMANCE INVESTMENTS

A basic principle in motivation theory is that people invest themselves in work in order to obtain desired returns or rewards.[6] Examples of that investment are time, physical energy, mental energy, creativity, knowledge, skill, enthusiasm,

---

[4] Lyman Porter, "Attitudes in Management: Perceived Deficiencies in Need Fulfillment as a Function of Job Level," *Journal of Applied Psychology,* vol. 46, p. 375, 1962.

[5] Basic provision for needs at this level seems largely guaranteed in our society.

[6] This discussion of participation and performance investments follows closely that which appears in T. J. Sergiovanni and David Elliott, *Educational and Organizational Leadership in Elementary Schools,* Englewood Cliffs, N.J.: Prentice-Hall, 1975, p. 138. See also T. J. Sergiovanni, "New Evidence on Teacher Morale," *North Central Association Quarterly,* vol. 42, no. 3, pp. 259–266, 1968.

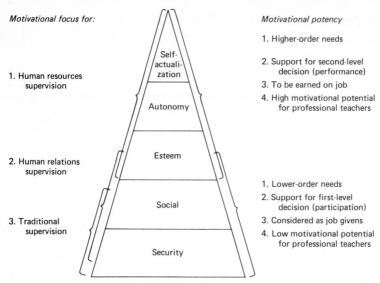

Motivational focus for:

1. Human resources supervision

2. Human relations supervision

3. Traditional supervision

Self-actuali-zation

Autonomy

Esteem

Social

Security

Motivational potency

1. Higher-order needs
2. Support for second-level decision (performance)
3. To be earned on job
4. High motivational potential for professional teachers

1. Lower-order needs
2. Support for first-level decision (participation)
3. Considered as job givens
4. Low motivational potential for professional teachers

Figure 8-1 The hierarchy of needs: A motivational focus for supervision.

and effort. Returns or rewards can take a variety of tangible and intangible forms, including money, respect, comfort, a sense of accomplishment, social acceptance, and security. It is useful to categorize expressions of investment in work as being of two types: first, a *participation* investment and, second, a *performance* investment.

The participation investment is required of all teachers and includes all that is necessary for the teacher to obtain and maintain satisfactory membership in the school. Meeting classes, preparing lesson plans, obtaining satisfactory-to-good evaluations from supervisors, following school rules and regulations, attending required meetings, bearing her or his fair share of committee responsibility, projecting an appropriate image to the public—in short, giving a fair day's work for a fair day's pay. Teachers not willing to make the participatory investment in work find themselves unacceptable to administrators *and* other teachers. On the other hand, one cannot command teachers to give more of themselves—to go beyond the participatory investment. In return for the participatory investment, teachers are provided with such benefits as salary, retirement provisions, fair supervision, good human relations, and security. In a sense, we are describing the traditional legal work relationship between employer and employee. We can think of no great institution in our society and no great achievements that have resulted from merely the traditional legal work relationship. Greatness has always been a result of employers' and employees' exceeding the limits of this relationship.

The performance investment exceeds the limits of the traditional legal work relationship. Here, teachers give far more than one can "reasonably expect," and in return they are provided with rewards that permit them to enjoy deep satisfaction with their work and themselves. When we speak of motivation to work, we speak of providing incentives that evoke the performance investment from teachers. It is important to distinguish between the kinds of return or rewards which evoke each of these investments. One does not exceed the limits of the traditional legal work relationship for more rewards of the kind one has been receiving. Supervisors and administrators cannot buy this second investment with more money, privileges, easier and better working conditions, and improved human relationships. These are important incentives as we shall see, but their potency is limited.

As we look to the needs hierarchy as a framework for prescribing the scope and content of supervisory behavior, it is helpful to visualize needs as falling into two categories: those described as lower-order needs (security, social, and, to some extent, esteem), and those described as higher-order (esteem, autonomy, and self-fulfillment), as illustrated in Figure 8-1. The lower-order needs are those which are available to teachers as they make the participation investment in schools. The school exchanges money, benefits, position, friendship, protection, interpersonal gratification, and the like, for satisfactory participation of teachers.

The higher-order needs are those whose fulfillment is exchanged for service which teachers give to the school and its clients as a result of the performance investment. Teachers tend not to be concerned with the pursuit of higher-order needs without consistent and considerable satisfaction of the lower-order needs. Since meaningful satisfaction of the esteem, autonomy, and self-fulfillment variety is intimately connected to performance, teachers will need to earn rewards of this kind through efforts toward the achievement of school goals. Supervisors who rely on reward structures characteristic of the higher-order needs are tapping potent motivational levels in teachers.

The motivational base for human resources supervision consists of needs of each of the five levels but focuses on those which we describe as higher-order. The limited motivational basis for traditional and, to some extent, contemporary supervision is totally inadequate for providing personal and professional growth opportunities which professionally oriented teachers seek.

COMPETENCE AND ACHIEVEMENT: PROFESSIONAL MOTIVES

Maslow's theory provides an integrated view of interdependent need structures, but some scholars have tended to focus on one need, often to the exclusion of other needs. Two such efforts seem to have particular relevance to understanding teacher behavior and teacher need. One effort explores in detail the competence motive—the desire for mastery—and the other, the achievement motive—the desire for success. The first effort, developed and popularized by Robert White,[7] presumes that people wish to understand and control their environment and wish to be active participants in this environment. This need is traced by White to early infancy and childhood experiences and is observed in the seemingly random and endless searching, feeling, tinkering, exploring, and investigating which

---

[7] Robert W. White, "Motivation Reconsidered: The Concept of Competence," *Psychological Review,* vol. 66, no. 5, pp. 297–333, 1959.

characterize this age. White claims that the years 6 to 9 are critical ones in developing this motive. If early experiences prove successful, people are likely to continue developing and extending their competence motives. As adults, they behave in ways which permit them to test and reconfirm the adequacy of their competence. The competence test reoccurs as successes are compiled, and each new test is usually at a level which is more challenging than that of a person's previous success.[8]

Many teachers have lost the capacity to strive for competence largely because of a history of failure. They are less ready to try something new or to undertake a more difficult assignment, for fear of additional failure. Schools benefit by developing and encouraging the competence motive, since teachers and other professional workers typically express a desire for job mastery and professional growth. A useful exercise for readers is to identify those aspects of the curriculum, the classroom management system, and the school management system which prohibit, delimit, or otherwise frustrate the opportunity for teacher and students to develop, express, and confirm the competence motive. When this motive is reinforced in teachers, personal satisfaction for the human organization and high-quality performance for the human school can be expected.

The second need, the achievement motive, is one studied intensively by David C. McClelland.[9] In commenting on McClelland's work, Gellerman describes a person who is "blessed" or "afflicted" with high need for achievement as follows:

> He tries harder and demands more of himself, especially when the chips are down. Consequently, he accomplishes more. We find, for example, that college students who have a strong achievement drive will usually get better grades than equally bright students with weaker needs for achievement. Executives "on their way up" in their companies are usually driven by stronger achievement needs than those who do not rise so quickly. The stronger the achievement drive, the greater the probability that the individual will demand more of himself.
>
> *Perhaps the most fascinating aspect of the achievement motive is that it seems to make accomplishment an end in itself.* If anything, it is the person who has little achievement motivation who expects a tangible reward for greater effort. While the achievement-motivated person does not spurn tangible rewards and even has a rather unexpected use for them, they are not really essential to him, either. He takes a special joy in winning, in competing successfully with a difficult standard; this means more to him than money or a public pat on the back. He is not an altruist: He simply finds enough delight in doing difficult things that he does not need to be bribed to do them.[10]

Teachers with a strong need for achievement have much to contribute to school effectiveness. They display an entrepreneurial behavior pattern which McClelland describes as being characterized by: (1) moderate risk taking as a func-

[8] As people perceive themselves as becoming increasingly competent, they evoke the self-fulfilling prophecy.

[9] David C. McClelland et al., *The Achievement Motive,* New York: Appleton-Century-Crofts, 1953; also, David C. McClelland, *The Achieving Society,* Princeton, N.J.: Van Nostrand, 1961.

[10] Saul Gellerman, *Motivation and Productivity,* New York: American Management Association, 1963, p. 124.

tion of skill rather than chance, (2) energetic or novel instrumental activity, (3) individual responsibility and accountability for behavior, (4) the need for knowledge of results—or for money as a *measure of success,* and (5) anticipation of future possibilities.[11]

Teachers with a strong need for achievement demand a great deal from the school. They need opportunities to display behavior manifestations which McClelland describes above and resist attempts to limit this behavior. Often if achievement needs cannot be expressed in the school, an individual seeks expression (1) organizationally in a "negative" fashion, (2) extraorganizationally in teacher associations and unions, or (3) in noneducational organizations and institutions. Teachers with a strong need for achievement can often be troublesome for many administrators and supervisors, but they have the potential to give fully and in a spirit of excellence to the school and its efforts.

MOTIVATING TEACHERS: SOME EVIDENCE

What do teachers want from their jobs? What do teachers need in order to be stimulated to extraordinary performance? Do needs and wants vary as the years go by? Do teachers at different career stages, different age levels, and of different sexes vary in their perception of needs? Is there an "overkill" approach to need fulfillment—that is, do we provide teachers with too much of one or another kind of satisfaction? What is the relationship between needs and wants and job satisfaction and job dissatisfaction? Are these related to increases or decreases in performance? Can the reward system currently available to teachers adequately provide for their needs? These and other questions are considered as we examine some evidence related to the important topic of satisfaction and need fulfillment in teaching. Our treatment of this subject is far less than definitive. More questions are raised than answered. Nevertheless, our hope is that supervisors will come to better understand the problems of human motivation as they relate to teachers and students.

THE NEED-DEFICIENCY CONCEPT

As those who supervise approach the problem of motivation through the Maslow need hierarchy, an early concern or question that comes to mind is the identification of the present level of focus or operation for most teachers.[12] At which levels are teachers adequately provided for, and where do the largest gaps exist?

In one attempt to measure need levels of educators, teachers and administrators in a school district were asked to report on perceptions of need deficiencies in their work environment.[13] The educators responded to a 13-item need defi-

---

[11] McClelland, *The Achieving Society,* p. 207.

[12] The concept of individual differences, particularly as it relates to needs, applies as well to teachers as it does to students. The concept is often ignored for both groups, but more so for teachers. Teachers as a group tend to focus on one level primarily (the esteem level), but at one time or another span the Maslow hierarchy. The Maslow theory suggests that as esteem needs become more easily satiated, teachers will focus increasingly on autonomy and self-actualization need levels.

[13] Francis M. Trusty and Thomas J. Sergiovanni, "Perceived Need Deficiencies of Teachers and Administrators: A Proposal for Restructuring Teacher Roles," *Educational Administration Quarterly,* vol. 1, pp. 168–180, Autumn 1966.

ciency questionnaire which was modeled after the Maslow theory. For each item respondents were asked to indicate: (1) how much of the particular characteristic was currently available in their jobs (*actual,*) and (2) how much of this same characteristic they thought should be available in their school positions (*ideal.*) Responses were given on a 7-point scale with the item's need deficiency score determined by subtracting *actual* response from *ideal* response. Thus an *actual* response of 3 to the social-need item "the opportunity to develop close friend-ships in my school position" subtracted from an *ideal* response of 5 yields a need deficiency score of 2. Table 8-1 gives sample items for each of the five need categories.

The larger the perceived need deficiency for an item or for a need level, the higher the assumed index of dissatisfaction. Smaller scores, on the other hand, indicate relative satisfaction with the level of need fulfillment for that item. Some of the findings from the study are presented in Table 8-2. This table presents mean need deficiency scores for each of the Maslow-type need levels by age group of respondents and again by sex of respondents.

Note that in every case except one (the 45-and-over age group) the esteem level accounts for the largest need deficiences. In all cases, for both age and sex categories, esteem, autonomy, and self-actualization items account for larger need deficiencies than items which compose the security and social need levels. Fulfillment at the social level, for example, though a popular concern of human relations supervisors, seems not to be of concern to educators in this study at all.[14] If one views deficiencies in need as measurements of job satisfaction, then supervisors should work to restructure reward systems in schools so that they focus more adequately at the levels where the largest deficiencies exist.

Two other observations can be made in reference to the data reported in

[14] This observation may very well represent an indictment against a seeming overemphasis on human relations and against our concern for "groupiness" and togetherness in schools.

TABLE 8-1. *NEED DEFICIENCY INDEX: SAMPLE ITEMS*

Category	Item
Security	The feeling of security in my school position
Social	The opportunity, in my school position, to give help to other people
Esteem	The prestige of my school position inside the school (that is, the regard received from others in the school)
Autonomy	The opportunity, in my school position, for participation in the setting of goals
Self-actualization	The opportunity for personal growth and development in my school position

The items which constitute the Need Deficiency Index are adapted from those developed by Lyman Porter for use with business management personnel. See his "Job Attitudes in Management: I. Perceived Deficiencies in Need Fulfillment as a Function of Job Level," *Journal of Applied Psychology*, vol. 46, pp. 375–384, December, 1963.

TABLE 8-2. PERCEIVED NEED DEFICIENCIES OF EDUCATORS

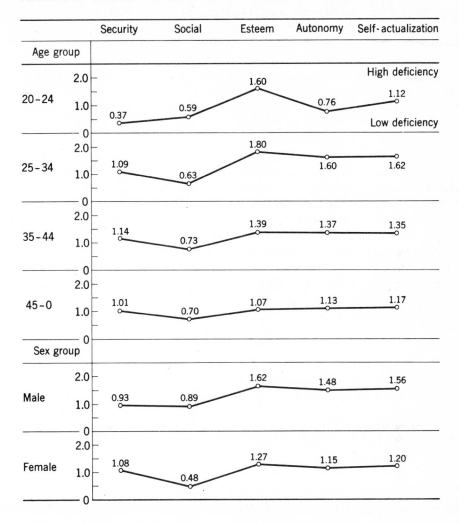

Table 8-2. The age data suggest a deficiency curve with smallest deficiencies reported by educators in the 20–24 age group and largest deficiencies in the 25–34 age group; a tapering trend is noticed in the 35–44 age group, with moderate need deficiencies reported by those 45 or over. A similar satisfaction age curve is reported by Herzberg in his 1957 comprehensive review of job satisfaction research. He notes that employees (from a variety of occupational groups) under 20 are relatively satisfied, with greatest dissatisfaction reported by those in the 20–29 age group. The curve tapers for the 30–39, with those 40 and over reporting as relatively more satisfied than others.[15] Nancy Morse observes that "in general,

[15] Frederick Herzberg et al., *Job Attitudes: Review of Research and Opinion,* Pittsburgh: Psychological Service of Pittsburgh, 1957, pp. 5–13. Herzberg further comments as follows: "From a lifetime

the shorter the time the employee has been with the company the more satisfied he is with his salary and his chances for progress in it."[16]

Generally speaking, women educators seem more satisfied with their school jobs than men do. Table 8-2 shows that, except for the security level, women perceive small need deficiencies. Each of these cases can be explained by differences in levels of aspiration and differences in individual and professional expectations which people face or feel as a result of age or sex. The 25–34 age group seems well aware that promotions and advancements occur at this point in their careers. As chances diminish, they apparently rationalize job wants and needs, lower aspirations and expectations, and accept the available and prevalent reward system. On the basis of these studies we can conclude that men seem to have higher levels of aspiration than women and, indeed, are expected to advance more than women are. As a result, men seem more difficult to please.[17] What would a study of need deficiencies conducted today reveal? Would women and men react similarly? As a group women in education would probably respond similarly, though the reaction of many would be less timid. For those who responded to the dreams of sex equality by raising their expectations for fulfillment in education to advancement to administration and supervision, their disappointing progress may have resulted in levels of dissatisfaction exceeding that of any other group.

As part of a larger study which investigated relationships between innovativeness, complexity, and job satisfaction in 36 large high schools (with between 1,500 and 2,500 students), 1,593 high school teachers responded to the Maslow-type need deficiency index described earlier.[18] The mean need deficiency scores for this group for each of the five levels of the Maslow-type hierarchy are given in Table 8-3.

of diverse learning, successive accomplishment through the various academic stages, and periodic reinforcement of efforts, the entrant to our modern companies finds that, rather than work providing an expanding psychological existence, the opposite occurs; and successive amputations of his self-conception, aspirations, learning, and talent are the consequences of earning a living."

[16] Nancy Morse, *Satisfactions in the White Collar Job,* Ann Arbor: University of Michigan Press, 1953, p. 68.

[17] James G. March and Herbert A. Simon offer a classic discussion of the relationship between aspiration, expectation, and satisfaction in *Organizations,* New York: Wiley, 1958.

[18] Fred D. Carver and Thomas J. Sergiovanni, "The School as a Complex Organization: An Analysis of Three Structural Elements," Mimeograph, University of Illinois, Department of Educational Administration, June 1968. See also, Fred D. Carver and T. J. Sergiovanni, "Complexity, Adaptability and Job Satisfaction in High Schools: An Axiomatic Theory Applied," *Journal of Educational Administration,* vol. 9, no. 1, pp. 10–31, 1971.

TABLE 8-3.   PERCEIVED NEED DEFICIENCIES OF HIGH SCHOOL TEACHERS

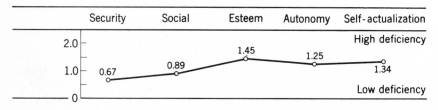

These findings suggest again that teachers are generally well satisfied with the two lower-order needs, but they express appreciably less satisfaction with respect to the three higher-order needs. The trend in need deficiency tends to follow that proposed by Maslow, but the least satisfaction for these high school teachers was reported for esteem. The investigators conclude as follows:[19]

> Relatively, the opportunity for higher-order need satisfaction is not available to teachers to the same extent as lower-order need satisfaction. While this observation does not speak to the expected or observed relationship it suggests that teachers (as a professional group) are ready to move up the Maslow-type needs hierarchy and derive satisfaction from the positions themselves. Further, the mean satisfaction scores suggest that immediately the most pressing needs of teachers is the need for esteem—internal and external to the high school. We would hypothesize that as esteem needs are met, perhaps as a result of increased salary and benefits derived through flexing of teacher organization muscles, teachers will move to satisfy autonomy and self-actualization needs. The implication for administrators is clear—provide teachers with opportunities to make independent educational decisions and encourage personal and professional development.

Of course many changes have taken place since these studies were conducted in 1966 and 1968. The economic climate of the seventies combined with declining enrollments and job shortages has produced a recession in education. Could it be that economic and other security-related conditions are now more important to teachers? Can the teacher militancy movement be interpreted as a demand for autonomy? What effect has the women's liberation movement had on raising the expectations of female teachers? Are they now less immune to job dissatisfaction? More work needs to be done in understanding more fully and in updating existing data relating to the phenomena of human need and teacher satisfaction.

THE MOTIVATION-HYGIENE THEORY

An examination of human need and an analysis of need deficiencies in teachers provides us with important concepts for understanding the bases of and need for emphasizing motivation and commitment of teachers as a key concern for supervisors. In this section a more operational approach to motivation-commitment is presented in the form of the motivation-hygiene theory as proposed originally by Frederick Herzberg and his associates.[20]

All of the paragraphs which appear below are descriptions of important features of the motivation-hygiene theory.[21] They are stated first, in an attempt to

[19] Ibid., 1971, p. 27.

[20] Frederick Herzberg, Bernard Mausner, and Barbara Snyderman, *The Motivation to Work,* New York: Wiley, 1959; Frederick Herzberg, *Work and the Nature of Man,* New York: World Publishing, 1966.

[21] This discussion follows closely Sergiovanni and Elliott, op. cit., pp. 139–148. See also T. J. Sergiovanni and Fred D. Carver, *The New School Executive: A Theory of Administration,* New York: Harper & Row, 1973, chaps. 4–8. The motivation-hygiene theory is not without its critics. See, for example, M. D. Dunnelle, J. P. Campbell, and M. D. Hakel, "Factors Contributing to Job Satisfaction and Job Dissatisfaction in Six Occupational Groups," *Organizational Behavioral and Human Performance,* vol. 2, pp. 143–174, 1967. For support, see D. A. Whitsett and E. K. Winslow, "An

sketch out the nature, scope, and potency of the theory. Their description is followed by an analysis of theoretical and research findings that provide the origins of the theory.

1   There are certain conditions in work that teachers expect to enjoy. If these conditions are present in sufficient quantity, teachers will perform adequately, but only adequately. If these conditions are not present in sufficient quantity, teachers will be dissatisfied and work performance will suffer.

2   The conditions in work which teachers expect as part of the traditional legal work relationship are called *hygienic factors*. Their absence results in teacher dissatisfaction and poor performance. Their presence maintains the traditional legal work relationship but does not motivate performance. Hygienic factors are associated with the participation investment in work.

3   The factors which contribute to teachers' exceeding the traditional work relationship are called *motivators*. The absence of motivators does not result in dissatisfaction and does not endanger the traditional work relationship. Motivational factors are associated with the performance investment in work.

4   Motivational factors and hygienic factors are different. Motivation to work does not result from increasing hygienic factors.

5   Hygienic factors are associated with the conditions of work and are extrinsic in nature. Examples are money, benefits, fair supervision, and a feeling of belonging. Motivational factors are associated with work itself and are intrinsic in nature. Examples are recognition, achievement, and increased responsibility.

6   Hygienic factors are important, for their neglect creates problems in the work environment. These problems can result in dissatisfaction and lowered performance. Taking care of the hygienic factors prevents trouble, but these factors are not potent enough to motivate people to work, to evoke the performance decision.

7   Hygienic factors meet the human need to avoid unpleasantness and hardship. Motivational factors serve the uniquely human need for psychological growth.

8   Satisfaction at work is not a motivator of performance per se, but results from quality performance. Administrators and supervisors should not use satisfaction as a method of motivating teachers, but satisfaction should be thought of as a goal that teachers seek, one that is best obtained through meaningful work.

9   Administrators and supervisors who use job satisfaction to motivate teachers are practicing human relations. This has not been proven to be an effective approach. Human relations emphasize the hygienic factors.

10   Administrators and supervisors who consider job satisfaction as a goal that teachers seek through accomplishing meaningful work and who focus on enhancing the meaningful view of work and the ability of teachers to accomplish this work are practicing human resources supervision. This has been proven to be an effective approach. Human resources development emphasizes the motivational factors.

Analysis of Studies Critical to the Motivation-Hygiene Theory," *Personnel Psychology,* vol. 20, no. 4, pp. 391–415, 1967. Our review of motivation-hygiene studies leads us to conclude that the theory is indeed appropriate for white-collar and professionally oriented workers but less appropriate for other workers.

11 True, not all teachers can be expected to respond to the motivation-hygiene theory, but most can.

In summary, the theory stipulates that people at work have two distinct sets of needs. One set of needs is best met by hygienic factors. In exchange for these factors, one is prepared to make the participatory investment—to give a fair day's work. If hygienic factors are neglected, dissatisfaction occurs, and one's performance on the job decreases to a level below the acceptable. Another set of needs is best met by the motivational factors which are not automatically part of the job but which can be built into most jobs, particularly those found in elementary schools. In return for the motivational factors, one is prepared to make the performance investment, to exceed the limits of the traditional legal work relationship. If the motivational factors are neglected, one does not become dissatisifed, but one's performance does not exceed that typically described as a fair day's work for a fair day's pay.

The Motivation-Hygiene Factors

Hygienic factors are those largely extrinsic in nature and associated with our lower-order needs, and motivational factors are those largely intrinsic in nature and associated with our higher-order needs. Now let us examine the factors themselves.

Motivation-hygiene theory results from the research of Frederick Herzberg.[22] The model for his research is an interview method whereby workers are asked to describe job events associated with satisfaction and dissatisfaction at work. Further, the effects of these feelings and events on one's performance at work are examined. Dozens of studies have been conducted using this approach with a variety of workers, from scientists to assembly-line workers, in a number of countries.[23]

In the majority of cases, studies reveal that traditional linear notions regarding satisfaction and dissatisfaction at work are in need of modification. Traditionally, it has been assumed that if a cause of dissatisfaction is identified, elimination of this cause results in job satisfaction and motivated workers. Teachers unhappy with school policies, the kind of supervision they are getting, money matters, and class scheduling will move to a state of satisfaction and motivation if these deficiencies are remedied. Motivation-hygiene studies by and large show that this is not the case. Remedying the deficiencies that cause dissatisfaction brings a person up to a level of minimum performance that includes the absence of dissatisfaction. Satisfaction and motivation are the results of a separate set of factors. The factors associated with satisfaction, but not dissatisfaction, are called motivators because of their ability to stimulate performance. The factors associated with dissatisfaction, but not satisfaction, are called hygienic because of their ability to cause trouble if neglected.[24]

[22] Herzberg et al., *The Motivation to Work.*
[23] See, for example, Frederick Herzberg, *Work and the Nature of Man,* New York: World Publishing, 1966.
[24] Frederick Herzberg, "The Motivation-Hygiene Concepts and Problems of Manpower," *Personnel Administration,* vol. 27, no. 1, p. 3, 1964.

The Motivation-Hygiene theory of job attitudes began with a depth interview study of over 200 engineers and accountants representing Pittsburgh industry. These interviews probed sequences of events in the work lives of the respondents to determine the factors that were involved in their feeling exceptionally happy and conversely exceptionally unhappy with their jobs. From a review and an analysis of previous publications in the general area of job attitudes, a two-factor hypothesis was formulated to guide the original investigation. This hypothesis suggested that the factors involved in producing job satisfaction were separate and distinct from the factors that led to job dissatisfaction. Since separate factors needed to be considered depending on whether job satisfaction or job dissatisfaction was involved, it followed that these two feelings were not the obverse of each other. The opposite of job satisfaction would not be job dissatisfaction, but rather *no* job satisfaction; and similarly the opposite of job dissatisfaction is *no* job dissatisfaction—not job satisfaction. The statement of the concept is awkward and may appear at first to be a semantic ruse, but there is more than a play with words when it comes to understanding the behavior of people on jobs. The fact that job satisfaction is made up of two unipolar traits is not a unique occurrence. The difficulty of establishing a zero point in psychology with the procedural necessity of using instead a bench mark (mean of a population) from which to start our measurement has led to the conception that psychological traits are bipolar. Empirical investigations, however, have cast some shadows on the assumptions of bipolarity; one timely example is a study of conformity and noncomformity, where they are shown not to be opposites, but rather two separate unipolar traits.

The factors Herzberg associates with motivation and hygiene are shown in Table 8-4. The findings of his original study are illustrated in Figure 8-2. Factors to the right of the zero line contribute predominantly to satisfaction, and factors to the left of this line contribute predominantly to dissatisfaction. The longer the line associated with a factor, the more often respondents cited this factor as contributing to job feelings. The greater the width of the line—in the diagram a box—the longer the duration of the attitude. Thus while respondents cited achievement more often than responsibility as a source of positive feelings about

Table 8-4   The Motivation and Hygiene Factors*

Motivation (Found in the work itself)	Hygiene (Found in the environment of work)
Achievement	Salary
Recognition	Possibility of growth
Work itself	Interpersonal relations (subordinates)
Responsibility	Interpersonal relations (superiors)
Advancement	Interpersonal relations (peers)
	Supervision—technical
	Company policy and administration
	Working conditions
	Personal life
	Status
	Job security

*The factors were identified and reported by Herzberg in F. Herzberg et al., *The Motivation to Work*, New York: Wiley, 1959.

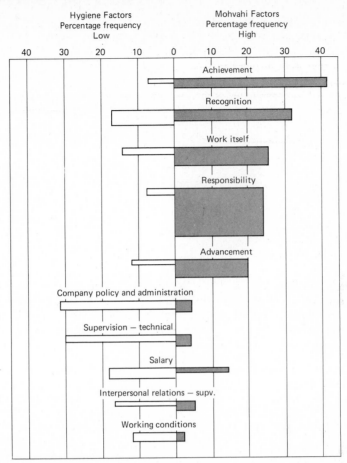

Figure 8-2 Comparison of motivation and hygiene factors. *(From Frederick Herzberg et al., The Motivation to Work, New York, Wiley, 1959.)*

a job, when responsibility was cited, the feeling lasted longer than in the case of achievement.

Achievement, recognition, work itself, responsibility, and advancement are the factors identified by Herzberg as contributing primarily to satisfaction. Their absence tends not to lead to dissatisfaction. These are the motivators—the rewards which one seeks in return for the performance investment.

Policy and administration, supervision, salary, interpersonal relationships, and working conditions are the factors that Herzberg identifies as contributing primarily to dissatisfaction. There are the hygienic factors—conditions which workers expect in return for a fair day's work.

In the separate teacher study illustrated in Table 8-5 achievement and recognition were identified as the most potent motivators.[25] Responsibility, although a

[25] Thomas J. Sergiovanni, "Factors Which Affect Satisfaction and Dissatisfaction of Teachers," *The Journal of Educational Administration*, vol. 5, no. 1, pp. 66–82, 1967.

Table 8-5 Percentages for the Frequency with Which Job Factors Contributed to High Attitudes as Compared with Low Attitudes for Teachers

Job factors	Percentage of highs NR = 142	Percentage of lows NR = 142	P
1. Achievement	30*	9	.01
2. Recognition	28*	2	.001
3. Work itself	11	8	
4. Responsibility	7*	1	.05
5. Advancement	0	1	
6. Salary	2	3	
7. Possibility of growth	6	2	
8. Interpersonal relations (subordinates)	7	20*	.01
9. Interpersonal relations (superiors)	3	4	
10. Interpersonal relations (peers)	1	15*	.001
11. Supervision—technical	1	10*	.01
12. School policy and administration	2	13*	.01
13. Working conditions	2	6	
14. Personal life	0	5*	.05
15. Status	0	0	
16. Security	0	1	

N = 72 teachers; NR = Number of responses
*Significant factor.

significant motivator, appeared in only 7 percent of the events associated with satisfaction. We do not take advantage of the motivational possibilities of responsibility in education—this factor is relatively standardized for teachers, in that responsibility does not vary very much from one teacher to another. Work itself did not appear significantly more often as a contributor to satisfaction. Apparently, elements of the job of teaching as we currently know it are inherently less than satisfying. Among these are routine housekeeping, attendance, milk money, paper work, study hall, lunch duty, and the like. The negative aspects of police, clerk, and custodial roles seem to neutralize professional teaching and guidance roles for these professionals. Poor interpersonal relations with students; inadequate, incompetent, insensitive, and close supervision; unfair, rigid, and inflexible school policies and administrative practices; poor interpersonal relations with other teachers and with parents; and incidents in their personal lives were the job factors found to contribute significantly to teachers' dissatisfaction.

Herzberg found in his original study with accountants and engineers[26] that, although recognition and achievement were mentioned most often as motivators, the duration of good feelings associated with these rewards was very short. Work and advancement seemed to have medium effects, but good feelings associated with responsibility lasted more than twice as long as those associated with work and advancement, and more than three times as long as those from achievement

[26] Herzberg et al., *The Motivation to Work.*

and recognition. Negative feelings associated with neglected hygienic factors were generally of short duration.

Teachers as Individuals

The motivation-hygiene theory provides simplified answers to rather complex questions. This is a bold theory which provides broad and general guidelines to administrators and supervisors interested in evoking the performance investment from teachers.[27] Its boldness and its broad propositions require intelligent caution in the application of the theory to practice. For example, while the theory suggests that by and large only the satisfiers motivate, it would be wrong to conclude that some people are not motivated by the dissatisfiers. Some individuals are indeed motivated by the dissatisfiers, but under ordinary circumstances it is not natural to be so motivated. The implication is that healthy individuals respond to the motivation-hygiene dynamic, while those less healthy do not. Further, healthy individuals who are deprived of work satisfactions on the job will seek these satisfactions elsewhere—at home through family membership, hobbies, community activity, sports, and the like. Attention to these aspects of life is important to all of us, but the world of work seems the more natural place for professional workers to find satisfaction for their needs of esteem, competence, achievement, autonomy, and self-fulfillment.

Teachers who seem more interested in hygienic factors than motivational factors can be categorized as follows: (1) those who have the potential for motivation seeking, but are frustrated by insensitive and closed administrative, supervisory, and organizational policies and practices; (2) those who have the potential for motivation seeking, but who decide to channel this potential into other areas of their lives; and (3) those who do not have the potential for motivation seeking on or off the job. Those in the second and third groups use their jobs as a means to achieve goals not related to the school.

The second group includes many teachers whose goals are buying a second car or a vacation house, supplementing their spouse's income to achieve a higher standard of living, putting their spouse or children through college, and so on. Men in this group often use the teaching occupation as a means to step into another job, such as coaching, counseling, or administration.[28]

The third group includes individuals who seem fixated at lower need levels. In a sense, they could be described as obsessed with avoiding unpleasantness and discomfort to the point that they have not developed the ability to seek satisfaction through the motivators and at higher need levels. Many psychologists regard this obsession as a symptom of poor mental health; if this is the case, then

[27] This discussion of teachers as individuals follows closely Sergiovanni and Elliott, op. cit., p. 147. See also T. J. Sergiovanni, "Human Resources Supervision," in Sergiovanni (ed.), *Professional Supervision for Professional Teachers,* Washington, D.C.: Association for Supervision and Curriculum Development, 1975, pp. 19–21.

[28] Simpson and Simpson maintain that semiprofessional women are far less committed to work careers than are most men of comparable attainments. They note that "a fairly mild economic pressure is often enough, however, to keep them [women] at work. Relatively few of them would face utter destitution if they stopped work. The pressure is more often the desire to maintain a standard of comparative luxury, to help the family move into a larger house, or to save toward the children's

selection procedures should be devised to identify and filter out teachers of this type. Tenured teachers of this type will need to be heavily supervised.

Teachers who have the potential for motivation seeking, but who elect to seek satisfactions of this kind outside of the school, are by and large good teachers who give honest labor in exchange for what they hope to gain from the school. Extraordinary performance is lacking among them, however, for such teachers do not have a strong commitment to the school and its purposes. Teachers of this kind will be with us for a long time, but they cannot be depended upon to substantially upgrade the nation's schools or to display much interest in becoming full partners in the school enterprise, unless they can become attracted to the motivational factors. Teachers interested primarily in hygienic factors, but who have potential for being influenced by the motivation factors, can make significant contributions to the school's work if kindly, but firmly and competently, supervised, or when combined with motivation seekers in schools with differentiated roles and responsibilities for teachers. Hygienically oriented teachers who have the potential for motivation seeking, but who are frustrated by the school and its administration are unfortunate casualties. When we deny teachers opportunities to channel motivation expressions they desire, we not only waste valuable human resources, but deny youngsters important opportunities for growth in their schooling. In general, hygienically oriented teachers think of their jobs too much in terms of salary, working conditions, supervision, status, job security, school policies and administration, and social relationships.

VROOM'S EXPECTANCY THEORY OF MOTIVATION

One approach to motivation which takes into account differences in the desires and needs of others and which does not prescribe a one best motivational strategy but which shares some features of the motivation-hygiene theory is Vroom's expectancy theory of motivation.[29] Vroom's is a contingency theory in that he views motivation as a response in a person's needs to a specific goal that person seeks. Performance on the job, in his view, is a means by which the person can achieve a personal goal. This view is consistent with human resources supervision

---

college education. . . . Work for women is no longer considered a tragedy; it is an acceptable alternative but it is not the first choice for many."

They further note: "It is true that educated women whose husbands' incomes are high often re-enter the labor force after their children are beyond early childhood, and many of these appear to be motivated by a wish for self-expression apart from economic consideration. But the need for self-expression which these women say they feel appears to be occasioned more by the boredom of finding themselves with an empty nest rather than by strong identification with the world of work."

Richard L. Simpson and Ida Harper Simpson, "Women and Bureaucracy in the Semi-Professions," in Amitai Etzioni (ed.), *The Semi-Professionals and Their Organization*, New York: Free Press, 1969, pp. 217, 218.

[29] Victor H. Vroom, *Work and Motivation*, New York: Wiley, 1964. See also Vroom, "Organizational Choice: A Study of Pre and Post Decision Processes," *Organizational Behavior and Human Performance*, vol. 1, pp. 212–225, 1966; and J. Galbraith and L. Cummings, "An Empirical Investigation of the Motivational Determinants of Task Performance: Interactive Effects Between Instrumentality—Valence and Motivation—Ability," *Organizational Behavior and Human Performance*, vol. 2, pp. 237–257, 1967, for studies which substantiate aspects of Vroom's theory.

in that it assumes that performance is a means to satisfaction rather than satisfaction being viewed as a means to performance. Since personal goals for individuals are likely to vary, no one set of motivational factors is identified. The basic components of expectancy theory are illustrated in Figure 8-3.

Basically, individual motivation is viewed as a function of a person's perception that his or her increased performance will result in certain rewards which will help him or her attain personal goals. If a teacher's goal is to be more influential in educational decision making (to attain more expert power), motivation will depend upon that teacher's perception that increased performance (volunteering for difficult curriculum work and doing a good job of it) will lead to appropriate rewards (winning the professional respect of colleagues) which will enable the teacher to achieve this goal. By the same token, another individual with personal goals of group acceptance may not be motivated to volunteer for additional work, and if assigned work, may not be motivated to perform in an extraordinary way unless that behavior is associated with group acceptance.

Since personal goals differ, rewards which appeal to some teachers may not appeal to others. It is therefore necessary, on the one hand, to individualize rewards to match personal goals which are consistent with those of the school and, on the other hand, to help build greater consistency between personal and school goals. Further, the relationship between individual performance, organizational rewards, and personal goals is not always clear to teachers, and clarification of their parts by supervisors may be necessary.

SUMMARY

This chapter focused on the human organization of the school. The human organization was considered as the connecting link (in the synthesizing theory, the set of mediating variables) between how supervisors think, believe, and behave and school progress toward the achievement of its goals. The highly motivated teacher was listed as a high-priority concern of supervisors, and it was argued that quality education is largely dependent upon the presence in schools of competent administrators, teachers, and students who are internally committed and motivated to work.

Maslow's theory of human motivation was then discussed. Needs were classified into a hierarchy of prepotency with lower-order needs identified as security, social, and aspects of esteem, and higher-order needs as esteem, autonomy, and self-fulfillment. In addition to "professional" needs, achievement and competence were discussed because of their particular relevance to teachers. The concept of need deficiency was also introduced, and studies by Porter, and Trusty and Sergiovanni were explained in an attempt to map patterns of need deficiencies in teachers.

Figure 8-3 Basic components of expectancy theory.

Teachers were described as being faced with two levels of decisions in their jobs—a participation-level decision and a performance-level decision. The participation-level decision was described as the decision to continue in the traditional legal work relationship which exists between employer and employee, and the performance-level decision as a commitment to exceed this relationship. The motivation-hygiene theory, as developed by Herzberg, was then described as a means to identify motivating factors associated with the performance decisions and hygiene factors associated with the participatory decisions. Motivation factors are concerned with aspects of the work itself, such as the amount of achievement and recognition available to teachers. Hygiene factors, on the other hand, are related to the work context and include security and general working conditions.

The discussion of the motivation-hygiene theory concluded with the caveat that though by and large only the motivation factors motivate, it would be wrong to conclude that some people are not motivated by the hygiene factors. Vroom's expectancy theory of motivation was then discussed as being a theory that is able to account for individual differences. Vroom's is a contingency theory in that he views motivation as a function of a person's perception that his or her increased performance will result in certain rewards which will help him or her attain personal goals.

STUDY GUIDE

Recall the concepts, ideas, and meanings associated with each of the following phrases and terms included in this chapter. Can you discuss each of them with a colleague and apply them to the supervisory context of your school? If you cannot, review them in the text and record the page number for future reference.

1 Achievement motive _____
2 Autonomy _____
3 Competence motive _____
4 Expectancy theory _____
5 Hierarchy of prepotency _____
6 Higher-order needs _____
7 Hygiene factors _____
8 Job context _____
9 Lower-order needs _____
10 Maslow's theory of motivation _____
11 Mediating variables _____
12 Motivation factors _____
13 Motivation-hygiene caveats _____
14 Motivation-hygiene theory _____
15 Need deficiency _____
16 Participation investment _____
17 Performance investment _____
18 Staff stability _____
19 Vroom's definition of motivation _____
20 Work itself _____

EXERCISES

1   Using the Maslow needs hierarchy, give specific examples of ways in which schools can help teachers to meet each of the five needs. As administrators and supervisors, consider the motivation question using Maslow's theory. What implications does the prepotency feature of the theory have?

2   Describe one or two teachers whom you know who are making only the participation decision at school. Contrast this with teachers who are making the performance decision.

3   The data summarized in Tables 8-2 and 8-3 were collected in 1966 and 1968. In what ways would a survey conducted today provide similar and different results? Take into account such recent developments as womens' liberation, teacher militancy, declining enrollment, and reduction in force.

4   What cautions should you keep in mind in developing motivational strategies based on Herzberg's motivation-hygiene theory?

Chapter 9

Group Effectiveness
and Supervision

It initially appears that the work of the school is accomplished by accumulations of individual efforts of students, administrators, teachers, supervisors, and other school personnel. Administrative work, for example, is done in the absence of teachers, and, indeed, administrators are often thankful for that quiet work time they have the first hour or two after classes begin. Further, students are expected to work alone, and cooperative effort is often discouraged and punished. Moreover, teachers tend to work alone, as their daily dispersion to isolated classrooms suggests.[1]

But there are many opportunities for teachers and other school members to function in groups. Formal group opportunities include grade-level meetings, curriculum councils, department meetings, and ad hoc committees. "Coffee klatches," "smokers," "old guard," and "newcomers" are labels that suggest the multitude of less formal but nevertheless potent groups that may appear in a given school. As a matter of fact, group life is a natural, necessary, and integral part of the organizational life of schools. Indeed, while the day-by-day role per-

---

[1] Teachers tend to function in their professional roles by themselves, having little direct opportunity to display their skills and techniques before colleagues. Miles refers to this phenomenon as "role performance invisibility." Matthew Miles, "Planned Change and Organizational Health, Figure and Ground," in Richard Carlson et al., *Change Processes in the Public Schools,* Eugene: University of Oregon, Center for the Advanced Study of Educational Administration, 1965, p. 24.

formance of teachers may take place in relative isolation, for many teachers, the character, content, and quality of this performance are directly related to their organizational group life.

GROUP SUPERVISION

The person-to-person pattern of supervision has been the predominant superviso-ry method since the beginning of schooling in America. Since teachers usually work alone and in physical environments which encourage isolation, supervisors function on a person-to-person basis as they move from class to class and from teacher to teacher. Two major flaws exist in person-to-person supervision: (1) this pattern resembles an inspectorial system and, as such, typically evokes negative responses from teachers,[2] and (2) this pattern locks in a one-way client-consul-tant relationship, with teachers always assuming the role of client and supervisors always assuming the role of consultant. Group patterns of supervision minimize power visibility as they replace inspection with problem solving. Further, the supervisory relationship is considered an interchangeable one, with actors assum-ing client or consultant roles as circumstances warrant and as functional authori-ty changes.

The concept of group supervision is often threatening to supervisors and other school officials. This is particularly true for those who feel they need to rely on formal authority and established hierarchical arrangements as means to pro-tect their interests and position in the school and to maintain control over subor-dinates. In our estimation, the absence of group supervision in schools is extreme-ly costly. This absence denies to the staff the maximum opportunity for personal and professional growth, frustrates the improvement of the educational program, and decreases the potential for student self-fulfillment. The cost of maintaining present person-to-person supervisory patterns is high.

"GROUP" DEFINED

Cattell describes a group as "an aggregate of organisms in which the existence of all is utilized for satisfaction of the needs of each."[3] Bass defines a group as a collection of persons which is mutually reinforcing.[4] Groups are characterized by the extent to which participants find group membership rewarding. In return for some form of need satisfaction, group members are expected to provide the group with loyalty, effort, and interest. An awareness of the relationship between rewards and investments is fundamental to understanding groups. Individual group participants will tend to become marginal group members or to withdraw

[2] Teachers may recognize and accept a hierarchy and thus attribute power and prerogatives to supervisors, but our egalitarian culture and professional norms insist that such power be displayed only minimally. High-power visibility evokes negative responses from the human organization. See our discussion of "Gouldner's model" in Chapter 3, where we consider unanticipated consequences of bureaucratic behavior.

[3] Raymond Cattell, "New Concepts of Measuring Leadership in Terms of Group Syntality," *Human Relations,* vol. 4, pp. 161–184, 1951.

[4] Bernard Bass, *Leadership, Psychology and Organizational Behavior,* New York: Harper & Row, 1960, Chap. 3.

from the group when their rewards cease or become out of proportion to their contributions to the group. Further, some individuals abandon group membership when the group is no longer potent enough to provide the kind of need satisfaction that they require. This relationship is not a balanced one. Investors must perceive that the rewards they earn as a result of their active membership exceed their investment in the group.[5] As indicated in Figure 9-1, investors need to get more out of group membership than they put into the relationship.

Many departments and other units in schools are better characterized as a collection of individuals rather than as a group.[6] Though strictly speaking a collection of teachers may qualify as a physical group if they are located in the same area of the building or as a department or grade-level group if they all teach in the same academic level or area, they do not qualify as a psychological group. In a psychological group, members share common purposes, interact with each other, perceive themselves to be a group, and obtain satisfaction of their needs as a result of group membership.

When a department or unit gets together, we can only be sure that a physical group is assembled. If only some of the teachers share common goals, interact with each other, share a group identity, and get needs met as a result of membership, then we have a psychological group within a physical group. Psychological groups are concerned with both "body and spirit"—physical groups are concerned only with body. Perhaps the deciding factor for most teachers as to whether they are merely physical members or are psychological members of a group is whether their needs are met as a result of group membership. Teachers will tend to become marginal group members or withdraw from the group when rewards cease or when rewards are not worth the contributions they are currently making to the group. In return for rewards teachers are expected to provide the group with loyalty, effort, and interest.

---

[5] Homans refers to this phenomenon as the "theory of distributive justice." See, for example, Leonard Sayles and George Strauss, *Human Behavior in Organizations,* Englewood Cliffs, N.J.: Prentice-Hall, 1966, p. 99. The theory works in either direction—the group ceases its reward granting behavior when it no longer values or requires the commitment of individuals, and individuals cease their commitment when rewards, in their view, are not sufficient to warrant their commitment.

[6] See, for example, T. J. Sergiovanni, *Handbook for Effective Department Leadership,* Boston: Allyn & Bacon, 1977, pp. 97–138.

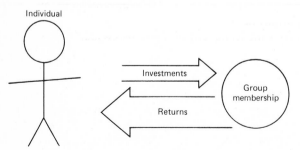

Figure 9-1 The investment exchange. Active group membership ceases (or becomes marginal) when investments in the group are equal to or exceed returns for members.

The development of a unit into a psychological group is a critically important first step, but in itself is not enough. Psychological groups are not necessarily effective work groups. Consider, for example, a group of teachers who share a common purpose, *the maintenance of things the way they are;* who interact regularly, *to discredit attempts to change their school;* who identify as a group, *the regulars;* and who find group membership comforting and satisfying, *sort of a mutual protection society.* This group indeed qualifies as a psychological group but probably does not qualify as an effective work group.

A physical group is a collection of individuals. A psychological group is a collection of individuals who share common purposes, interact with each other, perceive themselves to be a group, and who find group membership rewarding. Effective work groups are always psychological groups, but psychological groups are not always effective work groups. In an effective work group the purposes which members share are consistent with school objectives, and interaction between and among members is usually concerned with job-defined tasks, purposes, and activities. There is high identity with and commitment to school objectives, and task effectiveness is high.

PROPOSITIONS ABOUT GROUP FUNCTIONING

Let us consider several general propositions and assumptions which are basic to understanding groups.

1 Groups exist because they have to exist. Group life is a natural form of social organization for human beings. We influence groups and are influenced by groups throughout our lives. In the long run, more harm is done when schools work to frustrate and discourage group activity (among teachers *and* students) than when schools allow groups free expression.

2 Groups are neutral. In and of themselves, groups are neither good nor bad. While school groups can be powerful forces which work to achieve school goals, they can be equally powerful in working against school goals. For example, a teaching faculty with high morale may obtain satisfaction by working to frustrate school goals—and perhaps by discrediting the principal in the bargain—or by working to enhance school goals. Indeed, many student groups receive satisfaction in their dedication to frustrate the school's operation, while others are equally satisfied working for or with the school.

3 Groups have unique "personalities" which are conceptually similar to individual personalities. This group personality stems from and is composed of characteristics which individuals bring to the group. Thus, two school faculties or two departments with similar goals differ markedly because their membership differs.

4 As part of the group's personality, a group culture emerges which includes norms of behavior and a value system or belief pattern which are unique to the group. This belief pattern provides the cement which holds the group together and which regulates group behavior. We refer to the belief pattern as the group's *dynamic center.* A zone of freedom exists which permits individuals to stray somewhat from the dynamic center but still maintain group membership (see Figure 9-2). When group members move beyond the zone of freedom, they

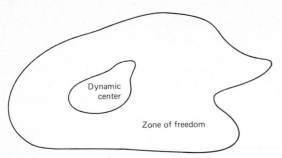

Figure 9-2   The group and its boundaries. *(From Harold Wilson et al., "The Group and Its Leaders," unpublished manuscript, Columbus: Ohio State University, Center for Educational Administration, Dept. of Education, 1963.)*

cross the group's boundary and forfeit membership. The closer a group member is to this dynamic center, the more influential that person will be. In Figure 9-3 we show various positions of group membership and levels of agreement in relation to the group's dynamic center. One who holds marginal membership in a group can improve his or her position by adopting more of the group's culture, thus moving closer to the dynamic center, or by moving the dynamic center of the group closer to himself or herself. This second strategy is difficult in that those who are removed from the dynamic center are often perceived by other group members as having little influence.

   5   Individuals behave differently when they assume roles as group members from the way they behave when they operate as free agents. Groups influence people. As a result of this influence, people behave differently—they react to group pressure. This phenomenon is suggested by Heron when he contrasts the actions and demands of workers as groups with their desires as individuals:

> The opinion polls almost always show that the most prominent desires of the individual employee relate to the most important thing in the world—*himself,* his personality, his recognition, his security, and his progress. He wants recognition, for his skills, his suggestions, his attention and energy, his performance and production.
>
>   But when he gets together with his fellow workers—who want exactly the same things—they agree almost unanimously to demand standard wage rates for all work-

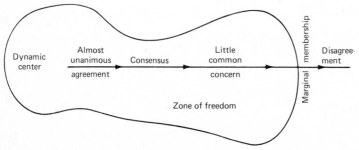

Figure 9-3   Group membership and movement. *(From Harold Wilson et al., "The Group and Its Leaders," unpublished manuscript, Columbus: Ohio State University, Center for Educational Administration, Department of Education, 1963.)*

ers on the same job, the prohibition of piecework and incentives, and uniform increases in all wage rates.

He wants fair treatment, as an individual, in job assignments and promotions. He resents favoritism or any process of selection which seems to overlook his abilities and gives the foreman job to someone less competent. He wants to be rewarded for his merit.

But in united action with his fellow workers he will demand that in promotions, layoffs, or rehirings, the principles of seniority shall strictly apply. He will stand on this demand with almost emotional devotion.[7]

As a result of this phenomenon, one may conclude that group pressures result in group conformity. Conformity in turn stifles creativity and individual expression. Therefore, as this argument develops, groups have negative and frustrating effects on individuality. Indeed, groups do have enormous potential for applying normative pressure to individuals. Further, these pressures often require some conformity from group members. Conformity, however, if viewed moderately, is the strength in groups that supervisors should seek. Conformity is not inherently bad. Indeed, a group norm may be one of creative expression by its members. Thus members conform by expressing their individuality. This position is effectively argued by Cartwright and Lippitt as follows:

It is important, first, to make a distinction between conformity and uniformity. A group might have a value that everyone should be as different from everyone else as possible. Conformity to this value, then, would result not in uniformity of behavior but in nonuniformity. Such a situation often arises in therapy groups or training groups where it is possible to establish norms which place a high value upon "being different" and upon tolerating deviant behavior. Conformity to this value is presumably greater the more cohesive the group and the more it is seen as relevant to the group's objectives.[8]

6 Goals held for the group but not by the group tend to be rejected by the group. The zone of freedom for a group is similar to the concept of self for individuals. A behavioral change for individuals is best accompanied by broadening one's concept of self to include the change. Groups change by broadening zones of freedom to include new alternatives. Even the most forceful leadership is frustrated if it overlooks this important concept.

GROUP EFFECTIVENESS

In this section characteristics which describe the ideal group and components of group effectiveness are presented. This ideal model should serve as a goal for supervisors to pursue as they work with school groups, and the effectiveness model suggests how this ideal might be accomplished.

This group maximizes its effectiveness, according to Likert, when it is characterized as follows:[9]

[7] Alexander Heron, *Why Men Work,* Stanford, Calif: Stanford University Press, 1948, p. 20.
[8] Dorwin Cartwright and Ronald Lippitt, "Group Dynamics and the Individual," *International Journal of Psychotherapy,* vol. 7, no. 1, p. 95, 1957.
[9] Abridged from Rensis Likert, *New Patterns of Management,* New York: McGraw-Hill, 1961, p. 166. Likert's list is much more illustrative and comprehensive.

1 The members are skilled in all the various leadership and membership roles and functions required for interaction between leaders and members and between members and other members.

2 The group has been in existence sufficiently long to have developed a well-established, relaxed working relationship among all its members.

3 The members of the group are attracted to it and are loyal to its members, including the leader.

4 The members and leaders have a high degree of confidence and trust in each other.

5 The values and goals of the group are a satisfactory integration and expression of the relevant values and needs of its members. They have helped shape these values and goals and are satisfied with them.

6 Insofar as members of the group are performing linking functions, they endeavor to have the values and goals of the groups which they link in harmony with one another.

7 The more important a value seems to the group, the greater the likelihood that the individual member will accept it.

8 The members of the group are highly motivated to abide by the major values and to achieve the important goals of the group.

9 All the interaction, problem-solving, decision-making activities of the group occur in a supportive atmosphere.

10 The group is eager to help each member develop to his or her full potential. It sees, for example, that relevant technical knowledge and training in interpersonal and group skills are made available to each member.

11 Each member accepts willingly and without resentment the goals and expectations that he or she and the group establish for themselves.

12 When necessary or advisable, members of the group will give other members the help they need to accomplish successfully the goals set for them. Reciprocal help is a characteristic of highly effective groups.

13 The supportive atmosphere of the highly effective group stimulates creativity. The group does not demand narrow conformity as do the work groups under authoritarian leaders.

14 There is strong motivation on the part of each member to communicate fully and frankly to the group all the information which is relevant and of value to the group's activity.

15 There is high motivation in the group to use the communication process so that it best serves the interests and goals of the group.

16 Just as there is high motivation to communicate, there is correspondingly strong motivation to receive communications.

17 In the highly effective group there are strong motivations to try to influence other members as well as to be receptive to influence from them.

It seems useful to differentiate between two major sources of rewards for group members. One reward source is the mutual satisfaction, or reinforcement, that individuals get from interacting with other individuals. The more satisfaction for group members as a result of this interaction, the higher the interaction effectiveness of the group. Interaction effectiveness is an important characteristic of a psychological group. Another source of rewards for group members comes from actual implementation of the group's purposes. The more satisfaction for group members as a result of doing the task, the higher the task effectiveness of the group. Task effectiveness and interaction effectiveness compose group effectiveness. The more satisfaction for group members as a result of interaction effectiveness and task effectiveness, the higher the group effectiveness.[10]

The Components of Group Effectiveness

Interaction effectiveness refers to the quality of group sentiment which exists for a given group. It includes such evasive concepts as morale, cohesiveness, communication ease, and so on. Bass suggests that this dimension of group effectiveness can be assessed by (1) the amount of harmony present and the absence of conflict, (2) the amount of satisfaction for members as a result of interaction, and (3) the perceived congruence between actual and expected relations among group members.[11]

Interaction effectiveness is facilitated by a number of variables, each having the strength to increase the potential for group members to interact. For example, collections of individuals about the same age, with similar educational backgrounds, and with similar interests will tend to have high interaction potential. The more homogeneous the group, the higher the interaction potential of the group. Exposure to contact, size, and pressures to participate are other variables affecting interaction potential.[12] Perhaps the most indicative factor of interaction potential is mutual predictability among group members. That is, a given group member is able to predict what other group members will do. The higher the mutual predictability among group members, the higher the interaction level of the group.

Consider, for example, a group of special teachers in an elementary school. One would suppose that this group, being somewhat homogeneous, manageable in size, having frequent opportunities for exposure to each other, and possessing common sentiments in terms of educational philosophy and school organization, would enjoy high interaction effectiveness. It is more difficult, however, to predict whether this group—or any other school group, for that matter—will use its energies, its power, its pressures, and its unique reward system on behalf of the school's purposes. Perhaps this group of special teachers will harness its energies to provide the very best services that it can to the school. Or perhaps this same group may decide that it is more rewarding to be a thorn in the principal's side. Another possibility is that this group may simply enjoy its unique informal reward system at the expense of doing more than a minimum job, if it does a job at all.[13]

---

[10] The notion of group effectiveness containing a task dimension and an interaction dimension is borrowed from Bernard Bass. Bass feels that *either* dimension or both dimensions may result in group effectiveness. Our view is that *both* dimensions are necessary for group effectiveness. Bernard Bass, *Leadership Psychology and Organizational Behavior,* New York: Harper & Row, 1960, Chap. 3. This discussion follows that which appears in Thomas Sergiovanni, "Group Effectiveness: Human Relations Is Not Enough," *Illinois Elementary Principal,* pp. 15–17, September 1967.

[11] Bass, op. cit., p. 46.

[12] See James G. March and Herbert A. Simon, *Organizations,* New York: Wiley, 1958, pp. 68–71, for an interesting and comprehensive discussion of factors which affect frequency of interaction.

[13] Dubin discusses subversive, cooperative, and neutral groups in his analysis of informal organization. Robert Dubin, *Human Relations in Administration,* 2d ed., Englewood Cliffs, N.J.: Prentice-Hall, 1961, pp. 84–87.

The direction and orientation of a school group hinge on another aspect of group effectiveness, the accomplishment of task. *Task effectiveness* refers to activity which promotes, defines, clarifies, pursues, and accomplishes relevant school goals. It is described in terms of the rewards that group members get from doing or completing a task. Challenging work; responsibility; intrinsic satisfaction; autonomy; feelings of success, achievement, and competence; recognition for task efforts; bolstering of self- and group esteem; and individual and group status are words and phrases which best describe the flavor of the reward system that characterizes task effectiveness.

A group whose primary reward system rests with task effectiveness will have at its disposal an arsenal of weapons to encourage, to motivate, and perhaps even to pressure group members to work on behalf of the school and its purposes. On the other hand, a group deprived of the reward system resulting from task effectiveness may divert its efforts away from work-centered activities and tend to concentrate on seeking satisfaction solely from the interaction-effectiveness domain. The group, not the job, becomes the focus of an individual's attention. Group norms which conflict with the purposes of the school may be established. Conformity to the group and its norms becomes necessary if one wishes to benefit from the group's reward system. This conformity may require that teachers do not exert more than a minimum effort in their jobs.[14] Such groups take a passive, rather than negative, stand in relation to school purposes and tasks. They expend energies, talents, and efforts primarily to maintain the group as a source of personal enjoyment for members. We conclude that groups high in interaction effectiveness but low in task effectiveness not only tend to be lacking in function, but may indeed be dysfunctional.

Interaction effectiveness and task effectiveness are not at opposite ends of a continuum. The effective group is highly successful in its task endeavors and uses its interaction potential on behalf of the task. Such a group would tend to reap rewards (acceptance, affiliation, belonging, and security, for example) while at the same time deriving satisfaction from getting a job done. This combination would best describe group effectiveness.

THE SUPERVISOR AS KEY

Supervisors are frequently in a position to make group effectiveness a reality. Their position is unique in that they affect *both* task and interaction effectiveness. They can foster interaction effectiveness by recognizing informal groups, by helping to initiate and promote interaction patterns within and between groups, and by planning formal groups in terms of their interaction potential. Much can be done by deliberately linking subgroups so that together they constitute an identifiable whole and develop a sense of cohesiveness as a faculty.[15]

---

[14] The rate-buster phenomenon and the sanctions which follow have been well documented in industry. We suspect that the analogy works for education, too. For example, elementary school teachers often mentioned that too much effort, too many displays, noticeable project work, elaborate bulletin boards, taking work home, and other signs of rate busting frequently result in informal and formal sanctions from the group.

[15] Rensis Likert, op. cit., proposes a plan of organization which is characterized by overlapping work groups, linked together by individuals who serve the original group but are also represented in

Interaction effectiveness tends not to be potent enough, however, to provide the kinds of rewards that nourish professional individuals. Professionals tend to need and actively seek the kinds of satisfaction that only task effectiveness can bring. Admittedly there are exceptions to this tendency. Some teachers tend not to be professionally oriented and may seek only relatively shallow levels of need fulfillment. These types would be quite content with the limited rewards available from interaction effectiveness.[16] Other teachers and teacher groups may focus on interaction effectiveness by default—that is, because this is the only source of rewards left open to them.

The implementation of group task effectiveness requires that supervisors encourage groups, formal and informal, to identify with and accept the school, its tasks, and its purposes. Task identification appears to be related to the extent to which individual teachers and groups of teachers are given responsibility and autonomy for participating in decision making and for participating in the development and implementing of teaching programs. Further, task identification appears to be related to the extent to which individuals perceive that they have opportunities to develop their professional skills. These variables are likely to increase opportunities for individual, group, and professional success.[17] Promoting task identification requires that supervisors, principals, and others be committed to faculty and student involvement and collaborative management, and that they willingly appreciate the authority which teachers and other school members bring to the school.

Group Effectiveness Summarized

The relationship between interaction effectiveness and task effectiveness in school groups is initially one of dependence. The consistent accomplishment of group tasks requires the establishment of interaction effectiveness. Once initial group effectiveness is achieved, the relationship changes to one of interdependence. That is, task effectiveness over time depends upon sustained interaction effectiveness, and sustained interaction effectiveness depends upon task effectiveness. The components of group effectiveness are summarized in Figure 9-4.

Interaction effectiveness, according to the model, is largely dependent upon communication frequency. The more homogeneous the group, the more opportunities for group-member contact; and the greater the mutual predictability among group members, the greater the frequency of communication. It should be noted that when creativity is valued as a group goal, more heterogeneity will need to be introduced, even at some loss to interaction frequency.[18] The rewards available to teachers through interaction effectiveness are feelings of affiliation,

---

groups at the next level. Likert's notion represents a proposal for organizing schools and other agencies on the basis of group structure.

[16] See our discussion of the motivation-hygiene theory which appears in Chapter 8 and our caveat regarding the universal application of human resources supervision in Chapter 1.

[17] March and Simon, op. cit., p. 77.

[18] Heterogeneous groups are preferred when tasks are extremely complex, when time is plentiful, when the consequences of error in judgment are grave, and when creativity is desired. Homogeneous groups are preferred when time is scarce, when production is important, when tasks demand cooperation, and when problems are routine. See Bernard Bass, *Organizational Psychology,* Boston: Allyn & Bacon, 1965, pp. 204–213.

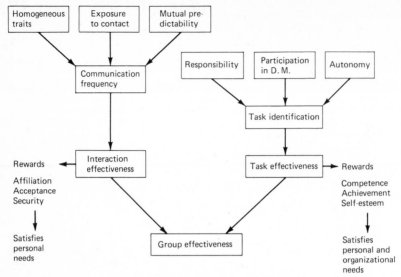

Figure 9-4   Basic components of the concept of group effectiveness.

acceptance, and security. These rewards tend to focus on personal need satisfaction but tend not to directly effect organizational need satisfaction.

The key component of task effectiveness is task identification. As group members identify with the task goals of the group, performance increases. March and Simon suggest that the greater the amount of perceived autonomy and responsibility of group members, and the more opportunities that exist for participation of group members, the greater the task identification of the group. Rewards available to teachers through task effectiveness are feelings of competence and achievement and the bolstering of group and individual self-esteem. This reward system is unique in that the basis for personal need satisfaction is the satisfying of organizational needs. Task effectiveness and interaction effectiveness constitute group effectiveness.

GROUPS IN ACTION

This section examines the group in action by describing phases which groups must transcend if they are to successfully accomplish their work. This is followed by an analysis of leadership functions as they apply to groups. A taxonomy and description of roles which may be assumed by group members is then presented.

Group Phases

It is useful to visualize the group as having certain fundamental interpersonal needs much like those associated with the individual personality. Groups and individuals must provide for these needs before they can function properly. Schutz identifies group and individual needs as follows: "There are three fundamental interpersonal needs—*inclusion, control,* and *affection*—and in order for an individual to function optimally he must establish and maintain a satisfactory relation in all three areas."[19] Individuals need to include others and to be included, to control others and to be controlled, to love others and to be loved, and the exact mix of needing or wanting to express each of these variables differs for each person. Indeed, inclusion, control, and affection are phases through which groups must successfully pass if they are to be characterized by sustained effectiveness in accomplishing their goals. The phases are arranged into a relatively loose hierarchy, with the attention of the group being given first to inclusion, then to control, and finally to affection. Problems associated with each of these are never solved by the group but are at least reasonably settled. This settling is not unlike a simmering pot, which is characterized by relative stability but is subject to a periodic eruption of bubbles. The phases, indeed, overlap (Figure 9-5), with the group generally moving forward but occasionally vacillating from one phase to another.

Each of the phases is examined separately below:

Inclusion   A group needs to define its boundaries and to work to include people within them. The inclusion phase requires that the group know who is in the group and who is not. Further, in view of the group's dynamic center, the group must communicate and delineate to members an expression of required behavior and forbidden behavior. Part of this phase includes identifying and articulating group goals and subsequently testing members to see if they are in agreement with these goals. The group works to win commitment from its members or excludes those who express disinterest in its goals. This exclusion may be physical, if possible, or mental, if necessary.

Control   Once the inclusion phase of group activity has been relatively settled, the group turns its attention to matters of control. Members need to decide problems of leadership, solve status arrangements, assign and agree upon roles to be played, distribute and consolidate power, provide for a workable and acceptable chain of command, and otherwise arrange themselves. While the control phase may not solve manifest control problems, hidden agenda problems, and other interpersonal problems, it works to solve them for the moment—to contain them. Whether such problems stay solved or not depends upon a group climate which is supportive, open, cooperative, and honest.

[19] William Schutz, "The Ego, FIRO Theory and the Leader as Completer," in Luigi Petrullo and Bernard Bass (eds.), *Leadership and Interpersonal Behavior,* New York: Holt, 1961, p. 57.

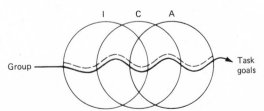

Figure 9-5   Natural group phases: inclusion, control, and affection.

Affection   The inclusion and control phases of group activity are seldom characterized by tranquility. Defining the dynamic center of a group and delineating its borders require a great deal of interpersonal expenditure. The control phase seems always characterized by tension. People are hurt as a result of the inclusion and control phases, and the group must heal its wounds if it is to function properly. The affection phase, then, is characterized by working to build a cohesiveness based on acceptance, forgiveness, and love.

The Hidden Agenda

Much of the group's activity, as it works through the inclusion, control, and affection phases, can be scheduled on the group's agenda and carried out through formal or overt procedures. A substantial amount of this activity, however, takes the form of an undercurrent which permeates the group's life. The official reasons for people coming together to form a group—the publicly stated and agreed-upon tasks to be accomplished—are referred to as the group's *public agenda*.[20] Beneath the public agenda there are a number of hidden agendas, often ignored but nevertheless most powerful, which are not openly recognized. Such private agendas are held by group members, group leaders, and, indeed, the group itself. Bradford describes the hidden agenda as follows: "Unlabeled, private and covered, but deeply felt and very much the concern of the group, is another level. Here are all of the conflicting motives, desires, aspirations and emotional reactions held by the group members, subgroups, or the group as a whole that cannot be fitted legitimately into the accepted group task. Here are all of the problems which, for a variety of reasons, cannot be laid on top of the table."[21]

Hidden agendas are an issue in each of the phases of group activity, but their influence is most strongly felt in the control phase. Hidden agendas need to be dealt with in one way or another. At one extreme they can be smothered or steamrollered by strong leadership, and at the other extreme they can be brought to the surface and "understood," as can happen in human-encounter or sensitivity groups.

Bradford offers a number of suggestions for supervisors in confronting the problem of handling hidden agendas. Among them are (1) to be aware of, to look for, and to recognize hidden agendas—those of the supervisor and those of other group participants; (2) to recognize that the group works continuously and simultaneously at both levels—hidden and public; (3) to work to bring hidden agendas to the surface; but (4) to be sensitive to the group's readiness to force some hidden agenda items, for many have potential for hurting the group more if they are made public; (5) to accept hidden agendas without evoking feelings of guilt; (6) to help the group work out methods of solving or settling hidden agendas in the same way that they develop methods of handling their surface agenda; and (7) to help the group evaluate its progress in handling hidden agendas.[22]

---

[20] This discussion follows that which appears in Leland P. Bradford, "The Case of the Hidden Agenda," *Adult Leadership*, pp. 3–7, September 1952.

[21] Ibid., p. 3

[22] Ibid., p. 7.

FUNCTIONAL ROLES OF GROUP MEMBERS

The question of leadership is one that cannot be avoided for long in an examination of groups. Traditionally, the group leader is considered the key determiner of a group's effectiveness. Good leaders, according to this view, are those who point direction for group activity, clarify goals, make relevancy judgments as they guide group discussion, keep people on the track, are the agenda watchdogs, push for full participation, and force decisions. Good leaders get things done! Their tools are their official role as chairpersons, an acceptable agenda, group know-how, and guided discussion.

Human resources supervision suggests that designated group leaders (teachers, chairpersons, supervisors, consultants, principals, and so on) come to conceive of their role primarily as one of providing service rather than direction to the group. For example, while traditional supervisory patterns require that the leader get things done (presumably by using the group and its resources), human resources supervisors work to help the group accomplish its tasks. Within this context, leaders do not merely solve the group's problems but focus on the group solving its problems; they do not merely move the group forward but help the group as it moves forward. But somebody must get the group going, must initiate discussion, define problems and goals, evaluate, summarize, monitor, provide information, and the like. Indeed, the group will not accomplish its goals without these and other leadership roles being fulfilled. Human resources supervisors are concerned with these roles but hold no monopoly on them. *Leadership functions are considered to be the responsibility of the entire group—not just of the designated leader.* The discussion which follows focuses on leadership and other group roles which are needed in effective groups rather than on who should assume what role. Roles are best assumed by those most capable of assuming them.[23]

Group roles are often classified into three broad categories depending upon whether they support group task effectiveness, support group interaction effectiveness, or exist solely for the satisfaction of the role incumbent. The first category, group task roles, includes roles which facilitate and coordinate the selection and definition of a common group problem and help in solving this problem. The second category, group-building or -maintenance roles, includes roles which are oriented to the functioning of the group as a group. The third category, individual roles, includes roles not primarily directed toward the group or the task but toward the individual participant.

Each of these roles is further described and illustrated below as we present

[23] At least two kinds of "capabilities" must be considered in deciding who assumes leadership in a given situation. Indeed, first and foremost is expert capability. Human resources supervision requires that ability authority be a prime consideration in the leadership decision. Another important dimension, particularly in reference to assigned or legitimate leaders as opposed to ad hoc or informal leaders, is the personality inclination or leadership propensity, given certain circumstances. Certain situations, for example, require one style of leadership and other situations another style. Who can best provide the needed leadership style for a given situation is an interesting and intriguing question. We consider this question later in the chapter when we discuss formal leadership in groups.

Kenneth Benne and Paul Sheats's now-classic taxonomy of functional roles for group members.[24]

Group Task Roles

The following analysis assumes that the task of the discussion group is to select, define, and solve common problems. The roles are identified in relation to functions of facilitation and coordination of group problem-solving activities. Each member may, of course, enact more than one role in any given unit of participation and a wide range of roles in successive participations. Any or all of these roles may be played at times by the group "leader" as well as by various members.

a The *initiator-contributor* suggests or proposes to the group new ideas or a changed way of regarding the group problem or goal. The novelty proposed may take the form of suggestions of a new group goal or a new definition of the problem. It may take the form of a suggested solution or some way of handling a difficulty that the group has encountered. Or it may take the form of a proposed new procedure for the group, a new way of organizing the group for the task ahead.

b The *information seeker* asks for clarification of suggestions made in terms of their factual adequacy, for authoritative information and facts pertinent to the problem being discussed.

c The *opinion seeker* asks not primarily for the facts of the case but for a clarification of the values pertinent to what the group is undertaking or of values involved in a suggestion made or in alternative suggestions.

d The *information giver* offers facts or generalizations which are "authoritative" or relates his own experience pertinently to the group problem.

e The *opinion giver* states his belief or opinion pertinently to a suggestion made or to alternative suggestions. The emphasis is on his proposal of what should become the group's view of pertinent values, not primarily upon relevant facts or information.

f The *elaborator* spells out suggestions in terms of examples or developed meanings, offers a rationale for suggestions previously made and tries to deduce how an idea or suggestion would work out if adopted by the group.

g The *coordinator* shows or clarifies the relationships among various ideas and suggestions, tries to pull ideas and suggestions together or tries to coordinate the activities of various members or subgroups.

h The *orienter* defines the position of the group with respect to its goals by summarizing what has occurred, points to departures from agreed upon directions or goals, or raises questions about the direction which the group discussion is taking.

i The *evaluator-critic* subjects the accomplishment of the group to some standard or set of standards of group functioning in the context of the group task. Thus he may evaluate or question the "practicality," the "logic," the "facts," or the "procedure" of a suggestion or of some unit of group discussion.

j The *energizer* prods the group to action or decision, attempts to stimulate or arouse the group to "greater" or "higher quality" activity.

k The *procedural technician* expedites group movement by doing things for the group—performing routine tasks, distributing materials, or manipulating objects for the group, e.g., rearranging the seating or running the recording machine, etc.

[24] Kenneth D. Benne and Paul Sheats, "Functional Roles of Group Members," *The Journal of Social Issues,* vol. 4, no. 2, pp. 43–46, 1948.

l   The *recorder* writes down suggestions, makes a record of the group decisions, or writes down the product of discussion. The recorder role is the "group memory."

Group Building and Maintenance Roles

Here the analysis of member functions is oriented to those participations which have for their purpose the building of group-centered attitudes and orientation among members of a group or the maintenance and perpetuation of such group-centered behavior. A given contribution may involve several roles, and a member or the "leader" may perform various roles in successive contributions.

   a   The *encourager* praises, agrees with and accepts the contribution of others. He indicates warmth and solidarity in his attitude toward other group members, offers commendation and praise and in various ways indicates understanding and acceptance of other points of view, ideas, and suggestions.

   b   The *harmonizer* mediates the differences between other members, attempts to reconcile disagreements, relieves tension in conflict situations through jesting or pouring oil on the troubled waters, etc.

   c   The *compromiser* operates from within a conflict in which his idea or position is involved. He may offer compromise by yielding status, admitting his error, by disciplining himself to maintain group harmony, or by "coming half way" in moving along with the group.

   d   The *gate keeper* and expediter attempts to keep communication channels open by encouraging or facilitating the participating of others ("we haven't got the ideas of Mr. X yet," etc.) or by proposing regulation of the flow of communication ("why don't we limit the length of our contributions so that everyone will have a chance to contribute?" etc.).

   e   The *standard setter* or *ego ideal* expresses standards for the group to attempt to achieve in its functioning or applies standards in evaluating the quality of group processes.

   f   The *group-observer* and *commentator* keeps records of various aspects of group process and feeds such data with proposed interpretations into the group's evaluation of its own procedures.

   g   The *follower* goes along with the movement of the group, more or less passively accepting the ideas of others, serving as an audience in group discussion and decision.

"Individual Roles"

Attempts by "members" of a group to satisfy individual needs which are irrelevant to the group task and which are nonoriented or negatively oriented to group-building and maintenance set problems of group and member training. A high incidence of "individual-centered" as opposed to "group-centered" participation in a group always calls for self-diagnosis of the group. The diagnosis may reveal one or several of a number of conditions—low level of skill training among members, including the group leader; the prevalence of "authoritarian" and "laissez faire" points of view toward group functioning in the group; a low level of group maturity, discipline and morale; an inappropriately chosen and inadequately defined group task, etc. Whatever diagnosis, it is in this setting that the training needs of the group are to be discovered and group training efforts to meet these needs are to be defined. The outright "suppression" of "individual roles" will deprive the group of data needed for really adequate self-diagnosis and therapy.

a The *aggressor* may work in many ways—deflating the status of others, expressing disapproval of the values, acts or feelings of others, attacking the group or the problem it is working on, joking aggressively, showing envy toward another's contribution by trying to take credit for it, etc.

b The *blocker* tends to be negativistic and stubbornly resistant, disagreeing and opposing without or beyond "reason" and attempting to maintain or bring back an issue after the group has rejected or by-passed it.

c The *recognition-seeker* works in various ways to call attention to himself, whether through boasting, reporting on personal achievements, acting in unusual ways, struggling to prevent his being placed in an "inferior" position, etc.

d The *self-confessor* uses the audience opportunity which the group setting provides to express personal, nongroup oriented, "feeling," "insight," "ideology," etc.

e The *playboy* makes a display of his lack of involvement in the group's processes. This may take the form of cynicism, nonchalance, horseplay and other more or less studied forms of "out of field" behavior.

f The *dominator* tries to assert authority or superiority in manipulating the group or certain members of the group. This domination may take the form of flattery, of asserting a superior status or right to attention, giving directions authoritatively, interrupting the contributions of others, etc.

g The *help-seeker* attempts to call forth "sympathy" responses from other group members or from the whole group, whether through expressions of insecurity, personal confusion or depreciation of himself beyond "reason."

h The *special interest pleader* speaks for the "small business man," the "grass roots" community, the "housewife," "labor," etc., usually cloaking his own prejudices or biases in the stereotype which best fits his individual need.

Groups need to work for balance among the three types of roles. Surely task roles depend upon maintenance roles, and maintenance roles are legitimized and become purposeful as a result of task roles. Our "hidden agenda" discussion explains why individual roles are played in groups. A mature group permits its members to occasionally assume individual roles. Sustained behavior of this type by one or another group member suggests malfunctions in the group's climate. The more information members have about group roles and their own performance in groups, the more likely they are to improve this performance.

SIZING UP YOUR GROUP

One can size up a group by examining eight critical items:

1 The amount of enthusiasm and commitment which exists for group goals and purposes
2 The quantity and quality of teacher contribution to the group
3 The quality of listening by teachers to each other
4 The amount of creativity exhibited in problem solving
5 Ways in which conflict and disagreements are handled
6 The quality and nature of leadership which exists

7 The methods and means of making decisions
8 The ways in which the group evaluates its performance[25]

Using these critical items, we have provided several descriptions of groups at work. These descriptions are adapted from W. J. Reddin 3-D Team Mode Theory and are related to his 3-D Theory of Leadership discussed in Chapters 5 and 6.

The *problem-solving* group is a group that attempts to examine problems as broadly and deeply as possible and thus reach an optimal solution to which all are committed. Due consideration is given to both the task at hand and the feelings of group members. Ideas are of high quality and are highly relevant to the task. When a group operates this way, the supervisor usually functions as an *executive.*[26]

The *productive* group is a task-oriented group whose primary concern is the immediate task. Contributions come from those who push for their own ideas. Disagreement occurs frequently but is usually useful. Discussions about productivity may be dominated by a few members, but their leadership is beneficial. Evaluation is usually focused on making the group more efficient. When a group operates this way, the supervisor usually functions as a *benevolent autocrat.*

The *creative* group is a group which focuses primarily on developing its members and their ideas. Much attention is paid to the minority opinion and to an attempt to incorporate the ideas of all members in the decision. Disagreement, although rare, is looked into closely so that benefit is derived from it. Evaluation of the group's efforts usually is aimed at improving group creativity. When a group operates this way, the supervisor usually functions as a *developer.*

The *procedural* group is a group that follows procedures and established patterns. Creativity and contributions, although forthcoming within defined procedures, are sound. Members listen politely, and disagreement is handled in a formal manner. Leadership is routine. Evaluation usually amounts to a comparison of the group's efforts to those of other groups. Evaluation is, however, functional. When a group operates this way, the supervisor usually functions as a *bureaucrat.*

The *mixed* group is a group that attempts to compromise between getting the task done and sparing people's feelings. The result is less effective. The group lacks focus on the problem, its members' comments are often irrelevant, and attempts at creativity usually fail. Disagreement exists but serves no useful purpose. Leadership is often absent when needed and present when not needed. Evaluation is weak. When a group operates this way, the supervisor usually functions as a *compromiser.*

The *fight* group is a group characterized by conflict and argument. The conflict is not functional, as contributions and creativity are usually blocked by

---

[25] W. J. Reddin, 3-D Team Mode Theory as summarized in *Team Style Diagnosis Test Instructions: Team Consensus Method,* Fredericton, N.B., Can.: Managerial Effectiveness Ltd., 1972.

[26] Refer to Chapters 5 and 6 for an explanation of various effective and ineffective leadership styles associated with Reddin's 3-D Theory of Leadership. He identifies four effective (executive, benevolent autocrat, developer, and bureaucrat) and four ineffective (compromise, autocrat, missionary, and separated) leadership styles.

argumentative group members. Leadership is dominated by one or two individuals, often those with the loudest voices. Disagreement between individuals sometimes becomes personal rather than being based on the issues. Evaluation of the group's efforts usually amounts to attacks on group members. When a group operates this way, the supervisor usually functions as an *autocrat*.

The *dependent* group is a group whose byword is harmony. More attention is paid to avoiding conflict than to discussing the problem. Most of the contributions are ones with which everyone can be expected to agree, and creative ideas are blocked when they are seen as possible criticisms of members or the group as a whole. Disagreement, even when obviously functional, is avoided. Leadership sometimes evolves, but it is usually friendly and weak. Evaluation of the group's efforts is usually in the form of compliments. When a group operates this way, the supervisor usually functions as a *missionary*.

The group in *flight* is a group that displays little interest in getting the job done. Conflict is kept at a minimum because of the energy it requires. Creativity and contributions are low, and leadership appears to be absent. Usually the decision is, in effect, not a decision but a rewording of the problem as it originally existed. There is rarely any effort made to evaluate or improve group performance. When a group operates this way, the supervisor usually functions as a *deserter*.

Groups may operate very close to one of Reddin's descriptions most of the time, but probably most groups shift operating styles occasionally, given certain issues. The problem-solving, productive, creative, and procedural groups are indeed very different in operating styles, but nevertheless each is effective in its own way. On the other hand, the mixed, fight, dependent, and flight groups, although different in operating styles, are each relatively ineffective. The contingency variables associated with choice of leadership styles presented in Chapter 6 can help supervisors to select a team mode and group operating style most consistent with the problem, tasks, and circumstances facing the group at a given moment.

SUMMARY

Groups are a natural, necessary, and important part of the organizational life of schools. In this chapter group supervision was offered as an alternative to person-to-person supervision as a means to more effectively achieve school purposes. Three types of groups were identified: physical groups, psychological groups, and effective work groups. Physical groups were defined as collections of individuals. Psychological groups were defined as collections of individuals who share common goals, interact with each other, view themselves as a group, and obtain satisfaction from group membership. Effective work groups were defined as psychological groups whose common purposes are consistent with those of the school.

Several propositions about group functioning were discussed, including such concepts as group necessity, neutrality, personality, culture, and normative structure. The characteristics of an effective work group, as proposed by Likert, were then presented as ideal standards for group supervision. Two key components of group effectiveness, interaction effectiveness and task effectiveness, were identified. Factors contributing to the establishment of these components and the supervisor's role in maintaining and developing them were proposed.

The discussion then shifted to the group in action. Using Schutz's Firo Theory, inclusion, control, and affection were offered as the natural cycle through which groups must travel before being able to fully work on tasks. The "hidden agenda" was then discussed as an example. It was suggested that leadership functions and roles as opposed to leadership prerogatives associated with one's position are emphasized in effective groups. A list of critical group task, maintenance, and self roles was then discussed. The chapter concluded with guidelines for sizing up a group and for determining its effectiveness. These guidelines were related to Reddin's 3-D Theory of Leadership presented in Chapters 5 and 6.

STUDY GUIDE

Recall the concepts, ideas, and meanings associated with each of the following phrases and terms included in this chapter. Can you discuss each of them with a colleague and apply them to the supervisory context of your school? If you cannot, review them in the text and record the page number for future reference.

1 Affection phase _____
2 Control phase _____
3 Creative group _____
4 Effective work group _____
5 Group dynamic center _____
6 Group maintenance roles _____
7 Group task roles _____
8 Group supervision _____
9 Hidden agenda _____
10 Inclusion phase _____
11 Individual roles _____
12 Interaction effectiveness _____
13 Investments returns _____
14 Leadership function _____
15 Likert characteristics _____
16 Marginal membership _____
17 Person-to-person supervision _____
18 Physical group _____
19 Problem-solving group _____
20 Psychological group _____
21 Sizing up the group _____
22 Task effectiveness _____
23 Zone of freedom _____

EXERCISES

1 How would you describe the group life in your department, unit, or school? How would your group measure up to the characteristics of group effectiveness suggested by Likert?

2 In sizing up your group, in what ways do you find it to share characteristics and features of the eight group types suggested by Reddin? Which of the four effective group types best fits your own leadership inclinations?

3 What are the consequences for a supervisor who fails to recognize the natural group tendencies which exist in schools?

4 What are the consequences for a supervisor who recognizes natural group tendencies in schools but who views them as undesirable and therefore works to subvert or discourage group activity?

Part Two

Human Resources and Educational Leadership

INTRODUCTION: SUPERVISING THE HUMAN CURRICULUM

Part One of this book deals with the exercise of organizational leadership. It attempts to point out those supervisory behaviors which lead to self-fulfillment of all organizational inhabitants. Many behavioral dynamics described in Part One can be applied to actual instructional practices in the classroom. Granting, now, that a school were willing to adopt the supervisory processes described in Part One, we must take up more precise educational concerns with which supervisors must deal. That is, what essential educational considerations should be uppermost in the supervisor's work with teachers and students?

While the authors propose a process of supervision which promotes the fuller development of all the human resources of the school community, they also assume that supervisors are concerned with more than process. That is to say, supervisors ought to have some ideas of their own about how education *ought* to be—how, for example, a good course might be structured, or how educational programs ought to nurture a variety of learning experiences. To be sure, the supervisor will not be the only source of ideas in the school. On the other hand, the supervisor ought to be working from some informed basic operational convictions about what constitutes good educational practice.

Assuming that human resources supervision is essential for developing a more humane school, what central ideas about the nature of human growth, the nature of learning, the nature of educational programs, and indeed the essential purposes of schooling will guide the supervisor? Without turning this book, or a supervision course in which it might be used, into a series of discourses on educational philosophy or curriculum development, the authors nonetheless believe that those preparing for, or engaged in, supervisory roles must articulate their convictions on these central issues. What follows in Part Two then is a series of chapters which pose critical educational questions for supervisory personnel. Their responses may be tentative and open to modification by discussions and experimentation with their colleagues in the schools. But supervisors should nonetheless develop some provisional principles by which to chart the course of their supervisory practice.

The questions posed in these chapters assume that readers have already been exposed to some treatments of the basics of curriculum development, learning theory, and educational philosophy. Our intention is to focus the reader's attention on some of the more important educational questions supervisors will face. There will be issues left out—for example, those issues relating to human development and the appropriate curricula for different stages of growth as outlined by Piaget, Bruner, Kohlberg, and Fowler.[1] Neither will we discuss supervising teachers and programs with a specialized focus, such as those dealing with special education or early childhood education. What is discussed in this section, however, would have relevance in that it touches upon some essential questions facing all supervisors.

Our contention is that supervisory behavior, whether exercised by a building principal, a department chairperson, a central office staff person, or a teaching colleague, is beginning to be seen as the locus for upgrading the educational achievement of a particular school. Individual teachers will take responsibility for continuing their efforts at improving program and instructional effectiveness. But supervisory personnel as individuals, and more so as teams, will be the key people in improving the whole school or the whole system's educational effectiveness.

To be sure, we have moved beyond the days when teachers were grossly underprepared in their own education for the tasks of teaching. In those days, the supervisor was expected to continue, through in-service and informal guidance, the education of those teachers. Today, teachers are better prepared than ever before. The tight job market has further squeezed out the less competent in the teaching profession.

[1] Jean Piaget, *The Language and Thought of the Child,* New York: Harcourt, Brace, 1926, and *The Child's Conception of the World,* New York: Harcourt, Brace, 1928, and *The Science of Education and the Psychology of the Child,* New York: Viking, 1970; J. S. Bruner, J. J. Goodnow, and G. A. Austin, *A Study of Thinking,* New York: Wiley, 1956; L. Kohlberg, "Stages of Moral Development as a Basis For Moral Education," in C. Beck, B. Crittenden, and E. Sullivan (eds.), *Moral Education,* New York: Newman, 1971, and "Development as the Aim of Education," *Harvard Educational Review,* pp. 42, 449–496, 1972; James W. Fowler, "Stages in Faith: The Structural-Developmental Approach," in Thomas C. Hennessy (ed.), *Values and Moral Development,* New York: Paulist Press, 1977.

Nevertheless, the schools as educational communities are floundering. Outstanding teachers are there in the school, but as a whole, faculties in many schools are being accused of not getting the essential job done. Supervisory personnel will be called on more and more to bring about significant improvement in the educational effectiveness of the whole school enterprise. If this is to happen, then people in supervisory capacities will have to roll up their sleeves and mobilize the talent, imagination, and enthusiasm of the faculty and help them pull together as a team, or as clusters of teams, to bring about schoolwide or systemwide improvements.

One of the perspectives of Part One of this book is that organizations and bureaucracies are not necessarily bad things. If one knows how they work, then one can use the organization and bureaucracy to do what they were set up in the first place to do. A school as an organization or bureaucracy brings together very talented and very committed people and brings together resources—money, learning materials, libraries, and labs—so that this organization can do what an individual teacher is unable to do. Yet teachers behave frequently as though they want as little to do with the organization as possible. Usually because of some hurtful or frustrating experiences with administrators, teachers become more and more individualistic. They set up their classroom as a private kingdom and work overtime to protect that private domain.

That kind of individualism is necessary in a bureaucracy gone mad, and some large urban systems seem to be moving in that direction. Yet that very isolationism cuts the teacher off from the potential enrichment of her or his work by preventing the sharing of ideas and resources which a large system makes possible.

Supervisors, because of their positions between teachers and the higher-level administrators, can intervene and interpret for both levels. They can effect the sharing of ideas and resources both vertically and horizontally in the organization, which will enrich the educational environment. In our opinion, no other person is in a better position to do this. Hence our repeated claims, especially given circumstances in the schools today and in the future, that supervisory leadership is the key to improved educational activity in the schools.

As people with supervisory responsibility move into the contemporary arena of education, they will find educational purposes and programs of every shape and hue. In order to assist others in bringing clarity to their thought and work, supervisors will have to have some clarity of their own. They will have to have taken time to step back from the everyday concerns of the school and the classroom to develop frames of reference and basic operating principles which would guide and make sense out of their everyday experience. The following chapters try to develop some of these frames of reference and principles which would allow the supervisor to exercise educational leadership.

Chapter 10 locates the supervisor in the midst of controversies which daily divide or accentuate divisions between teachers and other school personnel, not to mention school boards and parent groups. These controversies deal with the purposes, organization, and curriculum of schools. Where does the supervisor stand on these issues, and how will that stance affect his or her supervisory practice?

Chapter 11 highlights the importance of the supervisor's *platform*—that constellation of assumptions and beliefs about children and youth, about learning, program development, school climate, and the purposes of schooling. Some sources for the development of a platform are suggested.

Chapters 12 and 13 suggest critical questions supervisory personnel need to ask about curricular programs and the environment of learning. In working with individual teachers, departments, or schoolwide curriculum committees, as well as school administrators, supervisors enjoy unique advantages for creative intervention and advocacy.

In Chapter 14, the question of student and program evaluation occupies center stage. The role of supervisors in assisting in the development of useful forms of student and program evaluation is developed.

Chapter 10

The Controversial Context
of Supervision

When even slight cultural shifts are taking place in any society, they are bound to affect the education of the young. Changes in clothing style or work habits of adults will lead some in the schools to tighten controls lest the young be infected by the pernicious invasion of these subversive attitudes. Other educators will claim that youth must be prepared for changing times and therefore will openly discuss the advantages of these cultural innovations. We can, perhaps, recall with amusement the battles over women's voting rights or the early efforts of labor to unionize, and how many arguments raged in faculty lounges and school board meetings over the potentially good or evil influences these controversial changes would have on the education of youth.

Over the past two decades, however, schools at the local, state, and national levels seem to have been the center of controversy over a constellation of dramatic shifts in our culture. Integration, busing, teacher strikes and collective bargaining, law suits over student rights, drugs, the counter culture, prayer in the classroom, civil rights, and nonviolent social activism—these and many other easily recognizable phenomena have started debates and not a few riots, and have cost teachers and administrators their jobs and some students their lives. Now, there is not a great deal that anyone in education can do about social and cultural shifts of this magnitude—to prevent, control, or resolve them. Most of them will be resolved or absorbed in a disjointed and haphazard political give-and-take between various groups in the community. Educators can play a part in this give-and-take, dealing with individual students or groups of students or their parents or adults in the neighborhood as problems arise. But educators do not control these cultural shifts and so, more often than not, are primarily in a reactive position.

ORGANIZATIONAL CONTROVERSY

There are, however, many things that educators, collectively and individually, do control. Class schedules, variable instructional space, variable grouping of students, variable staff assignments, budget allocations, weekly and yearly calendars, curriculum design, and pedagogy—these and other organizational variables can be arranged in a variety of constellations to serve a variety of purposes.

However, not everyone agrees as to the one best fit between all of these variables. The disagreement almost always goes beyond efficiency considerations to more philosophical opinions. Let us consider a few of the controversies, examine some of the underlying pros and cons, and then indicate some implications for supervisory behavior.

One basic controversy deals with the structuring of space in schools. What is the most appropriate size and setting for instruction? The structuring of space for instruction or for learning is found on a continuum from a totally self-contained classroom with one teacher to a totally open school or campus, with the larger community seen as a legitimate place for learning and instruction. In between these two extremes, one finds more variety: schools with self-contained classrooms for different subject areas, each equipped with its own instructional resources; some self-contained classrooms for some subjects and some open areas for other subjects, where students are freer to move around among different small groups or to work at different tasks; some schools with only open-space learning areas, but which are themselves self-contained buildings or on self-contained campuses; and some schools which have partially open campus arrangements on a regular basis for learning and instruction in the community.

Underlying the choices for one or another use of space for learning and instruction are some assumptions and beliefs about teaching, about learning, about discipline, about child and adolescent development, about a lot of things. These assumptions operate below the surface until someone changes the space arrangement. Then all kinds of charges are made: "Kids will waste time." "It will be too noisy." "I won't be able to take attendance." "Kids need to be working on the same thing together." "No, this creates teamwork." "Kids will spend all their time at McDonald's." These assertions may or may not be true. But they indicate how strongly people feel about such a seemingly simple variable as space.

And, indeed, they might well feel strongly about this issue, for it raises several other issues such as: if instruction and learning can legitimately take place in a variety of settings, then perhaps there are a wide variety of ways to teach and ways to learn; if that is so, then the stress on the relative uniformity of teaching and uniformity of classroom size and class times may be inappropriate and, indeed, counterproductive. But if there is no uniform model for teaching and no uniform setting for learning, then who is to say what *is* legitimate or appropriate teaching, or what setting *is* legitimate or appropriate? And if we do not know the answers to those questions, or if we know that the answers are not *educational* answers but political answers, then what are supervisors supposed to do?

Supervisors were always thought to know what constituted good teaching; and, since their observations were always made during a traditional class period in a traditional classroom, they knew the best way to make use of *that* space. But what if there is no classroom as such to visit? What if the teacher being supervised is working in a very large, open-space room with four other teachers, and they interchange groups and teaching tasks and are always moving about this large room dealing with seven or eight groups of students of different sizes and different ages working on different tasks? How does this supervisor, using the traditional checklists, evaluate this teacher?

Suppose, for example, you are supervising a mountain-climbing project with 15 students. You are out in the mountains with them, hiking up narrow paths and clinging to cliff faces all day long. This is quite different from supervising learning activities in a biology laboratory. Imagine all the ways in which the style and method of supervising the mountain-climbing project differ from classroom supervising.

Or suppose you are supervising a wide diversity of "intensive education" experiences, which take the form of mini-courses. These mini-courses cover, unlike more standard courses offered in any large senior high school, field experiences such as working in orphanages, the city tax office, an architect's office, the water board offices. Are there uniform categories you could use to assess whether genuine learning was taking place in all of these field experiences? How would you validate these categories? What would be appropriate instructional strategies in each one of these field experiences?

Besides the fights over appropriate instructional space, other organizational controversies present the supervisor with further questions about his or her behavior. Assume that you are a new supervisor in an elementary school. Instead of traditional grade divisions, students are grouped in multiage, multigrade groups. This multigrade grouping or nongraded grouping is based on the mastery of certain skill levels, and promotion or advancement is not from one grade to another, but from the mastery of certain skill-related tasks or constellation of such tasks to new learning tasks. Some students might achieve mastery and advance to another group within 1 year. Others might take 3 years.

You are accustomed to a more standard supervisory situation: one teacher in one classroom all day long. When you had post-class-visit conferences with your teachers in the other schools, it was fairly easy to point out strengths and weaknesses in that setting. But now, the teacher you are observing is dealing with learning-activity packets in small groups of students, giving 5 minutes of instruction, and then leaving the students free to teach one another and to work on their own as she moves on to another small group. Even to keep her in view, you have to move around the different configurations of movable partitions and bookcases which act as partial space dividers in the large room. Should you follow her around, trying to catch some of her oral instructions to the small groups? Should you sit in on one of the small groups after she has gone to see how well it is doing? Suppose the room is noisy. Is that good or bad? Some kids leave the room without asking anyone's permission. What do you think about that? As you retreat to your office to prepare for your afternoon conference with this teacher, where will you begin?

When the conference begins, you discover that this teacher is part of a team working with a master teacher. Two of the other people in the large room were volunteer parents. This teacher's work was focused on a follow-up exercise to a multimedia presentation given by the master teacher that morning. After faking your way through the conference, you sit back and try to sort out all the questions chasing each other around your head: In order to evaluate this teacher, do I need to evaluate how the whole team works? Suppose the master teacher is dull. How does that affect the reaction of the students to the other teachers? This teacher I've just spoken with had a very specific task to do—explain the instructions on the learning packet to each group. The two volunteers were to drift around and answer other questions and, when necessary, help a group work through the learning task. Now suppose this teacher is really good at giving instructions, but weak in other teaching skills? How will he or she know that? Does the master teacher vary the tasks of the team? And the noise in that room! Can children actually learn anything with everyone talking like that and people getting up and leaving the room? Perhaps they can, but how do I find that out if teachers don't give out grades in this arrangement? Well then, how does one tell the smart ones from the dumb ones? Do kids get marked for effort, or only for achievement?

Anyway, the teacher seemed pleased that you visited her learning area. She said that you were the first one to observe her teaching in the three years since her first teaching assignment. Now, what is your next move?

This hypothetical situation is closer to the reality for more and more supervisory personnel. With diversification of staff roles, no one person is the supervisor in a school, nor is one uniform method applicable to such diversified staff roles. With diversification of instruction settings, a standard supervisory process can no longer be uniformly applied to each setting. With diversification of pacing, grouping (multiability, multiage, large-small, etc.), instructional strategies designed for different learning styles, learning packages or diversified contracts, and with more and more emphasis on individualized learning and education by appointment, it becomes clear that supervisor personnel, at whatever level, have to be extremely flexible and adaptive in trying to assess where the real learning might be taking place.

Not only does the supervisor need flexibility, he or she also requires a discriminating sense of judgment. Simply because schools have developed more complex and diversified organizational structures, processes, and programs, it does not mean that "anything goes." Being a supervisor does not mean accepting any type of activity, no matter how sloppy or disorganized, as legitimate educational activity under the rubric of experimentation or "field education" or individualized learning. Unstructured, unsupervised, aimless "free time" during the class day may be called "independent study," but sometimes that means a few extra hours for teachers to sip coffee in the faculty lounge and a few extra hours of playtime for students. Some free play is certainly appropriate for students of any age. But don't label that time with some grandiose title like "advanced research time" or "independent exploratory module for creative inquiry" (in the daily schedule abbreviated to IEMFCI). In other words, the supervisor should exercise discretion in deciding whether some teacher and student activities are as appropriate as others. Sixty percent of the school day devoted to free play, for example, would seem unacceptable under normal conditions. Granted that there are exceptions to every general rule of thumb; nonetheless, the supervisor has to be able to say "no" to certain proposals or activities. In themselves they may be worthwhile, but at a given time and place, they may be less appropriate educational activities than others.

This leads to the sticky question of the basis for decision making. Assume that you are supervising a group. Frequently the group will choose to make the decision. They will agree unanimously to do something a certain way, and you agree with their decision. Sometimes the group is not clear which decision to make. You as the supervisor take them through a problem-solving exercise, and they then see what the solution should be. Sometimes, however, the group will be divided on a decision, but the decision must be made. They agree to abide by your decision as long as you can give some reasons for your decision. That situation arises frequently in a school setting. And that situation calls upon you to decide on your strongest convictions as an educator.

As was said in the chapter on leadership, leadership through supervision requires a vision of what is possible, a belief about what is best or better in educational activities, a clear view of the purposes of education, and a willingness to stand on those convictions. Having convictions as a supervisor does not mean that one imposes them autocratically on one's subordinate. A person can have convictions and respect the convictions of others who disagree. Neither does having convictions about purposes and activities in education imply a necessary disdain for research and experimentation. Without some provisional convictions about what is important in education, however, a supervisor's interaction with subordinates turns to jelly; it becomes dominated by the wishes or convictions of the subordinates or by the least common denominator among their convictions. Supposedly, one gets appointed to supervisory roles because of some demonstrated competence as an educator, competence that flows out of a sense of purpose. One does not surrender that sense of purpose when moving into a supervisory position. Instead, that sense of purpose can be the key source of the supervisor's effectiveness.

CURRICULUM CONTROVERSY

Besides various controversies surrounding the efficacy of various organizational arrangements in the school, supervisory practice takes place amidst the crosscurrents of curriculum controversies. For the sake of clarification we will consider three sets of arguments going on in almost any school. Protagonists or debaters will not usually fit into one camp exclusively on every issue. The position or point of view is seldom proposed in its pure form; it is more a question of emphasis. By highlighting each position or school of thought in what follows, however, we wish to provide the prospective supervisor with some analytical lenses for interpreting why educators espouse some educational activities and oppose others. We also wish to challenge the readers to examine their own convictions. Where do they stand on these issues? How will their supervisory behavior be influenced by their convictions? What supervisory style will be most consistent with each of the differing schools of thought?

We will group the controversies in three sets of arguments:

Arguments between behaviorists and humanists
Arguments between those advocating a child-centered program and those advocating a society-centered school
Arguments between academicians and moralists

By lumping many positions together in paradigmatic groups or schools, we are obviously overlooking their many and varied nuances. We do so only to emphasize, by oversimplification, some of the larger differences between the various groupings. It is our belief that none of the six schools in their pure form provides sufficient basis for a total educational program. It would be difficult to find a school anywhere which reflected only one of the six positions. Neither could one find any theoretician who would advocate any one of the six positions in a pure form.[1]

Behaviorists versus Humanists

Two competing groups of thinkers and educators who have influenced both teaching methodology and program design can be listed as behaviorists and humanists. The scholars in both schools express a variety of points of view, but they clash on essentials. The behaviorists attempt to establish empirically verifiable links between teacher-student interaction, prescribed course sequences, and logical and rationally definable states of knowledge or student learning. In contrast, the humanists insist that personal, moral, aesthetic, and intellectual development involves internally dynamic processes of growth far more complex than the mechanistic, stimulus-reinforcement model of the behaviorists. The behaviorists are concerned much more with statistically valid research on the improved effectiveness of instruction in reaching predefined cognitive understandings and skill levels. The humanists reply that reality is too multidimensional to be treated in this reductionist fashion. They contend that learning, as it relates to the total develop-

---

[1] Much of what follows dealing with these six competing schools of thought is adapted from Robert J. Starratt, "Curriculum Theory: Controversy, Challenge, and Future Concerns," in William Pinar (ed.), *Heightened Consciousness, Cultural Revolution and Curriculum Theory,* Berkeley, Calif.: McCutchan, 1974, pp. 17–23. Reprinted by permission of the publisher. A differently nuanced treatment of conflicting positions in the curriculum field can be found in Elliot W. Eisner and Elizabeth Vallance (eds.), *Conflicting Conceptions of Curriculum,* Berkeley, Calif.: McCutchan, 1974.

ing consciousness of the individual, is too multidimensional and idiosyncratic to be profitably analyzed by limited statistical correlations, which cannot capture the simultaneous and preconscious nature of learning that is continuously taking place. And, even if the behaviorists could analyze learning behavior at this complex level through computerized measurement of multiform simultaneous responses that children have to instructional exercises and curricular materials, the humanists would consider this an unnecessary proof of the unique individuality of every student, which they hold to be self-evident already.

Some behaviorists, like Benjamin Bloom, do not appear to be as narrow-minded as some humanists might think they are. Rather, they have taken a rather hardheaded approach to learning and seem to be saying, "Look, I can't study everything all at once; instead, I am trying to take a look at the possibility of children mastering some skills and basic understandings. Yes, probably there *are* any number of other variables involved in learning, and there is more complex learning going on all the time inside students. But there are some students who don't acquire mastery of even some very basic skills which form the building blocks for more complex learnings—skills like the use of language syntax and reading. I'm trying to discover effective ways to promote mastery at least in these areas. Our research seems to show that if you alter the time requirements, improve instructional communications, and specify what precisely it is you are trying to get students to do so that *they* know when they're making progress, we can demonstrate cognitive and emotional growth."[2]

With that kind of interpretation, the humanists can have very little to argue with, as long as the behaviorists do not then universalize or absolutize their research findings as the *one* or *complete* explanation of all human learning, or claim that their definitions of specific behavioral outcomes encompass the whole range of possible or desirable learning outcomes.

Nor is the charge that behaviorists are concerned with mere training as opposed to education entirely fair. Again, it depends on whether the behaviorists will admit that they have carved out a limited domain of the educational enterprise, while insisting that their work deserves attention as *at least one way* of approaching some *fundamental* learning problems. The willingness to leave their effort open to the judgment of empirical evaluation, moreover, is often more than can be said for the proposals of some humanists.

Humanists, in differing from behaviorists, tend to affirm human spirit, higher forms of intelligence, imagination, creativity, and feeling, as well as lower-level intellectual activities as legitimate components of learning activities. Learning which involves interpersonal relations, self-image, creative expression, exploration of feelings, discussions of conflicting values—all of these—must be relatively open-ended types of learning, the results of which cannot be preprogrammed. *Man: A Course of Studies* would be an example of a humanist, rather than a

---

[2] Cf. Benjamin S. Bloom, "An Introduction to Mastery Learning Theory," paper read to the AERA Symposium, "Schools, Society, and Mastery Learning," held on Feb. 28, 1973, New Orleans, as part of the Proceedings of the AERA Annual Meeting. See also James H. Block (ed.), *Mastery Learning: Theory and Practice,* New York: Holt, 1971.

behaviorist, type of curriculum.[3] The behaviorist would criticize this curriculum because the course objectives were not specified in terms of student behavior and because the organization of the lessons are not logically linked together in a sequence in which each lesson builds on the concepts and skills developed in the previous lesson.

Whether one exercises a supervisory role from the central office or in a classroom, one's convictions about the issues of this debate will color one's behavior. As a teacher supervising student learning activities, will you insist on carefully articulated student learning objectives? Will they *all* be spelled out in empirically observable and behaviorally specific detail, or will some be more general or open-ended? If you are a department chairperson supervising the teaching of the members of your department, what pedagogical principles will you insist on, if any? And what will be your approach to your own supervisory behavior—will your own supervisory goals be spelled out in observable activities? If you have strong convictions about the efficacy of behavioral objectives, how will you deal with teachers who have equally strong convictions about humanistic pedagogy? Consensus-building exercises may carry you only so far, and then the philosophical convictions may sharply diverge.

Personal Freedom versus Social Adaptation

Another dispute, which has continued for years and is still continuing, involves those who would focus primarily on the individual personal freedom of the student, and those who would focus on social adaptation and citizenship. The heavy emphasis by some on individualized instruction, on letting the student choose when and what he or she will study on the basis of his or her own interests and curiosity, tends to relegate social requirements such as cooperation with legal structures and parental authority to the background. On the other hand, those who argue for social adaptation and the development of good citizenship can appear to minimize attention to the need for personal freedom of conscience, for affective relationships, and for individual self-fulfillment.

We can perhaps evaluate the argument by pointing to the philosophical roots of these differing points of view.[4] The personal-freedom group seem to side with the philosophical position of Jean Jacques Rousseau. Rousseau, with his "noble savage" concept of man, conceives of man as inherently good, noble, and innocent but as eventually being corrupted by society, its rules and regulations, its taboos and neurotic fears, its compromises, and its hypocritical social roles and mores. If parents, educators, government authorities, and other adults with power would leave children alone, children would naturally develop their healthy emotions of affection, trust, compassion, and sense of justice. Many of these assumptions seem to be present in the writings of the personal-freedom group.

The social-adaptation group seems, on the other hand, to side more with the philosophical position of Thomas Hobbes. Hobbes considered man inherently

---

[3] Cf. Elliot W. Eisner's analysis of this curriculum in Elliot W. Eisner and Elizabeth Vallance (eds.), *Conflicting Conceptions of Curriculum,* Berkeley, Calif.: McCutchan, 1974, pp. 193–200.

[4] Regarding the philosophical positions, see John E. Longhurst, *Essay on Comparative Totalitarianisms: The Twin Utopias of Hobbes and Rousseau,* Lawrence, Kan.: Coronado Press, 1966.

selfish and aggressive. In order for men to live together in society with some kind of order and peace, individuals had to surrender, through a social contract, some of their own freedoms to the state, so that they, in return, would be protected from exploitation at the hands of others. Although they do not put it so explicitly, the social-adaptation group seems to assume that society has the right to expect schools to indoctrinate youth into the requirements of adult life, to channel them into socially productive work roles, and to condition them for the responsibilities of parenthood, voting, material consumption, and middle-class social behavior.

To one who observes in passing the actual practice in large public junior and senior high schools, this conflict is sometimes glaringly evident. The social system of the school (the system of sanctions, discipline, rewards, rules and regulations, and legal and professional authority)—what some have called the hidden curriculum—is thoroughly Hobbesian in tenor, while the curriculum-instruction system is often based primarily, though implicitly, on Rousseau's image of man. Usually the social system within the school completely undermines whatever impact the curriculum might have in developing curiosity and free inquiry. Students grow cynical about teachers' exhortations to creativity and autonomy when they are forced to request a pass to go to the bathroom.

Ironically enough, we find someone like Jonathan Kozol bitterly criticizing the romantics who follow A. S. Neil in their efforts to promote freedom and spontaneity in youth. He does not disagree that these are ideals which in an ideal world would be worthwhile; rather, he claims that Summerhill-type schools are havens for the spoiled children of the wealthy, who do not have to face up to the harsh reality of an oppressive environment. Kozol's type of "free school," on the contrary, would provide a strict and demanding environment, for that is the only way the children of the poor can be toughened and trained to deal politically with the discriminatory use of power against them.[5]

The education-for-ecstasy people, the schools-without-failure people appear to speak from an upper-middle-class and utopian bias which refuses to acknowledge that the exercise of freedom requires *constant* political negotiation, or that there is a paradoxical principle operative in society—namely, that to ensure the basic freedoms of individuals, laws, sanctions, and institutions must be established which, by their nature, demand that the individual negotiate his or her behavior according to *their* ground rules and not his or her own spontaneous desires. As Schwab cogently remarks:

> A curriculum based on a theory about individual personality which thrusts society, its demands, and its structure far into the background or which ignores them entirely can be nothing but incomplete and doctrinaire, for the individuals in question are in fact members of a society and must meet its demands to some minimal degree since their existence and prosperity as individuals depend on the functioning of society.[6]

One can agree with the individual-freedom group's criticism of the misuse of

[5] Jonathan Kozol, *Free Schools,* Boston: Houghton Mifflin, 1972, and Jonathan Kozol, *The Night Is Dark and I Am Far from Home,* Boston: Houghton Mifflin, 1975.

[6] Joseph J. Schwab, *The Practical: A Language for Curriculum,* Washington, D.C.: National Education Association, Center for the Study of Instruction, 1970, p. 23.

authority, power, and laws in education, without accepting the *abolition* of authority, power, and law: reform yes, deschooling no.

While cautioning against an exclusive concentration on individualized personal growth to the neglect of the complementary social-adaptation orientation, one must agree with Harold Shane[7] that what is presented in educational literature as teaching the democratic process reflects the *folklore* of democracy, not its reality as it is practiced in this country. Such naïveté among educators receives support from social theorists such as Talcott Parsons and his followers who assume a basic rationality in their analysis of social dynamics.[8] Parsons seems to assume that decision making follows the logic of the scientific method and technological efficiency, and that social change takes place primarily in a rational fashion.

A rather different perspective of social change and the art of politics, however, derives from viewing it through the conflict model. From this vantage point, social change occurs only when those who have less power confront those who have more power and, through legal and political strategems or through more aggressive means, wrest some of it away from them.[9] In our country, moreover, the concrete practices of our economic system seem to dominate government and politics much more than the ideology of egalitarian democracy does. Most Americans in their public lives are constantly engaged in power trade-offs, and in highly competitive quests for personal gain, and will use every trick in the political game to attain those ends—egalitarianism be damned. Ask the critical thinkers among minorities what democracy means to them, and they will tell you it is the pious rhetoric used by the majority to cloak their entrenched opposition to increased political and economic equality for minorities.

Those interested in the social-adaptation goals of education, therefore, must strive for an honest appraisal of how free-enterprise economics has distorted the democratic ideals of this country. These educators need to be more aware of the need for constant reformation of the political process to protect the rights of all segments of our society. The personal-freedom group very seldom alludes to the need for young adults to act responsibly as *citizens,* to promote the welfare of all members of the community, to engage in an ongoing reform of the political process. The wealthy, perhaps, can withdraw into a private world to tend to their health gardens and frivolities, but schools should not contribute to a withdrawal of the majority of citizens from active participation in the political process.

Supervisors frequently find this conflict impinging on their work day. The vice-principal in charge of discipline is usually after younger teachers who do not hand in attendance records. He or she comes to you, the supervisor, asking you to "straighten these teachers out." At the same time, you recognize the importance of a teachers gaining the trust of the children. They may need some time to

[7] Harold G. Shane, "Looking to the Future: Reassessment of Educational Issues of the 1970's," *Phi Delta Kappan,* vol. 54, no. 5, p. 332, January 1973.

[8] Talcott Parsons, *Essays in Sociological Theory,* New York: Macmillan, 1959.

[9] Ralph Dahrendorf, *Class and Class Conflict in Industrial Society,* Stanford, Calif.: Stanford, 1959; Paulo Freire, *Pedogogy of the Oppressed,* New York: Herder & Herder, 1970.

work out a system with the children which conforms to school regulations but which does not put the teacher in the role of police officer. Other teachers may need some firm advice about their blatantly unprofessional attitudes toward a reasonable concern for order. The supervisor cannot take a different position on this issue every day. Rather, the supervisor needs to take the leadership in getting these conflicting positions out in the open and helping the faculty and administration develop realistic policies which all can accept and live by.

Academicians versus Moralists

Finally, a third major conflict in the schools takes place between academicians and moralists. The academicians tend to come from within the classical liberal arts tradition, and would promote hardheaded intellectual rigor, logical rationality, and concentration on the traditional disciplines, such as the natural and social sciences and the humanities. The moralists would claim that education's primary task is to build character and maturity and to build virtuous and healthy men and women, and that schools should therefore engage students, by example and by practice, in efforts to clarify and appreciate values, to develop heroic and altruistic attitudes, and to accept responsibility for their personal and public lives.

The academicians have always found champions among college and university professors, from the Committee of Seventeen to the promoters of the "structures of the disciplines" of the last decade. The great headmasters of the private Ivy League prep schools, as well as progressive educators of the twenties and thirties who talked about "educating the whole child," and, more recently, people like Carl Rogers or Arthur Foshay or Lawrence Kubie could broadly be considered in the moralist school. To make their point about the questionable exclusive concentration on the academic disciplines, the moralists can point to what Kubie calls "the idiot-savant, a man who is a scholar in his field, but humanly speaking an ignoramus . . ."[10] The academicians counter that their job is not to play baby-sitter, handholder, or amateur counselor, but that the primary purpose of schooling is to develop the mind and an appreciation for human achievements in the scholarly and cultural fields—let parents, psychologists, and clergymen look to the moral development of youth. Foshay seems to strike a healthy balance in his curriculum proposals for the seventies, although he does seem to promote the naive concept of democracy, based on the folklore of democracy, mentioned earlier.[11]

Once again, supervisory personnel can easily get caught in this crossfire. Having counseled a teacher that a certain book was acceptable for supplementary reading, you may find yourself embroiled in a controversy with the school board which claims that the book is dangerous to the morals of the children. Or, you may tear your hair out trying to convince a teacher that she or he needs to

---

[10] Lawrence S. Kubie, "Research in Protecting Preconscious Functions in Education," in Harry Passow (ed.), *Nurturing Individual Potential,* Washington, D.C.: Association for Supervision and Curriculum Development, 1964, p. 31.

[11] Arthur W. Foshay, *Curriculum for the 70's: An Agenda for Invention,* Washington, D.C.: National Education Association, Center for the Study of Instruction, 1970.

spend time after class talking with a student who is having a particularly difficult time at home with alcoholic parents. The teacher, on the other hand, may insist that if the child were *really* interested in learning compound sentence structure, she would not let the unpleasantness at home get in the way.

Again, the supervisor needs to be clear about his or her own beliefs on this issue. These will obviously influence the ways in which certain behavior of subordinates is perceived, valued, and rewarded.

SUMMARY

In this chapter we have attempted to situate the supervisory process in a realistic educational context. Anyone in a supervisory position in schools or school systems will be expected to take a stand on some fundamental organizational and curricular issues. Taking a stand on issues, however, does not mean autocratically imposing those positions or beliefs on subordinates. Rather, the supervisor's own clarity on the pros and cons of a controversy should enable subordinates to reach some agreement about their behavior.

Some controversies involve organizational aspects of the school, such as space and time utilization, diversified groupings, open classrooms, weekly and yearly calendars, and diversified staffing. Any one of these organizational variables can drastically affect the style and methodology of supervisory behavior. Some organizational changes will call for totally new supervisory strategies for educators.

Other controversies revolve around school purposes and curricular emphases. Various proponents of one position or another can be grouped—though awkwardly in many instances—into arguing camps: the behaviorists versus the humanists, the personal-freedom advocates versus the social-adaptation advocates, and the academicians versus the moralists. Supervisors will act differently in their relationships with subordinates depending on where they stand on these issues. Frequently, supervisors will be called upon to negotiate between different factions in the school which cannot resolve their differences on these issues. By being able to clarify what some of the underlying assumptions are behind these different positions, the supervisor may enable people in the school to come to some working agreements about what will be acceptable behavior of teachers in the school.

STUDY GUIDE

Recall the concepts and meanings associated with each of the following phrases and terms included in this chapter. Can you discuss them with a colleague and apply them to the supervisory context of your school? If you cannot, review them in the text and record the page number for future reference.

1 Academicians _____
2 Behaviorist views _____
3 Curriculum controversy _____

4 Humanist views _____
5 Moralists _____
6 Organizational controversy _____
7 Personal-freedom views _____
8 Social-adaptation views _____

EXERCISES

1 What is the basic difference between an organization controversy and a curriculum controversy?
2 As a teacher who supervises student learning, how would your supervisory behavior differ between *(a)* supervising a biology laboratory and *(b)* supervising a 3-day mountain-climbing expedition with the students?
3 Role-play the situation on page 187, with the roles of the teacher, vice-principal for discipline, and the supervisor all holding conflicting organization and curriculum positions.
4 Analyze three controversies during the past 2 years that have taken place in the schools in your state or home town, according to the organization or curriculum distinctions of this chapter. Then list the implications, if any, for supervisory personnel.

Chapter 11

The Supervisor's Educational Platform

Supervisory personnel can expect to face a wide variety of educational settings in today's schools. Even within the same school system, one can find traditional schools and highly innovative schools. Because of strongly felt expectations about education in the community, many school systems have purposely designed a variety of programs and settings in order to provide families with clear options for the education of their children. Educators moving between or within school systems will be required to shift gears and adjust, for example, to different systems of discipline, grading, scheduling, and class grouping. Supervisory personnel, therefore, must prepare for versatility in their methods of supervision, in order to match their methods to the educational setting.

This increased demand for versatility can be very unsettling. Supervisors accustomed to one method of supervision which seems effective in one particular school setting may have so identified sound pedagogy and effective learning experiences with that one setting that they cannot imagine any other setting being equally effective. By and large, however, the research indicates that no significant difference in learning outcomes can be traced to one setting or organization of programs and pedagogy rather than another.[1]

---

[1] Two exceptions to this generalization would be the research of Bloom and his associates on mastery learning, and very highly controlled experimental research on the learning of very precise

Nevertheless, it is painfully evident how frequently one way of organizing a schedule or a system of grading or a mixture of courses is defended with metaphysical certitude as the only valid and effective way in which children and youth can learn. Or, among supervisors, one supervisory strategy assumes a rigid orthodoxy, and it is believed that this strategy must be applied to any and all educational settings.

How, then, can one avoid either extreme of this dilemma? Does one become a total relativist, accepting any form or method or pedagogy or school organization as being as valid as any other? Or, does one choose one way as *the* one way to educate? Educators can easily get caught up in running battles with their colleagues, with parents, and with the school board on this issue as long as they stick to the *surface* realities. What is needed is some firm footing in principle. Some have called our often unexpressed constellation of principles a platform.[2] Just as a political party is supposed to base its decisions and actions on a party platform upon which it seeks election, so, too, supervisory personnel need a platform upon which, and in the light of which, they can carry on their work. With a clearly defined platform, they can begin to take a position relative to educational practices, looking beyond the surface behavior to probe for the real consequences of a variety of school practices.

To talk about the educational platform behind supervisory practice, however, raises the question of authority once again. The synthesizing theory of supervision places great stress on understanding how mediating variables within the school organization influence the effectiveness, or output, variables.[3] This theory criticizes the "direct" approach of supervision, where, for example, a principal moves from desire for an innovation (initiating variable) to mandating of the attitudes, opinions, or competencies of the teachers (mediating variables). If now we advocate that the supervisor clarify his or her *own* educational platform, does this mean that his or her own platform will be imposed on the school?

On the contrary, if the supervisor is to draw out the genuine talent and leadership of subordinates as we propose in human resources supervision, the supervisor needs to know what his or her own basic opinions, values, beliefs, and principles are. Without any commitment to some basic educational ideas, how can the supervisor or the subordinates develop some sense of direction as they work together to achieve their educational goals? Having a platform of one's own does not necessarily mean that the supervisor is the *most* knowledgeable instructional expert. Indeed, we propose that the role of teachers as instructional leaders should be supported, with supervisors exercising more managerial or growth-inducing leadership. On the other hand, the supervisor can best assist subordinates in clarifying what their educational platform is or ought to be, only if the supervisor has clarified his or her own.

To be more specific, then, what does an educational platform consist of? It

---

and very limited behavior. See James H. Block (ed.), *Mastery Learning: Theory and Practice,* New York: Holt, 1971.

[2] Decker Walker, "A Naturalistic Model for Curriculum Development," *School Review,* vol. 80, no. 1, 1971.

[3] Cf., Chapter 2.

consists of a series of assumptions or beliefs usually expressed in declarative, or sometimes normative, statements. These assumptions or beliefs deal with the way children and youth grow, with the purposes of schooling, with the nature of learning, with pedagogy or teaching, with educational programs, and with school climate.

In the previous chapter we examined what amount to platform positions on the purposes of schooling. These platform positions result in very observable structures, programs, and behaviors within the school. Classroom control, or discipline, for example, will differ considerably between schools and teachers who espouse the platform of social adaptation at the expense of personal growth and freedom and those who espouse the platform of personal freedom at the expense of social adaptation. Or to put it more clearly, when personal growth is defined as identical with social adaptation, then uniform compliance with school rules and regulations will tend to be interpreted as primary evidence that children's personal growth is proceeding on schedule. Or in a school stressing academic achievement the reward system of grades, teacher approval, awards banquets, etc., will focus on that to the neglect of recognition for achievements in other areas, for instance, those of social, moral, and personal growth. Frequently, a supervisor may encounter a policy dispute which actually stems from a conflict between the administration's platform position on the purposes of schooling and that of teachers, or between platform positions of teachers on the same faculty.

One way of bringing such conflicts into the light for rational discussion is for the supervisor to clarify the assumptions and beliefs which lie behind these disagreements. Normally, such discussions disclose the legitimacy of the other point of view and lead toward a more balanced integration of competing platforms. In other words, the supervisor can bring people out of their entrenched positions, dissolving "either-or" thinking and opening the way to a "both-and" platform position that allows for a differentiation which complements rather than excludes other points of emphasis.

What follows are two examples of at least partially developed platforms. They tend to focus on the primary emphasis of the platform. The first example places the central focus of the platform on the individual student and her or his activity in the schooling process. The second example exhibits more of an emphasis on the teacher's view of the universe, in which the teacher encourages students to participate.

FOCUS ON THE INDIVIDUAL STUDENT

1 The student is unlike input factors in system designs of industrial or military organizations, for instance a piece of steel which arrives at the "input station" all neatly measured and qualified and stable. Steel and wood and stone do not grow and change during the very time when the production worker is trying to manipulate them. Students do.

2 The school makes a difference in a child's growth, but not *that* much difference. If the school were nonexistent, other influences and experiences would "educate" the child. Besides, human beings are dynamic and constantly growing, despite their best efforts to the contrary. The school simply speeds up the growth process and channels it in supposedly beneficial directions, rather than leaving the student to random, trial-and-error growth.

3   Curricular-instructional programs should be designed in conformity to the growth patterns of students. The human growth needs of students should never be subordinated to objectives dictated by the needs of society and the demands of the disciplines. Theoretically, these three concerns—human growth, achievement of disciplined skills and knowledge, and fulfillment of social responsibilities—should not be in conflict. In practice, however, they frequently are in conflict, and the concern for human growth usually is the one to be sacrificed. This practice should be reversed.

4   The educator's primary function is to become obsolete. The job of the educator is to so influence students that the students will gradually but eventually reach the point where they do not need the teacher, where they can pursue their own learning on the basis of their acquired knowledge and skills.

5   Indirectly related to the above assumption is the further assumption that *active* pursuit of knowledge and understanding, an actual dialogue with reality, will produce the most significant and long-lasting types of learning. Whenever possible, therefore, the student must actively search, actively inquire, actively discover, and actively organize and integrate. The teacher's job is to guide and direct this activity toward specified goals.

These five basic assumptions place the individual student at the heart of this platform.

In order to clarify our platform beliefs about the growth patterns of the individual, the following conceptual diagrams attempt to sketch in broad strokes a picture of this growing human being. Despite their resemblances to cave drawings of prehistoric man, they might provide a helpful visual image of the student as he or she moves from infancy toward maturity.

Figure 11-1 attempts a rudimentary, three-dimensional model of growth

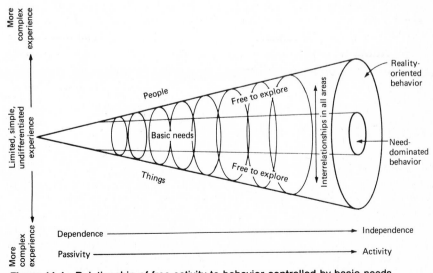

Figure 11-1   Relationship of free activity to behavior controlled by basic needs.

which emphasizes the individual's gradual increase in freedom to explore his or her world. Initially, the behavior of infants is almost entirely dominated by their biological needs, such as needs for food, warmth, sleep, and basic sensory stimulation. As these needs are regularly taken care of, and as infants become able to provide for these needs themselves, they have more time and energy to seek more complex sensory stimulation and to move away from purely self-centered concerns toward whatever makes up their environment. Their environment, they discover quite early, is made up of people and things. Animals populate their early "people world," but gradually they, too, become part of the nonhuman world. The exploratory behavior of infants is called *reality-oriented behavior* because through it, they move toward discovering things and people in their *own* right and not simply as gratifiers of their physical needs. As they move toward things and people in their own right, infants discover that reality is quite complex—that they have to deal with each situation and each person in different ways at different times.

As individuals mature physically, they discover that they can, and are expected to, manage many of the things which parents and siblings provided in their infancy, such as feeding, washing, dressing, returning toys to the toy closet, and so forth. Moreover, they are allowed more freedom to explore their environment, first outside their crib and playpen, then outside the house, and eventually outside the neighborhood. This pattern of continued movement away from dependency toward independence to interdependence, and from passivity to increased activity, is basic to the process of maturing, of becoming a developed human, and this process involves both emotional and cognitive development as well as physical development. And, unless severe physical or emotional restraints are imposed on individuals, they will develop along these lines naturally. There is a natural internal dynamism in human beings toward this kind of growth.

In Figure 11-2, the same three-dimensional model of growth forms the basis for sketching Maslow's descriptive categories of growth. It may be helpful at this point to review our earlier treatments of Maslow's motivational theory and Porter's adaptation of Maslow's categories into a hierarchy of needs.[4] What was stated in Chapter 8 as applying to the growth needs of teachers applies equally, in this platform, to the individual student.

As was stated earlier in Chapter 8, Maslow's need dimensions, or levels, build on one another. That is, as a lower need is relatively well satisfied, the next

[4] Cf. Chapter 8.

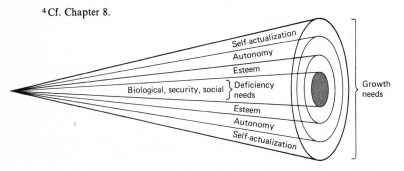

Figure 11-2 Human growth: Deficiency needs and growth needs.

higher need emerges and begins to occupy a person's conscious attention. Thus, as students move from satisfied security needs, they seek more social satisfactions by belonging to a group, by making friends, and by striving for acceptance within a circle of acquaintances wider than their own family.

As the social needs become relatively satisfied, students begin now to seek recognition for their own achievements. Here we notice the link between lower social needs and higher autonomy needs. Their acceptance into a group as they sought to satisfy their need for affiliation was itself a recognition that they were not absolute boors—that they had some likable or useful qualities. Their later quest for more autonomy will have its roots in this earlier desire to stand out from the group by being respected for some skill or quality in which they excel.

Many students falter at the esteem level. Since they experience either failure in their schoolwork or little esteem—or sometimes indifference—from their teacher and an almost total lack of trust communicated by the disciplinary system of the school, they perceive that their need for esteem cannot be satisfied by participating in school activities. The only school activities that do grant them a measure of recognition are primarily athletics for the boys and cheerleading for the girls.[5] But this recognition comes not so much from teachers and administrators as from the students' peers at school. Except for the very bright and creative, therefore, and the athletes and cheerleaders, schooling usually does not provide sufficient esteem for most students. No wonder, then, that many students seek other sources of esteem—in becoming socially popular, in outside activities with gangs, in outside jobs, in private hobbies, and in other activities.

If the schooling experience, on the other hand, could provide more experiences of achievement, of competence, of respect, and of status, then students could feel more enthusiastic about learning. They would come to seek more esteem through schoolwork and, because this was provided, would gradually accept more autonomous responsibility for their learning. In other words, through the esteem and recognition granted them for their unique talents by *school* personnel (teachers and administrators), and not solely their peers, they might come to identify more closely with the objectives of schooling and to seek fulfillment and self-actualization through learning activities.

Gradually, however, students will grow restless over learning experiences which were exclusively under the control and direction of the teacher and the department. If they are to develop their potential more freely, they must have more opportunities for self-expression and for creative exploration on their own. Once again, even many "progressive" schools stop short of allowing these self-actualizing attempts on the part of students. Certainly the curricular-instructional program requires structure and organization for the less mature students, but it should not penalize those students who are eager to pursue more adventuresome goals.

Figure 11-3 is rather self-explanatory. It simply attempts to chart the different people and things individuals encounter as they move from their passive and

[5] James S. Coleman, *The Adolescent Society,* New York: Free Press, 1961, documents this convincingly.

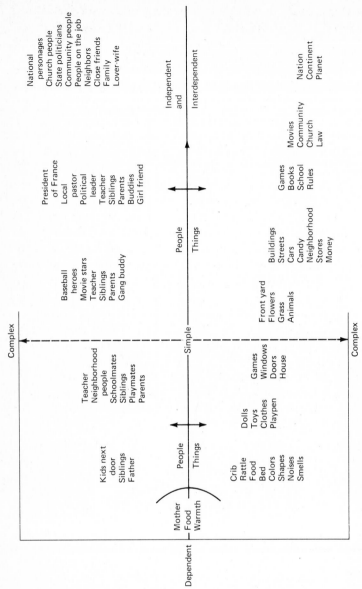

Figure 11-3 Environmental interaction chart.

dependent condition into more active and independent participation with their environment. Reflection on the numerous skills and learnings required to deal with these people and things in their expanding environment leads to the development shown in Figure 11-4.

Figure 11-4 attempts to indicate the development of habits, skills, and understandings which allow individuals the freedom to explore and participate in their environment. By mastering and internalizing any skill, individuals no longer have to consciously think about each minute part of the behavior involved in the performance of a skill. Rather, it becomes natural, like breathing or walking, and thus the conscious energies of individuals are freed to explore new areas of their environment, which they gradually assimilate into new skills, new understandings, and new interpretive maps of their environment. As they develop these skills and understandings, they are increasingly able not merely to explore the environment, but to interact with it—to develop deeper friendships, for example, or to take on part-time jobs, or to solve problems in school assignments.

These basic learnings include social skills, such as learning appropriate manners for different occasions, learning something about sex, age, and authority role-relationships, learning to delay gratification in order to achieve a higher goal, and so forth. Other basic learnings involve physical skills, such as manual dexterity, visual and auditory perceptual differentiation, correct speech habits, athletic skills, and so forth. Besides developing symbolic skills, methodologies for inquiry, and attitudes and values, individuals accumulate a repertory of personal meanings. These are derived from experiences whose intensity left a lasting, and frequently highly emotion-laden, impression. Finally, the emerging self-concept lies at the heart of the developing core of individuals and suffuses all of their accumulated learnings. Together, these elements of the developing core of the

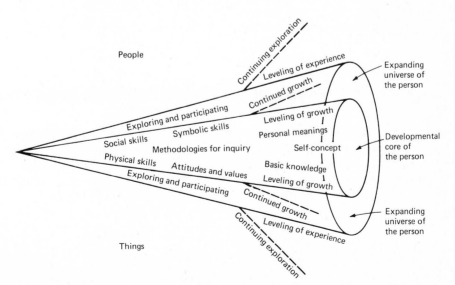

Figure 11-4 Developing freedom to explore and participate in the human environment.

person determine the quality and degree of the freedom of individuals to participate in their human environment.

Notice that these growth processes can level off after a while, as the result of a variety of circumstances. Everyone is familiar with people who have stopped growing—who simply do not go beyond a certain point either in exploring their universe or in pursuing more intense human experiences. People sometimes caustically remark about this phenomenon: "Oh, you mean John X. Well, he died 5 years ago, but he's doing all right, I guess." When the core of the person stops growing, individuals' experience of their environment levels off, and they settle into a daily routine where things seldom change, except for the worse.

Again, the stress of this platform is on the intrinsic dynamism of human growth. A corollary of this stress is that teachers should appeal to the natural curiosity of students, presenting them with exciting and imaginative learning tasks which will immerse the student in learning activity. Rather than continuously imposing the teacher's own agenda, leaving the student in a passive state while the teacher engages in the activity which the *student* should be performing, this platform emphasizes that the drive to learn and grow is already there in the student. This is not to say that the demands of the logical sequence of learning activities within a specified discipline of knowledge will be ignored. But much more leeway will be given to students to rummage about within the discipline of knowledge, frequently leapfrogging over logical steps to new insights and discoveries. Students can go back and fill in what they have left out; indeed, frequently they will come to recognize this need on their own. The emphasis is, however, on giving the students their head, encouraging them as they experience the excitement of the search or the puzzle. Obviously this leads to another corollary: the necessity of a highly individualized form of instruction, using learning-activity packets, exploratory projects, and expressive activities, and employing a variety of media adapted to different learning styles.

One can go on from this basic platform emphasis to postulate the kind of learning environment which this emphasis would require, including teacher-student relationships, student groupings, daily and weekly schedules, grading systems, learning materials, etc.

FOCUS ON THE TEACHER'S CONSCIOUSNESS

Another quite different platform places the teacher more in the forefront. This example is taken from a speech in which a teacher attempts to describe his sense of values and the consciousness which lies at the heart of his teaching activity. This platform rests on one basic assumption—that the primary impact of a teacher on a student results from the teacher's ability to entice students to enter the universe of a teacher's consciousness, to begin to apprehend and appreciate reality as the teacher does. While much of the initial student learning may be primarily imitation or extrinsic appropriation, gradually the student begins to choose to look at the world in the way the teacher does. In other words, the teacher convinces the students that reality makes sense and has a value when observed, experienced, and dealt with from that frame of reference. Notice in what follows how this platform goes beyond the categories of the positions described in the previous chapter, but is open to encompass many of them.[6]

As a teacher, I find myself a stranger in my own homeland—a stranger somewhat in the sense of the character Meursault in Albert Camus' novel *The Stranger*. Many of the communities I could belong to—suburbia, political parties, the counter culture, the business corporation, the bureaucracy of the school—are involved in causes I cannot fully endorse, or with illusions of value and meaning I cannot support, or with life lived—from my perspective—at the level of half truths. Like the Israelites of old, I have tried out different versions of the promised land, joined in the worship of modern-day golden calves, only to find them wanting, discovering that, wherever the promised land was, it wasn't there . . . at least not for me.

In a sense my teaching forces me always to continue the search, for I find that students are *also* searching for the promised land, and we both know enough to discover at least where it is not. As a teacher, then, it seems to me that I have a responsibility to my students, not only to help them learn their numbers, and correct spelling, and the history of the novel, and the reliability tests for research design. Somehow I have to be involved with their search for "what life is all about," their "pursuit of happiness," their probing of the mysteries of living . . . however you want to put into words what lies at the heart of human living. Kids not only want to unlock the mysteries of the universe, they want to know what's worth striving for, what the good life is all about, what to *do* with their lives. Though my experience in the classroom has been with high school youth and graduate students, I have heard younger children also framing the question, if only by the bewildered look in their eyes. They want to know what's real and what's phony about the adult world—the world which for them means the real world where life eventually makes sense and gets lived in earnest.

But whom can I speak for? Whose version of the promised land do I propose? Their parents' version? I had chosen not to live in the world of the factory or of business, or of government or of welfare. The good life for most of my students' parents was not something I could agree with—a better job with fewer indignities; membership, for the most part, in a silent majority; a better castle in the suburb; evenings being assaulted and insulted by television; weekends filled frequently with trivialities; a life unembarrassed by suicide and political corruption and the outrageous inequities between rich and poor. Since I had chosen not to identify with that world, how then could I propose that illusion of living to my students?

On the other hand, neither do the rites of passage of children or youth offer me a universe worth living in, for the point of teaching, it seems to me, is to guide them *through* the pain and terror of the passage into something better. The teacher, rather, stands between the world of children and youth and the world of adult concerns— between the sandbox, Alice in Wonderland, Rock and Roll music, the junior prom *and* the adult world of careers, politics, homebuilding, paying taxes, making ends meet, getting ahead, deciding how the world will be run. But the limited universe of both does not provide me an adequate place to live: the perspectives, attitudes, values and habits of both worlds cannot entirely contain or exhaust what I believe the promised land to be.

[6] This platform was enunciated in a paper by Robert J. Starratt at a Fordham University meeting of Phi Delta Kappa, January 1977.

As a teacher I ought to be able to justify what I do with kids, why I choose to teach them history or biology or poetry. Why teach this, rather than that? Whose history do I teach? Which scientific metaphors make the most sense out of the universe? Whose economics do I support? Whose view of patriotism do I teach? Why teach music rather than alchemy?

The school board has a set of answers to these questions. The PTA may have a different set of answers. The teachers union hardly perceives the questions. But the Chamber of Commerce knows what the answers are . . . or the child psychologists or university professors. . . .

But none of their answers touch my concern—that's why I feel a stranger. I still ask: Why do you teach, how do you touch the lives of kids, how do you open doors with them to new possibilities, how do you help them discover who they are, how do you help them find the way, or at least help them through the night?

To do this, I need to live somewhere, to know what I'm about, to have a sense of direction. If I am a stranger in the city, in the suburbs, in this culture, in the bureaucracy, in the academic discipline, in the union, in the counter culture, in the youth culture, who do I relate to, what do I see as truly meaningful, to what promised land do I point the way?

Well I'll tell you where I think the promised land is if you promise not to have me put away. OK?

It's here. It's inside you, it's all around you. Maybe not with all the promises yet fulfilled, but certainly the makings are there. Basically, our problem amounts to not being in touch with what's there.

Perhaps a few examples will clarify what I'm getting at. Let's think of a blind person. Let's call him Joe. Joe has been blind for twenty years. He's learned how to get about, he reads braille and has even earned a college degree. Let's suppose an eye specialist comes up with a way to repair whatever causes Joe's blindness. The operation is successful and Joe can now see. Imagine his feelings as he lives through the first month with his sight: looking at the stars, at the faces of his family and friends, watching a sun set, staring at a rose. Suppose Joe was trying to explain to a friend, a medical student, what it's like to see, what a beautiful, miraculous—yes, holy experience it is to see. And suppose his friend were to explain that, well sight is not so miraculous, it's simply a matter of light waves reflected off surfaces which activate rods and cones in the eye, which trigger interior sensory response patterns—or some such explanation. No miracle . . . nothing great . . . we just break down the experience into the constitutive physical properties and, you see, it's all rather common, rather predictable. Do you think that will explain away Joe's sense of ecstasy in his new-found ability to see and admire?

Well, let's ask a social science friend of his. Oh, he'll tell Joe that his feelings are quite understandable; in fact, that his responses to his Questionnaire on Seeing correlate at the .01 level of significance with others who experienced a similar cure; he'll explain how Joe's organism responds to certain stimuli and that the emotional valence related to his perceptions are a result of his imitating cues he has learned from his environment.

Or perhaps Joe will enroll in a class called Seeing Skills I. In this class he will learn color and shape discrimination. His performance objectives are reviewed, after his pre-test, and then he is put before a screen on which various colors are flashed. At the end of the first class, Joe's teacher is overheard in the teachers' room criticizing Joe's apparent slowness in working through the exercises; he seems fixated by colors. He refuses to finish his assignments on time. He has a motivation problem, probably. He'll probably get a C in seeing.

Just imagine yourself as Joe . . . what it would be like to *see* after all those years of total darkness . . . and how difficult it would be to understand how people could take this gift so lightly.

What I'm talking about is what we take for granted—our own bodies, our own senses, our own minds and imaginations. And all around us—what we take for granted: the sky, the sun, trees and flowers and rivers and stars . . . and other people. How seldom we are startled by the amazing complexity of the universe. How easily we accommodate to tragedy and the pain of other people; by naming it, usually with a euphemism, we think we understand it. And so experience of things and people is always *superficial;* for all practical purposes the world is invisible, or it's paper thin, an op-art celluloid covering over the void.

"Well, that's all a consequence," you say, "of science and technology. We have lost our innocence, yes. We are no longer immersed in the naive universe of the primitive where everything had magical qualities. We have moved beyond anthropomorphism to objectivity. Now we know that electromagnetic forces account for certain phenomena which used to be interpreted as signs from God. And the balances between the id, superego and ego explain madness and sanity as well as guilt, sanctity and heroism." We explain miracles with metaphors rather than with divinities, and that, of course, reduces them from the status of miracle to the status of fact. Gravity is not miraculous; it is a fact. The structure of the atom is not unusual; it is a fact. There is nothing wonderful about babies—they are simply fertilized ova coming to full growth.

The world can be looked at as simply being there—simply a collection of rocks, land masses, soil, trees, rivers, buildings, roads, people. And *me.* Just there, hanging around so to speak, waiting for something to happen, but expecting that nothing will. And the human mind comes along and bestows, in its benign largess, names for things, arranges things into a pattern or order, and creates coherence and relationships.

Or . . . the world can be looked upon as alive, as inviting us to discover the truth about it by listening to the words it whispers to us. Suppose we listened to the music of water and trees and human sadness and watched the dancing of summer wheatfields and ocean swells and children's minds.

Suppose in fact the whole of nature was a dance of energy giving thanks to be what it is, each part adding its energy to the ballet. Then sunsets become a recapitulation of the meaning of the day, and birdsong echoes the joy of life, and the spirit of God broods over the surface of the waters.

Suppose, rather than being anthropomorphic in applying human characteristics to animals and trees and rocks, it worked the other way around for us? Rather than our bestowing human characteristics on nature, suppose that we are cosmomorphic, that in our being are fingerprints of the enormous cosmic struggle of energy toward self-reflection? Let us take evolution seriously and argue that we can hear the messages sent by inanimate and animate nature because we were *there* once? Then thought becomes a response to what's there, rather than an invention, and knowledge involves loving, caring for the things we seek to know because we *belong to each other*.

Or, if that's too heavy, at least the universe can be a gift for us. Nothing that I encounter is something I have *earned*. I can't really own anything ultimately. It is more given to me than deserved. So when I come to know someone or something, I can accept the experience with reverence, with gratitude, with awe. Like the power to see; like my intelligence; like flowers and friends and sunlight. Why should not learning erupt in surprise that things should thus disclose themselves to me? Why should not learning be like opening a gift? Why should not learning lead me to celebration? Why should not learning be an encounter with a miracle? Why should learning not transform my life because I live in a universe where promises are not broken? Promises are not broken by God or by the universe. We have been blessed beyond all measure with life. We are the ones who break promises. The promised land is here, now, everywhere. But we must *live* in it, not deny its existence, not camouflage the miracle with metaphors that break the larger miracles into smaller and supposedly more objective miracles.

Someone out there in the audience will argue:

"But, yes, you just said it—the problem is with society. Society breaks promises. And that's because society is divided into the haves and have-nots. The sociology of knowledge and Marxist analysis illuminate the real source of the problem. We are victims of our class. We belong to either the oppressors or the oppressed. Some people have power and wealth and the good things of life and others are denied these. So it's a struggle, class warfare whether overt or covert. A dog-eat-dog world. That's the way it is. That's the way it will always be."

But what is it, I ask you, that the "haves" have and the "have-nots" lack? Think about that. This is not a defense of such inequities. Rather, I would challenge the values attached to terms of the inequities. Is their definition of the "good life" real or illusory? Think about that. What is it we "have"? What is it we lack?

Social theorists and anthropologists can present a picture of society that is based on irrational aggressions, competition for scarce resources, or a struggle for territorial ownership or the power to dominate. If we accept this explanation as the whole truth about human society, we accept a society that is not only subhuman but, I submit, a society that is demonic. If, rather, we accept these social and cultural analyses as partial and biased descriptions of humankind on a journey toward the promised land, we are closer to recognizing the obligation we as a people have to the past and to the future. For we are Prometheus as well as Caliban and, like Lear, we enter a world of madness when we lose our vision. To lose our innocence leads not to objectivity; it leads rather to the worship of other gods, whether they be called science, facticity, or anthropological theory.

Knowledge is not opposed to innocence; rather knowledge reveals how marvelously the promise is fulfilled.

"What a rosy world," you say, "sugar-coated, embarrassing in its enthusiasm. We have been too often betrayed to believe in that fantasy. Better the locked doors, the barricaded heart, the objectivity of statistics that filter out ugliness and terror. Better a mindless routine that smothers curiosity. The Garden of Eden we left long ago."

And we think that lets us off the hook. But that is my point. We are not off the hook. There is no safe exit from the promised land. Once you recognize that you're there, you recognize that you are commanded by a word spoken in the depths of your being to take responsibility for it. And the flight from that responsibility leads inescapably to genuine self-destruction. We live in a promised land that only becomes our promised land (not my promised land, but ours, yours and mine) when we accept the gift with reverence and love and do something with it. Do something with it. Bring the promise to further fulfillment, whether that means devising a better economics which shares the wealth of the promised land more equitably; whether it means drawing from nature future medicine to heal human disease; whether it means involvement in a politics of shared responsibility for the common good; whether it means searching out the logic of madness which can cure the pain, or illuminating the madness of compulsive normalcy in order to free those imprisoned by that illusion.

Living in the promised land is not a simple rollercoaster ride through ecstasy. The ecstasy of finding your home here brings the burden of living out the promise, saying no to triviality, celebrating the gift by giving it away freely in the face of laughter and derision.

And so when I walk into a classroom, the challenge is there. There are the messengers from the past who forgot the message, asking you to restore the vision, to help them discover the promise and its implications, wanting to *own* the message so they can pass it on to their children.

We all have read about, if not experienced, moments in the lives of people that gave birth to hope, birth to a dramatic change in their lives which they can point to with reverence and say, "I think I began to see, to walk upright, to dance *then*." Or we know of others who point to similar moments and say, "That's when I gave up, caved in, threw in the towel; that's the encounter which broke my spirit and the bleeding has never stopped." And frequently, all too frequently, those moments come in an encounter with a teacher. It is a scary thing to wonder how many kids began to die today because of what I did or did not do, or to know that perhaps some kid began to live today, began to see the promise unfolding and reached out for it.

Life or death in the classroom. That is what teaching in the promised land means to me.

Living in this kind of promised land I can finally be a teacher. I know at least a part of the message and what I need to do. I don't teach my students to despise suburbia, or their parents' work, or science, or Hollywood, or the banks. My job rather is to put them in touch with the promised land inside them and all around them, to let them sink their roots in that soil, breathe deeply that air, wonder over the miracle of sight and blood and springtime, test the loyalty of rain and mountains and trees, experience the magnanimous love within the fabric of the universe that offers them *itself* as a gift. And then let them go out into their neighborhoods and families to live and preach the good news.

> So the blind will see
> and the lame and crippled can stand on their own feet
> so prisoners can be set free
> and the poor receive the news of their inheritance.

In conclusion, let me restate my thesis. Our integrity as persons is always at stake in the classroom. We are the messengers from the past with a message for our children and for their children. The promised land is here, is offered to us. Those who accept that inheritance are qualified to be teachers. For in teaching we either replenish or frustrate a wondrous expectation. Ultimately, teaching is aimed at one thing . . . celebration.[7]

In this platform, the teacher is much more at the center than in the previous platform. Also, there is a definite value orientation to the teacher's activities. On the other hand, this platform would not necessarily rule out a considerable amount of individualization. It would mean, however, that the individualized learning would always or usually lead to appreciation as its primary goal.

THE SUPERVISOR'S PLATFORM

In stressing the importance of the supervisor's explicating his or her own platform, we realize that it may or may not come out as theoretical or as poetic as the two contained in this chapter. These were drawn in considerable detail for the sake of clarity. On the other hand, the effort to elucidate one's platform is of primary importance to the supervisor's task. Without sufficient clarity on what one really believes important in schooling, it will be really difficult to assist teachers in clarifying what their educational platforms are. As we will see in subsequent chapters,[8] the process of clinical supervision we propose involves this clarification process. If the teacher is to profit from the interaction with the supervisor and to move clearly and decisively toward sharply focused growth objectives, then the effort at platform clarification, and perhaps at platform amplification, will be one of the supervisor's primary concerns.

What are some practical guidelines, then, which might assist supervisors to draw up their platform? First we will look at some of the key ingredients which should make up an educational platform and then add some that belong specifically to a supervisor's educational platform. Then we will suggest some methods of drawing up and using one's platform.

We can identify 10 major ingredients that should be included in any educational platform.[9] Using these as benchmarks, supervisors could identify the key elements of their own platforms and those of teachers they supervise.

1 The aims of education—Here, the treatment of the schools of thought discussed in the previous chapter would help to clarify where one stood in terms of one's emphasis. Here it would help to set down, in order of priority (if possi-

---

[7] Abraham J. Heschel, *Who Is Man?* Stanford, Calif.: Stanford, 1965, and Peter Berger, *The Homeless Mind,* New York: Random House, 1973, were especially influential on the tone of this presentation.

[8] See Chapters 15 and 16.

[9] We have been helped in identifying these ingredients by the categories used by Zvi Lamm in *Conflicting Theories of Instruction,* Berkeley, Calif.: McCutchan, 1976. We have modified these categories and the interpretation Lamm gives them, however. In his provocative treatment, Lamm attempts to expound the logic behind what amounts to three educational platforms. Unfortunately, in our opinion, he has so stereotyped two of them as to render his analysis inapplicable for our purposes.

ble), the three most important aims of education—not simply education in the abstract, but education for the youngsters in our school system.

2 Major achievements of students this year—Bringing these aims down to more specific application, identify the major achievements of students that one deals with desired by the end of the year. (For example, some might put down mastery of some academic skills up to a certain level; others might put down the acquisition of certain basic principles which would govern behavior; others might put down more personal achievements, such as increased self-awareness or self-confidence, or trust and openness.)

3 The social significance of the student's learning—Here one might find that he or she emphasizes learning for entering the world of work; others might focus more on the utilization of learning for good citizenship; still others might focus on the acquisition of the cultural heritage of our civilization. This element may also draw a response which denies any direct major social significance to the student's learning because of a predisposition to view the individual in a highly individualistic sense.

4 The image of the learner—This element tries to uncover attitudes or assumptions about how one learns. Is the learner an empty vessel into which one pours information? Some may view the learner in a uniform way—as though all learners are basically the same and will respond equally to a uniform pedagogy. Some may use "faculty" psychology to explain how students learn. Still others will differentiate among various styles and dispositions for learning which point to a greater emphasis on individualization of learning.

5 The value of the curriculum—This element touches upon attitudes about what the student learns. Some will say that the most important learnings are those most immediately useful in "real" life. Others will say that any kind of learning is intrinsically valuable. Others would qualify that latter position and consider some learnings, such as the humanities or the school subjects to be intrinsically more valuable, because they touch upon those more central areas of our culture. Others would claim that the learning of subjects has value only insofar as it sorts out people of different abilities and interests and channels them in socially productive directions. Some might even claim that the curriculum helps youngsters to understand God better.

6 The image of the teacher—What basically is a teacher? Is a teacher an employee of the state, following the educational policies and practices dictated by the local, state, and federal government? Or is a teacher a professional specialist whom a community employs to exercise his or her expertise on behalf of youngsters? Or is a teacher a spokesperson for tradition, passing on the riches of the culture? Or is a teacher a political engineer, leading youngsters to develop those skills necessary for the reform of their society? This element tries to elicit assumptions about the role of the teacher.

7 The preferred kind of pedagogy—This element should be fairly clear. Will the teacher dominate the learning experience? Some assume that inquiry learning is the best way to teach. Others assume that each discipline lends itself better to some forms of pedagogy than others and that, therefore, the discipline will dictate the pedagogy. Some would opt for a much more permissive, student-initiated learning enterprise. While there would understandably be some reluctance to focus on *one* pedagogical approach to the exclusion of all others, nonetheless, we usually tend to settle on two or three as the more effective approaches.

8 The primary language of discourse in learning situations—This element frequently concerns the levels and quality of learning involved.[10] Does the language focus on precision of verbal definitions or the precise measurement of phenomena, or does it rather stress imaginative relationships? Frequently the difference between the question "How do you feel about that?" and the question "What do you think about that?" reveals a basic orientation toward the kind and level of learning being emphasized. Frequently a metaphor that is used gives away some underlying attitude, whether it be concerned with exact precision, the moral use of knowledge, or artistic sensibility.[11]

9 The preferred kind of teacher-student relationship—This element involves the quality of interpersonal relationships preferred by the teacher and student. Some would prefer a very caring kind of relationship in which the "needs of the whole child" are attended to. Others would prefer much more distance, leaving the personal needs of the students for someone else to attend to, stressing more the academic discipline. Still others would be very nondirective, allowing the spontaneous, felt needs of the child to direct the relationship, with the teacher being more of a resource person. Others might prefer a group orientation in which the teacher works primarily to facilitate the work of the group.

10 The preferred kind of school climate—Here, some of the organizational considerations touched upon in the previous chapter would come into play. This element concerns a constellation of factors such as schoolwide and classroom discipline, student pride in the school, faculty morale, the openness of the school community to divergent life styles, expressive learnings, and individualistic ways of thinking and behaving. Some would opt for order and predictability. Others would prefer a more relaxed climate, perhaps more boisterous but also more creative and spontaneous. This element would be very much related to what is valued in the curriculum and to the social consequences of learning.[12]

It becomes obvious as one tests out one's assumptions under each of the categories listed above that there tends to be an intrinsic logic to them. That is, there tends to be a consistency between assumptions about the nature of the learner and the preferred kind of teacher-student relationship, which in turn relates logically to one's beliefs about the aims of education.[13] As one clarifies one's assumptions, beliefs, and opinions under each of these 10 categories, the platform one uses in one's everyday actions in the school should begin to become apparent. That is to say, we usually make practical decisions about our professional practice as educators based upon convictions, assumptions, and attitudes which are not that clearly or frequently articulated. Nevertheless, they do influence, some would even say dominate, our actions. By bringing these convictions, assumptions, and attitudes out into the open for our own reflection, we can

---

[10] Benjamin S. Bloom, *Taxonomy of Educational Objectives: The Classification of Educational Goals, Handbook I: Cognitive Domain,* New York: McKay, 1956.

[11] Dwayne Huebner, "Curriculum Language and Classroom Meanings," in James B. Macdonald and Robert R. Leeper (eds.), *Language and Meaning,* Washington, D.C.: Association for Supervision and Curriculum Development, 1966, pp. 8–26.

[12] The material in Chapter 13 very much relates to questions about school climate, although there the focus is primarily on the classroom setting rather than the schoolwide setting.

[13] Again, we wish to acknowledge Lamm's *Conflicting Theories of Instruction* as the recent reminder of the logic inherent in our educational platforms.

evaluate their internal consistency and cogency. We can also check whether we are satisfied with our platform, or whether, perhaps, we have not taken important factors into consideration. By clarifying the underlying rationale for our actions, we might see a need to grow in specific areas in order to increase our effectiveness as well as to broaden our human capacities.

Two other categories round out the supervisor's platform. That is to say, the above analysis of key elements in a platform has been dealing with an educational platform. This educational platform focuses on what one believes ought to happen in a process of formal education. It could belong to a teacher, a student, an administrator, or a supervisor. The supervisor can elaborate his or her own educational platform, but it becomes complete when the supervisor adds his or her convictions about how the activity of supervising is supposed to help such a platform influence the realities of a school. The two categories that concern supervision are the following: the purpose of supervision, and the preferred process of supervision.

In a sense this whole book deals with the purpose and the process of supervision. Chapters 1 and 2 cover material that could be used to elaborate one's purpose or goals in being a supervisor. Chapters 4 to 6 deal with material that relates to the basic process of supervision in the organizational framework of the school.

11   The purpose or goal of supervision—Some would answer from a neo-scientific orientation. Others would speak from a human relations perspective. Still others would utilize the human resources rationale.

12   The preferred process of supervision—Some would express a preference for the clinical supervision approach.[14] Others would prefer a more permissive process which does not involve any evaluation or feedback, but only periodic reports by the teacher on what is being done in the classroom.

Again, the point of clarifying one's convictions and unspoken assumptions about the nature of supervision is to open the door for growth, for the sharing of ideas, and for supervisory performance that operates out of a clear sense of direction. Ideally, these last two elements of the supervisor's platform should perhaps be written down at the beginning, before one reads this book, and then at the end, after one has read the book. If the analysis of supervision presented between these covers has an effect, it would show up in the differences between the two platform statements.

APPROACHES TO PLATFORM CLARIFICATION

Many supervisors may find the initial efforts at platform clarification very frustrating. It is not something they do often, and therefore there can be a feeling of awkwardness. Yet everyone has an unexpressed platform. Were a sensitive observer to follow the supervisor around for a day or two on the job, it would be relatively easy to guess that supervisor's beliefs about how youngsters learn best,

---

[14] See Chapters 15 and 16.

about what is important to learn, about good teaching and inferior teaching, etc. Our actions usually reveal our assumptions and attitudes quite clearly.

Many will find the orderly process of filling out where one stands on the 12 elements of the platform the most convenient approach to take. The categories provide guidance in identifying the essential characteristics of one's platform. One can also check the internal consistency between statements under each category.

Others will prefer a less structured approach, letting their assumptions come out as they are felt and recognized, rather than having to force them into categories with which they are uncomfortable.[15] They will have a more difficult time expressing their platform, perhaps, but this approach may be far more rewarding for them.

Sometimes it helps to find a quiet place and to write down one's reflections. Normally, these will come out in a jumble, in no particular order of priority. Once we have written down the elements of our platform, we can with further reflection begin to group them in clusters and place them in some order of importance. Almost everyone with any experience in education, however, will feel several times during this exercise the need to qualify and nuance those general statements. "Which teaching strategy I'd use in a given situation depends a lot on a youngster's background. But by and large, I'd choose this approach." "While I'd place my major emphasis on mastery of basic intellectual skills, I still think it's important to spend some time teaching kids good manners." "I almost always prefer to start a lesson with a colorful advance organizer. That usually stirs up the kids' curiosity. But there are times when I run plain, old-fashioned memory drills."

Others will find the writing exercise too tedious and will seek out a colleague to discuss this whole question. The free flow of shared ideas frequently stimulates the process of clarification. In those instances, having a tape recorder along may help for subsequent transcription of the conversation. Others may find a combination of dialogue and writing the better way. Still others may go to a formal statement of goals which the school or system has in print to begin the process. By studying the goals and *probing the assumptions behind them,* the supervisor may discover areas of disagreement or agreement.

COMPARING PLATFORMS

However one goes about clarifying his or her platform initially, two other steps will prove helpful. After the first tentative statement of the platform, the supervisor should compare his or her platform with those of two or three colleagues, to test out areas of agreement or disagreement. Sometimes this may lead to modification of one's platform. It may also lead to a greater acceptance of diversity of perspectives. It certainly will help supervisors to build teamwork. Knowing the

[15] People in this group may identify with many of the sentiments expressed in William Pinar (ed.), *Curriculum Theorizing: The Reconceptualists,* Berkeley, Calif.: McCutchan, 1975. The authors there break new ground, using different categories to lend intelligibility to their educational platform.

basic biases of each other's approach will enable them to understand, at least, why they differ, and may also encourage them to work together in areas where they agree or might complement one another.

When the supervisors have discussed their platforms together, they should then compare them with the school's or the system's platform. That may not exist in a written document, but, as in their own cases, it exists implicitly in the operational policies of the school or school system. Frequently, they may find some genuine discrepancies between what the goal statements profess and what the school practices. Bringing those discrepancies to light, in itself, would be a service to the school. The purpose of examining against each other the expressed and unexpressed (but operative) platforms of the school, however, is aimed more at a comparison between the school's platform and the supervisor's platform. If they find striking divergences between them, then the supervisors will have to seek some means of reconciling the divergences, or of modifying one or the other to make them more compatible.

The point of this exercise is not to introduce frustration and cynicism but on the contrary to reduce it. It may be that the platform of the school and that of the supervisor are incompatible. In our opinion, the supervisor should leave the school in that case, and go to one which is more compatible. But if the supervisor or supervisory group in a school or school system are to exercise their potential influence in upgrading the quality of education, then they must be generally in agreement with the platform of the school or school system. Where that agreement exists, then supervisors can work with teachers and programs to achieve commonly agreed-upon goals. This does not mean uniformity in its oppressive sense. Rather, the supervisors can mobilize the talent and enthusiasm of the teachers, along with the technical support system of the school to move in an agreed-upon direction.

SUMMARY

In this chapter we have taken up the concept of the educational platform. When two examples of educational platforms were given, it became apparent that a platform is made up of those basic assumptions, beliefs, attitudes, and values which are the underpinnings of one's behavior an as educator. The examples were elaborate, yet highly personal. It was left to the reader to draw out from those platform statements a series of general statements which could make up a more skeletal platform.

Some time was spent suggesting ways in which supervisors could draw up their own platform. Ten essential elements to the platform were outlined, with two additional ones added for supervisors. With these as guidelines, supervisors can then begin to draw up their own educational platform. Again, the logic and basic intelligibility which flows from platform clarification to one's supervisory practice was stressed as the point of the whole exercise.

With this as a foundation, we can now move on to other concerns for the supervisor's exercise of educational leadership.

STUDY GUIDE

Recall the concepts and meanings associated with each of the following phrases and terms included in this chapter. Can you discuss them with a colleague and apply them to the supervisory context of your school? If you cannot, review them in the text and record the page number for future reference.

1 Educational platform _____
2 Environmental interaction chart _____
3 Human growth model _____
4 Maslow's motivation theory _____
5 Porter's hierarchy of needs _____
6 Reality-oriented behavior _____
7 Student-oriented platform _____
8 Teacher-oriented platform _____
9 Ten elements of an educational platform _____
10 Two elements of a supervisor's platform _____

EXERCISES

1 What is the difference between need-dominated behavior and reality-oriented behavior? Give three examples of each. Is one *necessarily* better than the other?
2 In your experience with teachers, pick out two whom you know pretty well and try to write down their platform according to the 10 categories.
3 Imagine you were talking with the teacher who spoke of his promised land. Role-play it out with someone else in the class.
4 Write out your platform only for your own eyes. After you have completed it, ask yourself whether it would differ much if you had to show it to your superintendent.

Chapter 12

Supervising Varieties of Curricula

The thesis of Part Two of this book is that educational supervision deals not only with the school as an organization but as an organization established for the purposes of education. Educational supervision, therefore, of necessity involves the supervisor in educational theory, in regard to both the general purposes of education and the means to achieve these purposes, the curriculum-instructional program. In this chapter we wish to summarize some of the more important issues supervisors face when, in their interaction with subordinates, they move into the arena of curriculum and instruction.

Curriculum has been often separated from instruction, or pedagogy, for purposes of analysis, research, and evaluation, as well as for professional course work in graduate schools. The supervisor, however, will most often encounter it in its living form, that is, embodied in the behavior of a teacher. Yet what the supervisor encounters in the instructional behavior of the teacher may not be immediately intelligible beyond a surface impression of the teacher's physical actions and interactions with students. Without some frames of reference provided either by the teacher or by his or her own study and experience, the observer may not be able to interpret the significance of the sequence of class activities, or why the teacher chose to introduce the topic in such and such a manner.

One way of attempting to understand curriculum and its influence in what goes on in the classroom is to review the textbook and other materials being used in the class. Another way, which gets one closer to the reality of what one is supposed to be supervising, is to study the teacher's lesson plans, not only for that day, but for the classes that follow. While these two steps are helpful, the observation and analysis of the actual instructional activity lie at the heart of the activity of educational supervision. It is in this instructional activity that the supervisor sees the teacher putting into action the teacher's integration of his or her educational platform with the goals of the school, the goals of this course, the specific objectives of this particular unit or lesson, and his or her knowledge of the ability, interests, and personalities of the students in the class. All these influences are uniquely synthesized, integrated, and molded, and then put into action in the teacher's instructional activity. Therefore, one observing that activity somehow has to be very sensitive to the intentions of the teacher to see how the activity of the teacher reflects this complex integration or synthesis. In other words, the supervisor must try to observe how the curriculum or the teacher's perception of it is, in fact, one of the controlling influences in what the teacher *does* in that classroom.

Perhaps an example will clarify. You may attend a performance of the ballet. In order to interpret, understand, and appreciate what the dancers are doing, the audience needs to know something about the story or the message which the dance interprets. That is, the audience tries to understand what the dancers are trying to express through their motions and pace. The dancer can sit down with you before or after the performance and explain the mood or the symbolism of such and such a part of the dance, but it is only when you observe her or him actually expressing that in motion in performance that you perceive and know what she or he means. You then can make some judgment about the quality of the performance and whether you think the movement reflected and communicated to you what the dancer intended.

So, too, one does not understand the teacher's instructional activity without some idea of how the curriculum is influencing that activity. Neither, on the other hand, does one understand how the curriculum actually gets transmitted to, or appropriated by, the students unless one observes it alive in an instructional transaction. In order to suggest how supervisors might interpret instructional activity by means of more sophisticated cognitive maps, or analytic lenses, we will now take up some perspectives and questions on curriculum.

CURRICULUM-INSTRUCTIONAL ACTIVITY

The term "curriculum" has many definitions, as does the term "instruction." For our purposes, we will define *curriculum* as that which the student is supposed to encounter, study, practice, and master—in short the "stuff" of what the student learns. That can be many things, from a basic skill like counting numbers, to spelling 100 words correctly, to memorizing the multiplication tables, to understanding the biological explanations of photosynthesis, to playing the piano, to writing verse, to comparing Plato's *Republic* with Augustine's *City of God* in a doctoral dissertation. We acknowlege that there is always a hidden or informal curriculum being taught in the classroom as well as elsewhere in the school. But we wish here to restrict curriculum to the formal or overt curriculum.

Instruction we will define as that process by which the student is led to encounter the curriculum to the desired degree of mastery. Not only must the instructional process lead the student to the curriculum, it must so structure that encounter that the student does not move on to something else before a predetermined level of mastery is achieved. Instruction, then, can be something a teacher does, or it can be built into a programmed textbook or into a computer or a learning packet.

In general, we will speak of curriculum as "what is to be learned" and instruction as "how it is to be taught." One must be aware, however, that these are loose and pragmatic ways of speaking. To say that instruction means how something is to be taught can be misleading. For example, someone could say: "I learned that by hard work, by breaking that problem down myself into the small pieces until I could find where the loose wire was. . . . I taught myself how to do that." In that instance there was no external instructor. In a sense, the person instructed herself. Or perhaps the person had earlier learned a generalizable problem-solving skill which in turn taught her a way of attacking other problems. In that instance, what she learned (the problem-solving skill) taught her in subsequent experiences *how* to learn other things. For our purposes, however, we will use instruction primarily to refer to a process in which a teacher is interacting with a student.

OBSERVING INSTRUCTIONAL ACTIVITY

Now, let us suppose you are having a busy day supervising. You visit the classes of five teachers. You discover that each teacher is using quite different methodologies. One teacher has his class divided into small groups and they spend most of the class discussing how best to go about studying the wave versus the particle theories of light. In another, the teacher is showing an animated cartoon which illustrates the different properties of light but concludes by leaving the students in a quandary over which theory of light is correct. In another class, the teacher is relating Newtonian particle physics to individualistic theories of society, and contrasting that with field theory physics and more communal views of society; toward the end of class the students get into a lively discussion of the low level of student morale and the prevailing tendencies of people at the school to "do their own thing." In the fourth class you find the students in the physics laboratory performing an experiment with a ripple tank, carefully following the instructions in their lab books and recording their measurements carefully in their notebooks. There is no class discussion; the teacher merely walks around the lab, occasionally pointing out a faulty measurement notation or telling one student team to stop "goofing off" or he will send them to detention hall. In the fifth class the students have been reading a biography of Isaac Newton and the teacher has assigned teams to prepare a model replication of Newton's laboratory. The class begins with the teacher questioning the students about the antecedent scientific knowledge to which Newton had access which might have shaped much of Newton's approach to his experiments.

You come back to your office at the end of the day with a half hour before you must leave to referee the girls' basketball game in the league quarter finals. Tomorrow you will be scheduled for individual conferences with all the teachers you have observed today. Besides all the routine aspects of class management such as the lighting, ventilation, noise levels, pupil attentiveness, and so forth, what will you say about the approach the teacher is using, especially as that relates to the curriculum that is supposed to be taught? Granting the observable strengths and weaknesses of each teacher in putting on the instructional performance (self-confidence, good tone of voice, good use of questions, etc.), can you say that one approach was better than the other? If you say none of the approaches is necessarily better, do you mean that they are all interchangeable, that it does not really matter which approach one uses? Or does each approach come out of a different idea of what the curriculum is or is supposed to be? Are these approaches mutually exclusive? Is the content learned in one approach totally different from the content learned in another? Or are there some common learnings one finds embedded in each approach? Is it fair, however, to give one departmental exam covering material taught in such divergent ways? How would these students score on a national physics test? Does it make much difference to you if the teacher does not care that much about national test scores? Before you begin to put some order into these bewildering issues, the bell rings and you must dash over to the gym to catch the bus for the girls' basketball tournament. (Jogging across the parking lot, you wish now you had put more time in on your graduate supervision course when these issues were discussed!)

Let us leave our distraught supervisor and return to our more dispassionate and reflective environment to put some order, sequence, and logic into this task. For example, what were some of the questions that did *not* occur to our frantic supervisor? It might be a good test of our own frames of reference if we were to pause at this point, close the book, and place ourselves in the situation, without the press of time and the girls' basketball game distracting us. Perhaps we could generate 10 other questions of major importance. After we put them down in the haphazard order in which they occur to us, we might order or group them in some sequence, e.g., moving from the more abstract to the more particular, or from those dealing with curriculum to those dealing with student achievement, to those dealing with the teacher's platform, etc.

OTHER QUESTIONS

An exercise such as the above will yield a variety of results. One salutary effect of going through the exercise and then sharing the results with others is that one quickly recognizes how many potentially useful questions there are. It becomes clear that classroom observation must be preceded by at least one lengthy conference in which the teacher can indicate what his or her intentions for the class are.

Our own first attempt to complete the exercise yielded the following questions. They are by no means exhaustive. We shall see subsequently that the kinds of questions we ask will emerge out of a variety of frames of reference about curriculum. But for the present let us consider the following questions for purposes of illustration.

1 *Methods and instructional effectiveness.* Are any of these five ways the most effective way to teach this? Is there another way that would be demonstrably the *most* effective way to teach that material? Suppose that the students might have had the opportunity to travel to a nearby government research lab doing interplanetary research on light signals? Or might the teacher have invited the director of the lab to come to the school to put on a demonstration lab, using all the latest sophisticated technology involved in spectroscopy?

Does the teacher always or usually use this method? If the teacher uses other methods, what are they? Are they related to specific curricular objectives, or are they used primarily to relieve boredom (which could also be a curriculum objective)?

2 *Instructional activity and curriculum-instructional objectives.* What is the teacher trying to do? Is the teacher trying to teach one thing or several things simultaneously?

What precisely is it that she or he wants to teach? To what level of mastery? Was that clear to you? Was it clear to the students? Why did the teacher choose this precise activity as the best or at least as a good means to bring the students into a learning encounter with the curricular material? In your judgment, was the means effective? How effective was it? Was it effective for all the students or only for some?

What level of mastery was evidenced by the students? How do you know that?

How does what the teacher is doing today flow out of what the class has been doing in previous classes? Is there a sequential order to the course, and if so, how does this part fit into the sequence? How much time does the teacher plan to spend on this matter of theories of light? To what level of mastery does the teacher wish to bring the students? Is the time being spent adequate for this purpose? Is that degree of mastery required to grasp the material coming later? Is there a balance between the time spent on this topic and the time spent on earlier and later topics? Who decides that? Who ought to decide that?

Is the teacher aware of the hidden, or informal, curricula involved in this approach?

3 *Curriculum-instructional units and departmental or school objectives.* How does this class and this course fit in with the departmental or school objectives? Is there a particular focus or emphasis to the objectives which each course is supposed to reinforce? If so, was there evidence of that reinforcement in this class? Why does the department or school support, or at least tolerate, such divergent methods of teaching? Are there specific objectives which are served by these differing approaches? Are these approaches the only methods encouraged in the department or school, or are there others?

4 *Methods and teacher-supervisor platforms.* How does this teaching method or approach fit with the teacher's platform? Are there obvious discrepancies between the observable behavior and the platform? If there are, are there legitimate reasons for the discrepancies? How does the teaching method fit with your (the supervisor's) platform? Are you aware of your comfort or discomfort, plea-

sure or displeasure over the fit or lack of it? Did these feelings, perhaps unacknowledged during the classroom observation, lead either to perceptions of only weak points of the class or perceptions of only strong points? Do you need to review your observations to weed out at least some of the bias that comes from your own platform?

If you knew nothing about the teacher's platform prior to the observation, could you infer what it was from the instructional activity you observed?

If you knew nothing of the teacher's class plan, could you infer what the primary instructional objectives of this class were?

If you knew nothing of what preceded this class, what could you infer that students already knew about the topic? What could you infer about their possession of skills and understandings necessary for learning the topic of the class?

By comparing your questions with these and those developed by others, you may begin to see some pattern or points of emphasis developing. But where do these questions come from, and why are they important? A little reflection will indicate that many of them come from our concepts or beliefs about the nature of learning, about what a curriculum is supposed to be, about the nature of the academic discipline, etc. In order for the supervisor to know at least some of the important questions to ask, he or she ought to have some clear ideas about curriculum and how supervisors can affect its improvement or effectiveness in an instructional setting.

BEYOND DOGMATISM

One of the more refreshing innovations in teacher training appears in the work of Bruce Joyce and Marsha Weil dealing with models of teaching.[1] They have studied a variety of teaching styles, processes, and interaction schemes and have come up with 16 models of teaching. Each model has some theoretical underpinnings to it, has a recognizable sequence of activities and a major orientation or a set of educational objectives, requires a consistent type of classroom interaction and a type of support system, and has, finally, general applicability to either specific purposes or many purposes.

Each one of these models also presumes a curriculum. That is, the models of teaching are not concerned exclusively with methodology, but imply a curriculum, at least in a general sense. Frequently, a theory of learning is embedded in the model. In some of the models a theory of groups or of society is also implied. These models are touched upon here to provide the prospective or practicing supervisor with some mental maps or schemata for use with teachers or others involved in the instructional system, rather than to propose any particular model as the best model.

It is our belief that different models are applicable to the demands of different situations. In that sense, using one model or approach may be "better," not in an absolute sense, but in the sense of its being more appropriate to a given set of circumstances. If a teacher engages in instructional activity that remains always

[1] Bruce Joyce and Marsha Weil, *Models of Teaching,* Englewood Cliffs, N.J.: Prentice-Hall, 1972.

the same, there may be circumstances in which that activity is counterproductive for at least some, if not all, of the students. Or a teacher's repertory of instructional strategies may be larger, consisting of three or four, but even then the teacher may still lack the versatility to respond to given situations that arise in a classroom.

In like manner, a supervisor may be working with a limited number of models in mind. In a given situation where a teacher asks a supervisor for help in tackling a difficult instructional task, this lack of versatility will limit the instructional options which the two of them produce. Moreover, some familiarity with a wide diversity of possible curriculum-instructional approaches will render the supervisor better prepared for the unexpected. When the unexpected occurs, we usually react negatively, because it does not fit our categories, our mental maps. If, for example, we conceive of art education only as discrete encounters with discrete art forms, then we might be upset by an art teacher whose class is involved in "environmental" art projects in which several art forms and media are simultaneously employed. Familiarity with a broad range of curriculum-instructional options enables the supervisor to appreciate truly unique and creative approaches.

Joyce and Weil initially identified more than 80 positions on learning which could be used in some way as models for teaching and curriculum development. As they began sorting through the potential models, they began to group them according to four basic families which represent different orientations toward the learner and the environment.

> Although there is much overlap among families (and among models within families), the four are: (1) those oriented toward social relations and toward the relation between man and his culture and which draw upon social sources; (2) those which draw on information-processing systems and descriptions of human capacity for processing information; (3) those which draw on personality development, the processes of personal construction of reality and the capacity to function as an integrated personality as the major source; (4) those developed from an analysis of the process by which human behavior is shaped and reinforced.[2]

Joyce and Weil then selected exemplars of each basic family as a way of explaining each basic approach and some of the possible varieties within the basic approach. They propose 16 models, although they assert that these by no means exhaust the universe of potential models. In Table 12-1 they list the models along with the major theorist associated with the model, the family or basic orientation of the model, and the purposes for which the model is applicable.

As you study the variety of models proposed, you may find some that are quite unfamiliar to you. Further reading in the curriculum field may be called for. It should also be clear that the models presented are representative, and that not all varieties of teaching or curriculum frameworks are represented here. It

---

[2] Bruce Joyce and Marsha Weil, *Models of Teaching,* Copyright 1972, p. 8. Reprinted by permission of Prentice-Hall, Inc., Englewood Cliffs, N.J.

Table 12-1   The Models of Teaching Classified by Family and Mission

	Model	Major theorist	Family or orientation	Missions or goals for which applicable
1.	Inductive Teaching Model	Hilda Taba	Information Processing	Primarily for development of inductive mental processes and academic reasoning or theory-building, but these capacities are useful for personal and social goals as well.
2.	Inquiry Training Model	Richard Suchman	Information Processing	
3.	Science Inquiry Model	Joseph J. Schwab (also much of the Curriculum Reform Movement; see Jerome Bruner, *The Process of Education,* for the rationale)	Information Processing	Designed to teach the research system of the discipline but also expected to have effects in other domains (i.e., sociological methods may be taught in order to increase social understanding and social problem-solving).
4.	Jurisprudential Teaching Model	Donald Oliver and James P. Shaver	Social Interaction	Designed primarily to teach the jurisprudential frame of reference as a way of processing information but also as a way of thinking about and resolving social issues.
5.	Concept Attainment Model	Jerome Bruner	Information Processing	Designed primarily to develop inductive reasoning.
6.	Developmental Model	Jean Piaget, Irving Sigel, Edmund Sullivan	Information Processing	Designed to increase general intellectual development, especially logical reasoning, but can be applied to social and moral development as well. (See Kohlberg.)
7.	Advance Organizer Model	David Ausubel	Information Processing	Designed to increase the efficiency of information-processing capacities to meaningfully absorb and relate bodies of knowledge.
8.	Group Investigation Model	Herbert Thelen John Dewey	Social Interaction	Development of skills for participation in democratic social process through combined emphasis on interpersonal and social (group) skills and aca-

Table 12-1   The Models of Teaching Classified by Family and Mission (Continued)

Model	Major theorist	Family or orientation	Missions or goals for which applicable
			demic inquiry. Aspects of personal development are important outgrowths of this model.
9. Social Inquiry Model	Bryon Massialas Benjamin Cox	Social Interaction	Social problem-solving primarily through academic inquiry and logical reasoning.
10. Laboratory Method Model	National Training Laboratory (NTL) Bethel, Maine	Social Interaction	Development of interpersonal and group skills and through this, personal awareness and flexibility.
11. Nondirective Teaching Model	Carl Rogers	Person	Emphasis on building capacity for self-instruction and through this, personal development in terms of self-understanding, self-discovery, and self-concept.
12. Classroom Meeting Model	William Glasser	Person	Development of self-understanding and self-responsibility. This would have latent benefits to other kinds of functioning, i.e., social.
13. Awareness Training Model	William Schutz Fritz Perls	Person	Increasing personal capacity for self-exploration and self-awareness. Much emphasis on development of interpersonal awareness and understanding.
14. Synectics Model	William Gordon	Person	Personal development of creativity and creative problem-solving.
15. Conceptual Systems Model	David E. Hunt	Person	Designed to increase personal complexity and flexibility. Matches environments to students.
16. Operant Conditioning Model	B. F. Skinner	Behavior Modification	General applicability. A domain-free approach though probably most applicable to information-processing function.

Source: Bruce Joyce and Marsha Weil, *Models of Teaching*, © 1972, pp. 11–13. Reprinted by permission of Prentice-Hall, Inc., Englewood Cliffs, N.J.

would seem, for example, that expressive learnings in the arts are given somewhat short shrift in this collection. For our purposes, however, this listing of a variety of curriculum-instructional models illustrates the broad range of types and styles that are possible and indeed desirable in a school setting. The supervisor who is familiar with a wide range of curriculum-instructional models will more readily recognize what the teacher is doing or intending to do—what the frame of reference is. The supervisor can then more easily interpret and evaluate how the teacher's activity within that framework is consistent and effective.

BLOOM'S TAXONOMY

Bloom's *Taxonomy* provides another useful interpretive map, or conceptual frame of reference, for the supervisor.[3] Within the cognitive domain, especially, Bloom's analysis of levels of learning can illuminate the focus of the instructional activity. The six cognitive levels proposed by Bloom and widely used in educational circles are:

1 Knowledge—ability to recall information from memory; knowledge of specific facts, definitions, symbols, formulae, conventions and steps in a process.
2 Comprehension—understanding. Ability to translate, rephrase, interpret, recognize essentials, extrapolate or recognize implications and limitations.
3 Application—(some call this transfer). Ability to use knowledge and understanding in a novel situation to solve problems.
4 Analysis—breaking a whole into its elements. Analysis of relationships, organizational principles, multiple causation, etc.
5 Synthesis—putting together elements and parts to form a new whole.
6 Evaluation—making judgments in a field using internal evidence or external standards.

With these levels of learning in mind, one can read through a teacher's manual, or a lesson plan, or a curriculum guide and quickly perceive the objectives of learning units or parts of units. Likewise, by observing the questioning patterns of teachers in an instructional setting, one can quickly see whether the teacher is focusing on simple recall or memory of terms, or whether he or she is asking for more. All too often, teachers test for memory only, and seldom go beyond that to require students to think. On the other hand, supervisors need to caution the inexperienced teacher who expects third graders to handle an abstract analysis of energy transfers in electronics. The ideal instructional objective would be to gear the learning tasks to the levels of cognitive development that students at their age level should have achieved. Most of the learning exercises should allow the student to employ those cognitive structures which have developed at his or her age level with increasing facility, providing enough repetition to solidify the learning and ensure a feeling of competence and enjoyment. The supervisor, on the other hand, should encourage the teacher to stretch the abilities of the students from time to time, to place expectations on their performance

---

[3] Benjamin S. Bloom, *Taxonomy of Educational Objectives: The Classification of Educational Goals. Handbook I—Cognitive Domain,* New York: McKay, 1956.

that go just a little bit beyond what they can comfortably handle. Thus, in observing the instructional interaction, supervisors should look for clear evidence that teachers are stimulating the students' learning transactions to move to deeper or broader levels of understanding, application, and analysis.

A whole area of learning that is frequently neglected, even in the best of schools, has to do with *evaluation*. Evaluation can be considered to apply to two distinguishable levels of learning or learning experiences. One involves a type of analysis that leads to judgments of value. Such and such a poem is a "good" poem because it combines startling metaphors with appropriate rhythms to create a unified effect on the listener. Such and such a political decision by such and such a President was decidedly contrary to the Constitution, as Supreme Court decisions two generations later showed. In the above two instances, the learning experience culminates in a judgment of value (as opposed to a judgment of fact). Evaluation in this sense predominantly involves rational factors. Another learning experience one could label "evaluation" has more to do with *appreciation*. Whether the learning involved mastering a piece of music on the piano or completing a complex mathematics problem or reviewing the intricacies of the physical and psychological processes of sight, the learner dwells in, or simply experiences, the pleasure, harmony, mystery, and complexity of what he or she is doing or observing. The learner in this instance experiences the value intrinsic to the learning transaction itself and enjoys it for its own sake.[4]

Supervisors, again because of their broader perspectives on learning and their view of the constellation of influences upon the students throughout the school, need to encourage teachers to spend more time on those learning experiences involved with evaluation. It does not necessarily require an older student to move into this level of learning. Of course, as students' cognitive structures develop greater capacity for depth, complexity, and breadth, the levels of evaluation will mature. Yet at all levels of schooling one does not need much experience before the importance of motivation becomes apparent. Frequently students dislike the learning tasks of the school because they seldom move into the level or the experience of evaluation. Sometimes learning ought to culminate in genuine enjoyment.

By placing Bloom's taxonomy of cognitive education objectives, or levels of learning, in relationship with Joyce and Weil's curriculum-instructional models, we can see that each of those models can in fact be viewed as stimulating learnings on each of the six levels.

We could cement our awareness of the varieties of curriculum-instructional possibilities by transposing Figure 12-1 into a large chart and writing in examples of learning tasks or student activities in each intersection of a model and a level of learning. (The curriculum-instructional models listed in Figure 12-1 are detailed in Table 12-1.) Such an exercise would easily convince us of the enormous universe of teacher strategies and student learning activities, many of which never are realized because they have never been thought of.

---

[4] We shall consider such learnings in more detail in Chapter 13.

	Knowledge	Understanding	Application	Analysis	Synthesis	Evaluation
Inductive reasoning						
Inquiry training						
Science inquiry						
Concept attainment						
Developmental stages or reasoning						
Advanced organizers						
Jurisprudential reasoning						
Group investigation						
Social inquiry						
T-group learning						
Nondirective learning (student initiated)						
Reality learning in classroom meeting						
Awareness training Human fulfillment learning, encounter						
Synectics						
Operant conditioning						

Figure 12-1 Taxonomies of educational objectives applied to curriculum-instructional models.

GENERAL PRINCIPLES OF CURRICULUM AND INSTRUCTION

We have looked at a diversity of instructional strategies with which supervisors should be familiar. Now, however, we raise the question of whether there are some general principles which should apply to all or almost all units of instructional activity. Research and experience answer affirmatively. We propose the following series of normative principles which should be evident in any instructional setting and which supervisors would do well, gently and persistently, to insist on.

1 Students must be given the opportunity to practice the kind of behavior implied by the learning-teaching objective. In the case of simple memorization of terminology, students should be called on rather often to repeat that terminology precisely and accurately. In the case of the learning objective of application, students must be given the opportunity to make several applications, and to return from time to time to other applications to reinforce the learning desired. In all of this first principle, we stress the importance of the activity of the students.

Unless they are actively involved in learning, they will not learn except in the most superficial way.

2   The learning experience must give students the opportunity to deal with the content implied by the objective. If the objective is to develop the skill of inductive scientific reasoning, then the learning experience must place students in a genuinely scientific setting where they encounter scientific data which can be analyzed by means of appropriate scientific instruments. Insofar as that learning experience lacks specifically scientific content, then the experience becomes diluted, or thinned out.

3   Students must obtain satisfaction from carrying out the behavior implied by the objective. This principle insists on some sense of successful closure in the learning episode. One of the major problems in nonindividualized instructional settings is that one-third of the class seldom catch up with the rest of the class; they only partially complete their assignments. Their grades usually reflect the penalties imposed and lead to further loss of sense of worth and interest in the learning tasks.

4   The desired learnings or level of performance must be within the range of possibility for the students involved. This principle calls for an awareness on the part of both teachers and supervisors of the development stages and levels of cognitive, moral, and psychosocial growth. Some teachers expect fourth and fifth graders to engage in democratic group decision making. They will severely punish the miscreant who destroys the phony harmony of a simulated town meeting by laughing at the "goody-goody" who is simply trying to imitate the teacher. This is not to say that teachers should not introduce simple concepts of democracy. This principle holds for appropriate expectations of pupils' performance—appropriate to their level of development.

5   There are many particular experiences that can be used to attain the same objectives. Frequently teachers settle on only one or two examples or one or two ways to look at the problem or concept. This principle encourages more concern for diversity of student learning styles, or cultural or ethnic backgrounds. It also encourages the teacher and supervisor constantly to be enlarging their repertory of teaching aids and resources, their bag of tricks, so to speak, in order to provide the student with a new approach to a learning task when another one has failed to bring about the desired results.

6   The same learning experience will usually bring about several outcomes. Not infrequently a student's response to a question will take the teacher completely by surprise. Instead of responding that that was the wrong answer, the teacher should ask the student to clarify how he or she came up with that response. Frequently students come to quite legitimate learning or insights which the teacher had not foreseen as flowing from the assignment. This principle also alludes to the hidden, or indirect, curriculum. Sometimes the teacher unwittingly communicates a value, an attitude, or a reward system that is quite contrary to the objectives of the instructional activity. Supervisors can be especially helpful in pointing this out to teachers.

7   Student learnings will be strengthened, deepened, and broadened if a skill, a concept, relationships, principles, etc., are encountered and used repeatedly in several disciplines or discrete frameworks of learning. This principle points to the importance of a teacher's knowing what other teachers are teaching and have taught to their students. In that way the teacher can draw many comparisons, contrasts, and examples from the student's own experience. Consistent repetition in the use of learning and expressive skills will not only lead to their habitual use, but to their refinement and broader scope as well. Not enough attention has been given in the literature on teaching and learning to the importance of repetition and review. The rhetoric of the literature on learning and teaching leads the inexperienced teacher to believe that instructional activity must always move into new material after initial mastery has been achieved. This often results in a wide but shallow coverage of many topics rather than a solid and usable mastery of the learning task. This principle seeks quality, not quantity, in instructional activity.

THE SUPERVISOR AND THE EDUCATIONAL PROGRAM

Sometimes the function of supervision is completely separated from the function of curriculum development. Sometimes the same person is involved in both, such as a building principal or a department chairperson. In either event the supervisor, who normally would focus primarily on the instructional activity of teachers and the use of their instructional materials, of necessity must observe the effectiveness of the curriculum in action. Where one and the same person, such as a department chairperson, is involved with both supervision and curriculum development, the information about the effectiveness of the curriculum on classroom learning comes immediately through the observation of instructional activity.

The department chairperson, observing teachers use the new textbook which the department had chosen that year, not only observes the teachers' adaptation of the textbook, but the influence of the textbook on the teachers, on the flow of learning tasks, and on the attention, interest, and attitudes of the students. Through such observation, the supervisor may discover a considerable gap between two major sections of the text, a gap which the students were having difficulty crossing. With this information, and from discussions with the teachers, the chairperson may design a transitional unit to help teachers and students bridge the gap. This would be a clear example of the activity of supervision involved not only with the instructional activity of the teacher, but, in a real sense, with the educational program. From this perspective, then, it is appropriate to speak of supervising the curriculum or the educational program.

The distinction between supervision and curriculum development can still remain. The activities relating to both can be assigned to different roles in the school system, if that seems best. Nonetheless, the supervisor can act as one of the main sources of feedback information to the curriculum developer. The supervisor observes both the instructional activity of the teacher and the learning activity of the student. From such a vantage point, the supervisor can make some valid inferences about the effectiveness of the curriculum design, its scope, its sequence, its pedagogical appeal, its pace, and its effective marshaling of available learning resources. The supervisor may not be in a position to suggest *another* way of designing the curriculum, but he or she can at least point out what works and what does not.

In some cases, such as that of the department chairperson, this feedback information can immediately begin to generate modifications in the sequence, the pace, the clarity or dramatic appeal of the advanced organizers, etc. A department usually is self-enclosed enough that programs can be modified quickly and easily enough.

In other instances, a supervisor may be working with an age or grade cluster of teachers and students, say grades 1 through 4. It may happen that the sequence of curriculum materials between grades 3 and 4 is causing considerable problems for the youngsters, and therefore problems for the teachers who have run out of alternative strategies to effect the learning encounter. The supervisor can huddle with teachers from all 4 years and try rearranging the learning units, with the end result that the second-grade teacher will now spend twice as much time teaching and reinforcing the learning of a specific spatial concept, the grasp of which is required for the third graders to handle related conceptual material. Or, the supervisor and teachers may decide to remove those one or two learning units from the curriculum altogether and place them in the sixth-grade curriculum where the youngsters' cognitive structures will have developed adequately to handle such cognitively complex material.

In other instances, several supervisors from different grade or school levels or from different discipline areas may be in a position to address a curricular problem common to each of their areas of responsibility. By teaming up to attack the problem, they may come up with at least a clear identification of what the problem is (say, lack of software resources to support such a curriculum), where it is primarily located (say, in the seventh grade when the inquiry method is introduced), and what needs to be done about it. By taking this kind of action, the supervisors, even though their primary responsibility is not in curriculum development, can effect beneficial changes in the curriculum.

THE CENTRAL ORGANIZATIONAL POSITION OF SUPERVISORS

In systems where different people are responsible for supervision and for curriculum development, such cooperation and mutual support are necessary for both in order to maximize their common objectives—the best opportunities for the most appropriate growth of youngsters. From the human resources perspectives of supervision which the authors advocate, the supervisor appears in a key position to bring complementary influences to bear on the instructional tasks of the school. The supervisor can be an advocate for the students vis-à-vis the teacher. The supervisor can be an advocate for the teacher vis-à-vis the administration (say, in urging a different class schedule). The supervisor can also be an advocate for the teacher vis-à-vis the curriculum developer *and vice versa.* In other words, the supervisor frequently stands between the instructional activity and the organizational resource staff and administration. The supervisor is, in a sense, the link. He or she sends messages in both directions. While within the organization chart the supervisor may not appear to, he or she occupies what is perhaps the key position in the school system. The supervisor is close enough to the instructional activity of the school and yet sits in on most of the important administrative meetings. Both by the relative prestige attached to various supervisory positions as well as by the range of contacts within the school system, the supervisor occupies a key position in the organizational network from which it is possible to marshal and channel all the best resources the system possesses toward more effective instruction. In small systems where the supervisor is also the chief administrator, the concentration of this potential in one person (there being no need for numerous meetings with different bureaucratic layers of support staff) offers the possibility of rapid program change. And, as the literature on instructional leadership has urged for the past 50 years, that kind of administrator ought to spend much more of his or her time doing instructional supervision.

SUMMARY

This chapter has attempted to focus the supervisor's attention on the curriculum influences on the instructional activity under observation. Besides the more general platform of beliefs, theories, and attitudes upon which teachers habitually base their instructional activity, teachers also bring to the instructional setting their knowledge of the subject matter or discipline and their strategies for bringing the student into a genuine encounter with some aspect of it. In the examples cited, we saw how five different teachers approached the teaching of the nature of light. The group inquiry approach, the historical approach, the experimental approach, the conceptual approach through a lecture or film, the analogy approach—all provide access to the reality of light and to theories to explain the physical properties of light. The supervisor needs to be able to move freely into the frame of reference of the teacher and student in order to support the genuine learning and sound instruction that can and does take place within that perspective. Hopefully, the supervisor will be able to rummage about in his or her own repertory of curriculum-instructional strategies to come up with additional suggestions to enrich, enliven, and open up to even further possibilities the teaching and learning that could be occurring within that framework.

Joyce and Weil's inventory of curriculum-instructional models can further enlarge the supervisor's repertory. It provides additional maps, or paradigms, to enable the supervisor to interpret the instructional activity being planned or under observation. Bloom's *Taxonomy* reminds the supervisor that any instructional activity can be pointed to various levels of learning. By examining the levels of learning possible within each of the curriculum-instructional models, the supervisor is equipped for a kind of two-dimensional analysis or interpretation of the teacher's instructional activity.

Regardless of the type of its instructional activity, the following seven principles should apply to every instructional unit.

1 The student must be given the opportunity to practice the kind of behavior implied by the learning-teaching objective.
2 The learning experience must give the student the opportunity to deal with the content implied by the objective.
3 The student must obtain satisfaction from carrying out the behavior implied by the objective.
4 The desired learnings or levels of performance must be within the range of possibility for the students involved.

5 There are many particular experiences that can be used to obtain the same objectives.

6 The same learning experience will usually bring about several outcomes.

7 Student learnings should be reinforced by being used in different settings and disciplines, and by being used repeatedly.

Finally, the role of the supervisor, while remaining distinguished from that of the curriculum developer, was studied in terms of its potential for curriculum revision. It is legitimate to speak of supervising the curriculum. The supervisor, because of his or her central position in the organizational network of the school, can have considerable influence on curriculum reform.

STUDY GUIDE

Recall the concepts and meanings associated with each of the following phrases and terms included in this chapter. Can you discuss them with a colleague and apply them to the supervisory context of your school? If you cannot, review them in the text and record the page number for future reference.

1 Curriculum activity _____

2 Hidden curriculum _____

3 Instructional activity _____

4 Model families _____

5 Models of teaching _____

6 Normative instructional principles _____

7 Supervision and curriculum development _____

8 Taxonomy of educational objectives _____

EXERCISES

1 Pool the resources of the class to see whether cumulatively the class can explain the major characteristics of the curriculum-instructional models Joyce and Weil have assembled.

2 Observe a film of a teacher teaching a class. Does that teaching fit into one of the models listed? Go back and see which of the levels of learning are getting most of the teacher's attention. Go back a third time and see whether the seven instructional principles are being followed.

3 What kinds of other questions are generated by viewing the film? Imagine that you would be meeting with that teacher within an hour of the post-observation conference. Divide up into teams of three and plan your strategy for the conference. Perhaps someone could role-play the teacher.

4 Consider all the classes you attend in your college or graduate program. How would you analyze and describe the instructional activity that goes on in them? Are they effective in the instructional strategies employed?

5 Ask someone who is involved in curriculum design and development where he or she receives most of the feedback on the curriculum's effectiveness. Ask a practicing supervisor how often she or he gets involved in curriculum revision.

Chapter 13

An Environmental Design
for the Human Curriculum

Our thesis throughout this book has been simple. The productivity of the organization increases as it encourages the human growth of its participants. Moreover, the job satisfaction of the participants increases as they channel their energy into the fulfillment of organizational or professional goals. When applied to supervisory practices in the school, this thesis means that essential to the supervisory role is a commitment to the human growth of teachers and students through satisfying and fulfilling experiences in the educational process. This implies that supervisory personnel not only must employ those supervisory styles most conducive to human development, but must also bring to their work an idea of a human curriculum—that is, a general model of a school program which offers those educational experiences which will lead students to human maturity.

As should be obvious, the proponents of humane organization are not in the health and recreation business. Whether talking about banking, advertising, or educational organizations, they envision effort and hard work leading to significant results, but in a human way, not in a machinelike or hyperrationalized system. An assumed premise through this book is that the one-dimensional view of schools based on the means-end model or the systems model is inadequate (though useful). That view is based on technological rationality: the objectification of the world and of persons through an abstractive process which categorizes and interprets schooling in a cause-and-effect, statistically quantified series of relationships. This results in an instrumental view of humanity itself which is somewhat spuriously justified by some advocates of the purely functional man or woman, the goal-oriented, need-directed organism proposed by behavioristic psychology.[1]

Rather than cling to that arthritic view, which denies any validity to technological rationality, we wish to assert not only its limitations when it is infelicitously proposed as the only form of rationality, but also its considerable power when employed in the service of human growth. Jails can be models of technological efficiency and yet waste enormous resources of human potential.

Curriculum theorists, as well as sociologists, psychologists, and philosophers, present telling criticisms of the ineffectiveness of present school programs, despite the attempts at curricular innovations. Goodlad, one of the foremost spokesmen for curricular changes, admits that there is a notoriously low correlation between academic success and personal stability, leadership, family happiness, and honest workmanship.[2] Despite conflicting reviews of his findings, James Coleman's massive study of educational achievement raises serious doubts about the effectiveness of even the most prestigious school programs. His study suggests that individuals' self-concepts, and consequently their perceptions of their own control over their futures, is the single most important factor in achievement.[3] His earlier study of adolescent subculture underlines the tenacious attempts of adolescents to frustrate the designs of the system of schooling precisely because it communicates so little respect for them as persons, and because it fails to provide them with genuine opportunities for personal commitment. The works of Friedenberg,[4] Kozol,[5] and Holt[6]—even if one argues that they overstate their case—point to serious lack of human concern on the part of teachers and administrators.

This mounting disquiet over the inability of the curricular changes to make a bigger difference is not so much a proof of any *intrinsic* weakness of newer curricular approaches but represents, rather, a growing awareness that other human factors—besides the purely intellectual and academic—play as great a part, if not greater, in effecting mature and genuine human growth. The evidence from developmental psychology, as well as the more normative statements of anthropologists and philosophers, points to those *personal* human variables which lead to genuine human growth.

---

[1] Dwayne Huebner, "New Modes of Man's Relationship to Man," in Alexander Frazier (ed.), *New Insights and the Curriculum,* Washington, D.C.: National Education Association, Association for Supervision and Curriculum Development, 1963, p. 145.

[2] John I. Goodlad, "The Education Program to 1980 and Beyond," in Edgar Morphet and Charles Ryan (eds.), *Implications for Education of Prospective Changes in Society: Designing Education for the Future,* no. 2, New York: Citation Press, 1967, p. 49.

[3] James Coleman, *Equality of Educational Opportunity,* Washington, D.C.: U.S. Dept. of Health, Education and Welfare, 1966; and James Coleman, *The Adolescent Society,* New York: Free Press, 1961.

[4] Edgar Friedenberg, *The Dignity of Youth and Other Atavisms,* Boston: Beacon Press, 1965; and *The Vanishing Adolescent,* New York: Dell, 1959.

[5] Jonathan Kozol, *Death at an Early Age,* Boston: Houghton Mifflin, 1967.

[6] John C. Holt, *How Children Fail,* New York: Pitman, 1964.

In this chapter we shall attempt to summarize some descriptions of these human variables and to construct a theoretical model of the human context of learning. As we shall see, such a model facilitates a critical analysis of the shortcomings of current curriculum-instructional programs and provides a framework for promoting curriculum-instructional units which are more adapted to a variety of learning experiences. As the supervisor works with teachers or students, such a theoretical framework will provide a valuable source for discussing objectives and specific units of the instructional program.

B COGNITION AND D COGNITION

Abraham Maslow outlines some of these other human factors.[7] In Maslow's description of human growth, an individual moves from the satisfaction of basic biological and security needs to the satisfaction of higher human needs, such as self-esteem, autonomy, and self-actualization. As individuals approach personal maturity, they become more capable of transcending those lower needs of self-gratification, security, and social acceptance. Instead of being *completely* absorbed in the process of *becoming*—of "becoming someone," of "making something out of life," of "striving for success"—they are able to enjoy *being*—being who they are and where they are—and at the same time to enjoy and appreciate others for what they are and to appreciate the world and objects in it for their own sake (not in order to use persons and objects to solve problems or satisfy lower needs). A completely future-oriented, instrumental approach to learning deprives the present of its intrinsic value, in much the same way as the hero of Henry James's novel *The Beast in the Jungle* was blinded to the potentialities of the present by his fear and anticipation of the beast.

According to this distinction, then, between "being" and "becoming," Maslow differentiates cognitions as B cognitions and D cognitions.

D cognition can be defined as the cognitions which are organized from the point of view of basic needs or deficiency needs and their gratification and frustration. That is, D cognition could be called selfish cognition, in which the world is organized into gratifiers and frustrators of our own needs with other characteristics being ignored or slurred. The cognition of the object, in its own right and its own being, without reference to its need-gratifying or need-frustrating qualities, that is, without primary reference to its value for the observer or its effects upon him, can be called B cognition (or self-transcending, or unselfish, or objective cognition). The parallel with maturity is by no means perfect (children can also cognize in a selfless way), but in general, it is mostly true that with increasing selfhood or firmness of personal identity (or acceptance of one's own inner nature), B cognition becomes easier and more frequent. (This is true even though D cognition remains for *all* human beings, including the mature ones, the main tool for living-in-the-world.)[8]

B cognition is less structured, more a grasp of the wholeness and immediacy

    [7] Abraham H. Maslow, "Some Basic Propositions of a Growth and Self-Actualization Psychology," in Arthur W. Combs (ed.), *Perceiving, Behaving, Becoming,* Washington, D.C.: National Educational Association, Association for Supervision and Curriculum Development, 1962, pp. 34–39.
    [8] Ibid., p. 41.

of the object or person, more contemplative in posture, less instrumental or prob-
lem-oriented (with the subsequent splitting up of the object or person by abstraction). This is not to identify B cognition solely with a passive state of mind. B
cognition can also involve action—not only intense intellectual concentration,
but also the active exercise of manual and technical skills. It can also involve the
reciprocal self-revelation and appreciation of friendship.[9] What differentiates B
cognition from D cognition, or B activity from D activity, is the end intended. B
cognition or B activity seeks no end outside itself, outside the sheer satisfaction
intrinsic to the knowledge or activity, whereas D cognition or D activity is instrumental—is used to solve problems or answer questions or gain a specified objective.

Maslow is quick to draw curricular implications from this distinction.

> This development toward the concept of a healthy unconscious, and of a healthy
> irrationality, sharpens our awareness of the limitations of purely abstract thinking, of
> verbal thinking and of analytic thinking. If our hope is to describe the world fully, a
> place is necessary for preverbal, ineffable, metaphorical, primary process, concrete-
> experience, intuitive and esthetic types of cognition, for there are certain aspects of
> reality which can be cognized in no other way. Even in science this is true, now that
> we know (a) that creativity has its roots in the non-rational, (b) that language is and
> must always be inadequate to describe total reality, (c) that any abstract concept
> leaves out much of reality, and (d) that what we call "knowledge" (which is usually
> highly abstract and verbal and sharply defined) often serves to blind us to those
> portions of reality not covered by the abstraction. That is, it makes us more able to
> see some things, but less able to see other things. Abstract knowledge has its dangers
> as well as its uses.
>
> Science and education, being too exclusively abstract, verbal and bookish, do
> not have enough place for raw, concrete, esthetic experience, especially of the subjec-
> tive happenings inside oneself. For instance, organismic psychologists would certain-
> ly agree on the desirability of more creative education in perceiving and creating art,
> in dancing, in (Greek style) athletics and in phenomenological observation.[10]

He continues:

> This same tie between health and integration of rational and irrational forces (con-
> scious and unconscious, primary and secondary process) also permits us to under-
> stand why psychologically healthy people are more able to enjoy, to love, to laugh, to
> have fun, to be humorous, to be silly, to be whimsical and fantastic, to be pleasantly
> "crazy," and in general to permit and value and enjoy emotional experiences. . . .
> And it leads us to the strong suspicion that learning *ad hoc* to be able to do all these
> things may help the child move toward health.[11]

If Maslow's description of the healthy person appears somewhat lyrical, he
readily admits that the human condition also involves conflict, anxiety, frustration, sadness, and guilt. But as people mature, they are able to distinguish between neurotic or petty pseudoproblems and the "real, unavoidable, existential

[9] Cf. Huebner, op. cit.
[10] Maslow, op. cit., p. 44.
[11] Ibid.

problems inherent in the nature of man."[12] Considerations of these aspects of human life, including the unavoidable reality of death, belong in the human curriculum. Jerome Bruner and Ralph Harper, for example, offer some enlightened approaches to the topic of death as it might be included in a curriculum design.[13]

The mature person, then, lives in two worlds: an inner world and an outer world. The two worlds constantly interact with one another, but nevertheless one can point to relatively distinctive experiences and different processes in each. A curriculum that is concerned with only the outer world—with D cognitions and D activities, with extrinsically motivated behavior, and with the world of impersonal, functional, and objective relationships—will produce, other things being equal, immature and stunted young adults.

For our purposes, then, we may employ Maslow's terms to describe one dimension of human growth. We may represent this dimension diagrammatically on a continuum:

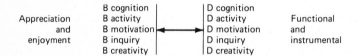

Appreciation and enjoyment	B cognition B activity B motivation B inquiry B creativity	D cognition D activity D motivation D inquiry D creativity	Functional and instrumental

PERSONAL MEANING AND CULTURALLY DEFINED MEANING

James Macdonald describes two other growth experiences found in the process of human development: the experience of personal meanings and the experience of culturally defined meanings.[14] When discussing the development of the self, he comments:

> The self as a reflection of ego-processes strives toward meanings. These meanings are of two general varieties; they are perhaps best described by the prescriptions "know thyself" and "know thy world." The self is not "actualized" in a vacuum but in a world. The world is, however, primarily as it is perceived by the self. For the world to become only what one feels it is is to retreat into psychosis; but for the world to be accepted only as it is defined, in terms of rational, cultural knowledge, is certainly a form of neurosis. In neither case is the ego integrated into a functional, open, and reality-oriented structure.
>
> It should be apparent to all that the growing self must have personal meanings and cultural meanings for adequate realization. Further, it follows from this that the two meaning systems are not separate compartments within the individual. They are (in a healthy state) functionally integrated into the purposive striving of the person.[15]

---

[12] Ibid., p. 45.

[13] Jerome S. Bruner, "Identity and the Modern Novel," *On Knowing: Essays for the Left Hand,* Cambridge, Mass.: Belknap Press, 1962; Ralph Harper, "Significance of Existence and Recognition for Education," in Nelson B. Henry (ed.), *Modern Philosophies and Education,* Chicago: University of Chicago Press, 1955, pp. 215–258.

[14] James Macdonald, "An Image of Man: The Learner Himself," in Ronald C. Doll (ed.), *Individualizing Instruction,* Washington, D.C.: National Education Association, Association for Supervision and Curriculum Development, 1964.

[15] Ibid., p. 39.

Combs also emphasizes the importance of personal meaning, although he agrees with Macdonald on the need to integrate the two kinds of meaning.

> Any piece of information will have its effect upon behavior in the degree to which an individual discovers its personal meaning. To put this in more technical terms, we could say that the effect of any bit of information will depend upon its psychological distance from the self. Learning thus becomes the discovery of personal meaning. We might think of all the information a person needs in order to make an effective adjustment to life as existing on a continuum from that which is very close to self to that which is very far away from self. The problem of learning then becomes a problem of moving information from the not-self end of this continuum to the self end.[16]

He goes on to criticize the neglect of personal meaning in school.

> In our zeal to be scientific and objective, we have sometimes taught children that personal meanings are things you leave at the schoolhouse door. Sometimes, I fear, in our desire to help people learn, we have said to the child, "Alice, I am not interested in what you think or what you believe. What are the facts?" As a consequence, we may have taught children that personal meanings have no place in the classroom, which is another way of saying that school is concerned only with things that do not matter! If learning, however, is a discovery of personal meaning, then the facts with which we must be concerned are the beliefs, feelings, understandings, convictions, doubts, fears, likes, and dislikes of the pupil—those personal ways of perceiving himself and the world he lives in.[17]

Personal meanings are meanings that are organized and integrated with the self-concept and carry not only cognitive but affective content. These meanings are unique to each person and are derived from his or her life experiences. For a child who has spent every summer on Cape Cod, the meaning of Cape Cod would be illuminated by or saturated with personal intonations which a geographer describing the New England coast might not have. "Football" has a culturally defined meaning, but for a veteran professional quarterback that meaning would be colored and enriched by nuances from his own personal experience of the game. The most personal meanings, of course, are the concepts which the students have of themselves. Their relationships with others, especially with their immediate families, have molded over several years the students' self-images or concepts. Their sense of their own worth, of their capabilities, of their shortcomings and failures, and of what is worthwhile in life are a part of their self-images. All new experiences and learnings tend to be filtered by and through their self-concepts. While the educational program, mediated by the teacher, is meant to introduce students into the broad and various realms of culturally defined meanings, the teacher must remain sensitive and responsive to the broad range of personal meanings of the student in order to assist the student in the task of integrating the two realms of meaning. This process of integration will result in a

[16] Arthur W. Combs, "Personality Theory and Its Implications for Curriculum Development," in Alexander Frazier (ed.), *Learning More About Learning,* Washington, D.C.: National Education Association, Association for Supervision and Curriculum Development, 1959, p. 10.
   [17] Ibid., p. 11.

deeper grasp—both intellectual and valuational—of reality. The teacher, then stands between the two meaningful contexts and mediates and clarifies their integration. Macdonald asserts that the student's ego-integration is achieved "through the discovery and internalization of more and more productive meaning schemes in both spheres."[18]

Macdonald's categories differ somewhat from Maslow's B and D cognitions, for it is possible that personal meanings can be D cognitions and can be used for D activities. One obvious example of personal meaning used in D activities from daily classroom experience concerns the student's personal understanding of what he or she is trying to do. For all too many students involved in a particular classroom exercise, the point is not necessarily to learn something well, but simply to find out what the teacher wants him or her to say, and to say it. For that is how one gets good grades. Therefore the classroom exercise is, for the student, an exercise in grade getting.[19] The teacher who fails to understand this personal perspective of the student stands to suffer no small disillusionment. It is likewise possible that culturally defined meanings can be transformed into B cognitions and lead to B inquiry; for example, the student's insight into and appreciation of the tragic character of Othello, or his or her curious inquiry into the structure of the eye. Thus, we can represent these two dimensions in a conceptual model of curricular concerns:

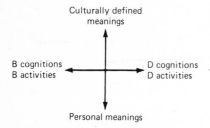

ACTIVITIES OF THE INDIVIDUAL, OF FRIENDS, OF THE GROUP

Up to this point we have spoken of elements in the growth process of the individual as an individual. But the individual does not exist isolated and alone in the world. Although the fully mature and self-actualized person can retreat within himself from time to time to be alone to dream or savor the peace of his or her own reflections, or to contemplate a spring landscape or sunlight dancing on the water, most of the time we exist as persons in relation to other persons.[20] We are invested with significance by others who have need of us. We give life to others and participate in their lives. "We live and move and have our being not in ourselves but in one another."[21] Novelists, philosophers, and social psychologists

---

[18] Macdonald, op. cit., p. 43.

[19] Marvin Grandstaff, "Situations as a Category of Curriculum Theory," a paper presented at the June 1968 Curriculum Conference of the Center for the Study of Instruction, Washington, D.C.: National Education Association, 1968.

[20] John MacMurray, *Persons in Relation*, New York: Harper, 1961, p. 211. Though difficult, this book offers a stimulating challenge to traditional views of knowledge.

[21] Ibid.

have described the variety of influences of others upon the individual. The individual's attitudes, values, aspirations, and accomplishments are all affected by the ebb and flow of the matrix of relationships in which he or she exists. Huebner accents the importance of the encounter with others in the growth process of the individual.[22] Unlike the human relations school generally, and theorists such as Likert in particular, Huebner stresses not so much the formation of attitudes by the group or group belongingness—which are not to be denied as critical supports for individual growth—but the importance, rather, of conversation between individual and individual. Real conversation is the bridge over the aloneness that each person experiences, is the gesture across the chasms that separate the particular universes of individuals, and the means by which they reveal themselves and transcend the limitations of their personal world. This is one of the reasons why childhood friendships are so important and, for the adolescent, why initial romantic experiences are so expansive. Today's school experiences being what they are, the only experience most students have with the miracle of their own personal uniqueness is found on a date or in informal relationships outside the school. Research into why this experience of friendship and trusting intimacy has been excluded in any and all forms from the classroom might reveal the purely instrumental and hyperrational environment of the curriculum.

Relationships are established through conversation. The conversation between friends differs from the conversation of a group; but in whatever setting, it is through conversation that the individual makes contact with other individuals. To quote Huebner: "Conversation is thus an art. Not only an art of language, by which man finds new, esthetically satisfying language forms and symbolizes the experience of his world; but also an art which leads to the forming of oneself and the other. By speaking and by listening, man can become aware of what he is and what he may become, and may help his fellow man do the same."[23]

Notice that conversation can both enhance the level of interpersonal relationships and thereby create friendship, and also be a means of discovering new and satisfying ways of symbolizing the world. Hence, conversation has an objective as well as a personal referent; that is, through dialogue with a friend, with whom I feel secure enough to explore new meanings and expressions, I may discover new relationships between aspects of reality, new ways of understanding and appreciating a hitherto vaguely understood aspect of reality.

We may then speak of a general dimension of human growth which moves from individual thought and action to conversation with another, to action and discussion in a group. All three experiences are formative of the person and make up that person's environment of learning. Group activities and discussions contribute to the person's ability to relate to others, to share in group goals, and to surrender selfish attitudes and values for the benefit of the group. Sometimes, however, group participation in school activities can be made a fetish. Conversation with another person can usually be carried on at a deeper level than discussion in a group and can lead to the formation of the stronger ties of friendship.

22 Huebner, op. cit.
23 Ibid., p. 152.

And there are times when it is good for a person to be alone, to work alone, to simply get away from all the talk and think things over on his or her own. This third dimension of human growth can be represented as a continuum moving from individual activity to conversation, and activity with a friend to discussion and activity in a group:

Individual ◄─────── Friend ───────► Group

We may then add this dimension of human growth to the two previously described dimensions. The resulting model provides the context of the human curriculum:

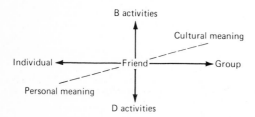

But what of the content of the curriculum? What about those structures inherent in and formative of the discipline that makes up the material of the curriculum? The model described above provides the context, the situation[24] in which the teaching and learning of core concepts and images, structural principles, and processes of inquiry and invention take place. The point is not to disparage curriculum content, but rather to place it in the context of *human* learning, and to insist that only by attention to the human context can curriculum content be integrated into the healthy personal growth of the student. One must reluctantly admit that knowledge is not virtue, but that, nevertheless, knowledge integrated with a humanizing educational process will be far more likely to lead to humane behavior than an impersonal process in which the student is manipulated by fear of failure and the bogus reward of academic honors in order to get him or her to some preconceived academically or socially defined goals.

The model of the human curriculum, then, will be made up of four elements, one substantive (the curriculum content; though the content will be embedded in the context, for purposes of analysis we shall treat it in abstraction) and the other three contextual. For purposes of clarification, the model is presented in its entirety and then broken down into its constituent parts in the following sets of diagrams (Figures 13-1 to 13-3).

CLARIFICATION OF THE MODEL

In order to clarify the model, we shall locate learning activities in each quadrant. For example, in diagram alpha (α) an activity in the individual–culturally defined

24 Grandstaff, op. cit.

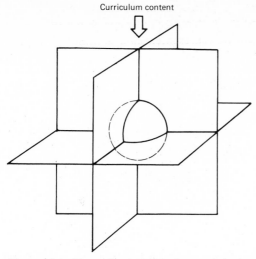

Figure 13-1 Three-dimensional context of the human curriculum. The three dimensions are represented by the three geometric planes. The curriculum content is represented by the sphere embedded in this three-dimensional space.

meaning quadrant would be the activity of a student studying alone in the library the events surrounding the Declaration of Independence. In this activity the student might check two or three sources, but the learning consists mainly of the acquisition of historical information and, probably, a culturally conditioned interpretation of the significance of the events. If the student attempts to reflect on the political freedom he or she and his or her family enjoy as a result of American

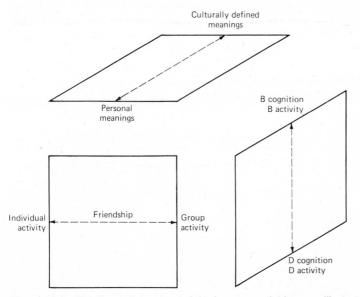

Figure 13-2 The three dimensions of the human curriculum are illustrated separately for visual clarification.

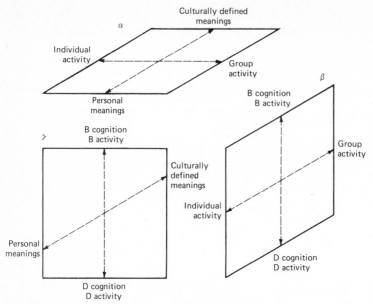

Figure 13-3 These sets of diagrams indicate how the three dimensions might be considered in pairs of two-dimensional constructs, again for conceptual clarification. Activities can be identified in each quadrant of each construct.

political democracy and on this freedom in contrast, say, to the political repressions in certain Latin American dictatorships, the kind of learning would be enriched by including personal meanings and interpretations. This learning activity, then, would begin with the individual more or less accepting culturally defined meanings and then continue by the individual's relating these to his or her personal experience.

Let us suppose, however, that the student is white and on relatively good terms with a black classmate, whose individual study project is concerned with colonial slavery. Later that week in the cafeteria, student W and student B just happen to ask each other how their individual study projects are progressing. The resulting conversation might bring student W to a different understanding of his classmate's ambivalent feelings about the uncritical patriotic tone of the textbook. This learning experience then involves culturally defined meanings and a critical analysis of them in the light of personal meanings in a dialogue with a friend. Had student B chosen the study project on the Declaration of Independence, the kind of learning which probably would have occurred would be quite different from student W's learning, even though student W and student B might give the same factual responses on a true-false test.

Let us suppose, again, that student W and student B attend the same class that day for a group discussion on the American Revolution. Let us suppose that, besides considering the oppressive military, political, and economic pressures on the early colonists in New England, New York, and Pennsylvania, the discussion turned toward the right of any people to rebel against political, economic, and military oppression. Perhaps the treatment of the American Indian by our government might be injected into the discussion. Or let us suppose that the Castro-led revolution in Cuba came up and was debated hotly in terms of communist influence and ideology. Perhaps the political outcomes of both revolutions might be contrasted and evaluated. Now student W's understanding of the significance of the Declaration of Independence might change as the debate of democratic versus communist political and economic ideology provided a contrasting contemporary background for its interpretation. In this instance the context of the learning experience is composed of both personal and culturally defined meanings and group discussion and analysis.

Learning in all of these contexts frequently takes place in a school setting but often by chance, especially as regards the injection of personal meanings. If teachers were more aware, however, of the personal meanings which each student brings to class, and of the enormous pedagogical effect of dialogue between two students, they could plan the instructional unit to be more responsive to these contexts of learning.

Other examples of learning which might take place in different quadrants of diagram α would be a study of occupations, a study by rural farm students of price controls on crops, an analysis of a film like *Sixteen in Webster Groves* by students from an affluent suburb, a study of genetic laws of heredity, and a study of the automobile industry. Depending on the context the teacher wanted to plan for, different emphases and therefore different learnings would take place.

In the beta diagram (β) one could locate the activity of an individual student memorizing vocabulary lists in French in the individual, D activity quadrant. The individual student's efforts to master any skill, whether it be penmanship or reading faster or mixing colors in art class, can usually be classified in that same quadrant. In almost any kind of testing and grading situation the same individual, D cognition context would be operative. In any group competition, say in a grade-level spelling contest or science project contest, the learning would take place in the group activity, D cognition quadrant. A moment's reflection would reveal the enormous motivational potential in these latter learning contexts. Group problem solving or project work, even without the overt competitive aspect, could also be considered as group D activities, for the group is still striving to use specific knowledge to come up with an answer or a construct which will measure up to the teacher's expectations and earn a good grade.

In the same β diagram, the examples of an individual student painting a picture in art class, listening to folk music, and studying the aerodynamics of the fruit fly out of curiosity or fascination would fall in the individual, B activity quadrant. This is not to say that all activities related to art are necessarily B activities. A student who is attempting to replicate a landscape by Van Gogh in order to satisfactorily pass an exercise in oil-color mixing demanded by his art teacher may very well be engaged in purely D activity. In learning activities, however, where the student engages in more contemplative and appreciative behavior, the context can be more readily identified with the individual, B activities quadrant. At this point, the reader might try to recall and list learning activities from his or her own past school experience which would fall in this quadrant. The list would probably be quite small.

A final example in the β figure to illustrate a learning context involving group activity and a B activity is a dramatic production by the group. Teachers by and large have not begun to use drama as a context for learning. Having students adapt a story from their literature or history books for a dramatic presentation often allows them a moving experience of conscious identification with a character. By trying to get inside the personality of the character they are portraying, students come to understand the situation of the play sympathetically; they can look out on the world and on the other characters in the play from the eyes of another person. By internalizing and then externalizing the conflict, comedy, or tragedy of the dramatic situation, students can develop an understanding and sensitivity to the problems, joys, and miracles in their own lives. Because of the atmosphere of make-believe—which is often a more intense reflection of reality—students are relieved somewhat of the threat of exposing themselves and yet can get a feeling for real interpersonal communication. To use the dramatic context for learning does not require a full-scale production similar to that of the annual school play. It may consist of impromptu dramatizations with the simplest of stage props to suggest the make-believe atmosphere. Often, the excitement such imaginative experiences arouse leads students to drop many of their defenses and to work as a team to put on the show. Anyone familiar with group dynamics would point to this kind of experience as critical in developing group spirit and cohesion, as well as in allowing students to bring forth a part of themselves which they customarily hide. This is not to say that dramatic productions should be used for therapy. The emphasis should be on the objective dramatic situation. But teachers should be aware of the group dynamics involved in these experiences in order to prevent them from getting out of hand and to assist and clarify whatever learnings take place.

In the gamma diagram (γ), one can again conjecture about a variety of possible learning situations. A student who constructs a montage in order to express what war or patriotism or autumn means to him would be learning in a context of B cognitions and personal meanings. Interpretive readings of poetry might also be classified in this context. A context involving personal meanings and D cognitions or D activities might be one in which a student whose father works with computers and who has some knowledge of the versatility of computers takes a course in computer programming. As she learns the several languages of the computer, she will no doubt be spontaneously thinking of several applications of particular codings. Another example of this context would be a biology class exercise on the reasons for certain dietary foods where one of the students might have worked in a hospital kitchen. If the teacher knows as much as possible about the backgrounds of the students, the teacher can utilize the experiences of students to help clarify some of the implications of the matter under study.

As was mentioned in Chapter 12, in the discussion of evaluation, significant learning occurs when the student is able to appreciate and "dwell in" what he or she has learned, to feel the human implications of some object or aspect of reality, or simply to marvel at its intricacy or simplicity. This kind of sympathetic knowing can be experienced not only in a love relationship but also in knowing other aspects of reality. Scheler points to the importance of this kind of knowing in a world where technological rationality threatens to cut off one's roots in nature.

> Hence the first task of our educational practice must be to revive the capacity for identification with the life of the universe, and awaken it anew from its condition of dormancy in the capitalistic social outlook of Western man (with its characteristic picture of the world as an aggregation of movable quantities). We must dissociate ourselves, firmly and unreservedly, from the gross error of regarding the sense of unity with the universe as merely an "empathic" projection of specifically human emotions into animals, plants, or inanimate objects—as sheer anthropomorphism, therefore, and a fundamental misapprehension of the real. On the contrary, it is man the microcosm, an actual embodiment of the reality of existence in *all* its forms, who is himself *cosmomorphic,* and as such the possessor of sources of *insight* into all that is comprised in the nature of the cosmos.[25]

Iredell Jenkins points to this kind of knowing in a person's aesthetic experience of a deeper participation in the world.

> Through aesthetic experience we become intimately involved with things, we participate actively in their interests and adventures, and so we see them as they see themselves. This point is most frequently put by saying that art deepens our sympathy for the things and situations—for the human persons and problems—it presents. It puts us more nearly in the place of the objects and personalities it depicts, and has us confront the world from their position rather than from our own. So it is held that through our appreciation of art we achieve a special sort of sympathetic understanding: we overcome the partiality of our prejudices and preconceptions, we live through situations from the inside instead of judging them from the outside, and so we are prepared to accept things on their own terms instead of rejecting them for not conforming with our demands.[26]

As the teacher prepares encounters with the central ideas or personages in a science or literature class, he or she should attempt to lead the students to these kinds of B cognitions. A student studying the dynamic gravitational relationships of the planetary system, for example, should be led to a sense of wonder at the mathematical precision of such a system. This would be an example of a learning context involving B cognition of culturally defined meanings. This experience could be coupled with D cognitions as the class studies the technical engineering problems of putting a space capsule into orbit around the moon.

These descriptive examples should indicate the rich variety of learning contexts which teachers can utilize to make their curriculum-instructional program more human. It would be an interesting exercise for readers to list their own series of activities appropriate to each quadrant of the three diagrams. Going beyond this exercise, readers might then attempt to construct from these lists a

---

[25] Max Scheler, *The Nature of Sympathy,* trans. by P. Heath, London: Routledge, 1959, p. 105.
[26] Iredell Jenkins, *Art and the Human Enterprise,* Cambridge, Mass.: Harvard, 1958, p. 130.

logically related sequence of learning experiences for a class unit focusing on one central idea. A complementary and equally fruitful exercise might be to select a topic from one of the discipline-oriented curriculum packages and construct classroom situations which would involve, either serially or simultaneously, all three dimensions of the learning context.

In Figure 13-4, nine subsets of the model have been encircled and labeled. Thus, the GBC subset refers to those activities involving group activity, B cognitions or B activities, and culturally defined meanings; the ICD subset refers to individual activity, culturally defined meanings, and D cognitions or D activities. And so on. The ninth subset includes all six poles of the three dimensions. This kind of activity or learning might be called a *peak* activity or learning, that is, that kind of extraordinary learning experience in which all elements in the human context become fused and integrated. A teacher is fortunate if she or he can stimulate such peak experiences once or twice a year.

As one searches for actual classroom experiences involving each one of these learning contexts, it becomes evident that the school in practice deals almost entirely with only two of these contexts: the ICD context and the GCD context. The other seven contexts of learning have been by and large neglected in both

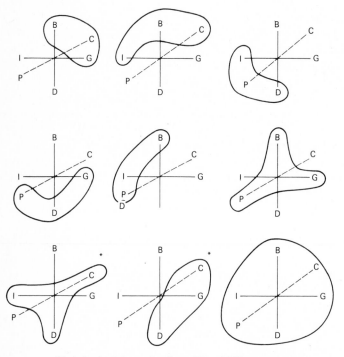

*Today's schools focus primarily on IDC and GCD contexts.

Figure 13-4 Nine possible contexts for learning. In the diagrams above, the letters stand for the poles of the dimensions described in the preceding pages. B stands for B cognitions; D stands for D cognitions; I stands for individual activity; G stands for group activity; C stands for culturally defined meanings; P stands for personal meanings.

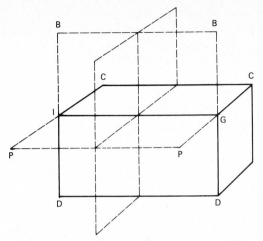

Figure 13-5 Today's schools use primarily ICD and GCD contexts and omit the following contexts: IBP, GCB, GPB, IPD, ICB, GPD.

curriculum design and teaching strategies. Perhaps these contexts are seen to be more appropriately dealt with by the student counselor. It may be that much counseling involves these contexts, but that is no reason for excluding them as genuine learning contexts for the classroom.

In Figure 13-5, we attempted to show how much of the human context of learning is neglected in curriculum design and in classroom practice. The space within the solid lines represents the ICD and GCD contexts; the space within the dotted lines represents those other six neglected contexts of learning. In this diagram, the limitations of designing a discipline-dominated curriculum based almost entirely on technological rationality become more apparent.

If we consider student learnings—the outcomes of encounters with curriculum content—as the area contained in the three-dimensional model, we can see in Figure 13-6 how much learning is neglected. This is not to say that learnings in

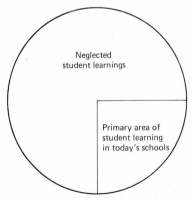

Figure 13-6 Learning in today's schools.

the shaded area of the figure are *entirely* neglected. Such a judgment would be unfair to those many teachers who are struggling to bring students to these learnings. The primary focus, however, of much of the recent thinking about curriculum, as well as of the practice in today's schools, is on learnings in the one quadrant.

SUMMARY

In proposing the human context of learning as a model by which supervisors might assist and evaluate classroom procedures and curriculum design, we must once again insist on the genuine value of programming, processes of inquiry, structural principles, and organizing centers. The curriculum movement rightly deserves the accolades of history for its significant clarification of these factors in the educational process. We hope to avoid, however, the blind acceptance of these insights as the panacea for achieving human progress. That is, by what magic formulae can we hope to "input" these insights into school programs and "output" an end to man's exploitation of man, an end to insane asylums, a reduction in alcohol and drug addiction, and a solution to the problems of poverty, racial conflict, and international tension? We need technological rationality, to be sure, if we are to confront these tragic human experiences, but we perhaps need even more a human community of trust and esteem and sympathy and forgiveness, and the foundation of this kind of community is to be discovered more in the realm of ethical and sympathetic rationality.

While an appeal to these basic human qualities of life is considered unscientific and sentimental by some, a curriculum which effectively programs these qualities of human life out of existence is self-defeating. To be fair, a curriculum focusing solely on interpersonal relations and aesthetic contemplation can produce a flaccid and ineffective personality. It is not a question, however, of either-or. The schools can provide an atmosphere and a curriculum for both intellectual and personal growth. And, consonant with the theme developed earlier, one can enter upon the greatest personal growth through *knowledge* of the world and can grow intellectually precisely by an internalization and integration of knowledge in one's personal life.

STUDY GUIDE

Recall the concepts and meanings associated with each of the following phrases and terms included in this chapter. Can you discuss them with a colleague and apply them to the supervisory context of your school? If you cannot, review them in the text and record the page number for future reference.

1   B cognitions _____
2   Personal meanings _____
3   Culturally defined meanings _____
4   Three-dimensional context _____
5   Technological rationality _____

6 IDC context _____
7 A peak learning experience _____

EXERCISES

1 Reflecting on your own educational experience can you recall a clear example of B cognition or a B learning experience? If not, can you recall a clear example of a B learning experience outside of your formal education? What were some of the features of this experience, as you remember it?

2 Reflect on your previous experience as a teacher. Did you foster learning in all of the nine contexts for learning? Which contexts did you tend to emphasize? What does that tell you about the assumptions you were making (your platform)?

3 If you were to attempt to introduce some of these learning contexts into a school you are familiar with, what changes in teacher behaviors and classroom organization would have to be effected?

4 Return to the film of a teacher's class viewed as part of the exercises in Chapter 12. Study the class to see which of the contexts were being used.

Chapter 14

Supervision and Evaluation

Supervision includes the monitoring of evaluation activities that go on in a school. Sometimes, supervisors themselves will be involved in evaluating activities directly, such as evaluating teachers' instructional abilities or school program effectiveness. Chapter 16 will deal with the evaluation of teachers' instructional activity. In our chapters on educational platform and on curriculum (Chapters 11 and 12), we have tried to raise essential questions which should be asked of any program.

Where it comes to program evaluation, it is our belief that most program evaluation more frequently concerns a specific course evaluation or a component of a course. Less frequently, a department or grade cluster will evaluate their whole program with a view to modifications. And even less frequently, a whole school or a school system will evaluate its total program (in order, for example, to introduce a form of mastery learning into all its courses). These latter decisions are usually influenced more by persons other than supervisors who have executive responsibilities or by outside experts. We will focus, therefore, on the more ordinary supervisory experience of monitoring the evaluation activities that take place in a course.

One could view evaluation as having different objectives. One objective, for example, would be to evaluate a course or student learnings in it with a view to introducing something new. For example, a course or a course unit could be evaluated to see how much mastery learning was taking place. Or the purpose could be to measure the compatibility of the conceptual content of the course with the cognitive developmental stages of the students. In both of these instances, the purpose of the evaluation is to bring the instructional activity, curriculum content, and student learnings much more into place with a set plan for improved student learning. And so evaluation can be analyzed according to its objectives: evaluation for needs assessment, evaluation for task analysis, evaluation as systems analysis, evaluation for change, or evaluation for evidence of racism or sexism.

Our primary focus in this chapter will be the supervisor's monitoring and assistance in the evaluation for improved student learning, for effective instructional planning, and for program (course) design. We will not go into detail on various testing methodologies or on how to interpret their results. Rather, we wish the supervisors to raise larger questions about how student learnings are evaluated, about what student learnings are not evaluated and why, and about the instructional uses of good evaluation processes.

THE ACTIVITY OF EVALUATION

Program and pupil evaluation formerly was thought of primarily as something that happened at the end of the term or the end of the year. At the conclusion of the course, students were evaluated on their progress in attaining the goals of the program by means of a test, a "final exam" of some kind or other. When the course was over, the teacher might have spent some time looking back over the curriculum and specific instructional strategies to see whether or not some units clearly were inappropriate and unsuccessful. In the case of a new course, or a course being taught for the first time, the teacher and supervisor might compare student achievement with the earlier course. They also would probably ask teachers in whose classes their students subsequently enrolled whether there was any noticeable difference after the new course.

Michael Scriven, in writing about curriculum revision, calls this type of evaluation *summative evaluation*.[1] It sums up, so to speak, the cumulative impact of the curriculum on learning, or it makes a general assessment of the cumulative learning of the whole curriculum by the student. He distinguishes summative evaluation from *formative evaluation* by positing formative evaluation as an ongoing process within the curriculum–instructional activity sequence. Through formative evaluation of the instructional program the teacher, learner, and curriculum designer can receive rapid feedback on the effectiveness of short-term segments of the program, rather than having to wait until the conclusion of the program for the more summative type of evaluation. Formative evaluation, since it goes on so close in time to the instructional activity and the learning encounter, can have a formative influence on the instructional activity and the learning encounter. In a given situation the teacher can see that use of a particular ad-

---

[1] Michael Scriven, "The Methodology of Evaluation," in Robert Stake (ed.), *AERA Monograph Series on Curriculum Evaluation,* no. 1, pp. 39–83, 1967.

vanced organizer or a demonstration simply is not getting the students' attention or, by questions from the students, that it is well over their heads. This kind of quick feedback will probably lead the teacher to discard that approach on the spot and to try a new tack. Or a student may discover that he has not yet mastered the rule on capital letters. He and the teacher can then set up some exercises to ensure a more adequate grasp of those rules.

Bloom and associates divide evaluation into three types: summative, diagnostic, and formative.[2] Diagnostic evaluation is closely related to both formative and summative evaluation, but it is distinguished by its purposes. Diagnostic evaluation is used to place a student properly in the level of instruction that best matches his entry behaviors and skills with learning objectives of the instructional unit. It is also used to determine the underlying causes or circumstances behind repeated deficiencies in a student's performance that have not responded to ordinary remedial measures.[3] Diagnostic evaluation usually employs some recognized standardized test or battery of tests which will highlight cognitive, affective, physical, psychological, and environmental factors in the student. With such information concerning how well the youngster is functioning in his or her stage of development, more appropriate resources can be made available. Some of the similarities and differences between diagnostic, formative, and summative evaluation as listed by Bloom and associates appear in Figure 14-1.

FORMATIVE EVALUATION

For the moment, we will consider the activity of formative evaluation, for the supervision of evaluation activity would seem more involved in that form of evaluation. A brief overview of formative evaluation of the curriculum points to particular activities of students, other activities of the teacher, and the formative use for both of testing. Depending on the situation, supervisors may or may not participate in the evaluation activities, but they will certainly be expected to monitor in some fashion the effectiveness of these evaluation activities.

Student Evaluative Activity: Evaluation of the Curriculum-as-Learned

Let us consider an ordinary class setting, say a self-contained classroom with 1 teacher and 24 students. The class has just concluded a comparison of two poems. Previous classes have dealt with aspects of poetry, such as mood, figures of speech, rhythm, unity, image, and symbol. They have seen a variety of poems and have done some analysis using these critical concepts. The objective of today's class was to have them use these critical concepts to compare two poems and to argue why one poem was a "better" poem than the other. This objective fit into the larger goal of the course that aimed at the students' developing a discriminating taste for superior literary expression.

Toward the end of the class the teacher felt satisfied that most if not all of the students reflected a good grasp of the analytical concepts and had applied

[2] Benjamin S. Bloom, J. Thomas Hastings, and George F. Madaus, *Handbook on Formative and Summative Evaluation of Student Learning,* New York: McGraw-Hill, 1971, p. 87 et passim.
[3] Ibid., p. 87.

Type of Evaluation

	Diagnostic	Formative	Summative
Function	Placement: Determining the presence or absence of prerequisite skills Determining the student's prior level of mastery Classifying the student according to various characteristics known or thought to be related to alternative modes of instruction Determination of underlying causes of repeated learning difficulties	Feedback to student and teacher on student progress through a unit Location of errors in terms of the structure of a unit so that remedial alternative instruction techniques can be prescribed	Certification or grading of students at the end of a unit, semester, or course
Time	For placement at the outset of a unit, semester, or year's work During instruction when student evidences repeated inability to profit fully from ordinary instruction	During instruction	At the end of a unit, semester, or year's work
Emphasis in evaluation	Cognitive, affective, and psychomotor behaviors Physical, psychological, and environmental factors	Cognitive behaviors	Generally cognitive behaviors; depending on subject matter, sometimes psychomotor; occasionally affective behaviors
Type of instrumentation	Formative and summative instruments for pretests Standardized achievement tests Standardized diagnostic tests Teacher-made instruments Observation and checklists	Specially designed formative instruments	Final or summative examinations

Figure 14-1 Similarities and differences between diagnostic, formative, and summative evaluation.

them well in arguing for the superiority of one poem over the other. In an attempt to further reinforce the learning and to test out her impressions that the class had pretty well achieved the instructional objectives she said, "Now let's all pause a minute and reflect what it is we learned today. What new thing struck us? What have we understood with greater clarity? How does what we've done today fit with what went on before? Of what practical use was this whole experience, anyway?"

The following answers came back:

"I learned that it makes a difference when you read a poem out loud. I could *hear* how much superior that first poem was to the other one."

"I learned that you can still like an inferior poem—I mean, yeah, the first poem is a better poem, by all the measures we apply to it, but I like the second poem because it expresses a feeling about being alone that I've had many times. Just because a poem is a mediocre poem doesn't mean it's no good at all."

"I learned that I had to read both poems at least four times before they made any sense to me. It seems that with poetry, kinda like music, you gotta acquire a kind of familiarity with it before it really says anything to you."

"I learned that all this art stuff isn't entirely a matter of feeling, you know, all from inside someone's fantasy. There's something to it, some kind of intelligence. And you can talk about poetry intelligently, instead of simply leaving it to subjective feelings of like or dislike."

"I learned that I have no poetic imagination. I never thought those kinds of thoughts. And I'm wondering how one gets to be a poet—are you born that way, or can you develop it?"

"I'm really having a hard time understanding what makes a poem 'unified.' It's a word that seems to me to mean perfect, or perfection. Like a perfect circle or something. So if a poem has unity, then it must mean that every word, every line is in perfect place. But who could ever decide that? Maybe I need to see examples of *really* unified poems and some that are a little off-center and maybe I'll catch on."

"I learned that it feels good to discover that a lot of people agree with my conclusions. Before the class started, I wasn't sure whether my picking the first poem as better was the right answer, you know. But when other people gave the same reasons as I had, I really felt good, because I figured—yeah, for the first time—that I'm understanding all the stuff we've been doing on poetry."

Suppose you were observing in that class. After the class you and the teacher sat down to review the class. What practical things would the two of you do as a result of those student responses?

The example illustrates a range of student learnings which reflected not only the achievement of the teacher's objectives, but also the many idiosyncratic, ancillary learnings that always occur. The example points to the importance of taking that kind of time to let students reflect on what they have learned. Obviously, the students in that honors poetry class had rather high levels of motivation and of verbal and abstractive abilities. Students in third or fourth grade will come up with simpler responses, to be sure. But getting them into the habit early of evaluating what they are learning will pay enormous dividends as it develops into ongoing reflective habits of mind and a genuine satisfaction over knowing that they are making progress.

Students' evaluation of their appropriation of the curriculum can lead to both cognitive and affective results. On the one hand, by reflecting on their grasp of the learning task, they can clarify what they know. Frequently, the simple recall of the class material or unit will reinforce the grasp of the material. When this reflection is done in a nonthreatening environment, students can also clarify and admit what they have not yet grasped or understood. They can trace back the instructional sequence until they get to the point where the teacher or the textbook lost them. This clarifying of what one does not know will often lead to a desire to learn that, to get at that the first thing in the next class.

On the affective level, students can also be encouraged to review what they learned, not so much for intellectual understanding but simply for enjoyment. The youngster who had to repeat the poems many times was discovering how poems are meant to be enjoyed. This kind of enjoyment is not limited to those subjects within the humanities. A sensitive biology teacher or a physical educa-tion teacher can lead students into a kind of repetitive appreciation of what they have learned. Sometimes that leads to genuine wonderment.

In either case, student evaluation of this learning can lead to ownership. Recognizing what they have learned, what it means, how it is related to what they have learned before, how they can use it, what a sense of excitement or enjoy-ment comes with that mastery of a skill or discovery of a surprising piece of information—all of this leads students to appropriate that learning as theirs. Once appropriated, the learning tends to be effective, which is to say the student owns it and can use it in many ways in the immediate future. Unfortunately, many teachers fail to take the time to encourage this sense of ownership. What they miss by omitting the encouragement of student self-evaluation is the genuine satisfaction of knowing how much actually gets absorbed and how fascinating it is to observe the individual coloring of the learning that was supposed to take place. Moreover, much of the formative evaluation the teacher engages in will not pick up the obvious clues which students put forth in their self-evaluation. A supervisor who helps a teacher to initiate student self-evaluation may have pro-vided a stimulus for instructional and program improvement more effective than several semesters of in-service lectures on the topic.

The Teacher's Formative Evaluation Activity: Evaluation of the Curriculum-as-Taught

By means of student self-evaluation, brief quizzes, questions right in the middle of instructional activity, by checking homework assignments, and through infor-mal out-of-class conversations, teachers can get an idea of the effectiveness of the curriculum unit design as well as of their teaching strategies. It will take a mul-tiplicity of feedback mechanisms rather than the single mechanism of an occa-sional test to provide the formative information. Sometimes a test will be the real problem because it has been poorly constructed.

In any event, the teacher's formative evaluation activity will have several foci. The teacher must try to evaluate how well the student is encountering and mastering the learning task. There may be several reasons why the student is having difficulty. There may be emotionally upsetting conditions at home; a fight in the school yard that morning could have made concentration on schoolwork impossible. But it may be that the pace of the class was too fast, or that the examples used were too strange, or that the student was distracted briefly at the beginning of the class and missed one of the initial steps in the explanation.

If most or all of the class is showing disinterest or confusion, then the teacher has to evaluate what in his or her teaching is lacking. Or is it the learning-unit design in the textbook that is confusing or flat? Sometimes the only way to identify the cause is to ask the students. From time to time, however, the teacher is not all that aware of the deficiency in the textbook or in his or her teaching. Sometimes the problem does not surface for a week or two, when a test shows up a consistent gap in the class's grasp of an essential part of the sequence of learning.

And then there are the teachers who are perpetually unaware of how they smother any student initiative in learning. Low grades are simply their way of punishing what they perceive as the recalcitrance and general laziness of youth. Here, the formative evaluation of the teacher is almost totally ineffective because the source of the problem is ignored.

Supervisors can help teachers address the difficult task of formative evaluation primarily by communicating to the teacher a sense of respect for the teacher's competence to refashion his or her curriculum-instructional plan more effectively. Frequently, teachers think that a textbook is too sacred to be altered one iota. On the contrary, the teacher is in the best position to know what will work with his or her youngsters and should deviate from the textbook when that is called for. The supervisor can work alongside the teacher, exploring alternative strategies, testing out an idea on one or two students before trying it with the whole class, and looking for gaps and blind spots and filling them in so that students can move easily from one thing to another. Once the teacher gains the self-confidence, then he or she will be much more likely to carry on such programs and self-corrective activities independently.

In cases where substantial program revision may be called for, the supervisor can enlist the assistance of someone more skilled in curriculum design to work with several teachers. The point is, however, that the teacher ought to be the central person in this kind of formative evaluation, not the supervisor. Frequently the most important activity of the supervisor is convincing the teacher that he or she can do it, and furthermore ought to, and finally, has to do it. Familiarity with a variety of evaluation techniques such as those presented by Bloom and associates[4] will equip the supervisor with a certain repertory of approaches, some of which may be useful to get the teacher started.

In this regard, a formative use of testing can be a key source of feedback data which will unlock the problems besetting both teachers and students. More often than not, quizzes and tests are not carefully reviewed. The grades are entered into the mark book, and the papers are handed back to the students, who

[4] Op. cit.

look at the grade at the top of the page, give off a whine, a curse, or a gleeful expletive, crumple up the paper, and toss it in the basket.

A careful review of tests and quizzes, however, can be turned into very effective learning. First, there is usually a high level of interest because of the grade involved. (We are assuming a non-mastery-learning setting. In the instance of mastery learning the papers would usually not have a grade.) By reviewing the quiz or the test, students have a chance to see where they made their mistake, thereby clearing up (hopefully) what could be a lingering problem if not corrected. It also provides the teacher some clues as to why some students failed to achieve the objective of the instruction. Such information often leads to more appropriate remedial exercises. In the exchange of information, the teacher can likewise score all kinds of other useful points, such as reinforcing the main point of the instruction, reviewing previous learnings leading up to the material under consideration, clarifying the level of exactitude or logic or basic English required in the course, pointing out the necessity to ask questions in class when points are unclear, etc., etc.

Students, even the ones who put down most of the correct answers, have an opportunity to review the essentials of the previous class or learning unit. For students whose low performance was due to one key deficiency, the opportunity is there to see the principle or concept or formula or rule as such, that is, as a generalization that applies to many particulars; through the repetition of the mistake which is underlined before them in glowing red, they can now have the insight that they could not grasp before.

Such review also allows the rhetoricians in the class an opportunity to debate the precise meaning of a word or phrase in the question that they took to mean something other than what the teacher intended. Sometimes a student has a legitimate complaint when the wording of the question allows for two different readings and therefore for two different responses. The teacher's review of the test can help clear up such problems before some disgruntled youngster goes home to enlist the support of his or her parents who in turn become disgruntled and demand an appointment with the principal.

Again, supervisors can help teachers get far more instructional mileage out of their tests and quizzes. Rather than being something extraneous to instruction, this kind of formative evaluation can become one of the regular tools of instruction. Only in this way can testing be restored to its proper place as an aid to instruction rather than being a specter dominating both instruction and student motivation.

The Supervisor in Formative Evaluation

As should be evident from the above, the role of the supervisor is that of evaluating the type and effectiveness of the formative evaluating activity that goes on in the classroom. By keeping uppermost in mind that this type of evaluation is intended to improve the learning of the student and the instructional effectiveness of the teacher and the curriculum program, the supervisor can help the teacher and student stay on target in their evaluation efforts.

Moreover, the supervisor should have enough distance from the evaluation activity itself to perceive the values that are brought into play by the type and style of the evaluation procedures employed by the teacher. That is to say, evaluation is a process of assigning value and significance to actions, things, answers, or questions. Behind any evaluation activity there are a whole host of assumptions which have value content. These assumptions usually go untested or unquestioned.

Some assumptions behind some forms of evaluation include the following: that knowing or understanding something means giving this response to that question; that this curriculum design or this text contains a legitimate approach (or the most legitimate, or the only legitimate approach) to this area of human knowledge (for example, modern Latin American history), and therefore a test of the student's knowledge of this approach indicates that he or she knows something true or objective or valid about that area of human knowledge; that using the language of public discourse in evaluation is the best means of measuring what the student has learned (rather than using poetry or music or graphics to measure it); or that teachers and other school officials have the authority and competency to decide the criteria for evaluating and ranking students.

Behind these assumptions, of course, are other assumptions: that learning primarily involves learning what others have discovered (and seldom the way they discovered it), and so evaluation monitors learning on that level; that there is always a causal connection between learning and instruction (rather than learning and the *students'* search, inquiry, practice, trial and error, or logical deduction), and hence evaluation of learning implies an evaluation of instruction; that the proper place for most learning is a classroom, and so evaluation never compares classroom learning (with all its constraints) with learnings in other settings. One could go on and on, describing assumptions behind assumptions. The point of listing these is to encourage supervisors occasionally to create enough distance from the evaluation activity for both the teacher and themselves so that they can perceive the value assumptions that are embedded in their evaluation procedures. If nothing else, such distancing can be a healthy antidote to dogmatism; at best it will encourage flexibility and more holistic approaches to evaluation.

Kunkel and Tucker propose five criteria by which supervisors and other evaluators might evaluate the quality of their evaluation activity.[5] These criteria were developed as part of their perception-based model of evaluation. Even without endorsing the theory of knowledge upon which the model is based, we believe these criteria can be applied to ensure quality evaluation in any evaluation scheme.

> Quality 1. *Holism.* The evaluation should avoid distortion of the total reality being evaluated by an undue emphasis on quantification or on only a few variables. Toward this end both statistical and existential forms of inference should be used.

[5] Richard C. Kunkel and Susan A. Tucker, "A Perception-based Model of Program Evaluation: A Values Oriented Theory," paper presented at AERA Annual Meeting, New York, 1977.

Quality 2. *Helpfulness toward program improvement.* This is really the key to formative evaluation, and what distinguishes it from summative evaluation. The primary purpose of formative evaluation is to assist the one responsible for the curriculum program. It looks to growth, improvement, increased effectiveness, rather than to ranking, judging, categorizing, criticizing.

Quality 3. *Acceptance of hard and soft data.* In order to reduce distortion through methodological rigidity or theoretical bias (e.g., positivism or mechanistic reductionism), the reality being evaluated should be described by both empirical and intuitive methodologies. The qualities of the phenomena as well as the quantitative properties deserve attention.

Quality 4. *Evaluation vulnerability.* The process of evaluation requires dialogue between the evaluator and the evaluated in which the theory and methodology of the evaluator are open to question. Rather than assuming an elitist posture, the evaluator must enter a shared enterprise with the evaluated in which perceptions are discussed and conclusions negotiated. The evaluator has to be as vulnerable as the evaluated.

Quality 5. *Vision of the future.* Since the purpose of the evaluation is the improvement of the program or the behavior being evaluated, the evaluator ought to be able and willing to disclose his view of the future context in which such improved programs or behaviors will function better. In this way, evaluation is seen as dynamic, as creative, and as open to the future, as in fact that essential activity that keeps an action system in a process of self renewal.[6]

These criteria will also be evident in our later treatment of clinical supervision.[7] For the moment, however, we can appreciate the necessity of the supervisor's awareness of the values embedded in any evaluation scheme. In the ongoing process of formative evaluation, it is possible to achieve a more holistic appraisal of teacher, student learning, and program. When one moves into summative evaluation, however, supervisors will have a much more difficult time preventing the exterior imposition of one exclusive set of values.

SUMMATIVE EVALUATION

In treating summative evaluation, we wish to distinguish between the *activity* of summative evaluation and the *reporting* of the results of summative evaluation. Frequently summative evaluation is spoken of exclusively as the reporting of results. Supervisors ought to monitor not only the reporting of results, but also how the activity of summative evaluation itself is designed and carried out. For example, a teacher may have a very fine method of preparing her students for a final exam, but may have a very one-sided approach to reporting results. Beyond the individual teacher's reporting of results, the supervisor needs to look at the system's use of these reports and the system's reporting procedures to outside agencies.

When dealing with summative evaluation of students, then, supervisors can help teachers realize the significant instructional activity and learning that can

[6] Ibid., pp. 2–4.
[7] See Chapter 17.

take place through summative evaluation. Teachers, for example, can encourage students to engage in a summative-type self-evaluation, aiming for the students' review of what significant things *they* think they have learned in the course. Some teachers will assign a final project of this type. Even in a more structured class review of the course prior to a final exam, the students can deepen much of what they have learned. Frequently the review provides the opportunity for a whole new synthesis of learnings. What was said in the discussion of formative evaluation about going over test results would also apply here; it would be the teacher's last chance to get the point across before the students move on.

When considering the reporting of summative evaluation results, we may wish that the five criteria mentioned earlier could be applied. There are many reasons why summative evaluation usually is far less complete than what the five criteria would require. Summative evaluation has as its primary purpose the reporting of results at the conclusion of a program or of a time span. Among the people reading these reports of summative evaluation are guidance counselors, principals, parents, college admission officers, employers, state licensing officials, etc. By and large, they are looking for brief reports using recognizable symbols of usually a quantifiable result. It would be impossible for this reporting system to work with substantially expanded reports that measured up to the five criteria. First, it would put an intolerable burden on teachers to prepare an extensive portfolio on each of their students. The agencies receiving these reports would have to hire additional personnel simply to read and code these reports. Given the political and legal climate surrounding information systems and their use, a more expansive summation of the pupil's achievements would open a Pandora's box of problems. While more holistic summative evaluation reports would be desirable for a variety of purposes, then, the practical difficulties involved would prevent any useful developments in this arena.

When we move into the *reporting* of summative evaluation of the teacher's effectiveness and the effectiveness of the curriculum, we move into a process fraught with problems and misunderstandings. Because of the neoscientific-management influences in education[8] and political and economic issues surrounding schooling, summative evaluation of teachers, instructional strategies, curriculum design, and instructional materials has been used for purposes other than what might be called scientific objectivity.

Recently, schools are being held accountable by local, state, and federal agencies. Teachers, supervisors, building principals, and superintendents are under increasing pressure to give an account of themselves to the taxpayers and legislatures. There is the simplistic assumption that if youngsters are falling behind in scores on standardized tests, then the fault can be laid exclusively on the school's doorstep.

Even if the schools were largely to blame, a conclusion certainly without any clear evidence, the methodologies of reporting and evaluation used in most accountability schemes, and the theory of knowledge upon which they rest, are

---

[8] To be taken up in more detail in Chapter 16.

highly simplistic and value-biased. First, the issue of accountability has become a highly political issue. It is impossible to assume that the evaluation, interpretation, and reporting of school results would remain untainted by political motives. Any claim to scientific objectivity in accountability reports will involve at least as much rhetoric as truth.

Secondly, the almost total reliance of accountability schemes on test scores or quantifiable aspects of learning rests upon a theory of knowing or learning that comes out of behavioristic psychology. The view of human beings reflected by behavioristic psychology would more than likely be rejected by most citizens as entirely too simplistic or reductionist. Yet measures of learning dictated by this model of humanity are used as the primary source of evidence that the schools are doing—or not doing—what these same citizens are paying taxes for. That the irony in this goes unnoticed or is ignored only points to the muddying of evaluation purposes by political concerns.[9]

Supervisors have recognized competence and expertise within the school system. They should use their authority and join forces with other supervisors and teachers to resist accountability schemes which take such a one-dimensional and biased view of learning and instruction. If supervisors and teachers allow accountability schemes to intrude more and more into the schools, the end result will be a program which leaves teachers and students little or no latitude in the classroom. Everything will already have been spelled out in a tightly systematic process leading to the achievement of preestablished behavioral objectives.[10]

Finally, supervisors and teachers (and, where possible, students) will engage in summative evaluation activities at the end of the course. Not only will they review what the final results were in student learnings, but they will review the results of their formative evaluations throughout the course. It is during the summative evaluation activity that one can see again the usefulness of the five criteria of good evaluation. The entire program should be reviewed as to the effectiveness of its scope and sequence. This comprehensive evaluation should also include an assessment of the adequacy of instructional materials such as films, slides, reference books, field trips, etc. Those involved in the evaluation should also question whether the use of time and space was helpful. Was the pace about right? Is there any way to revise the class schedule to allow for longer or shorter periods or for a more flexible schedule for large and small group sessions? Such a general overview should also include a look at the high and low points of the course and some guesses at the probable reasons for both. This comprehensive summation of the course or program will enable the teacher to make those necessary decisions about changes in the program next time around. Here is where the supervisor can be an enormous resource as the two come up with a

[9] Ernest R. House (ed.), *School Evaluation: The Politics and Process,* Berkeley, Calif.: McCutchan, 1973; Robert E. Stake, "Overview and Critique of Existing Evaluation Practices and Some New Leads for the Future," paper presented at AERA Annual Meeting, San Francisco, 1976; and Kunkel and Tucker, op. cit.

[10] Ernest R. House, "Beyond Accountability," in Thomas J. Sergiovanni (ed.), *Professional Supervision for Professional Teachers,* Washington, D.C.: Association for Supervision and Curriculum Development, 1975.

variety of program changes and test them out for logic and "fit" in the overall program. Such a program evaluation often becomes the starting point for the supervisor's agenda the following year.

SUMMARY

This chapter has taken up the supervisor's role in monitoring the evaluation activity of teachers. We established the distinctions between formative and summative evaluation. We saw that students can engage in their own self-evaluation process in both formative and summative evaluation. This is a central activity that reveals to the teacher how the student is personally appropriating the learning tasks. We saw how in the teacher's use of tests for both formative and summative purposes valuable learning could be taking place. In other words, we were stressing that evaluation can be and ought to be viewed as an intrinsic element in both teaching and learning.

While the supervisor acts in a manner supportive to the teacher's evaluation activities and occasionally becomes involved with the teacher in planning and designing evaluation activities, we saw that one essential activity of the supervisor is to keep enough distance from the evaluation activity to perceive the values embedded in the process. Some value assumptions behind rather standard evaluation procedures were highlighted. The five criteria for good evaluation were presented as a means for both teacher and supervisor to check that their evaluation activities were on target.

It is apparent, then, that evaluation is a critical aspect of the supervisor's professional responsibility. Evaluation must be continuous and not simply an end-of-year or end-of-semester assessment. It involves much more than rating the teacher according to the test results of students, and much more than the grading and promotion of students. Rather, the comprehensive evaluation process provides a continuous and responsible basis for decision making throughout the curriculum-instructional program. Only by means of an ongoing evaluation process can the program be improved and adapted to the human needs of students and hence result in more effective student learnings. The neglect of continuous and thoroughgoing evaluation on the part of supervisors, teachers, and students can be cited as the single most pervasive cause of stale and irrelevant instructional programs. Continuous and honest appraisal of the quality and effectiveness of the instructional program, on the other hand, can be the necessary catalyst for imaginative curriculum development itself, as well as for improved teaching strategies.

STUDY GUIDE

Recall the concepts and meanings associated with each of the following phrases and terms included in this chapter. Can you discuss them with a colleague and apply them to the supervisory context of your school? If you cannot, review them in the text and record the page number for future reference.

1 Diagnostic evaluation _____
2 Evaluating evaluation _____
3 Evaluation reporting _____
4 Evaluation activity _____
5 Formative evaluation _____
6 Misuses of testing _____
7 Student self-evaluation _____
8 Summative evaluation _____

EXERCISES

1 Inquire at a school you are familiar with about current accountability reports that the state requires. Do you think the taxpayers are receiving adequate information about the effectiveness of that school? Discuss your reactions in class.
2 Write out your own assumptions behind a method of formative student evaluation that makes sense to you.
3 In your formal education, have you been asked to evaluate what you have learned? How might a student encourage that practice with his or her teachers?

Part Three

A Human Resources Approach to Staff Development, Clinical Supervision, and Teacher Evaluation

INTRODUCTION: GROWTH-ORIENTED CLASSROOM SUPERVISION

The state of the art of classroom supervision is perhaps best illustrated by examining prevailing teacher-evaluation strategies. Teacher evaluation has typically meant the rating, grading, and classifying of teachers, using some locally standardized instrument as a yardstick. The instrument generally lists certain traits of teachers assumed to be important, such as "the teacher has a pleasant voice," and certain tasks of teaching considered to be critical, such as "the teacher plans well." The evaluator usually writes in comments as, increasingly, does the teacher.

This evaluation instrument is filled out after a classroom observation of the teacher, often lasting from ½ to 1 hour. The observation visit is usually preceded by a conference, which varies from a brief encounter to a session where lesson plans, objectives, and teaching strategies are discussed. Sometimes a postobservation conference follows, wherein comments and ratings are discussed and negotiated. Usually, the teacher-evaluation procedure is concluded when both parties sign the instrument. The instrument is then forwarded to the district archives. This teacher-evaluation procedure may occur once or twice a year for the tenured teacher and two to four times a year for novices. Many teachers report having been observed in the classroom only a handful of times, and reports of almost never being observed after achieving tenure are common. Though exceptions exist, and progress is being made, by and large neither teachers nor administrators and supervisors are satisfied with present procedures. More damaging, many supervisors privately view the procedures as lacking in credibility. What are the likely effects of participating in a system characterized by such doubts? The system takes on a certain artificial or mechanical quality, a routine functioning which becomes an end in itself.

The present state of classroom supervision can be attributed to *faulty ideology* and *faulty technology.* The dominant ideologies in supervision are those associated with human relations and scientific management. The effects of human relations have been to adopt laissez faire approaches which severely downgrade classroom supervision. Presumably, it is considered that teachers are professionals, and if treated nicely, but otherwise left alone, they will respond properly. The classroom is the castle of the teacher as a professional, and classroom supervision is viewed as threatening to, or usurping of, teacher authority. This argument is an attractive rationalization for many principals and supervisors who have good management skills and some interpersonal facility but are otherwise weak or uncomfortable in dealing with the educational side of the enterprise.

Increasingly, the emphasis in schools has shifted from classroom supervision to general supervision, and this is the scientific-management side of the ideology question. In the scientific-management view it is felt that if one can focus primarily on educational program administration and supervision through developing a materials-intensive curriculum, usually linked to a detailed curriculum syllabus or detailed predetermined objectives, then teachers can be supervised in classrooms by remote control. Teaching behavior becomes more predictable and reliable as teaching objectives and materials become more detailed, structured, and standardized. Thus we can control what teachers do by controlling the objectives they pursue, the materials they use, the curriculum they follow, the assignments and tests they give, and the schedule they follow. Granting that the existence of this kind of materials-intensive program is a means to control classroom practices, nagging questions born of the accountability movement remain. How can supervisors *be sure* that teachers are indeed performing prescribed duties up to standard? What evaluation technology can be used to answer this question? Technologies are associated with ideologies, and the language of scientific management (objectivity, rationality, reliability, precision) has been found by most Americans to be irresistible. The technology of classroom observation and evaluation, as most readers will attest, is shrouded in a sense of scientism not found even in the more legitimate sciences. This phenomenon is contrary to what most educators actually believe—*that teaching is far more an artistic enterprise than a scientific one.* Not willing to admit this publicly, we continue our deception by willy-nilly participation in a doubtful system of supervision and evaluation.

The pressure for accountability is, in our view, legitimate and cannot be ignored. Classroom supervision and evaluation is important and is needed and desired by teachers and the public alike. But the typical response to this pressure—tightening up a set of procedures with ideological and technical shortcomings, doing more of the same but now doing it with more intensity—needs to be reversed. These issues are discussed in Chapter 16, where more naturalistic approaches to supervision and evaluation more consistent with the values of human resources supervision and the nature of work in education are suggested. A caveat at this point is significant. Though we are strong advocates of more naturalistic approaches, we seek not to throw out the proverbial baby with the bath water. Present methods have value if viewed more modestly and intelligently, if applied in a more discriminating fashion, and if supplemented by more naturalistic approaches.

GENERAL VERSUS CLINICAL SUPERVISION

Most of the literature on supervision and textbooks on supervision tend to emphasize either (or some combination of) the organizational and behavioral aspects of general supervision or the educational program administration aspects of general supervision. Most notable in recent years are books by Harris[1] (educational program administration emphasis), Alfonso, Firth, and Neville,[2] and Wiles and Lovell[3] (organizational and behavioral emphasis). Parts One and Two of this book are also concerned with general supervision. Part One, for example, is concerned with the organizational-leadership aspect of general supervision and Part Two with the educational-leadership aspects of general supervision. The strong emphasis one finds in the literature on general supervision is related in part to the decline of interest in classroom supervision by scholars and practitioners.

In the interest of focusing attention anew on classroom supervision, some have attempted to distinguish between the two by referring to classroom supervision as clinical and out-of-class supervision as general. Cogan, for example, cites two purposes of clinical supervision in his popular book entitled *Clinical Supervision:* "The first is to develop and explicate a system of in-class supervision that, in competent hands, will prove powerful enough to give supervisors a reasonable hope of accomplishing significant improvements in the teacher's classroom instruction. The second purpose is to help correct the neglect of in-class or clinical supervision and to establish it as a necessary complement to out-of-class ('general') supervision."[4]

In a similar vein Goldhammer refers to clinical supervision as follows:

> First of all, I mean to convey an image of face-to-face relationships between supervisors and teachers. History provides the principal reason for this emphasis, namely, that in many situations presently and during various periods in its development,

---

[1] Ben N. Harris, *Supervisory Behavior in Education,* 2d ed., Englewood Cliffs, N.J.: Prentice-Hall, 1975.

[2] Robert Alfonso, Gerald Firth, and Richard F. Neville, *Instructional Supervision: A Behavioral System,* Boston: Allyn and Bacon, 1975.

[3] Kimball Wiles and John Lovell, *Supervision for Better Schools,* Englewood Cliffs, N.J.: Prentice-Hall, 1975.

[4] Morris L. Cogan, *Clinical Supervision,* Boston: Houghton Mifflin, 1973, p. xi.

supervision has been conducted as supervision from a distance, as, for example, supervision of curriculum development or of instructional policies framed by committees of teachers. "Clinical" supervision is meant to imply supervision up close.[5]

General and clinical supervision are, of course, interdependent. Meaningful classroom interventions are built upon healthy organizational climates, facilitated by credible leadership and premised on a reasoned educational program. Though general supervision is an important and necessary component of effective supervision, without clinical supervision it is not sufficient.

THE FOCUS OF CLINICAL SUPERVISION

Clinical supervision refers to face-to-face contact with teachers with the intent of improving instruction and increasing professional growth. In many respects, a one-to-one correspondence exists between improving classroom instruction and increasing professional growth, and for this reason staff development and clinical supervision are inseparable concepts and activities. How does evaluation fit into this picture? Evaluation is a natural part of one's professional life and occurs continuously. Every decision that teachers, administrators, and supervisors make is preceded by evaluation (often latent) of some sort. Evaluation is valuing, and valuing is judging. These are natural events in the lives of educational professionals and, of course, are critical aspects of clinical supervision and staff development.

But evaluation can take a number of foci, some of which are more compatible with events, purposes, and characteristics of educational supervision than others. Evaluation experts, for example, make an important distinction between *formative* evaluation and *summative* evaluation.[6] Teacher-evaluation procedures typically found in school can be classified as summative. Evaluation which emphasizes ongoing growth and development would be considered formative. Consider the following distinctions:

1 Summative evaluation of teachers has a certain finality to it—it is terminal in the sense that it occurs at the conclusion of an educational activity. In evaluating a teacher's performance, summative evaluation suggests a statement of worth. A judgment is made about the quality of one's teaching.

2 Summative evaluation is a legitimate and important activity which if done carefully can play a constructive role in a school's total evaluation strategy.

3 Formative evaluation of teachers is intended to increase the effectiveness of on-going educational programs and activity. Evaluation information is collected and used to understand, correct and improve on-going activity.

4 With respect to teaching, formative evaluation is concerned less with judging and rating the teacher than with providing information which helps improve teacher performance.

---

[5] Robert Goldhammer, *Clinical Supervision: Special Methods for the Supervision of Teachers,* New York: Holt, 1969, p. 54.

[6] Michael Scriven, "The Methodology of Evaluation," in Robert Stake (ed.), *AERA Monograph on Curriculum Evaluation,* no. 1, Chicago: Rand McNally, 1965. See also Benjamin Bloom, Thomas Hastings, and G. F. Madaus, *Handbook on Formative and Summative Evaluation of Student Learning,* New York: McGraw-Hill, 1971.

5 In the strictest sense formative and summative evaluation cannot be separated, for each contains aspects of the other, but it is useful nevertheless to speak of a formative focus and a summative focus to evaluation.[7]

The focus of clinical supervision should be on formative evaluation. The supervisor is first and foremost interested in improving instruction and increasing teachers' personal development. Does this emphasis conflict with demands that teachers be held accountable for their actions? We think not. A formative evaluation emphasis is entirely consistent with holding teachers accountable, but in a professional, not occupational, sense. Professional accountability is growth-oriented and implies a commitment to consistent improvement. Occupational accountability is not growth-oriented at all, but merely seeks to meet some predetermined standard. Presumably, once this standard is met—that is, once the teacher is judged to meet minimum standards of "satisfactory" teaching—the teacher's growth obligations cease.

From time to time supervisors will indeed be engaged in a more summatively focused evaluation. Though the supervisor's major commitment is to formative evaluation, occasional problems occur and incompetent teachers or teachers whose philosophy and orientation are disengaged from that of the school will be discovered. As a result, withholding tenure or dismissal of a tenured teacher may well be considered. Personnel actions of this sort are so intertwined with existing local administrative policies and state statutory restrictions and requirements, that a totally different mind-set is needed. Such a procedure is best placed in the hands of a line administrative officer of the district. In the case of a principal who assumes both a supervisory and administrative role, the teacher should be informed of the focus and the tone of the evaluation procedure which is to follow. The school attorney would most likely be consulted regarding due process if administrative guidelines on this question are wanting. Many state education agencies and state school board associations publish pamphlets and other guidelines on this touchy and increasingly legalistic problem.[8]

Practically speaking, if we are interested in improving classroom instruction, we must start with the teacher. Sustained changes in teacher behavior and sustained improvements in classroom functioning occur as a result of teachers who are committed to these changes. That being the case, supervisors are forced to depend upon the willing cooperation of teachers. Indeed the supervisor does not change teachers but helps them to change, a condition more suited to formative evaluation.

In addition to what is known about changing behavior, the supervisor needs to face up to the reality resulting from increased staff stability today and in the decade or so ahead. Good teaching jobs are increasingly difficult to find, and teachers are less likely to leave once they are employed. Low teacher turnover is often viewed initially as a blessing, particularly by those who just a few years ago

---

[7] Thomas J. Sergiovanni, *Handbook for Effective Department Leadership Concepts and Practices in Today's Secondary Schools,* Boston: Allyn and Bacon, 1977. p. 372.

[8] See, for example, Newell N. Jenkins, Terrence Barnicle, Gerald Dempsey, and J. Todd Franklin, *Formal Dismissal Procedures under Illinois Teacher Tenure Laws,* Springfield: Illinois Association of School Boards, 1975.

experienced difficulty in finding and keeping teachers. But in reality, low turn-over poses serious problems for schools. For example, dissatisfied teachers are now less likely to leave. Their reasons for staying in the job are too important.

With regard to change, in an expanding district one can impose changes on existing staff and by the process of staff attrition and careful replacement, transfers, and careful new assignments, obtain commitment to these changes. But under present conditions of stability, changes in educational programs and teaching practices must be accompanied by parallel changes in identity and commitment of the present teaching staff. And finally, many schools are faced with the prospect of a relatively young teaching staff likely to grow old together over the next 2 or 3 decades. Age in itself has the potential to provide natural benefits which accrue from experience and maturity. But this potential can be lost, unless marked by a commitment to continuous personal and professional development. The critical nature of staff-development needs in the decades ahead is a convincing argument for every school district to adopt a formatively oriented system of clinical supervision.

SUMMARY

In this introduction current practices relating to teacher evaluation were criticized. It was suggested that teachers and supervisors alike have doubts about the credibility and usefulness of current practices but seem nevertheless to participate in them. Doubtful participation results in the system being characterized by a certain mechanical, artificial, and routine quality, whereby the evaluation process becomes an end in itself. It was further suggested that defects in the system could be attributed to faulty ideology and faulty technology. The ideology of human relations seems to have resulted in a neglect of classroom supervision though present accountability pressures are intent on correcting this neglect. The technology of scientific management has armed the supervisor with an array of teacher-evaluation weapons which may not be as suited to the basically artistic nature of teaching as might be first assumed. More naturalistic practices, better suited to the educational enterprise, will be offered in Chapter 16.

In the interest of focusing attention anew on classroom supervision, a distinction was made between clinical and general supervision. The former refers to face-to-face contact with teachers intended to improve both the quality of instruction and teacher professional growth (Part Three of this book). The latter refers to the organizational and behavioral aspects of supervisory life (Part One) on the one hand, and educational programs administration and supervision (Part Two) on the other. It was claimed that an emphasis on educational programs administration and supervision to the exclusion of more than token clinical supervision, was akin to supervising teachers by remote control.

Formative and summative evaluations were then discussed. Though both emphases are inevitable in any system of supervision and evaluation, it was suggested that the proper and dominant focus of clinical supervision is formative. Formative evaluation is consistent with a growth-oriented approach to classroom supervision, and this approach is in turn consistent with a school district's commitment to professional rather than occupational accountability.

Chapter 15

Supervision as Staff Development

We are in a period of unprecedented interest in staff-development programs for teachers. This interest is fueled by the stark realization that a serious consequence of declining student enrollments and teacher surpluses has been an increase in staff stability. Simply put, when teachers land a decent job, they are likely to stay. Combine this phenomenon with a relatively young teaching force, and many districts are faced with large numbers of teachers who are likely to stay employed in the same school or system for the next 2 or 3 decades. One side of the staff-development coin then is keeping a staff growing in competence and excitement about their work. The other side is a realization that most newly graduated teachers are not fully developed and functional professionals.

Rubin speaks to these issues as follows:

> A teacher prepares to teach by spending four or five years at a training institution. There, in the existing order of things, he or she learns a sampling of all accumulated information, something about the theory of education, and a few prescriptions regarding the art and science of teaching. Even if this preparation were adequate, and it clearly is not, the training can become outdated in a very short time. Indeed, the moment teachers leave the training institution they embark upon a rapid journey to obsolescence. The eye of research may soon detect cracks in the foundation of old theory, lighten what were once dark voids, and illuminate new educational requirements. The social sciences are only now beginning to probe deeply into the dimen-

sions of human interaction. And we have recently come to realize, with incredible lateness, that schools can teach children to be failures as well as successes. Beyond affective considerations, the continuous modernization of substantive knowledge is an accepted fact. It has often been noted, and with good reason, that the teacher who has not studied, say biology, during the last five years no longer knows the subject. The odds are therefore good that such a teacher will fill students with misconceptions. Preservice training alone, then, cannot produce great teaching.[1]

Staff development in education has come of age. Its importance is undisputed. But what is the relationship between staff development and human resources supervision? In the sections which follow, we suggest that the relationship is intimate.

STAFF DEVELOPMENT AND IN-SERVICE EDUCATION

Though in-service education of teachers has a long history, present practices have many shortcomings and have not been met with enthusiasm by teachers.[2] Reasons often given for such reactions are that in-service programs are often too formal and bureaucratic, are viewed as administrative responsibilities and teacher duties, and are too centralized, having a high degree of dysfunctional administrative planning and scheduling.

One effect of formal in-service programs that reflects a high degree of administrative responsibility is that the emphasis shifts from education to program. A successful program becomes one that meets legal requirements and one that is executed smoothly, efficiently, and according to schedule. Further, such programs are often characterized by activities that are selected and developed for uniform dissemination without serious consideration of the purposes of such activities and of the needs of individual teachers. We are not proposing that typical in-service education programs be abandoned, for they have their place, as limited as it may be. We are proposing, however, that they be drastically curtailed, and that they be supplemented by staff-development approaches, programs, and activities.

What is the difference between a staff-development orientation and in-service-education orientation? *Conceptually, staff development is not something the school does to the teacher but something the teacher does for himself or herself.* While staff development is basically growth-oriented, in-service education typically assumes a deficiency in the teacher and presupposes a set of appropriate ideas,

---

[1] Louis J. Rubin, "The Case for Staff Development," in Thomas J. Sergiovanni (ed.), *Professional Supervision for Professional Teachers,* Washington, D.C.: Association for Supervision and Curriculum Development, 1975, p. 34.

[2] Ben Harris and Wailand Bessent, *In-Service Education: A Guide to Better Practice,* Englewood Cliffs, N.J.: Prentice-Hall, 1969, pp. 1–10; Henry J. Hermanowicz, "The Pluralistic World of Beginning Teachers," in *The World of Beginning Teachers,* Washington, D.C.: National Education Association, National Commission on Teacher Education and Professional Standards, 1966, pp. 16–25; Rubin, op. cit., pp. 35–38. This discussion of distinctions in orientation between in-service education and staff development follows that which appears in Thomas J. Sergiovanni and David Elliott, *Educational and Organizational Leadership in Elementary Schools,* Englewood Cliffs, N.J.: Prentice-Hall, 1975, p. 152.

skills, and methods which need developing. By focusing on these ideas, skills, and methods, in-service education works to reduce the teacher's range of alternatives—indeed, to bring about conformity. Staff development does not assume a deficiency in the teacher, but rather assumes a need for people at work to grow and develop on the job. Rather than reduce the range of alternatives, staff development works to increase this range.

Teacher growth is less a function of polishing existing teaching skills or of keeping up with the latest teaching developments and more a function of a teacher's changing as a person—of seeing himself or herself, the school, the curriculum, and students differently. One should not have to make a choice between the two, for both are important. But it is the latter sort of change which is the essence of the staff-development orientation. The former emphasizes keeping teachers up to standard, the latter the continual raising of quality.

The distinctions we make between an in-service education and staff-development orientation is a *conceptual* one designed to help supervisors gauge their own thinking and monitor their own activities with better balance, in the hope that we might be more responsive to teacher needs. *But having made the conceptual distinction, we now combine the two in practice.* The in-service orientation is necessary at times and seems best matched to formal intervention strategies. The staff-development orientation should receive major focus and seems best matched to informal intervention strategies. Though the emphasis of each may differ, both are concerned with remediation and growth.

A DESIGN FOR STAFF DEVELOPMENT

In the section which follows, a design for staff development in education is presented. This design is composed of five critical components. The components are *intents, substance, competency areas, approach,* and *responsibility.* The design requires staff-development planners to be concerned about program intents and substance and, in turn, to match these with appropriate approaches, competency levels, and responsibility designations. Let us consider each of the components separately.

Intents

Staff-development programs and activities are typically designed around such themes as presenting information of one kind or another, helping teachers understand this information, helping teachers apply this understanding in their teaching, and helping teachers to accept, and be committed to, these new approaches. Presenting information is a *knowledge*-level intent. A program, for example, might be designed to introduce a group of science teachers to the concept and nomenclature of inquiry teaching. Promoting understanding is a *comprehension*-level intent. The intent here might be to help teachers to understand how inquiry teaching might affect the way they presently plan and organize instruction. Using inquiry methods effectively in teaching a particular biology unit is an example of an *applications*-level intent. Though each of these levels is necessary, none is sufficient to gain sustained use of inquiry methods by teachers. Teachers may be able to demonstrate such methods on demand but are not likely to use them once out of the spotlight unless they believe in, and are committed to, such methods. Becoming committed to inquiry methods as a useful approach to science teaching is a *value-* and *attitude-integration*-level intent.

Often only knowledge and comprehension levels are legitimately appropriate focuses for staff-development programs. But programs specifically designed to meet intents at these levels are not likely to be sufficient for such higher levels as value and attitude integration. By the same token programs designed for higher-level intents, when only knowledge-level intents are necessary, may well be too elaborate, wasteful, and exhausting for both supervisors and teachers.

Substance

Rubin has identified four critical factors in good teaching, each of which he believes can be improved through appropriate staff-development activities:

> The teacher's sense of purpose
> The teacher's perception of students
> The teacher's knowledge of subject matter
> The teacher's mastery of technique[3]

Sense of purpose and perception of students are akin to a teacher's *educational platform* and as such represent values, beliefs, assumptions, and action theories a teacher holds about the nature of knowledge, how students learn, appropriate relationships between students and teachers, and other factors.[4] One's educational platform becomes the basis for decisions one makes about classroom organization and teaching, and, indeed, once a platform is known, key decisions the teacher will make can be predicted with reliability.

A teacher, for example, who considers his or her purpose to be imparting information is likely to rely heavily on teacher talk and formal classroom arrangements. Likewise, a teacher who perceives youngsters as being basically trustworthy and responsible is likely to share responsibilities for decisions about learning with the class. If a supervisor were interested in reducing teacher talk and/or increasing student responsibility, he or she would have to contend with the critical factor of purpose and perception of teachers. His or her target is the restructuring of educational platforms of teachers.

In describing the importance of knowledge of subject matter, Rubin notes:

> There is a considerable difference between the kind of teaching that goes on when teachers have an intimate acquaintance with the content of the lesson and when the acquaintance is only peripheral. When teachers are genuinely knowledgeable, when they know their subject well enough to discriminate between the seminal ideas and the secondary matter, when they can go beyond what is in the textbook, the quality of the pedagogy becomes extraordinarily impressive. For it is only when a teacher has a consummate grasp of, say, arithmetic, physics, or history that their meaning

---

[3] Rubin, op. cit., p. 44.

[4] The concept of educational platform and how its variants, teacher-espoused platform and teacher platform in use, might be used as part of a clinical supervision strategy are described in the next chapter.

can be turned outward and brought to bear upon the learner's personal experience. Relevancy lies less in the inherent nature of a subject than in its relationship to the child's frame of reference. In the hands of a skilled teacher, poetry can be taught with success and profit to ghetto children.[5]

Though content versus process arguments continue from time to time, both aspects of instruction are necessary for effective teaching. Our observation is that the less a teacher knows about a particular subject the more trivial the teaching and the more defensive the pedagogy. By defensive pedagogy we mean dominance by the teacher and strict adherence to curriculum materials. But one can have a great appreciation for a particular field of study and still not be able to disclose its wonder and excitement effectively. Mastery of technique, classroom organization, and management, and other pedagogical skills make up the fourth critical dimension of effective teaching.

These dimensions are the basis for deciding the substance of staff-development programs. Comprehensive programs are concerned with all four—the teacher's conception of purpose, sensitivity to students, intimacy with subject matter, and basic repertory of teaching techniques.

Competency Areas

What are the major competency areas for which teachers should be accountable? It is reasonable to expect that teachers, as is the case with other professionals, *know how* to do their jobs and to keep up with major developments. The areas of knowledge for professional teaching are suggested above—knowledge about purposes, students, subject matter, and techniques. But knowing and understanding are not enough. Teachers are expected to put their knowledge to work—to demonstrate that they *can do* the job. Demonstrating knowledge, however, is a fairly low-level competency. Most teachers are competent enough and clever enough to come up with the right teaching performance when the supervisor is around. The proof of the pudding is whether they *will do* the job of their own free will and on a sustained basis. Finally, professionals are expected to engage in a lifelong commitment to self-improvement. Self-improvement is the *will-grow* competency area. Self-employed professionals (doctors, accountants, etc.) are forced by competition and by visible product evaluation to give major attention to the will-grow dimension. Teachers, as organizational professionals whose "products" are difficult to measure, have not felt this external pressure for continuing professional growth. Increasingly, however, school districts are making the will-grow dimension a contractual obligation, and indeed teachers who are perfectly satisfactory in the know-how, can-do, and will-do competency areas face sanctions (including dismissal) for less than satisfactory commitment to continuing professional growth.

The relationships between competency areas, intents, and substance are shown in Figure 15-1. Let us begin explaining this figure with the know-how competency area. Knowledge- and comprehension-level intents are associated with this competency area, and the teacher is expected to know and understand

[5] Rubin, op. cit., p. 47.

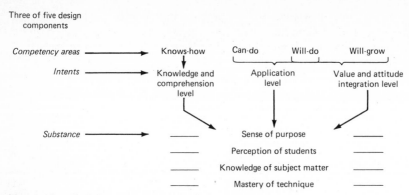

Figure 15-1 Building a design for staff development.

purposes, students, subject matter, and techniques. In the can-do area, teachers apply this knowledge of substance to their classrooms. The will-do area, however, requires not only ability to apply this knowledge but also an identity and commitment to the application. Staff-development programs aimed at the will-do dimension must have value and attitude integration as well as application intents. Will-grow is equally dependent upon value- and attitude-integration intents. It follows, then, that supervisors who are interested in working with teachers in the will-do and will-grow competency areas and who choose programs and strategies suited only to knowledge and comprehension (they invite an expert from the state university to speak to teachers about inquiry teaching) are not likely to be successful.

Approach and Responsibility

We have now discussed three of five design components for staff development: intents, substance, and competency areas. Two more remain: the strategy, or *approach,* to staff development and the locus of major *responsibility.* Approaches can be grouped into three general categories: traditional, informal, and intermediate. Traditional approaches are generally more formal and structured and are designed to meet specific and uniform objectives. Informal approaches, on the other hand, are very low in structure and rely on discovery and exploration techniques. Often objectives are not predetermined but are discovered or assessed after the fact. Intermediate approaches are moderately structured with a predetermined agenda which permits a great deal of flexibility. Let us consider each approach briefly.

Traditional Approaches and Administrative Responsibility Traditional approaches to staff development are well known to supervisors and administrators and need little elaboration. They seem best suited when a staff-development problem can be defined as a deficit in knowledge of some kind. Traditional approaches are typically accompanied by clear objectives and rely on conventional, though well-executed, instruction. Teachers generally assume passive roles and are exposed to logically structured programs or activities. Techniques most often used are lecture, illustrated lecture, demonstration, and observation, often followed by guided discussion activities.

Traditional approaches seem well suited to routine information updating of latest books, techniques, principles, and ideas relating to one's work. It is assumed not that a particular group is considering adopting something new, but that the group is only learning more about it. As intents change from learning to understanding, to applying, to integrating new things into one's repertoire of behavior, approaches will need to change if staff development is to be effective. If one were to generalize about intents of staff-development programs typically found in schools, the widespread use of traditional approaches to the virtual exclusion of other approaches would lead one to conclude that educators have an insatiable appetite for knowledge but are not interested in doing very much with this knowledge.

The locus of responsibility for traditional approaches to staff development is with the administration as it executes its personnel administration functions. In describing such functions Castetter notes that "*development* refers to provisions made by the school system for improving the performance of school personnel from initial employment to retirement. . . . Although it is recognized that personnel can and should improve their effectiveness without formal involvement of the system, attention here will be focused on those activities specifically planned and administered by school officials to facilitate staff development."[6] Though traditional approaches have a place and should remain administrative responsibilities, alone they represent a minimum commitment to staff development.

Informal Approaches and Teacher Responsibility Perhaps the most innovative and provocative approaches to staff development are those which rely on exploration and discovery by teachers. It is assumed that by providing teachers with a rich environment loaded with teaching materials, media, books, and devices, and that with generous encouragement and support from principals and supervisors, teachers will interact with this environment and with each other through exploration and discovery. Exploration and discovery can help many teachers to find themselves, to unleash their creativity, to learn more about their own capabilities as people and teachers, and at the same time to pick up new teaching ideas, activities, and methods.

Thelen notes that in the most useful staff-development programs "one finds intensity of personal involvement, immediate consequences for classroom practice, stimulation and ego support by meaningful associates in the situation and initiating by teacher rather than outsider."[7] Informal approaches seem best able to meet these criteria, and because of their enormous potential, such approaches should play an important role in school district staff-development planning.

Major responsibility for informal approaches rests with teachers. Such efforts can take a variety of forms. Two teachers sharing ideas, a team or family of

[6] William B. Castetter, *The Personnel Function in Educational Administration,* New York: Macmillan, 1971, p. 259.

[7] Herbert Thelen, "A Cultural Approach to In-Service Education," in Louis Rubin (ed.), *Improving In-Service Education,* Boston: Allyn and Bacon, 1971, pp. 72–73.

teachers working and planning together, teacher involvement in an in-building resource center, and participation in district or area teacher centers are examples. Informal staff-development approaches should be encouraged and supported. Indeed, the benefits derived from such approaches are a good reason for supervisors and administrators to advocate patterns of instruction which encourage teachers to plan and work together. Team teaching, schools within the school, and family grouping are examples of arrangements which naturally stimulate informal staff-development activities.

Teacher centers deserve special attention in that they represent fledgling, but promising, attempts to elevate and legitimize the role of teacher in accepting some of the responsibility for staff development. In describing such centers Kathleen Devaney notes:

> There is a notion of *teachers centers* which is essentially an image of a place—small, welcoming, hand-built—where teachers come voluntarily to make things for classrooms, to exchange ideas, and to learn in a format of one-shot or short-series workshops rather than semester-long courses based on lectures and texts. Because this place is non-institutional neutral ground, teachers can let down their hair, drop competitiveness and defensiveness, and thus find starting points for self-improvement and professional growth.[8]

Some centers indeed fit the "non-institutional neutral ground" pattern, but no hard and fast rules regarding location exist. A teacher center can be developed and operated in a surplus classroom or perhaps in an overlooked or poorly used basement location of a particular school. The center could be limited to only teachers of that school or perhaps expanded to serve district or area teachers. The closing of schools in many districts throughout the country lends itself to the establishment of a district or area teacher center in abandoned school buildings. Indeed, some centers are located in storefronts and warehouses. Regardless of scale or location, some common aspects exist, the most notable being that the locus of responsibility for planning and operation is with teachers. Further commonalities are suggested by Devaney:

> The common purpose which stands out as a bond linking widely dissimilar teachers centers is the aim to help teachers enliven, individualize, personalize, enrich, elaborate, reorganize, or re-conceptualize the curriculum within their own classrooms. Study of scores of teachers center program offerings and calendars demonstrates center leaders' belief that help to teachers in the area of curriculum is the most teacher-responsive service they can offer. These centers teach teachers how to use manipulative, real-world, exploratory, frequently individualized curriculum materials and how to gradually reorganize classroom space and time to accommodate greater student activity and interaction. They engage teachers in adapting packaged curriculum materials, making their own materials, or building classroom apparatus, and often they involve teachers in some new study—often math or science—or craft so as

---

[8] Kathleen Devaney, "What's a Teacher Center For?" *Educational Leadership,* vol. 33, no. 6, p. 413, 1976. This issue of *Educational Leadership* was guest-edited by Vincent Rogers, and its theme is teacher centers.

to reacquaint them with the experience of being active, problem-solving learners themselves.[9]

Changes of lasting quality in schools depend heavily on grass-roots processes. Further, it seems clear that teachers look to other teachers as important models for change. In two separate studies with similar themes both Haller and Keenan[10] asked teachers to identify to whom they go for help when they run into curriculum problems and to whom they could go for ideas and insights about teaching and learning. The Canadian and American teachers who responded to these questions were further asked which sources of new ideas were most credible. Choosing from such categories as principal, supervisor, central office staff, professor, research journals, and so on, the overwhelming choice in response to each question was *other teachers*. Teachers go to other teachers for help and for sources of new ideas, and they believe in each other—potent reasons why supervisors need to provide support for informal staff-development approaches.

Intermediate Approaches and Supervisory Responsibility   The cornerstone of a comprehensive staff-development program for any school or district is a *supervisory* system of staff development. Traditional approaches with administrative responsibility and informal approaches with teacher responsibility should be viewed as supplements to this primary thrust.[11]   Informal approaches are low-keyed, classroom-focused, teacher-oriented, and particularistic. Traditional approaches, on the other hand, are high-keyed, more formal, system- or school-oriented, and universal.

A supervisory system of staff development assumes an intermediate position whereby the supervisor enters into a relationship with teachers on an equal footing and assumes an active role along with teachers. The teachers' capacities, needs, and interests are paramount, but sufficient planning and structure is introduced to bridge the gap between these interests and school program and instruction needs.

Intermediate staff-development approaches usually have the following characteristics:

1   The teacher is actively involved in contributing data, information, or feelings, solving a problem, or conducting an analysis.

2   The supervisor shares in the contributing, solving, and conducting activities above as a colleague of the teacher.

3   In colleagueship the supervisor and teachers work together as professional associates bound together by a common purpose. The common purpose is improvement of instruction through the professional development of teacher and

[9] Ibid., p. 414.

[10] Emil J. Haller, *Strategies for Change,* Toronto: Ontario Institute for Studies in Education, Department of Educational Administration, 1968; and Charles Keenan, "Channels for Change: A Survey of Teachers in Chicago Elementary Schools," doctoral dissertation, Urbana: University of Illinois, Department of Educational Administration, 1974.

[11] As education becomes professionally mature, the cornerstone position will likely shift to informal approaches with administrative and supervisory approaches as supplements.

supervisor.[12] Neither the teacher's autonomy as a professional nor the supervisor's responsibilities as a professional are compromised in the process since the relationship is based not on authority but on a commitment to professional improvement.

4 Staff-development activities generally require study of an actual situation or a real problem and use live data, either from self-analysis or from observation of others.

5 Feedback is provided, by the supervisor, by other teachers, or as a result of joint analysis, which permits teachers to compare observations with intents and beliefs, and personal reactions with those of others.

6 The emphasis is on direct improvement of teaching and learning in the classroom.

For the remainder of this chapter and in Chapter 16 the focus will be on this intermediate approach to staff development in which supervisors play such an important part.

CHARACTERISTICS OF EFFECTIVE STAFF-DEVELOPMENT PROGRAMS

By way of summary, excerpts from a study of staff-development programs conducted under the auspices of the Florida State Department of Education are provided. The study suggests a number of clear patterns of effectiveness consistent with the recommendations provided above:

> School-based programs in which *teachers participate as helpers to each other and planners of in-service activities* tend to have greater success . . . than do programs . . . conducted by college or other outside personnel without the assistance of teachers.
>
> In-service education programs that have *differentiated training experiences for different teachers* (that is, "individualized") are more likely to accomplish their objectives than are programs that have common activities for all participants.
>
> In-service education programs that *place the teacher in an active role (constructing and generating materials, ideas, and behavior)* are more likely to accomplish their objectives than are programs that place the teacher in a receptive role. . . .
>
> In-service education programs in which *teachers share and provide mutual assistance* to each other are more likely to accomplish their objectives than are programs in which each teacher does separate work.
>
> Teachers are more likely to benefit from in-service programs in which they can *choose goals and activities for themselves,* as contrasted with programs in which the goals and activities are preplanned. [Italics added][13]

---

[12] Our definition of colleagueship follows Morris Cogan, *Clinical Supervision,* Boston: Houghton Mifflin, 1973, chap. 5. By contrast, the relationship between supervisor and teacher in traditional approaches is more clearly superordinate-subordinate, and in informal approaches the supervisor is more of a helper, facilitator, or passive supporter. In the intermediate approach the supervisor is neither dominating nor passive but is involved, side by side, with the teacher as a colleague.

[13] Roy A. Edelfelt and Margo Johnson, *Rethinking In-Service Education.* Washington, D.C.: National Education Association, 1975, pp. 18–19, as quoted in Devaney, op. cit., p. 416. The original report is Gordon Lawrence, *Patterns of Effective In-Service Education,* Tallahassee, Fla.: State Department of Education, 1974.

Notice the importance given to teacher involvement in planning, differentiated experiences for different teachers, active roles, using ideas, materials and behavior found in the actual teaching situation, teachers working with and helping other teachers, and teacher goals.

MAPPING STAFF-DEVELOPMENT STRATEGIES

We have now discussed the five critical components of staff development. In this section we arrange the components into a conceptual map, or design, to assist in understanding how the various components interact and to help in planning and decision making. This design for staff development is illustrated in Figure 15-2.

Before we begin to discuss this design, refer back to Figure 15-1 and note the relationship between three of the five design components. Here we suggested that staff-development intents at the knowledge and comprehension levels were suited to increasing teachers' knowledge; intents at the applications level, their can-do and to a lesser extent their will-do competence; and intents at the value and integration level, their will-grow competence. The content, substance, or "subject matter" of intents could be concerned with one or a combination of four aspects of effectiveness in teaching: purposes, perceptions of students, knowledge of subject matter, and technique. In Figure 15-2, two additional critical components, approach and responsibility, are included, and all five are illustrated in a fashion to help monitor existing staff-development programs or make decisions about new programs.

Let us consider the box in Figure 15-2 first. Notice that the box consists of four layers, each corresponding to aspects of teacher effectiveness. For illustrative purposes let us refer only to the bottom layer, mastery of technique, and specifically to the technique of inquiry teaching. Staff-development intents are shown across the top of the box and teacher-competency areas across the bottom of the box. If we are interested in only knowing about inquiry teaching, then we are concerned with knowledge-level intents and the know-how competency area. If we are interested in committed adoption and use of inquiry teaching, then we are concerned with value- and attitude-integration intents and will-do–will-grow competency areas.

The programs we develop for the latter intents should be different than those for the former. To the left of the box appear the approach and responsibility components of staff development. Traditional, intermediate, and informal approaches correspond to administrator, supervisor, and teacher responsibilities. The shaded box area directly to the right of each approach-responsibility designation suggests which intents and competency areas are likely to be effectively served by that approach. Traditional approaches seem best suited to knowledge-comprehension intents. Intermediate approaches seem best suited to comprehension, application, and value- and attitude-integration intents. Similarly, informal approaches point toward application intents though these seem most potent for value- and attitude-integration intents.

What approaches to staff development should be used for our inquiry-method example? Who should assume major responsibility for this approach?

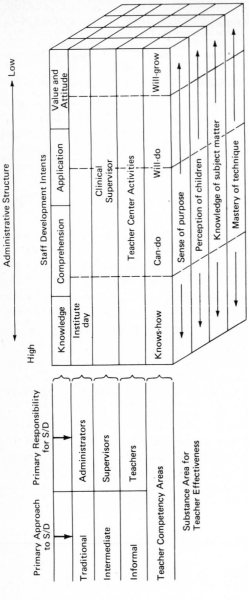

Figure 15-2 Design for staff development.

The answer depends on the kind of purposes or intents sought. If one were interested only in knowledge and comprehension, then an administrator-directed-institute day might be best. Clinical supervision might be a strategy if inquiry teaching were seen as important to the school and the intent were committed implementation of this technique by teachers. Though informal approaches are typically more potent than others, staff-development agendas in this approach belong to teachers, and they may not choose to pursue inquiry teaching. If they did, then the approach might well be the most effective for achieving committed implementation of this technique by teachers. An additional drawback of informal approaches is that they are often not effective at the knowledge level. It seems best therefore to view staff development in a more comprehensive fashion.

SUPERVISION AS STAFF DEVELOPMENT

Supervisors are involved in the more administrative aspects of district and school staff-development programs and are facilitators and supporters of more informal thrusts. However, they assume active roles in, and major responsibility for, intermediate approaches which rely heavily on face-to-face interaction with teachers at work in classrooms. In this effort, they rely heavily on materials and observations generated from the work itself in an attempt to promote professional growth and to directly improve classroom instruction.

As indicated in the introduction to Part Three, traditional involvement of supervisors in the classroom has generally boiled down to summative teacher evaluation characterized by a technology associated with the ideology of scientific management. Reliance on rating scales, "scientific" measurements of one sort or another, and evaluation based on behavioral objectives–oriented evaluation are examples. We suggested further that though administrators and supervisors publicly participate in this system of supervision, privately most have doubts about its effectiveness. The irony in using such methods of supervision and evaluation is that the methods tend not to match the nature of work in education. The heart of the mismatch is using quasi-scientific methods to evaluate activities which are basically artistic.

A number of alternatives, each with a more formative emphasis targeted to professional development and improvement, were suggested in the introduction. It is useful to group these alternatives into generations in an attempt to understand their evolution. First-generation alternatives rely heavily on involving teachers in target setting. Second-generation alternatives are associated with the cycle of clinical supervision popularized by Anderson, Cogan, Goldhammer, and others. Third-generation alternatives are the more naturalistic approaches to supervision. The use of educational connoisseurship based on the analogy of aesthetic criticism, as suggested by Eisner, as well as portfolio development and analysis and the collection of artifacts stand out as examples of more naturalistic approaches. Second- and third-generation alternatives are considered in the next chapter. Here we give brief attention to the use of target setting in supervision.

TARGET SETTING AND EVALUATION

One way in which a target-setting procedure might be arranged is as follows:

Step 1 *Target setting.* Based on last year's observations, conferences, and summary reports, on clinical supervision episodes, and/or on self-evaluation, teachers develop targets or goals they would like to reach in improving their teaching. Targets should be few in number and within reach—rarely exceeding 8 or 10, preferably 3 to 6. Estimated time frames are provided for each target. Targets are then shared with the supervisor.

Step 2 *Target-setting review.* The supervisor reviews each target and estimated time frame and provides the teacher with a written reaction. A copy of both may be forwarded to the principal for his or her review and comments. A conference appointment is made with the teacher.

Step 3 *Target-setting conference.* The teacher and supervisor meet together to discuss targets, time frames, and reactions, and to revise them if appropriate. A written summary of the conference is prepared.

Step 4 *The appraisal process.* This begins at the conclusion of the target-setting conference and continues in accordance with the agreed-upon time frame. The specific nature of the appraisal process depends upon each of the agreed-upon targets and could include formal and informal classroom observation, an analysis of classroom artifacts, videotaping, student evaluation, and/or interaction analysis. The teacher participates in this step by suggesting appraisal methods and by periodically conferring with the supervisor.

Step 5A *Summary appraisal.* The supervisor prepares a summary appraisal commenting on each of the targets and confers with the teacher.

Step 5B *Summary of appraisal procedures.* In addition to the summary appraisal the supervisor prepares a summary of appraisal procedures which details dates and frequency of contacts with the teacher, a general review of targets and progress noted, a summary of help given to the teacher, an indication of the comprehensiveness of the appraisal, and recommendations. This statement is also discussed in conference with the teacher, step 5A.[14]

The setting of targets, or supervision by objectives as some call it, is becoming a popular alternative to evaluation strategies which rely heavily on checklist rating scales in many schools. Target setting should not be confused with using student-oriented behavior objectives and evaluating teachers on the amount of pupil gain demonstrated for each objective. Widespread as this particular practice may be, it is regarded with suspicion by leading evaluation experts and is totally unacceptable as a primary or exclusive evaluation strategy.

Some school districts link the entire teacher-evaluation system to the target-setting strategy and others see target setting as a critically important component of a more comprehensive evaluation strategy. Either alone or in combination with other approaches, target setting can be a powerful means for linking teacher evaluation and supervision to continuous staff development.

---

[14] This section on target setting follows Thomas J. Sergiovanni, *Handbook for Effective Department Leadership Concepts and Practices in Today's Secondary Schools,* Boston: Allyn and Bacon, 1977, pp. 394–396.

Target setting is subject to abuses and has shortcomings which, if ignored, can seriously undermine the development of an effective evaluation strategy. The most serious problems arise from supervisors' rigid adherence to prespecified targets and autocratic imposition of targets on teachers. Rigidly applying the system unduly focuses the evaluation and blinds individuals to many important events and activities not originally anticipated or stated. Teachers may focus all their concerns and energy on the targets at issue and neglect other areas not targeted at the time. Target setting is meant to help and facilitate, but rigid application can actually hinder teacher growth.

Target setting should not be seen as a system of management control (although for weak teachers who show little or no capability for self-improvement, it might legitimately be used as a management system of close supervision) but as a cooperative system of self-improvement. Supervisors and teachers together should discuss events and participate in the development of targets, with the teacher assuming the primary role and the supervisor an influential but supporting role.

SUMMARY

This chapter was concerned with the supervisor's role in staff development. It was noted that current declines in student enrollments and shortages in teaching jobs have combined to increase the stability of teaching staffs. A relatively young and stable teacher force is requiring policy makers to focus anew on the necessity for staff-development programs in education.

Though no operational distinction was intended, a conceptual distinction was made between an in-service education orientation and a staff-development orientation. The former tends to focus on deficiencies in teachers and on bringing them up to standard. The latter tends to focus on professional growth and on raising the quality of performance.

A design for staff development consisting of five critical components was presented. The components were intents, substance, competency areas, approach, and responsibility. The relationships and interdependencies between and among intents were discussed. With respect to approach and responsibility three approaches to staff development with corresponding responsibility designations were described. Traditional approaches were seen as administrative responsibilities, intermediate approaches as supervisory responsibilities, and informal approaches as teacher responsibilities. Corresponding staff-development-program examples might be institute days, engaging teachers in clinical supervision, and developing a teacher center.

The chapter concluded with a discussion of more formative alternatives to traditional teacher evaluation which could be considered as intermediate staff-development approaches. Target setting was cited as a first-generation alternative, strategies associated with the cycle of clinical supervision as second-generation alternatives, and naturalistic approaches such as connoisseurship and criticism, and portfolio development, as third-generation alternatives. Target setting was then briefly discussed. Second- and third-generation alternatives will be discussed in Chapter 16.

STUDY GUIDE

Recall the concepts and meanings associated with each of the following phrases and terms included in this chapter. Can you discuss each of them with a colleague and apply them to the supervisory context of your school? If you cannot, review them in the text and record the page number for future reference.

1 Administrative approaches to staff development _____
2 Colleagueship _____
3 Competency areas _____
4 Critical factors in teaching _____
5 Design for staff development _____
6 First-generation alternatives _____
7 Ideology of scientific management _____
8 In-service-education orientation _____
9 Intermediate approaches to staff development _____
10 Second-generation alternatives _____
11 Staff-development orientation _____
12 Staff stability _____
13 Target setting _____
14 Teacher center _____
15 Third-generation alternatives _____
16 Value and attitude integration _____

EXERCISES

1 Though the distinction between staff-development and in-service organization is conceptual and not operational, try to classify activities and programs in your school into each of the two categories.
2 Develop a 10-item attitude questionnaire assessing teacher feelings about staff development in your school. Use the questionnaire to collect teacher impressions and views and to prepare a "state of the art" report on staff development in your school.
3 Prepare a short talk (10 minutes) to be given before a citizens' advisory committee or school board entitled "Staff Development: Important in the Seventies—Critical in the Eighties."
4 Using the design summarized in Table 15-2, select another topic for staff development, perhaps one from a teacher-effectiveness area other than mastery of technique. Work this new topic through the design, reaching staff-development decisions about approach—responsibility, types of intents, and competency areas.

Chapter 16

Clinical Supervision and Teacher Evaluation

In the introduction to Part Three a distinction was made between general supervision and clinical supervision. General supervision referred to the attention and concern supervisory leaders give to organizational factors such as healthy climate and supportive relationships, on the one hand, and the broad educational leadership and statesmanship responsibilities of supervision, on the other. Clinical supervision, by contrast, refers to face-to-face encounters with teachers about teaching, usually in classrooms, with the double-barreled intent of professional development and improvement of instruction. By this definition, the intermediate approaches to staff development discussed in Chapter 15 are integral parts of clinical supervision. In this chapter we refer more directly to clinical supervision and teacher evaluation, describing and advocating approaches more consistent with the aspirations of the introduction to Part Three.[1] This chapter complements the discussion of student and program evaluation which appears in Chapter 14.

[1] This chapter is based on, and follows closely, chap. 11, "Supervision and Evaluation of Teachers," in T. J. Sergiovanni, *Handbook for Effective Department Leadership: Concepts and Practices in Today's Secondary Schools,* Boston: Allyn and Bacon, 1977, pp. 372–387; "Reforming Teacher Evaluation: Naturalistic Alternatives," *Educational Leadership,* vol. 34, no. 8, pp. 602–617, 1977; and "Toward a Theory of Clinical Supervision," *Journal of Research and Development in Education,* vol. 9, no. 2, pp. 20–29, 1976.

PUBLIC AND PRIVATE VIEWS OF TEACHER EVALUATION

Assume that you are at a workshop for supervisors and others with responsibility for teacher evaluation. The workshop leader asks you to write three statements, each of which expresses a personal feeling or belief you have about teacher evaluation. First write a *public* statement which you would be willing to share with teachers, board members, and parents; next a *confidential* statement which you would be willing to share only with trusted colleagues; and finally a *private* statement which you would not readily share with others. Chances are that doubt in the credibility of present practices characterizes your confidential and/or private statements. If this is the case, you join many others with responsibility for teacher evaluation who share your doubts. Indeed these thoughts become major supervisory problems when one realizes that the same teacher-evaluation practices which raise doubts of credibility are today being implemented with more intensity and on a wider scale than ever before. Let us assume for a moment that our hypothesis that by and large supervisors and others responsible for teacher evaluation privately view the procedures as lacking in credibility is correct. What are the likely effects of participating in a system characterized by such doubts? We have noticed that the system takes on a certain artificial or mechanical quality, a routine function, which becomes an end in itself.

PREVAILING AND ALTERNATIVE ASSUMPTIONS

This section reviews some of the assumptions basic to present teacher-evaluation practices and contrasts these with alternative assumptions and practices which we believe hold promise for increasing meaning in the process of teacher evaluation and which seem more naturally compatible with the work of educational enterprises. This section should be read in conjunction with comments on present practices contained in the introduction to Part Three.

At present the dominant view of teacher evaluation is characterized by a commitment to technical-rational values. These values are expressed in the form of predetermination and the scientific method. Predetermination is evidenced, for example, by establishing, before a teaching episode, outputs such as specific objectives and competency levels to be exhibited and by otherwise specifying the rules of the game, or the blueprint for evaluation, before the evaluation takes place.

The scientific method is evidenced, for example, by an emphasis on empirical design characteristics in the evaluation process and on a primary concern for precision in measurement. Rating scales are often emphasized as means to measure predetermined competencies displayed by teachers, and effectiveness in teaching is often defined as accomplishing predetermined intents, sticking to predetermined rules, or displaying predetermined behavior.

In recent years a number of prominent program-evaluation experts have developed and begun to test alternatives to this technical-rational approach which rely far less on the scientific method and far more on the intuitions, aspirations, and capabilities of those involved at both ends of the evaluation.[2] Theirs is a more naturalistic approach which sees value in discovering as opposed to determining and in describing as opposed to measuring. Though the primary focus of this pioneering work is on program evaluation, its underlying assumption, characteristics, and design features apply to teacher evaluation as well.[3]

In Table 16-1 key assumptions and practices associated with technical-rational approaches to teacher evaluation are contrasted with those associated with more naturalistic approaches.

[2] See, for example, Robert E. Stake, *Program Evaluation, Particularly Responsive Evaluation,* paper no. 5 in Occasional Paper Series, Kalamazoo: Western Michigan University, Evaluation Center, November 1975; Robert E. Stake (ed.), *Evaluating the Arts in Education: A Responsive Approach,* Columbus, Ohio: Merrill, 1975; Elliot W. Eisner, "Emerging Models for Educational Evaluation," *School Review,* 80, no. 4, 1972; Decker Walker, "A Naturalistic Model for Curriculum Development," *School Review,* vol. 80, no. 1, 1971; Michael Scriven, "Goal-free Evaluation," in Ernest House (ed.), *School Evaluation: The Politics and Process,* Berkeley, Calif.: McCutchan, 1973; George Willis, "Curriculum Criticism and Literary Criticism," *Journal of Curriculum Studies,* vol. 7, no. 1, 1975; and John S. Mann, "Curriculum Criticism," *Teachers College Record,* vol. 71, no. 1, 1969.

[3] See, for example, Elliot Eisner, "The Perceptive Eye: Toward the Reformation of Educational Evaluation," Washington, D.C.: AREA, Division B, Curriculum and Objectives, 1975, invited address; Morris Cogan, *Clinical Supervision,* Boston: Houghton Mifflin, 1973; James Raths, "Teaching without Specific Objectives," *Educational Leadership,* vol. 18, no. 7, 1971; and Sergiovanni, "Toward a Theory of Clinical Supervision," op. cit.

Table 16-1

Technical-rational assumptions and practices	Naturalistic assumptions and practices
1. Evaluation is viewed as a process designed to determine the worth of something—a teacher, teaching episode, or performance.	1. Evaluation is valuing something. Before one can begin to value something fully, one needs to understand it. Therefore, evaluation is seeking to understand something. What is going on in this classroom and why? What does it mean?
2. The emphasis is on observing words and behavior and not on intuition and understanding. Indeed, intuition is something to be controlled because of its impressionistic rather than scientific nature, and understanding is a luxury which may distract the evaluation process from its true course.	2. Words and behavior are viewed only as proxies for understandings and meanings, and therefore much is missed by focusing only on the proxies. The evaluation is designed to inform the supervisor's intuition, not to replace it.
3. Evaluators follow a blueprint and evaluate the teacher according to the specifications called for in the blueprint.	3. Evaluators develop a representation of events which have taken place—a portrait of the teaching episode. Thus "specifications" not previously determined are included in the evaluation.
4. The blueprint designed for the evaluation specifies what is of value and defines meanings and understandings. This is an exclusive process.	4. The portrait characteristics of the evaluation assume that multiple and sometimes contradictory understanding and meanings exist. The evaluator's job is

to identify and describe them. Portraits of teaching episodes often reveal a hidden curriculum more potent than that intended and unanticipated consequences which may have more value than those intended by the teacher or specified in the lesson plan. This is an inclusive process.

5. What is important to the evaluation are the stated intents of the teacher and the predetermined objectives held for students.

5. What is important to the evaluation are the implicit assumptions and guiding platform statements which teachers bring to the class, the manner in which these assumptions and platform statements are articulated into classroom activities and practices, and the implications and effects of these activities and practices.

6. Evaluators are primarily concerned with their methodology. They ask, "How can I be sure that I can describe and measure, without error, the extent to which predetermined objectives are being met by the teacher and whether this teacher exhibits predetermined competency levels in teaching?"

6. Evaluators are primarily concerned with discovering, describing, and measuring important things which occur. They are willing to choose methods suited to important things even though these things may be weak or considered by others (particularly technical-rational evaluators) as subjective or impressionistic.

7. Evaluators rely heavily on rating scales and other teacher-evaluation instruments. These help them to be objective, to treat all teachers the same, and to ensure that the focus of the evaluation is on important events.

7. Evaluators believe that rating scales and other teacher-evaluation instruments often prevent them from fully understanding classroom events and prevent them and the teacher from becoming personally involved in the evaluation process. They prefer to use data from the situation at hand to help define the parameters of the evaluation and to help understand crucial evaluation issues. They prefer to use videotape, teacher and student interviews, artifact collections, and evaluation portfolios, and they consider these better methods of representation than instruments and rating scales.

8. Evaluators are primarily concerned with estimating the worth of a particular teaching performance and, by inference, the worth of the teacher. The teacher assumes a subordinate role in the process. The evaluators are the experts. Evaluation is something done to teachers by evaluators.

8. Evaluators are primarily interested in increasing understanding, in stimulating thought, and in extending the experience of the teacher being evaluated. The teachers assume a key role in the process. Evaluators and teachers share the expert role, and evaluation is something done together.

Source: Thomas J. Sergiovanni, "Reforming Teacher Evaluation: Naturalistic Alternatives," *Educational Leadership*, vol. 34, no. 8, 1977.

Why is it important to describe prevailing assumptions behind teacher-evaluation practices? Technologies are associated with ideologies, and the language and values of science (objectivity, rationality, reliability, and precision) have been found to be irresistible to educators. Present classroom observation and evaluation technology is shrouded with a sense of scientism often not even found in the more legitimate sciences. The irony in this is that most educators believe that teaching is far more of an artistic enterprise than a scientific one. That being the case, it may be that we have adopted a technology of teacher evaluation ill-suited to the nature of the educational enterprise.

In the sections which follow, several strategies for teacher evaluation more characteristic of naturalistic assumptions and more consistent with the artistic nature of the educational enterprise are described. Well-known traditional methods have a place in teacher evaluation, but they should play a minor role as compared with the alternatives we propose.

CLINICAL SUPERVISION

Earlier we referred to clinical supervision, which emphasizes working with teachers about teaching in classrooms, as an activity distinct from general supervision. There is, however, a special meaning associated with the phrase which refers to a cycle, or pattern, of supervision as pioneered by Anderson, Cogan, Goldhammer, and others and is perhaps best known through Cogan's book entitled *Clinical Supervision.*[4]

Born in the real world of professional practice this technique evolved from a series of problems faced by supervisors as they worked with teachers and would-be teachers. As problems were faced, a set of practices emerged, at first sporadically, then incrementally, and finally becoming a systematic form now known as the cycle of clinical supervision. The essential ingredients of clinical supervision, as articulated by Cogan, include the establishment of a healthy general supervisory climate, a special supervisory mutual support system called "colleagueship," and a cycle of supervision comprising conferences, observation of teachers at work, and pattern analysis.[5]

Clinical supervision is based on a number of assumptions different from those of traditional rating and evaluating and prescribes a pattern of action which departs substantially from present practice. In clinical supervision it is assumed, for example, that the school curriculum is, in reality, what teachers do day-by-day, that changes in curriculum and in teaching formats require changes in how teachers behave in classrooms, that supervisors are not teachers of teachers, that supervision is a process for which both supervisors and teachers are responsible, that the focus of supervision is on teacher strengths, that given the

---

[4] Clinical Supervision evolved from a series of techniques developed as a result of the pioneering work of Robert Anderson, Morris Cogan, and Robert Goldhammer in the Harvard MAT program of the late fifties and early sixties. Originally conceived as a component of preservice teacher education the technique has since been developed for in-service use. Morris Cogan, *Clinical Supervision,* New York: Houghton Mifflin, 1973.

[5] Our discussion of clinical supervision as originally articulated by Cogan and adapted by us follows closely Sergiovanni, "Toward a Theory of Clinical Supervision," op. cit., and "Supervision and Evaluation of Teachers," op. cit.

right conditions teachers are willing and able to improve, that teachers have large reservoirs of talent, often unused, and that teachers derive satisfaction from challenging work. These assumptions are consistent with those associated with McGregor's Theory Y as discussed in Chapter 5.

Following these assumptions clinical supervision is an in-class support system designed to deliver assistance directly to the teacher. In practice, clinical supervision requires a more intense relationship between supervisor and teacher than that found in traditional evaluation, first in the establishment of colleagueship and then in the articulation of colleagueship through the cycle of supervision. The heart of clinical supervision is an intense, continuous, mature relationship between supervisor and teacher with the intent being the improvement of professional practice.

THE CYCLE OF CLINICAL SUPERVISION

One cannot provide in a few pages all the techniques and know-how associated with clinical supervision. Competency will come with practice as supervisors team together in learning the skills of clinical supervision. The intent here is to describe the cycle of supervision, to provide some basic principles and concepts underlying clinical supervisory practice, and to suggest some techniques and tools which supervisors might find useful as they begin to develop competencies as clinical supervisors.

Cogan identifies eight phases to the cycle of supervision.[6]

1 *Phase 1 requires establishing the teacher-supervisor relationship.* This first phase is of particular importance, for upon its success rests the whole concept of clinical supervision. Teachers are suspicious of evaluation in general, and the intense sort of supervision prescribed by Cogan can be even more alarming. Further, the success of clinical supervision requires that teachers share with supervisors responsibility for all steps and activities. The supervisor has two tasks in Phase 1: building a relationship based on mutual trust and support, and inducting the teacher into the role of co-supervisor. Cogan believes that both tasks should be well advanced before the supervisor enters the teacher's classroom to observe teaching. Phase 1 establishes the colleagueship relationships deemed critically important by Cogan. This relationship is in a large part the focus of Part One.

2 *Phase 2 requires intensive planning of lessons and units with the teacher.* In Phase 2 teacher and supervisor plan, together, a lesson, a series of lessons, or a unit. Planning includes estimates of objectives or outcomes, subject matter concepts, teaching strategies, materials to be used, learning contexts, anticipated problems, and provisions for feedback and evaluation.

3 *Phase 3 requires planning of the classroom observation strategy by teacher and supervisor.* Together teacher and supervisor plan and discuss the kind and amount of information to be gathered during the observation period and the methods to be used to gather this information.

4 *Phase 4 requires the supervisor to observe in-class instruction.* Cogan em-

---

[6] Cogan, op. cit.

phasizes that only after careful establishment of the supervisory relationship and the subsequent planning of both the lesson or unit and the observation strategy does the observation take place.

5 *Phase 5 requires careful analysis of the teaching-learning process.* As co-supervisors, teachers and supervisors analyze the events of the class. They may work separately at first or together from the beginning. Outcomes of the analysis are identification of patterns of teacher behavior which exist over time and critical incidents which occurred which seemed to affect classroom activity, and extensive descriptions of teacher behavior and evidence of that behavior. It is believed that teachers have established persistent patterns of teaching which are evidenced and can be identified as a pattern after several carefully documented observations and analysis.

6 *Phase 6 requires planning the conference strategy.* Supervisors prepare for the conference by setting tentative objectives and planning tentative processes, but in a manner which does not program, too much, the course of the conference. They plan also the physical setting and arrange for materials, tapes, or other aids. Preferably, the conference should be unhurried and on school time. Cogan notes that it may well be necessary to arrange for coverage of a teacher's classroom responsibilities from time to time.

7 *Phase 7 is the conference.* The conference is an opportunity and setting for teacher and supervisor to exchange information about what was intended in a given lesson or unit and what actually happened. The success of the conference depends upon the extent to which the process of clinical supervision is viewed as formative, focused evaluation intended to understand and improve professional practice.

8 *Phase 8 requires the resumption of planning.* A common outcome of the first seven phases of clinical supervision is agreement on the kinds of changes sought in the teacher's classroom behavior. As this agreement materializes, the eighth phase begins. Teacher and supervisor begin planning the next lesson or unit, and new targets, approaches, and techniques to be attempted.

As one reviews the cycle of clinical supervision, it appears as though it describes that which many supervisors have been doing all along. But a quick review of the assumptions basic to clinical supervision, particularly the concept of co-supervisor, suggests that the resemblance may be superficial. The supervisor works at two levels with teachers during the cycle: helping them to understand and improve their professional practice and helping them to learn more about the skills of classroom analysis needed in supervision. Further, while traditional classroom observation tends to be sporadic and requires little time investment, clinical supervision asks that supervisors give 2 to 3 hours a week to each teacher. Supervisors can better manage their time by involving only part of the faculty at a time—perhaps one-third for 3 months in rotation. As teachers themselves become competent in clinical supervision and assume increased responsibility for all phases, they will need supervisors less.

TOWARD A THEORY OF CLINICAL SUPERVISION

It is not necessary, in our view, for supervisors to follow a specific or single set of procedures or phrases in implementing clinical supervision. Indeed, specific steps and procedures will depend upon the nature of classroom activity, the strengths of the teacher involved, and the inclinations of the supervisors. Underlying clinical supervision, however, are some basic ideas and concepts from which supervisors may develop suitable practices for their own unique situations.

Herbert Simon differentiates between natural and artificial sciences. "A natural science is a body of knowledge about some class of things—objects or phenomena—in the world: about the characteristics and properties that they have; about how they behave and interact with each other.[7] The artificial sciences, on the other hand, are created by human conventions.

In Simon's words, "The thesis is that certain phenomena are 'artificial' in a very special sense: They are as they are only because of a system's being molded, by goals or purposes, to the environment in which it lives." The study of human inventions such as formal organizations, the suburban family, and the professions (medicine, business, law, and education, for example) is the study of human creations rather than of natural phenomena. The design of these human inventions is artificial in the sense that they depend upon the goals which people seek and on their view of reality rather than on natural phenomena or natural laws.

On a smaller scale, the classroom can be seen as an artificial setting whose form and function are determined largely by the stated and implied assumptions, beliefs, and intents of individual teachers and by their attempts to adjust the classroom to their perception of a larger environment. This larger environment, equally artificial, is composed of the expectations and other conventions found in the school as an organization, in parents, in other professionals, and in the community and the society at large. Further, all the other people involved in the life of that classroom live in behavioral worlds of their own, artificial in the sense that it is influenced by their goals, needs, perceptions, and aspirations, and by their relationships with others.

We view clinical supervision as planned intervention in this world of the artificial. Its objective is to bring about changes in classroom operation and teacher behavior. The behavioral world of individual teachers is, in turn, shaped and influenced by their stated and implied assumptions, beliefs, and goals, and therefore successful changes in the former require changes in the latter.

This world of the artificial is further complicated by the incompleteness of knowledge which one has about oneself and the world in which one lives. "In actuality, the human being never has more than a fragmentary knowledge of the conditions surrounding his actions, nor more than a slight insight into the regularities and laws that would permit him to induce future consequences from a knowledge of present circumstances."[8] Clinical supervision therefore is not only concerned with teacher behavior and the antecedents of this behavior but with the incompleteness with which most of us view our assumptions, beliefs, objectives, and behavior.[9]

---

[7] Herbert A. Simon, *The Sciences of the Artificial,* Cambridge: M.I.T., 1969, p. 1.

[8] Herbert A. Simon, *Administrative Behavior: A Study of Decision-making Processes in Administrative Organizations,* 2d ed., New York: Free Press, 1957, p. 81.

[9] This section follows Sergiovanni, "Toward a Theory of Clinical Supervision," op. cit.

EDUCATIONAL PLATFORM

It is tempting to view the classroom enterprise as a rational set of activities, each generated in pursuit of clearly stated and understood objectives. Indeed, one is often led to believe that classroom activity is a logical process of determining objectives, stating them in acceptable form, developing learning experiences, and evaluating the outcomes of these experiences in relation to the predetermined objectives. This view assumes that the teaching arena is objective, and that teachers come to this arena with a clean slate, free of biases, willing and able to make rational choices.

In reality, however, most supervisors know that teaching is not nearly as antiseptic an enterprise as one might think. Indeed, teachers, supervisors, and others bring to the classroom a variety of agendas, some public, many hidden, and probably most unknown, each of which has a telling effect on educational decision making. The agendas which one brings to teaching tend to fall into three major categories: what one believes is possible, what one believes is true, and what one believes is desirable. Together the three are the essential ingredients of one's *educational platform*.[10] A platform implies something that supports one's actions and by which one justifies or validates one's own actions. An approximate analogy would be that of a political platform. This platform states the basic values, critical policy statements, and key positions of an individual or group. Once known, the political platform can be used to predict responses that a politician or political party is likely to make to questions on various campaign issues. The concept of educational platform, particularly as it affects curriculum and educational program matters, is discussed at length in Chapter 11. Here our attention is on platform as it relates to clinical supervision.

Assumptions, Theories, and Beliefs

The components of one's educational platform are the assumptions, theories, and beliefs one holds for key aspects of effective teaching, such as the purpose of schooling, perceptions of students, what knowledge is of most worth, and the value of certain teaching techniques and pedagogical principles. For purposes of illustration, let us consider each component below, recognizing that operationally they are inseparable.

Assumptions which teachers hold help answer the question "What is possible?" Assumptions are composed of our beliefs, the concepts we take for granted, and the ideas we accept without question about schools, classrooms, students, teaching, learning, and knowledge. Assumptions help the teacher to define what classrooms are actually like and what is possible to accomplish within them. Assumptions are important to the decisions that teachers make, because they set the boundaries for what information will or will not be considered and for other possibilities and actions at the onset of instruction.

Theories we hold help answer the question "What is true?" Theories are beliefs about relationships between and among assumptions we consider to be

---

[10] Decker Walker, "A Naturalistic Model for Curriculum Development," *The School Review,* vol. 80, no. 1, pp. 51–65, 1971.

true. Theories form the basis for developing instructional strategies and patterns of classroom organization.

Beliefs about what is desirable in classrooms are derived from assumptions and theories which one holds regarding knowledge, learning, classrooms, and students. What is desirable is expressed in the form of intents, aims, objectives, or purposes.

Consider, for example, a teacher whose educational platform includes the assumptions that "little or no knowledge exists which is essential for everyone to learn" and that "youngsters can be trusted to make important decisions." The two assumptions might well lead to the theory that "students who are allowed to influence classroom decisions will make wise choices and will become more committed learners." That being the case, a corresponding aim for that teacher might be "to involve students in shared decision making," or perhaps "to have students interact with subject matter in a manner which emphasizes its concepts and structure rather than just its information."

Contrast this with a teacher whose educational platform includes the assumption that "the only justifiable evidence of good teaching is student acquisition of subject matter as specified by the teacher" and the assumption that "motivation of students should reflect the realities of the world outside the school, where good behavior and performance are publicly rewarded and poor behavior and performance are publicly punished." The two assumptions might well lead to the theory that "students need to be motivated, on the one hand, and disciplined, on the other, by any means necessary to get the behavior and performance which leads to acquiring the most subject matter in the least amount of time." In this case a corresponding aim might be "to provide visible rewards and privileges to students who behave and perform to the teacher's expectations and visible punishment to those who do not."

Educational platforms are powerful determinants of the nature and quality of life in classrooms. For example, imagine the fate of students in the classrooms of people who consider themselves teachers of French or biology and not of students as compared with teachers who view instruction in a more holistic and integrated way. With the same example, consider the fate of the supervisor who wants the first sort of teacher to be more sensitive to individual differences of students and to emphasize more the joy of learning French or biology as well as mastery of subject matter, but does not take into account the educational platform of such teachers. Unless the supervisor is a master at behavior modification and the teachers witless enough to respond passively to stimuli from the supervisor, change in teaching behavior will require some altering of those persons' educational platforms.

Known and Unknown Platform Dimensions

In the world of the classroom the components of educational platforms are generally not well known. That is, teachers tend to be unaware of their assumptions, theories, or objectives. Sometimes they adopt components of a platform that seem right, that have the ring of fashionable rhetoric, or that coincide with the expectation of important others, such as teachers whom they admire, or of groups with which they wish to affiliate. Though teachers may overtly adopt aspects of educational platforms in this manner, covertly, or unknowingly, they are often likely to hang onto contradictory assumptions, beliefs, and theories. Publicly they may say (or espouse) one thing and assume that their classroom behavior is governed by this statement, but privately, or even unknowingly, they may believe something else which actually governs their classroom behavior. Indeed, teachers are not aware that often their classroom decisions and behavior contradict their espoused platform.

THEORIES GOVERNING TEACHER BEHAVIOR

It has been suggested that the classroom is an artificial setting where form and function are influenced largely by the stated and implied assumptions, theories, and aims of individual teachers. Together these beliefs form an educational platform which supports teachers' actions and by which they justify or validate their actions. As also has been suggested, many aspects of a teacher's platform are unknown or perhaps known but covert. When covert dimensions differ from espoused, the former are likely to constitute the *operational* platform for a given individual.

The clinical supervisor needs to be concerned with two theories which the teacher brings to the classroom—an *espoused theory* and a *theory in use*. As Argyris and Schön suggest:

> When someone is asked how he would behave under certain circumstances, the answer he usually gives is his espoused theory of action for that situation. This is the theory of action to which he gives allegiance, and which, upon request, he communicates to others. However, the theory that actually governs his action is his theory in use. This theory may or may not be compatible with his espoused theory; furthermore, the individual may or may not be aware of the incompatibility of the two theories.[11]

When one's espoused theory matches one's theory in use, they are considered congruent. Congruence exists, for example, for the teacher who espouses that self-image development in youngsters is desirable in its own right and is related to student achievement and whose teaching behavior and artifacts of that behavior confirm this espoused theory. Lack of congruence between a person's espoused theory and theory in use, *when known*, proposes a dilemma to that individual. A second teacher, for example, shares the same espoused theory regarding self-concept, but his pattern of questioning, his use of negative feedback, his marking on the bell curve, and his insistence on standard requirements may reveal a theory in use incongruent with his espoused theory. The social studies teacher who believes in and teaches a course in American democracy in a totalitarian manner represents another example of incongruency between espoused theory and theory in use.

[11] Chris Argyris and David A. Schön, *Theory in Practice: Increasing Professional Effectiveness,* San Francisco: Jossey-Bass, 1974, p. 7.

THE JOHARI WINDOW

A useful way of understanding how known and unknown platform dimensions of teachers fit into clinical supervision is by examining the *Johari Window* as it relates to espoused theories and theories in use.[12] This relationship is illustrated in Figure 16-1.

The Johari Window in this case depicts the relationship between two parties, teacher and clinical supervisor. The relationship revolves around aspects of the teacher's educational platform known to self and others, known to self but not others, not known to self but known to others, and not known to self or others. Four cells are depicted in the Johari Window, each representing a different combination of what the teacher knows or does not know about his or her teaching as contrasted with what the supervisor knows and does not know about that teacher's teaching.

In the first cell, *the public or open self,* the teacher's knowledge of his or her teaching behavior and other aspects of his or her professional practices corresponds with the supervisor's knowledge. This is the area in which communication occurs most effectively and in which the need for the teacher to be defensive, to assume threat, is minimal. The clinical supervisor works to broaden, or enlarge, this cell with the teacher.

In the second cell, *the hidden or secret self,* the teacher knows about aspects of his or her teaching behavior and professional practice that the supervisor does not know. Often the teacher conceals these aspects from the supervisor for fear

---

[12] Joseph Luft, *Of Human Interaction,* New York: National Press Books, 1969. The Johari Window was developed by Joseph Luft and Harry Ingham and gets its name from the first names of its authors.

	What the supervisor knows about the teacher	What the supervisor does not know about the teacher
What the teacher knows about himself	Public or open self 1	Hidden or secret self 2
What the teacher does not know about himself	Blind self 3	Undiscovered or subconscious self 4

Figure 16-1 Johari Window and educational platform. *(From Thomas J. Sergiovanni, Handbook for Department Leadership Concepts and Practices in Today's Secondary Schools, Boston: Allyn and Bacon, 1977.)*

that the supervisor might use this knowledge to punish, hurt, or exploit the teacher. The second cell suggests how important a supervisory climate characterized by trust and credibility is to the success of clinical supervision. In clinical supervision the teacher is encouraged to reduce the size of this cell.

In the third cell, *the blind self,* the supervisor knows about aspects of the teacher's behavior and professional practice of which the teacher is unaware. This cell, though large initially, is reduced considerably as clinical supervision for a given teacher develops and matures. This is the cell most often neglected by traditional teacher-evaluation methods.

In the fourth cell, *the undiscovered self,* aspects of teacher behavior and professional practice not known to either teacher or supervisor are hidden.

HELPING TEACHERS CHANGE

Creating a condition for change greatly facilitates the change itself. If, for example, individual teachers are unaware of inconsistencies between their espoused theories and their theories in use, they are not likely to search for alternatives to their present teaching patterns. One way in which search behavior can be evoked in a teacher is by surfacing dilemmas. Dilemmas surface as a result of teachers learning that their theories in use are not consistent with their espoused theory.

Dilemmas promote an unsettled feeling in a person. Their espoused educational platforms mean a great deal to people, and what they stand for and believe in is linked to their concept of self and sense of well-being. Dilemmas born of inconsistencies between these images and the actual behavior of individuals are upsetting and need to be resolved. Indeed they are likely to lead to a search for changes either in one's espoused theory or in one's theory in use.[13]

Readiness for change is a critical point in the process of clinical supervision. It is at this point that an appropriate support system needs to be provided. Part of this support system will be psychological and will be geared toward accepting and encouraging the teacher. But part must also be technical and will be geared toward making available teaching and professional practice alternatives to the teacher.

Argyris and Schön point out that congruence is not a virtue in itself. Indeed a "bad" espoused theory matched to a theory in use may be far less desirable, from the supervisor's point of view, than a "good" espoused theory insufficiently matched.[14]

SOME EVIDENCE

To this point in our discussion of developing a theory of clinical supervision we have hypothesized that:

[13] Leon Festinger, *Theory of Cognitive Dissonance,* Evanston, Ill.: Row, Peterson, 1975; and Milton Rokeach, "A Theory of Organizational Change within Value-Attitude Systems," *Journal of Social Sciences,* vol. 24, no. 21, 1968.
[14] Argyris and Schön, op. cit.

A teacher's classroom behavior and the artifacts of that behavior are a function of assumptions, theories, and intents the teacher brings to the classroom. Together these compose the teacher's educational platform.

Educational platforms exist at two levels: what teachers say they assume, believe, and intend (their espoused theory) and the assumptions, beliefs, and intents inferred from their behavior and artifacts of their behavior (their theory in use).

Espoused theories are generally known to the teacher.

Theories in use are generally not known to the teacher and must be constructed from observation of teacher behavior and artifacts of that behavior.

Lack of congruence between a teacher's espoused theory and the teacher's theory in use proposes a dilemma to the teacher.

Faced with a dilemma, a teacher becomes uncomfortable, and search behavior is evoked.

Dilemmas are resolved by teachers modifying their theory in use to match their espoused theory. It is possible that espoused theory will be modified to match theory in use, but because of the link between espoused theory and self-esteem, and self-esteem with the esteem received from others, the more common pattern will be the former.

Though a number of studies suggest that indeed teachers are likely to respond as suggested,[15] a number of caveats are in order. McGuire, for example, in reviewing the literature on consistency theory notes that search behavior is only one of several possible reactions to dissonance. Additional examples of dissonance reduction, he notes, are *avoidance*, whereby one represses the matter by putting the inconsistency out of mind; *bolstering*, whereby the inconsistency is submerged into a larger body of consistencies so as to seem relatively less important; *differentiation*, whereby one sees the situation causing dissonance to be different in a particular case ("I wasn't actually putting down the youngster but just giving her a taste of her own medicine"); *substitution*, whereby one changes the object about which he or she has an opinion rather than the opinion itself ("It is true that I said all school administrators are petty bureaucrats, and they are, but he is a statesman, not a bureaucrat"); and *devaluation*, whereby one downgrades the importance of the inconsistency in question, thus making it more tolerable.[16] The extent to which a teacher faces up to inconsistencies between espoused platform dimensions and those actually in use may well depend, as hypothesized earlier, upon the quality of climate and setting the supervisor provides—colleagueship in Cogan's language.[17] In an extensive review of the litera-

---

[15] Using Flanders's interaction-analysis techniques as a means of collecting information and as a basis for producing verbal feedback, Tuckman, McCall, and Hyman conclude that "behavior and self-perception of experienced, in-service teachers *can* be changed by involving a discrepancy between a teacher's observed behavior and his own self-perception of his behavior, and then making him aware of this discrepancy via verbal feedback." Bruce W. Tuckman, Kendrick M. McCall, and Ronald T. Hyman, "The Modification of Teacher Behavior: Effects of Dissonance and Feedback," *American Educational Research Journal,* vol. 6, no. 4, pp. 607–619, 1969.

[16] William J. McGuire, "The Current Status of Cognitive Consistency Theories," in Shel Feldman (ed.), *Cognitive Consistency, Motivational Antecedents, and Behavioral Consequents,* New York: Academic, 1966, pp. 10–14.

[17] Cogan, op. cit., p. 67.

ture Fuller and Manning conclude that self-confrontation and discrepancy analysis, though achieving uneven results, is by and large a powerful supervisory technique. In addition they note that "if the person is not too stressed, or closed, or anxious, or distracted, the self-confrontation experience 'takes,' i.e., the person notices some discrepancy. This is either a difference between what he thought he was doing and what he was actually doing (an incongruence discrepancy), or a difference between what he was doing and what he wanted to do (a deficiency discrepancy)."[18] This again highlights the importance of the climate which accompanies the process of clinical supervision. But as Fuller and Manning point out, a supportive climate is a necessary but not sufficient requirement for success: "Change is said not only to require the presence of facilitative conditions such as acceptance and empathy, but also 'confrontation'. . . . The teacher will not benefit from seeing her video tape alone since there is no confrontation. . . . Feedback that is not accompanied by some focus has been found to change behavior little, if at all."[19]

Alan Simon developed and field-tested a supervisory strategy which incorporates many of the features of clinical supervision described above.[20] Using videotaping techniques, Simon, as the supervisor, interviewed teachers, asking them to specify aspects of their espoused educational platform as it applies to education in general and to a particular lesson. He then videotaped the teachers actually teaching the lessons described. The videotape was then reviewed by the supervisor, sometimes with the help of outside experts not familiar with the teachers' espoused platform, and from this analysis a theory in use, as perceived by the supervisor, was constructed. This theory in use was also recorded on videotape. Together, the supervisor and teacher viewed the videotape now containing the teacher-espoused theory, an example of the teacher at work, and the supervisor's perception of the teacher's theory in use. The teacher was then interviewed to determine whether the videotaped espoused platform actually represented his or her thoughts before the lesson, whether the videotaped lesson represented his or her teaching, and whether the supervisor's videotaped rendering of the theory in use was fair and accurate. Overall the teachers verified the accuracy and fairness of the videotapes. Interviewing continued, to determine attitudes toward the process and to obtain perceptions of the effectiveness of the process from the teachers. Judges, listening to the audiotaped interviews, concluded that overall the teachers had positive attitudes toward the process and found it help-

[18] Frances F. Fuller and Brad A. Manning, "Self-Confrontation Reviewed: A Conceptualization for Video Playback in Teacher Education," *Review of Educational Research*, vol. 43, no. 4, p. 487, 1973.

[19] Ibid., p. 493.

[20] Alan Simon, "Videotapes Illustrating Concepts of the Argyris and Schön Model in Instructional Supervisory Situations," doctoral dissertation, Urbana: University of Illinois, Educational Administration and Supervision, 1976. See also Alan Simon, "Analyzing Educational Platforms: A Supervisory Strategy," *Educational Leadership*, vol. 34, no. 8, pp. 580–585, 1977. For a further extension of this work and its application to high school teachers see Michael Hoffman, "Comparing Espoused Platforms and Platforms-in-Use in Clinical Supervision," doctoral dissertation, Urbana: University of Illinois, Educational Administration and Supervision, 1977. Also, Michael Hoffman and Thomas J. Sergiovanni, "Clinical Supervision: Theory in Practice," *Illinois School Research and Development*, vol. 14, no. 1, pp. 5–12, 1977.

ful. Further, by rating teacher responses into defensive and open categories, judges concluded that indeed dilemmas had surfaced and that search behavior had been evoked.

NATURALISTIC EVALUATION

In Chapter 15 we referred to staff-development alternatives which emphasize formative evaluation and which involve teachers as partners in the process, as being of first-, second-, or third-generation varieties. Target setting and self-evaluation were considered to be first-generation, clinical supervision to be second-generation, and emerging naturalistic approaches to evaluation to be third-generation.

Many forms of clinical supervision resemble naturalistic approaches. Such forms are naturalistic when they rely heavily on developing a complete representation of a teaching episode and when they use this representation as a basis for making inferences and building understanding of events. Videotaping is the most common method of representation associated with clinical supervision. Clinical supervision uses the data at hand (actually generated from the environment and activities being evaluated) rather than data which fit a preconceived rating form or a set of instrument specifications, and it places the teacher in a key role as generator, interpreter, and analyst of events described.

Sometimes clinical supervisors take too seriously the need to "scientifically" and "objectively" document events. Sometimes they focus too intensely on the stepwise or work-flow aspects of clinical supervision. Sometimes they rely too heavily on predetermined objectives or on specifying detailed blueprints and plans which subsequently determine the direction of the evaluation. But clinical supervision can be geared to discovering and understanding rather than determining, and in that sense it has naturalistic potential. Additional naturalistic strategies which can be used either separate from clinical supervision or preferably, in our view, as a part of clinical supervision are described in the sections which follow. These techniques are powerful means for providing rich descriptions of classroom activity from which theories in use might be inferred.

CONNOISSEURSHIP AND CRITICISM

It is difficult to discuss naturalistic alternatives to present teacher-evaluation practices without reference to the work of Elliot Eisner.[22] Eisner is concerned

---

[21] Elliot Eisner, "Applying Educational Connoisseurship and Criticism to Education Settings," Stanford, Calif.: Stanford University, Department of Education, undated, mimeo; see also his "Emerging Models for Educational Evaluation," op. cit., and "The Perceptive Eye: Toward the Reformation of Educational Evaluation," op. cit. Eisner notes that, unfortunately, to many the word "connoisseurship" has snobbish or elite connotations, and criticism implies a hacking or negativistic attitude. In his words, "connoisseurship, as I use the term, relates to any form of expertise in any area of human endeavor and is as germane to the problem involved in purse snatching as it is to the appreciation of fine needle point." And, "criticism is conceived of as a generic process aimed at revealing the characteristics and qualities that constitute any human product. Its major aim is to enable individuals to recognize qualities and characteristics of a work or event which might have gone unnoticed and therefore unappreciated." Quoted from "The Perceptive Eye: Toward the Performance of Educational Evaluation," footnote 2. See also John Mann's discussion and application of Ian Ramsey's "disclosure" models of representation as compared with "picturing" models. Mann, "Curriculum Criticism," op. cit., p. 37.

with developing in supervisor and teacher the qualities and skills of appreciation, inference, disclosure, and description. He refers to these qualities as the cultivation of educational connoisseurship and criticism. It is through the art of connoisseurship that one is able to appreciate and internalize meanings in classrooms and through the skill of criticism that one is able to share or disclose this meaning to others. Eisner uses references to wine connoisseurship and art criticism as illustrations of these concepts. The art of appreciation is the tool of the connoisseur and the art of disclosure the tool of the critic. Cross uses the example of sports commentators and writers to illustrate the combined application of connoisseurship and criticism.

> Most of us are familiar with some of the techniques employed by commentators in describing and remarking on well-executed plays or potentially victorious stragegies. Plays executed with finesse are often seen in stop action, instant replay, slow motion or are recounted in stirring detail on sports pages. One of the major contributions of these commentators is their great knowledge of sports, familiarizing them with possibilities so they know whether a flanker reverse, off tackle run, screen pass or drawplay was used or has potential for gaining yardage in a given situation, or when the bump and run, blitz, or single coverage was used or likely to prevent gain. Knowledge about educational potentials is also necessary. The potentially worthwhile tactics of teaching or those in use—the bump and runs or flanker reverses of schooling—need to be described and conveyed.[22]

The commentator's ability to render play-by-play action in a fashion which permits us to see and feel the game as he or she does depends upon a feel of intimacy with the phenomena under study not permitted by mere attention to game statistics and other objective information and upon a quality of disclosure more vivid than a box score. And in education, the evaluator's ability to describe classroom life in a fashion which permits us to see and feel this environment as he or she does depends upon a similar intimacy with classroom phenomena (educational connoisseurship) and a rendering of this intimacy (educational criticism) well beyond that provided by a brief observation or two accompanied by a series of ratings or a teacher-evaluation checklist. Eisner maintains that educational connoisseurship is to some degree practiced daily by teachers and supervisors:

> The teacher's ability, for example, to judge when children have had enough of art, math, reading or "free time" is a judgment made not by applying a theory of motivation or attention, but by recognizing the wide range of qualities that the children themselves display to those who have learned to see. Walk down any school corridor and peek through the window; an educational connoisseur can quickly discern important things about life in that classroom. Of course judgments, especially those made through windows from hallways, can be faulty. Yet the point remains. If one knows how to see what one looks at, a great deal of information . . . can be secured. The teacher who cannot distinguish between the noise of children working and just plain noise has not yet developed a basic level of educational connoisseurship.[23]

---

[22] James Cross, "Applying Educational Connoisseurship and Criticism to Supervisory Practices," doctoral dissertation, 1977. Urbana: University of Illinois, Educational Administration and Supervision.
[23] Eisner, "The Perceptive Eye," p. 9.

Eisner believes that the existing level of connoisseurship found in teachers and supervisors can and should be refined, that perception can be enhanced and sharpened, and that understanding can be increased. He further points out that

> . . . connoisseurship when developed to a high degree provides a level of consciousness that makes intellectual clarity possible. Many teachers are confronted daily with prescriptions and demands from individuals outside the teaching profession that are intended to improve the quality of education within the schools. Many of these demands the teachers feel in their gut to be misguided or wrong-headed; the demands somehow fly in the face of what they feel to be possible in a classroom or in the best interests of children.[24]

In this context he notes: "Many teachers, if you ask them, are unable to state why they feel uneasy. They have a difficult time articulating what the flaws are in the often glib prescriptions that issue from state capitols and from major universities. Yet, the uneasiness is often not always, but often justified." And further: "Many teachers have developed sufficient connoisseurship to feel that something is awry but have insufficient connoisseurship to provide a more adequate conceptualization of just what it is."[25]

When applied to supervision, educational connoisseurship is a necessary but insufficient art. Classroom understanding needs to be described and communicated, and this aspect of the process, the art of disclosure, is what Eisner refers to as educational criticism. We have much to learn about cultivating the art of connoisseurship and the skills of disclosure. Much will depend upon our ability to regain confidence in ourselves, in our ability to analyze and judge, in our willingness to rely on intuition and perception—all today often considered dubious skills, ones to be ridiculed in the face of objective and scientific demands for accountability.

ARTIFACTS ANALYSIS AND PORTFOLIO DEVELOPMENT

Videotaping is a common technique associated with clinical supervision and with the arts of educational connoisseurship and criticism. Indeed, videotaping can provide a useful and readily accessible representation of teaching episodes and classroom activities. But because of the selective nature of lens and screen, this technique can also frame perception and evoke slanted meanings. Further, what the screen shows always represents a choice between possibilities and therefore provides an incomplete picture. And finally, some aspects of classroom life do not lend themselves very well to lens and screen and could be neglected.[26]

Artifacts analysis and/or portfolio development, when used in conjunction with videotaping, can help provide a more complete representation of classroom life and therefore can increase meaning.[27] These approaches, however, can stand apart from videotaping and indeed can stand apart from each other.

---

[24] Ibid., pp. 10–11.

[25] Ibid., p. 11.

[26] This discussion follows Sergiovanni, "Reforming Teacher Evaluation," op. cit.

[27] See Patricia Scheyer and Robert Stake, "A Program's Self-Evaluation Portfolio," Urbana: University of Illinois at Urbana-Champaign, Center for Instructional Research and Curriculum Evaluation, undated mimeo, for a discussion and application of this concept for program evaluation.

Imagine a classroom or school deserted suddenly 20 years ago by its teacher and students and immediately being sealed. Everything there remains exactly as it was at the moment of desertion—desks, chairs, interest centers, work materials, test files, homework assignments, reading center sign-up lists, star reward charts and other "motivational devices," bulletin boards, workbooks, student notebooks, grade books, plan books, library displays, teacher workroom arrangements, student lounge-area arrangements, and so on.

Twenty years later you arrive on the scene as an amateur anthropologist intent on learning about the culture, way of life, and meaning of this class (its goals, values, beliefs, activities, norms, etc.). As you dig through this classroom, what artifacts might you collect and how might you use these artifacts to help you learn about life in this classroom? Suppose, for example, you were interested in discovering what was important to this teacher, how this teacher viewed his or her role in contrast to that of students, what youngsters seemed to be learning and/or enjoying, and how time was spent? In each case what might you collect? What inferences might you make, for example, if you were to find most of the work of students to be in the form of short-answer responses in workbooks or on ditto sheets, no student work displayed in the class, all student desks containing identical materials, and a teacher test file with most questions geared to the knowledge level of the taxonomy of educational objectives?

Portfolio development represents a teacher-evaluation strategy similar to that of artifacts analysis but with some important differences. The intent of portfolio development is to establish a file or collection of artifacts, records, photo essays, casettes, and other materials designed to represent some aspect of the classroom program and teaching activities. Though the materials in the portfolio should be loosely collected and therefore suitable for rearrangement from time to time to reflect different aspects of the class, the portfolio should be designed with a sense of purpose. The teacher or teaching team being evaluated is responsible for assembling the portfolio and should do it in a fashion which highlights their perception of key issues and important concerns they wish to represent.

Like the artist who prepares a portfolio of his or her work to reflect a point of view, the teacher prepares a similar representation of his or her work. Together supervisor and teacher use the collected artifacts to identify key issues, to identify the dimensions of the teacher's educational platform, as evidence that targets have been met, and to identify serendipitous but worthwhile outcomes. A portfolio collection could be used, for example, to examine such issues as:

Are classroom activities compatible with the teacher's espoused educational platform and/or that of the school?

Do supervisor and teacher have compatible goals?

Are youngsters engaging in activities which require advanced cognitive thinking, or is the emphasis on lower-level learning?

Do youngsters have an opportunity to influence classroom decisions?

Is the classroom program challenging all the students regardless of academic potential, or are some youngsters taught too little and others too much?

Are the youngsters assuming passive or active roles in the classroom?

Is the teacher working hard? That is, is there evidence of planning, care in preparation of materials, and reflective and conscientious feedback on students' work, or are shortcuts evident?

Does the teacher understand the subject matter?

What is the nature and character of the hidden curriculum in this class?

Though portfolio development and artifacts analysis share common features, the most notable of which is the collection of artifacts, portfolio development is the responsibility of the teacher. The teacher decides what will be represented by the portfolio and the items to be included in its collection. Together the teacher and supervisor use this representation to identify issues for discussion and analysis.

In this chapter we have suggested that classroom supervision and teacher evaluation are shrouded with a false sense of scientism. Though present approaches have a place and can be helpful, as an exclusive or even primary strategy, they have not been effective, and, indeed, teacher evaluation is characterized by widespread doubt among teachers and supervisors.

The proposed solution is to tighten up existing procedures, to get serious, to increase objectivity—or to otherwise emphasize even more our present technical-rational procedures. What we may not realize, however, is that the defects of technical-rational views are not just in the procedures, but are inherent in underlying assumptions. The practices we suggest, those based on naturalistic assumptions, are emerging and are yet to be refined. Much more work needs to be done by *practicing supervisors* and their university counterparts in developing these ideas. One cannot promise that practices based on naturalistic assumptions will be more effective, but if our original hypothesis is true, the assumptions suggest alternatives worth trying.

SUMMARY

In this chapter it was hypothesized that by and large supervisors and others responsible for teacher evaluation privately view the procedures as lacking in credibility. The technology of present practices was characterized as scientific management and underlying assumptions as technical-rational. The internal integrity of these approaches was accepted, but their application to educational settings was described as ill-suited and inappropriate. The center of this mismatch is the willy-nilly application of the values of science to the art of teaching. Naturalistic assumptions and practices were suggested as alternatives more befitting the nature of work in education and the spirit of professional, as opposed to occupational, accountability in education.

Clinical supervision, in the specific sense of a supervisory cycle associated with Cogan, and adaptations of this process were presented as fairly well-developed techniques with naturalistic potential. It was argued that clinical supervision can and should take many forms, and that more experimentation with different forms is needed. A theoretical framework was offered as a means to conceptualize the process of clinical supervision. Basic to the framework was the assumption that teacher behavior is governed by the interplay of two theories: an espoused theory, which represents the teacher's public educational platform, and a theory in use, which represents the teacher's actual educational platform. Sometimes the actual platform is unknown to the teacher. Theory in use is inferred from classroom observations, analysis of videotapes, collected artifacts and portfolios, and other techniques. Confronting an individual with a theory in use inconsistent with that individual's espoused theory results in the surfacing of dilemmas which he or she seeks to resolve. This process acts as a stimulus to change and as a means to generate substantial change issues.

More emerging naturalistic techniques were then presented either as methods by which theories in use might be constructed or as techniques to be used independently of clinical supervision notions. These included concepts of educational connoisseurship and criticism and practices of artifact collecting and portfolio development. These ideas were not offered as tried and true practices but as alternatives worth trying. Universities have a role to play in developing and refining naturalistic approaches, but major headway is likely to depend upon the developmental efforts made by practicing supervisors.

STUDY GUIDE

Recall the concepts, ideas, and meanings associated with each of the following phrases and terms included in this chapter. Can you discuss each of them with a colleague and apply them to the supervisory context of your school? If you cannot, review them in the text and record the page number for future reference.

1 Artifacts analysis _____
2 Clinical supervision _____
3 Cogan's cycle of supervision _____
4 Connoisseurship in education _____
5 Criticism in education _____
6 Educational platform _____
7 Espoused theory _____
8 Johari Window in supervision _____
9 Portfolio development _____
10 Private views of evaluation _____
11 Public views of evaluation _____
12 Technical-rational assumptions _____
13 Theory in use _____
14 Surfacing dilemmas _____

EXERCISES

1 Our contrast of technical-rational assumptions and practices and naturalistic assumptions and practices deliberately separates the views in an opposing fashion and indeed sets up the technical-rational assumptions as "straw men." Rewrite this section, showing the contrast between technical-rational and naturalistic assumptions as complementary and supplementary rather than competing, with each set adding power and meaning to the other.
2 Refer to Figure 16-1. Assuming the role of supervisor, identify three teachers in your school. For each, prepare a list of "public or open self" traits of his or her teaching.

Compare the lists. Do the same sorts of characteristics appear in the "public self" for all three teachers? Repeat this procedure for the "blind self" quadrant. If you are a teacher, what sorts of characteristics would you write about your teaching in the "hidden or secret self" quadrant?

3 How would you describe concepts of educational connoisseurship and criticism to your superintendent?

4 Ask one or two teachers to prepare a portfolio collection over a span of 2 weeks of artifacts which highlight a particular issue, such as individualized instruction or whether youngsters are assuming more active roles in the classroom. How might the collection of artifacts and portfolio development be used to supplement more traditional "rating scale" approaches to teacher evaluation?

Chapter 17

What Lies Ahead: The Best
of Times, the Worst of Times

Over the past 10 years there have occurred rather dramatic assaults on the educational establishment, both public and private. In the late sixties and early seventies, there appeared to be a ground swell of protest against the rigidities, oppression, discrimination, and vested interests of the school bureaucracy. Many urban parents lost faith in the public school's ability to make good the promises they thought it had fulfilled for other minorities. Many young people saw the schools as wastelands, extensions of a basically alien adult world. Many educators gave up on "the system" and opted for alternative schools. There was a blossoming of new approaches to learning, some of which are still flourishing today on the fringes of "the system," some of which have found a home within it.

The last few years have seen a noticeable decline in the more strident assaults. That decline in criticism means many things, to be sure. It does not, however, signal an end to dissatisfaction with the schools. It does seem, on the other hand, that more people are willing to roll up their sleeves and get down to the painstaking work of reform. Whether this more constructive behavior is the result of the harsh realities of a tight job market, or the result of understanding better how organizations change and resist change, or a combination of the two, is difficult to say.

From our limited perspective, however, it does appear that most people are no longer stirred by tumult and shouting. It appears, on the contrary, that people in the schools and on school committees are ready for some quiet and effective improvements. The critics have in fact accomplished much. Funding has been provided for the education and hiring of teachers in multicultural education, special education, and bilingual education, and for any number of remedial or diagnostic specialists. Some experiments of the alternative schools enjoy a respectable place within the system. Some systems now have three or four varieties of schools (a "back-to-basics" school, a standard school, an alternative school, etc.) from which parents may select one for their children.

This is not to say that the schools are out of the woods, by a long shot. Substantial progress is being made, however, and this provides a basis for moderate optimism. There seems to be a more positive climate for working within the system, for making serious and long-range efforts at upgrading the quality of education.

SUPERVISORS AND EDUCATIONAL QUALITY

Yet schools are facing a declining enrollment and budget squeezes. Having to make the most out of less, schools are placing those exercising supervisory responsibility squarely in the middle of these efforts to upgrade the quality of education. As top administrators try to plan for optimal use of the tax dollar and engage more and more in the political give-and-take with community special-interest groups, they have less and less time for educational and instructional matters. Supervisors, as those closest to instructional activity after the teacher, will have to be the ones who assist in the planning, coordinating, executing, and evaluating of these efforts to improve the educational quality of the school.

From this perspective, then, these are the best of times for supervisors. That is, if our perceptions of what is and will be happening are correct, then supervision will become that cluster of activities upon which participants and publics will rely for overall schoolwide or systemwide educational improvement.

Not everyone agrees with this educated hunch about the immediate future. Others believe that because the problems of education are so massive and involve more and more powerful political blocs, the local school system and its community is too small to tackle them. With integration and busing still red-hot issues, teacher unions dominating the bargaining enterprise, urban deterioration continuing, and national levels of literacy steadily declining among other problems, the state and federal governments are seen as the only agencies with sufficient power and resources to respond adequately. There is more and more talk about the "public policy" domain in education, in which the study and formation of public opinion is involved. University professors, teacher-union representatives, parent associations, school board representatives, and citizens groups promoting this and that are journeying to the state assembly and to the United States Congress.

PUBLIC POLICY ORIENTATION

Establishing and then enacting public policy from the federal and state level is seen as the major answer to the schools' problems. Some of the best qualified graduate students in education are being encouraged to major in this young but rapidly growing field. That is where the action is, many claim, and where it will be for some time to come.

This, of course, shifts the picture considerably away from the school building or the school system in which supervisors are seen as key to the upgrading of educational quality. The arena of state and federal public policy formation involves political activity of a far more sophisticated nature than that on the local level, even in large cities. That is the "big leagues," so to speak. When public policy results in legislation with enormous appropriations of money, one realizes the stakes that are involved.

We nonetheless believe that the new focus on this larger political arena can blind us to the unavoidable need to have competent personnel on the local level who will carry out public policy. One does not legislate superior teaching and more humane learning. That is effected by competent professionals in the schools.

There need not be a quarrel between the two opinions. There could easily develop a quarrel, however, if those enacting public policy do not allow for sufficient local discretion to implement the policy. There could result a whole new layer of neoscientific management at the state and federal level which would simply smother the development and utilization of the human resources of the local school. If this happens, then it surely will be the worst of times for those exercising supervisory responsibility at the local level. One easily predictable outcome is that any supervisor not repeating the party line will quickly be replaced by one who will.

We maintain, however, that there need be no quarrel between the two schools of thought. They can, in fact, complement one another. How that could happen leads us to our final statement on the importance of human resources supervision, which we have been stressing in this book.

HUMAN RESOURCES SUPERVISION ESSENTIAL

We have tried to show how human resources supervision differs from, and goes beyond, other forms of supervision. We believe that there is sufficient—not extensive enough yet, but still sufficient—evidence from the field of organization and management research to validate this claim.

We believe that when human resources supervision is self-consciously exercised within an organizational setting, it can simultaneously increase the effectiveness of the people involved and their job satisfaction and human growth. The application of this form of supervision to schools leads to some obvious conclusions, which we have touched upon.

At the same time that we developed the rationale for this style of supervision, we were attempting to expose the reader to the dynamics of organizational life. The supervisor must function within that matrix of organizational and bureaucratic activity. If the supervisor knows how the organization works, then he or she can use the potential of the organization for educational purposes, rather than be victimized by unintended, perhaps, but actually dysfunctional aspects of the organization.

Because they are so often at a middle level in the organization, supervisors have access to top-level decision makers as well as to the instructional scene. Because supervisors can interpret the different levels to each other, serve as advocates of now one level, now the other, and tap and coordinate the very considerable resources of the organization as well, they can actually keep the organization on course.

The organization—the school or the school system—was set up to serve a purpose, to provide for the formal education of children. Those at the top are frequently distracted by financial or political concerns from that primary goal. Those individual teachers in the classroom are so close to their own activities that it is difficult for them to see other aspects of the school organization as deserving of equal attention. The supervisor is usually in the best position, then, to help the organization function the way it was intended to. And therefore it is essential, absolutely essential, that supervisors understand how organizations in general and schools in particular function. Without such understanding, they, and all the participants in the school organization, will end up floundering their way through crisis after crisis without knowing why things are always turning out so badly.

Every bureaucracy began, as Weber noted,[1] with a charismatic vision or an inspiration. The resulting organization or bureaucracy was a way of enfleshing that vision, making it operative, functional. Organization or bureaucracy ensured an orderly continuation of the vision and intentions of its founders throughout following generations.

Public schools as well as private schools were founded on such visions and inspirations. Some would call these inspirations myths, not in the sense of wild fancies or improbable superstitions, but rather in the sense of beliefs in a possibility that could not be empirically verified at the time, perhaps could never be empirically verified. We have argued that, besides understanding how organizations function and utilizing those managerial skills which will make the organization responsive to human beings, supervisors need to reestablish or clarify what that myth or that vision is for themselves. We have called it a platform because it is a term that is more manageable for our more empirical sensibilities.

Whatever one wants to call it, the organization does not function well when its participants lose sight of the basic purpose of the organization. One of the essential tasks of a human resources supervisor will be to encourage the formulation and/or review of these basic purposes as they are personally appropriated by the staff. In that way, many arguments over ancillary purposes can be put in their proper perspective and the major focus of people's energies can be kept on the educational purposes of the school.

Finally, human resources supervision acts on very basic beliefs about human nature. We think that these beliefs about human beings are most consistent with our most cherished political and religious beliefs as well as with the expressed

---

[1] S. N. Eisenstadt, *Max Weber: On Charisma and Institution Building,* Chicago: University of Chicago Press, 1968.

purposes óf the schools. We know from our own experience as well as from research findings that acting on those beliefs more often than not enables men and women to work together effectively.

These three characteristics of human resources supervision should be highlighted: it is founded on beliefs about human nature that center on human beings as active, responsible, and growing persons; it is exercised with a conscious understanding of organizational dynamics; and its logic and intelligibility are rooted in an educational vision and platform which is both personal and yet legitimated within educational tradition. These three characteristics of human resources supervision give it a power and a direction which we believe enable it to accomplish the upgrading of the quality of education in a local school or school system. And no matter at what higher level of government, plans, laws, projects, and policies are made for the improvement of education, the proof of the pudding will always be found at the local level. If it does not happen there, it does not happen.

Hence, those concerned with the formulation and enactment of public policy should recognize the need for qualified and committed educators at the local level. The local-level educators, moreover, need to appreciate the issues at stake in the deliberations of state and federal legislators. They will need to be more active in making their voices heard, as well as to listen carefully to the points of view being argued before the legislatures.

We close with this word. Supervision, in our opinion, is entering a phase bright with promise but also one in which supervisors will have to stay alert to the political arena as never before. It can be the best of times or the worst of times— but it will be an exciting time, a time for making history.

Index